Strange Victoriana

Tales of the Curious, the Weird and the
Uncanny from Our Victorian Ancestors

JAN BONDESON

AMBERLEY

Jan Bondeson is a senior lecturer at Cardiff University, and the author of many critically acclaimed books, including *Cabinet of Medical Curiosities*, *The London Monster* and *Buried Alive*. His previous Amberley titles include *Queen Victoria's Stalker*, *Amazing Dogs* and *The Lion Boy*.

First published 2016
This edition published 2018

Amberley Publishing
The Hill, Stroud
Gloucestershire, GL5 4EP

www.amberley-books.com

British Library Cataloguing in Publication Data.
A catalogue record for this book is available from the British Library.

ISBN 978 1 4456 8655 4 (paperback)
ISBN 978 1 4456 5886 5 (ebook)

Printed in the UK.

Contents

Preface

After the publication of my book *Queen Victoria's Stalker* in April 2011, it was to be featured in *Fortean Times* magazine. When submitting the feature, I suggested to the Editor of this magazine that perhaps I should also contribute a series of short articles featuring sensational stories and startling Victorian images from the 'worst newspaper in England' – the *Illustrated Police News*. This idea was acted upon, and the serial has gone on for more than five years, to considerable acclaim: the readers of the *Fortean Times* were treated to a monthly dose of Dog-faced Men, White Gorillas, Female Errand-Boys, ghosts and hermits, and assorted historical mysteries and oddities. In late 2015, I made arrangements to have this curious collection of weird Victoriana published in book form; about half of the stories have been published in the *Fortean Times*, although many have been revised and extended, and the other half consists of entirely new material. The present volume is the result of these exertions; I think it is a fine gallimaufry of Victorian eccentricity and freakishness, and wish it many readers.

1

The History of the
Illustrated Police News

The *Illustrated Police News* [henceforth *IPN*] was inaugurated on 20 February 1864; it would remain in publication, as a weekly Saturday newspaper, for not less than seventy-four years. The original incarnation of this newspaper had four pages, the first of which was devoted to illustrations of recent crimes; its news stories were often culled from other London papers. It was not, as has often been proclaimed, a forerunner in criminous journalism; in fact, the concept of such 'Illustrated Police' weekly papers dates back as far as the 1830s. *Cleave's Weekly Police Gazette* was published in 1835 and 1836, and so was the *People's Weekly*

An advertisement for the inaugural issue of the *IPN*, from the *Caledonian Mercury*, 15 February 1864.

Police Gazette; the *People's Hue and Cry, or Weekly Police Register* made an appearance in 1834 and the *People's Police Gazette* an even more brief appearance in 1841. *The Penny Sunday Times and People's Police Gazette* was published from 1840 until 1842, with many good and accurate illustrations of criminal affairs. Already back in the 1830s, there were illustrated weekly mainstream newspapers, like the *Weekly Chronicle*, the *Penny Satirist* and *Cleave's Penny Gazette*, which occasionally contained woodcuts of celebrated London crimes, like the unsolved murder of Eliza Grimwood in 1838 and the murder of Lord William Russell by his valet Courvoisier in 1840.

It is a matter of debate what event triggered the foundation of the *IPN*. The *Illustrated London* News was inaugurated in 1842 and still going strong in 1864, but it was priced at sixpence and aimed for a better class of reader with its elegant engravings. The year 1861 saw the foundation of the *Penny Illustrated Paper*, a downmarket version of the *Illustrated London News* that was published weekly at the price of one penny; it boasted a variety of rather crude illustrations, occasionally concerning recent crimes. The early proprietors of the *IPN*, the publisher Henry Lea and the businessman Edwin Bulpin, may well have been impressed with the apparent success of the *Penny Illustrated Paper*; in spite of its lowly price of a penny, it sold enough to stay in business and prosper. The great interest in crime and criminals from the lower classes of society would imply, Lea and Bulpin hoped, that a weekly 'Illustrated Police' newspaper priced at just a penny would enjoy a wide circulation among working men all around Britain. It would become a 'Newgate Calendar' for the present time, chronicling the recent criminous activities of humankind at home and abroad. A disapproving writer in the *London Review* of 1864 did not at all approve of the inauguration of the *IPN*, commenting that:

> During the past month, the hoardings of the metropolis have been covered with large bills, announcing that the *Illustrated Police News* would shortly be published. Several numbers of this periodical have now appeared, and we must say that we do not think the morality of the lower orders will be at all benefited by its publication. Wood engravings, very similar to the late Mr Catnach's Seven Dials pictures, illustrate the various murders and housebreakings that are narrated ...

Nor did an 1865 writer in *Punch* have anything good to say about the *IPN*: it was generally read among rogues and thieves, he asserted, and was popular among 'young rascals who delight in stories about exploits such as those of TURPIN and JACK SHEPPARD'.

We do not know much about the early years of the *IPN*, except that the paper managed to stay in business throughout the 1860s, which was no mean feat for a recently established newspaper in London's highly competitive publishing world. The politics of the *IPN* were largely populist, advocating socially conscious and radical concepts like the extension of suffrage, and fair wages and proper housing for working men. The early advertisements were for nerve tonics and patent medicines, for other books and newspapers published by Lea, and for shoes and leather wares produced by Bulpin. The railway murder of Mr Briggs by the German Franz Müller in October 1864 was prominently featured in the *IPN*, with woodcuts of Müller in court and on the scaffold. In early 1865, when some enthusiastic *IPN* readers wanted to purchase complete bound sets of the issues for 1864, there was odium when the careless publishers had forgotten to keep copies of all the issues; they had to insert a notice that they were willing to buy back clean copies of eighteen penny issues for their files.

* * *

In July 1865, the *IPN* was taken over by a much more formidable figure in London's publishing world, George Purkess Jr. His father George Sr was a prominent London bookseller and publisher, and George Jr went into business with him at an early age. When George Sr remarried a widow with two sons in 1851, he allowed both these sons to change their surname to Purkess and to join his business, something George Jr is

THE MURDERER CARRYING HIS VICTIM INTO THE HOP PLANTATION.   MURDER AND MUTILATION OF THE BODY.

THE BARBAROUS MURDER OF A CHILD AT ALTON, HAMPSHIRE.

The murder of Fanny Adams in 1867, a 'classic' illustration from the *IPN*, 31 August 1867.

unlikely to have approved of. In 1856, George Jr left his father's employ at the age of twenty-three and opened a newsagent's shop of his own at No. 16 St Alban's Place, Edgware Road, in partnership with a man named Walters. This business prospered, and although his father had left everything to his widow when he died in 1859, George Purkess was in a position to build up something of a publishing empire in the 1860s. It would appear that the *IPN* was the first newspaper he acquired. More business-minded than Lea and Bulpin, he offered readers to subscribe to the *IPN* for 8*s* 8*d* per annum; he did much to improve its circulation to newsagents and newspaper stalls all over Britain, and employed agents in Australia, Canada and South Africa to make sure that the paper would be available to crime enthusiasts all over the world. From late November 1867 onwards, all text was banished from the first page, which would henceforth contain illustrations only.

From his office in the Strand, George Purkess published a steady stream of books and pamphlets on crime, quackery and popular history. For many years, the mainstay of his firm would be the widely read *IPN*, which immediately established a firm rapport with the low-brow elements of the reading public. Its circulation was 150,000 copies in 1872, and 300,000 copies in 1877. Its success spawned a few competitors wanting to get in on the act, but the *Illustrated Police Gazette* did not last long in 1867, the *Police Record* was absorbed into the *IPN* in 1868, and the penny-pinching *Illustrated Halfpenny Police Budget* failed to make any impact in 1871. For many years, the *IPN* successfully protected its niche in Victorian publishing. Murders at home and abroad, assaults and outrages, accidents and macabre events were described with gusto. Each weekly issue consisted of four pages, the first of which was entirely devoted to lurid illustrations that advertised the stories lurking within. These remarkable and dramatic illustrations have become part of the cult of Victoriana. Expertly executed by skilful draughtsmen, they make the most of the sanguinary and macabre subject matter. Brains are blown out, skulls crushed with blunt instruments and limbs lopped off. In 'Singular accident to a parachutist', the end of the wretched aeronaut helplessly descending towards the ocean is precipitated by an enormous shark leaping up and seizing hold of his legs. In 'Outrage by a mad dog' a boy is bitten hard in the buttocks by the infuriated animal; the blood is spurting from the wound and the boy is yelling with pain. Women coming to grief in various ways were a favourite subject for the male-dominated readership of the *IPN*. A lady bicyclist is gored by a bull from behind and sent flying over the handlebars, her legs exposed for everyone to see.

The *IPN* was very much a working men's newspaper. It advocated patriotism and xenophobia and despised evangelism and temperance. Its ideal was Merry Old England, where every good, honest working man had his plate of roast beef and his tankard of ale, and where there were no dodgy foreigners lurking about. Although probably not much more anti-Semitic than the rest of the Victorian press, some of its illustrations of Jewish criminals and vagabonds could have been taken over, without alterations, by Mosley's Blackshirts. For the average reader of the *IPN*, there was nothing funnier than a clergyman being thrown by his horse, a well-dressed lady falling off an omnibus, a burglar being bitten by a bulldog, or the 'Hallelujah Lasses' of the Salvation Army being pelted with rotten tomatoes by a gang of young hooligans. Each issue of the *IPN* had several columns of advertisements at the end, mostly dealing with 'rubber goods' for amorous gentlemen, as well as patent medicines aimed to make the hair re-grow on balding pates or to restore sexual potency.

More than once, clergymen wrote to the newspapers to complain about the *IPN*: its lurid illustrations, unfastidious contents and indecent advertisements. Reading such a newspaper surely must entice young people into an immoral and criminal life, they reasoned. In 1868, the young railwayman Thomas Wells murdered his superior, the Dover Priory stationmaster Edward Adolphus Walshe, and he was duly arrested, tried and executed. There was newspaper speculation about the possible brutalising influence of a singular piece of reading-matter found in young Wells' pocket after he had been arrested – a copy of the *IPN*! In March 1870, a clergyman wrote to *The Times* to lament that in his country parish, the *IPN* had a very large circulation indeed. Recently, a murder had been committed by a man named Mobbs, who testified in court that he had read about a recent child murder in the *IPN* and paid close attention to the lurid illustrations. Surely there was a sinister connection here, and such a vicious newspaper should no longer be allowed to corrupt the minds of impressionable young people. The witty Purkess replied that he had once known a murderer who had been influenced by another piece of criminal literature given to him by his grandfather, one that featured the tale of Cain and Abel, among other sanguinary transactions! An author on the Penny Press in *Macmillan's Magazine* of 1881 was even more outspoken in his criticism of the *IPN*:

> There is an even lower depth, and it is an unflattering comment on our boasted civilisation that the worst papers have the largest circulation. The *Illustrated Police News* is to be found in every town and village of England. Its chief contents are reports extracted from the daily papers of proceedings at police courts, trials and inquests; its illustrations minister to the morbid cravings of the uneducated for the horrible and the repulsive, and its advertisements call for the intervention of the police.

In November 1886, after a newspaper poll had voted the *IPN* 'the worst newspaper in England', a journalist from the *Pall Mall Gazette* went to interview George Purkess. The office of the *IPN*, in the Strand, could be detected from some distance, due to the small crowd gathered outside, in front of the pictorial placard advertising the current issue. Purkess, described as 'a stout, comfortable-looking man of middle age', received the news of the vote with the greatest composure, being thick-skinned with regard to such criticism. He jovially invited his fellow journalist into his private office. The *IPN* had most buyers and subscribers in the Manchester, Liverpool and Birmingham areas; its London circulation was just one-eighth of the total issue. The circulation abroad was fairly limited, although a friend had recently sent Purkess a copy of the *IPN* that he had picked up in Hyderabad. Although the *IPN* was considered a working man's newspaper, Purkess claimed that a Dowager Marchioness was a permanent subscriber, and that an Earl had once ordered his biography of Calcraft the Hangman; several clergymen had also been known to request copies.

The main reason the *IPN* was such a scandalous newspaper was its lewd and graphic illustrations, which outraged many people. Heads were crushed and limbs lopped off; blood spouted from knife wounds; children screamed in agony when bitten by dogs, and wives desperately begged for mercy when beaten up by their brutal husbands. Images that would today seem amusing and burlesque, like some 'fast' women getting drunk, or a lady bicyclist flying through the air after being gored from behind by a bull, also infuriated the prudish Victorians. When interviewed, George

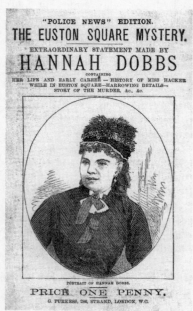

The 'Police News' edition of the autobiography of Hannah Dobbs, of recent Euston Square notoriety, published by George Purkess.

Purkess defended his *IPN* artists, whom he thought were as good as those working for any other rival journal, including the *Illustrated London News* and the *Graphic*. He had half a dozen artists on his staff in London, and occasionally employed seventy or more freelance artists in all parts of the country. Whenever a high-profile crime was committed, Purkess was able to dispatch one of his artists to the scene. Several times, he claimed, criminals depicted in the *IPN* had written back to compliment their excellent likenesses in the paper. Here he was not bragging, since during his ownership, the drawings in the *IPN* were both artistically to a high standard and of an admirable accuracy, with regard both to portraits of criminals and drawings of the houses where celebrated crimes had taken place.

***

By the 1880s, George Purkess was a wealthy man. Having a liking for quackery and popular medicine, he published *The Family Doctor and People's Medical Adviser*, a weekly journal that deplored the use of corsets and advocated rational female dress, and provided some quite dangerous-sounding health advice for the people; he also published an array of short handbooks on health and alternative medicine. Ever eager to make money on celebrated criminal cases, his printing company issued

A 'Ripper' issue of the *IPN*, from 22 September 1888.

pamphlets about Charles Peace, the burglar turned murderer; Henry Wainwright, the Whitechapel Road murderer; and the autobiography of Hannah Dobbs, the suspected Euston Square murderess of 1879. The *IPN* remained the jewel in the crown of his publishing empire, however, and the income from its very substantial sales helped to finance his various other publishing activities. The Jack the Ripper murders of 1888 were exploited by the *IPN*, with various gory illustrations, and the newspaper promoted the dubious hypothesis that the Whitechapel Murderer was still active in 1891, or even in 1893, prowling the East End streets and adding to his murderous tally with impunity.

After the death of George's first wife Elizabeth Purkess in 1882, he remarried Emily Elliot, who may well have been his long-time mistress and the mother of his illegitimate daughter, in 1885 and moved into No. 77 Gower Street [the house still stands, and is today the Arran House Hotel]. George Purkess was an enthusiastic theatregoer and a busy Freemason, a founding member of the Unity Club, and a contributor to many theatrical charities. Still he was an obscure figure in many respects: not much is known about his personal life, and no undisputed likeness of him exists, something that is strange for the proprietor of an illustrated weekly journal. George Purkess fell ill with tuberculosis of the larynx in the late 1880s and in spite of an attempt at surgical treatment in 1892, he

Another 'Ripper' issue of the *IPN*, from 20 October 1888.

died not long after, leaving £10,399, a veritable fortune that owed much to his long and successful management of the *IPN*. In his will, he directed that all his possessions apart from household items should be sold and the proceeds invested to provide an income for his wife and daughter.

The *IPN*, the main asset left by George Purkess, was purchased by a syndicate of businessmen. These individuals soon made detrimental changes to the newspaper: new draughtsmen were employed, and the quality of the illustrations declined markedly. In December 1894, the number of pages increased from four to eight, with illustrations on the front page as well as on pages four and five. The focus on crime gradually weakened, with columns on racing, boxing and music hall actresses being introduced, as well as serialised novels and mildly indecent 'saucy songs'. In June 1897, the number of pages was further increased to twelve, and the adulteration of the newspaper's contents continued: the criminals were now in a minority, and the bruisers, racehorses and music hall performers were in danger of taking over the newspaper altogether. The *IPN* was still capable of reporting a good murder, but its quality with regard to both journalistic prowess and the quality of its illustrations was in a decline in the post-Purkess era.

In June 1893, the *IPN* received a more determined rival, the *Illustrated Police Budget* [henceforth *IPB*], which was founded by the journalist Harold Furniss, who rather cheekily described it as 'The leading Illustrated Police Journal in Britain'. The *IPB*'s sleazy journalism and alternately gory and semi-pornographic illustrations appealed to the male working-class readership who used to buy the *IPN*, and it gradually managed to establish itself as Britain's second 'Illustrated Police' newspaper. As its very name suggested, the *IPB* did everything on the cheap. Whereas the *IPN* still prided itself on the quality and accuracy of its illustrations, those in the *IPB* were often based on imagination alone. Drawings of lantern-jawed bruisers and scantily clad, buxom female music hall performers abound in its pages; images of flagellation, or of women fighting or getting drunk, occur with a regularity that suggests a pathological appeal. Thus the *IPB* had all the faults of the *IPN*, but none of its merits: its crime reporting was plagiaristic and of low quality, its illustrations shoddy and inaccurate, and its lurid sensationalism unbridled. It was printed on very brittle, low-quality paper, meaning that few intact copies have survived in private hands. Still, the *IPB* survived well into Edwardian times as the only serious competitor of the *IPN*.

***

For the Fortean enthusiast, the *IPN* has a good deal to offer. Just like Charles Fort himself, the newspaper's editorial staff sifted an enormous amount of newspaper copy, from Britain, Europe and the United States,

THE·TOOTING·HORROR
MURDER OF A WIFE AND SIX CHILDREN — SUICIDE OF THE HUSBAND

The 'Tooting Horror' of 1895, in which the unemployed plasterer Frank Taylor murdered his wife and six of his seven children, before committing suicide, another 'classic' illustration from the *IPN*, 16 March 1895.

in their search for dastardly crimes and macabre events. When there were no recent murders, curiosities from the animal kingdom were sometimes used to bolster the paper's contents. A swan is eaten by a boa constrictor, a monkey scalds a cat with the teapot, a man is attacked by a furious magpie, and a burglar is confronted by a razor-wielding orang-utang. When an old tramp is attacked by some hooligans, he is defended by his large troupe of trained rats. Fish fall from the sky, sea monsters attack, and in two separate incidents, a child and a dog are abducted by large eagles.

When, in 2010, I came across a large, privately held collection of Victorian periodicals, I was cheered to find a substantial run of the *IPN*, and also three voluminous ledgers of cuttings from this and other newspapers, some of them dealing with celebrated murders, others with headings like 'Ghosts and Hauntings', 'Hermits and Misers', 'Lion Wagers', 'Trouble with Polar Bears', 'Cat Hoarders' and 'The Great Twiss Mystery'. I decided to make use of this material for the production of a series of short articles in *Fortean Times* magazine, to describe strange, macabre and uncanny episodes from the Victorian era. Care was taken to make use of the original *IPN* story as the inspiration only: other contemporary newspapers were consulted, as were later published sources, in print and online. Without the access to various fully searchable online Victorian newspaper repositories, to various scholarly databases and library catalogues, and to the vast array of online genealogical tools available at the National Archives, this book would have been a good deal shorter, and its stories would often have ended anticlimactically.

The *Fortean Times* serial is still ongoing in late 2016, to considerable acclaim: Dog-Faced Men are exhibited on stage, the doctors congregate around the bed of the Sleeping Frenchman of Soho, Miss Vint demonstrates her Reincarnated Cats, and scantily dressed Female Somnambulists tumble from the roofs. From the spectral world, we have the Haunted Murder House near Chard, the Ghost of Berkeley Square, the Jumping Spectre of Peckham and the Fighting Ghost of Tondu. The White Gorilla takes a swig from its tankard of beer, eagles come swooping from the sky to carry off little children, heroic Newfoundland dogs plunge into the waves to rescue drowning mariners, and the Rat-Killing Monkey of Manchester goes on a rampage in the rat-pit, swinging a hammer. After reading this book, your views on Victorian culture will change forever.

2

Medical Freaks

Somnambulists in Peril

The Victorians in general, and the readers of the *IPN* in particular, had a fascination for the conscious but immobile (female) body, at risk of being buried alive while in some strange trance-like state, but unable to move or cry out. This fascination also extended to the mobile but unconscious female body: sleepwalkers, or somnambulists as the Victorians called them, were among the favourite subjects for the *IPN*'s bawdy-minded draughtsmen. Male somnambulists may have been *news*, but they were never *Illustrated Police* news, even if they performed a tap dance on the roof of the House of Lords; the *IPN*'s somnambulists were all young, female and scantily clad. Whether they were saved in the last minute by some gallant male rescuer, or fell to their death screaming with terror, they helped to sell a lot of newspapers.

One of the earliest *IPN* somnambulists was the seventeen-year-old Clara Dalrymple, from a small village near Glastonbury. It was well known that she often went walking in her sleep, but in May 1868, she rose from her bed in her bedroom on the second floor and walked out on a plank that a workman had put between her father's house and the one opposite. She fell, but her dress caught in a lamp-post (which the careless artist left out) and she was saved. Dorothea Lessing, the daughter of a wealthy merchant in Budingen, Germany, went out sleepwalking in February 1870. She opened the window of her bedroom and went out on a small bridge connecting the second floors of two houses. Since the bridge had not been used for many years and was very rusty, she fell through it, although she remained suspended from one of her wrists. Although breaking a bone in her wrist and being almost prostrate with nervous exhaustion, she survived her ordeal. Madame Broneau, the French somnambulist, was less fortunate: she fell to her death in Belfast after walking out on the roof.

FEARFUL SITUATION OF A FEMALE SOMNAMBULIST IN SOMERSETSHIRE.

Above: The somnambulist Clara Dalrymple walks the plank near Glastonbury, from the *IPN*, 1 June 1868.

Right: Madame Broneau falls to her death, from the *IPN*, 9 February 1878.

DEATH OF A SOMNAMBULIST

In 1885, a Kidderminster police constable heard screams from the roof of a house and he observed a young lady somnambulist, dressed only in her night-shirt, who had got through a window out onto the roof, where she awoke. Her father and the police constable threw her a rope and she was rescued from her perilous position. In 1888, a scantily clad lady somnambulist walked into the sea in Brighton, but she awoke in the cold water and was eventually saved. Finally, in 1897, the pretty somnambulist Miss Charlton took a walk on the parapet of her family's house in Manchester, with a lighted candle in her hand. Fortunately, she fell only four feet, onto the flat roof of a neighbouring property, and thus survived her ordeal without any permanent harm being caused.

FRIGHTFUL POSITION OF A SOMNAMBULIST

The Kidderminster somnambulist is saved, from the *IPN*, 8 August 1885.

FEARFUL POSITION OF A SOMNAMBULIST.
NARROW ESCAPE.

Miss Charlton falls from the roof, from the *IPN*, 17 April 1897.

Andrian, the Dog-Faced Man, 1874

In 1874, the London newspapers announced that two of the greatest human curiosities of the present time had arrived at the Metropolitan Music Hall in Edgware Road: Andrian the Russian Dog-faced Man and his son Fedor. A reporter and a draughtsman from the *IPN* were present to provide a feature about these strange beings. The fifty-five-year-old Andrian was a quiet, morose individual, who spoke only Russian. He was of medium height, strongly built and dressed in rather dirty-looking Russian garments. His eyes were a curious yellow and his skin an

ANDRIAN THE DOG FACED MAN AND HIS SON
SINGULAR BEINGS FROM THE KOSTROMA FOREST. RUSSIA

Andrian the Dog-faced Man and his Son: an original drawing from the *IPN*, 7 February 1874.

unhealthy grey. Young Fedor, who was on show with him, was actually Andrian's illegitimate son, the impresario said, although many of the female visitors to the exhibition must have experienced a frisson of horror that even a sex-starved Russian peasant woman had once consented to copulate with such a monster. Andrian was like a man half changed into an animal, a spectacle destined to strike horror into Victorian people. His face was entirely covered with hair, like that of a Skye terrier.

A doctor was impressed to see Andrian drink a pint of undiluted vodka with relish, as he carved his beefsteak at the exhibition. He showed little affection for his son, and much resented when some visitors to the exhibition spoke to the lively young Fedor and tipped him handsomely, and then passed by the smelly father with horror. The showman said that ever since he had first put Andrian on show before the curious in St Petersburg, Paris and Berlin the year before, the hairy man had vowed to return to his native village as soon as his tour of the European capitals was over, and to spend all the money he had earned entirely on strong drink. According to another, slightly more prepossessing version, Andrian was a devout member of the Russo-Greek Church. Since others in that faith had told him that he must surely have been cursed by the Devil, poor Andrian spent all his money on the purchase of prayers from a devout community of monks near Kostroma, 'hoping one day to be able to introduce his frightful countenance in the court of heaven', as the exhibition pamphlet flippantly expressed it.

If many visitors to the exhibition were disgusted or horrified by the debauched, unkempt spectacle of Andrian, all were charmed by his little son Fedor. Although just four years old, he was more intelligent, and much more sprightly and vigorous, than his wretched father. The growth of down on his face was not yet so heavy as to conceal his features, but the medical men who saw him did not doubt that he would one day become just as hairy as his father. Fedor's hair was white and as thick as that of an Angora cat, and he had long whiskers and a tuft of long hair at the outer angle of either eye. He liked to travel and to meet new people, and was already getting spoilt and petulant. He spoke French, and in spite of his tender age, gave rational replies to questions from the audience. The dentition of both Adrian and Fedor was very defective. Andrian had only the stump of a tooth in the upper jaw and four rotten teeth in the lower jaw. Fedor had a perfectly edentulous upper jaw, with no alveolar processes, and only four incisors in the lower jaw.

Andrian and Fedor remained in London until early April 1874, and then spent ten days in Liverpool. According to the *Liverpool Mercury* of 14 April, the jolly young Fedor pointed at the bald head of a doctor in the audience and suggested that it would have been an improvement if some of the hair on his own face could have been transferred to the savant's bald pate! Andrian died later in 1874, probably from cirrhosis of the liver brought on by his excessive drinking of spirits. Fedor's later distinguished career in the American sideshow, under the name of Jo-Jo the Dog-faced Boy, has been described in my book *Freaks*. Jo-Jo toured the world with Barnum & Bailey's Greatest Show on Earth until his death, from pneumonia, in 1912.

Conjoined Twins in the *Illustrated Police News*

The iconography of conjoined twins owes much to the popular press: whereas most articles about them in medical journals were without images, those in popular magazines were often well illustrated. When there was a scarcity of criminal news, the *IPN* took an interest in popular amusements and occasionally featured conjoined twins exhibited in the London sideshow.

The original Siamese twins, Chang and Eng, were born in 1811 and lived united for sixty-three years. They were omphalopagus twins, joined at the abdomen. It was more than once debated whether they could be separated, but when they were younger, the twins themselves were unwilling to submit to such an operation. When the Siamese twins grew older, they became afraid that after the death of one of them, the other would be tied to a corpse, and during a journey to London and Edinburgh they consulted several eminent surgeons. The verdict of Sir William Ferguson, among others, was that it was inadvisable to attempt a surgical separation. At autopsy, it was seen that the Siamese twins' liver and several major vessels were shared, and although they could have been separated with ease if they had lived today, an attempt at operation with nineteenth-century techniques would probably have been fatal. The Siamese twins do not appear to have made it into the *IPN* while alive, but after their death, a standard drawing of them in old age was published with their obituary.

The original Siamese twins, from the *IPN*, 31 January 1874.

Medical Freaks

The conjoined twins Rosa and Josepha Blazek were born in rural Bohemia in 1878. Much astonished by this monstrous birth, their parents consulted the local witch, who recommended that the children should be kept without food for eight days. The twins survived this cruel treatment, however, and after this impressive demonstration of resilience, even the witch agreed that they should be kept alive. Several showmen applied to Rosa and Josepha's parents to get permission to exhibit them for money. In November 1880, the two little girls were on show at the Egyptian Hall in London. The *IPN* journalist thought them bright, intelligent children, and reproduced a good drawing of them and their parents. Rosa and Josepha were pygopagus twins, joined at the hips. They later went on to make a career for themselves, of course preferring life in gay Paris to the drab existence in the Bohemian backwoods in the cabin of their rustic parents. They were called 'Le pygopage du Théatre de l'age Gaité', and were a well-known attraction at the Paris stage, amusing the audience with singing and playing violin duets. Later, they passed out of public notice until they consulted the surgical clinic at the Prague General Hospital in 1910, after Rosa had noticed a large and rapidly growing abdominal swelling. She was asked whether she might be pregnant, but denied it vehemently; her sister, who certainly was in a position to know, supported her denial. But before the investigation was brought any further, Rosa was delivered of a healthy son. Later, the two inseparable sisters married the same man and moved to the United States; they died there in 1922 at the age of forty-three.

The Blazek twins, from the *IPN*, 27 November 1880.

THE DOUBLE CHILD AT THE EGYPTIAN HALL

The *IPN* also featured another, more obscure pair of conjoined twins. The two little girls, Radica and Doodica, were born in Orissa, India. Just like the original Siamese twins, they were omphalopagus conjoined twins, joined by the abdomen. The superstitious residents of their village saw the girls as symbols of divine wrath and demanded their immediate expulsion. Distraught at the appearance of his daughters, their father wanted to physically separate the girls with his own hands, but local officials restrained him and rescued the infants. Later, the monks of a local temple took over their care. In 1892, Radica and Doodica began their exhibition career at the Royal Aquarium, under the London showman Captain Colman. The *IPN* journalist thought them intelligent and bright; although they had only been taught English for a few months, they understood what he said. According to their impresario, they were on the way to the World's Fair in Chicago. Their career as travelling exhibition objects continued until 1902, when Doodica developed tuberculosis. In Paris, Dr Eugene-Louis Doyen surgically separated the sisters, in an effort to save Radica. Doyen was a pioneering medical filmmaker and filmed the twins' surgery as 'La Separation de Doodica-Radica'. The operation was initially considered a success; although Doodica soon expired from tuberculosis, Radica seemed to thrive. However, she had already contracted tuberculosis, and died from it a year later; the final months of her life were spent in a Paris sanatorium, alone.

The Orissa twins, from the *IPN*, 17 September 1892.

Buried Alive!

Another favourite subject of the *IPN* was the danger of apparent death and premature burial. Having looked through a folder of cuttings from this newspaper, I found not less than twelve illustrated stories of people being buried alive or narrowly escaping this dire fate. For at least thirty years, the *IPN* reproduced horrific stories from all over Europe, about knocking sounds from the vault, nails scraping against unyielding coffin lids, and prematurely buried women giving birth to children inside their coffins.

The debate about the certainty of the signs of death, and the risk of being buried alive by mistake, had raged in continental Europe since the 1740s. In Germany, the authorities had financed the erection of waiting mortuaries, where corpses could be incubated awaiting the onset of putrefaction, since this was considered the only certain sign of death. In France, Spain and Italy, among other countries, there was a vigorous debate whether to trust the medical profession, or follow the same negativist path. In France, several newspapers were agitating in favour of burial reform. Their journalists frightened their readers out of their wits by reproducing the most ghastly tales of prematurely buried people awakening in their coffins and suffering the most horrible tortures.

As I have demonstrated in my book *Buried Alive*, many of these newspaper accounts were culled from the foreign press, others 'recycled' stories from old newspapers, and yet others were pure inventions. One favourite story for the anti-premature burial campaigners can be called 'the lucky escape'. An individual is declared dead either by a layperson or by a doctor, but wakes up before or during the funeral and makes his or her resuscitation known. The more horrific version has the enfeebled victim of catalepsy knock on the coffin lid just as the earth is thrown at it; in the 'amusing' version, the next of kin think that the resuscitated 'corpse' is a ghost and flee yelling.

The earliest tale of a 'lucky escape' in the pages of the *IPN* concerns a Mrs Smithson of Leathford, of whom it is briefly told, without any source given, that she woke up in her coffin after being declared dead, and that her husband and children thought she was a ghost. The illustration has her accost her startled relatives dressed only in her shroud, like Poe's Lady Madeline Usher. The tale of Mrs Smithson may well have been true, but I have not been able to verify it using alternative sources. Another story, concerning an unnamed woman in San Francisco who woke up after being declared dead, seems even more dubious.

A more reliable account comes from Wembdon near Bridgwater, where a labouring man named George Chilcott collapsed in September 1884. Since he was still and death-like, his family took him to church to be buried, without wasting any money on calling the doctor. The vicar of

Mrs Smithson of Leathford comes walking
into the parlour, wearing her shroud, and
frightens her husband and children, from
the *IPN*, 11 April 1874.

Wembdon, the Revd Arthur Newman, thought Chilcott too warm to be
dead, however, and although his family was keen to have him decently
buried as soon as possible, the parson kept the coffined 'corpse' in the
church. After a three-day wake, Chilcott was observed to move slightly.
He was taken out of his coffin and medical aid was finally called for.

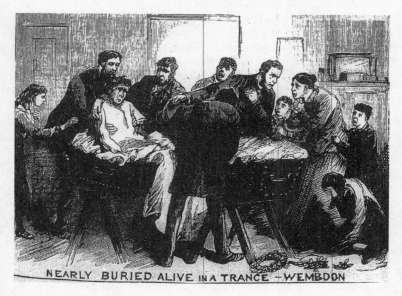

George Chilcott of Wembdon rises from the dead, from the *IPN*, 4 October 1874.

The account in the *IPN* ends here, but the relevant issues of the *Bridgwater Times* have some further interesting things to add. Not only is the story absolutely true, but Chilcott eventually recovered completely. Parson Newman was known to be quite eccentric, being more fond of hunting, shooting and fishing than looking after his parishioners, but this time he had done one of them a real service. Chilcott is unlikely to have appreciated his family's great urgency to have him put underground, however.

Rescuing George Chilcott was Parson Newman's first newsworthy action; his second came in 1900, when he absconded from the parish without warning. The locals soon found out that he had gone to America, taking his mistress with him. After a few months, this odd parson returned to Wembdon, hoping to resume his duties, but his irate parishioners had had enough of him. The exact words of the disgraced parson when he read the petition they had nailed to the church door, barring him from his ministry, have unfortunately not been recorded. But if this forthright West Country parson, whose predilection for coarse language was well known, had remembered the dramatic events from 1885, he may well have exclaimed, 'You may bury each other as you wish now, yer buggers!'

In May 1895, a woman at Limoges was declared dead after suffering a cataleptic fit. When her coffin was carried into the church for the funeral

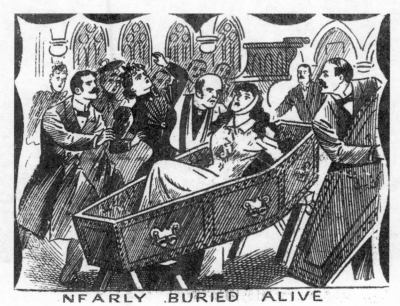

Nearly Buried Alive, from the *IPN*, 25 May 1895.

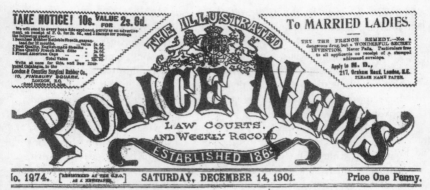

SENSATIONAL SCENE AT A GRAVESIDE.
A LADY IS VERY NEARLY BURIED ALIVE.

Sensational Scene at a Graveside, from the *IPN*, 14 December 1901.

A woman buried alive at Llanelly, from the *IPN*, 28 June 1884.

ceremony, a distinct knocking sound was heard from inside. The lid was prised off and the woman taken out alive. This story was also reported by some mainstream British newspapers, and it does not seem entirely unlikely. It originated in the French newspaper press, however, and in *Buried Alive*, I demonstrated that a considerable proportion of these French newspaper yarns had been invented by unscrupulous journalists. In December 1901, Donna Maria Galvago made it to the first page of the *IPN*, after she had revived inside her coffin just when it was to be buried, but this is yet another 'from our Foreign Correspondent' story that cannot be independently verified.

On 28 January 1905, it was time for the strange story of Mrs Alice Holden, the Accrington cataleptic. She had fallen into a decline after being knocked on the head by some poultry thieves and gradually faded away. A doctor certified her dead, but when the undertaker was called

The careless colleagues of the prematurely buried gendarme in Grenoble belatedly pay their respects, from the *IPN*, 26 January 1889.

in to measure her for the coffin, he saw her eyelids flutter and she was restored to life. She did not sue the careless doctor, but warned him to be more careful in the future when declaring people dead, particularly since she had herself twice been laid out for burial before, once as a child and once when fifteen years old. The *IPN* improves on the story by having her clutch the hand of the startled undertaker, who well-nigh has a fit himself. In the illustration, she looks quite fit and healthy, and very unlike a cataleptic. In real life she was very frail and weak, however, although later strong enough to go on an extended tour of various northern music halls, where a showman told her pathetic story as she reclined in a chair.

The second type of premature burial yarn in the pages of the *IPN* is that of the corpse or skeleton found in a strange, unnatural position, having attempted to break out of the unyielding coffin. As I have demonstrated in *Buried Alive*, these stories were a mainstay for the French anti-premature burial propaganda. The year 1874 supplied a 'shocking case of premature interment' originally reported in the *Messager du Midi*. An unnamed young woman at Salon had been certified dead by a doctor and buried in a vault straight away due to the heat. After a week, her mother wanted to see the remains and the vault was opened. The coffin had burst and the corpse was lying in the middle, with dishevelled hair and linen torn to pieces (gnawed in agony, it was presumed). The mother was so shocked by the dreadful spectacle that the doctors feared for her reason, if not her life. Later in 1874, it was reported that an unnamed Jewish lady in Brody in Galicia had been hastily buried after being declared dead. After a week the grave was opened and it was observed that the linen was soaked with blood – clearly evidence of another dreadful case of premature burial.

In 1886, the *IPN* supplied yet another horrific account of a premature burial, this time from closer to home and verified by a much more reputable source. Canon Williams, the vicar of Llanelli, had been called by a gravedigger who had opened a brick tomb in the churchyard to put a coffin in the empty space in a tomb made for two persons. He was shocked to see that the lid of the coffin already in the tomb had been forced open, and that the right arm and leg of the corpse inside were hanging out through the opening. The Canon found out that this woman had been presumed to have died eleven years earlier; the cause of death was marked as 'unknown' and there was no evidence of any medical man being called to see her. Clearly this woman had been buried alive, the Canon wrote in a letter to the *Lancet*, and the possibility of such horrors occurring regularly was too dreadful to contemplate. Modern medical science would not agree with the Canon, however, since post-mortem putrefactive changes can cause the body to swell and change position, and even to burst open a coffin.

In 1889, the *IPN* had another sinister tale to tell. A gendarme near Grenoble drank excessive amounts of potato brandy and fell into a death-like trance. His colleagues believed him to be dead after a wake of just twenty hours, put him in a coffin and took him to the local mortuary. In the middle of the night, the sexton heard moans and knocks from the coffin! He tried to prise off the lid but it had been too tightly fastened. Instead, he bored some holes in the coffin to let in air, before running off to fetch assistance. When they finally were able to knock off the lid, the gendarme had ceased to breathe. His forehead was terribly lacerated from his frantic attempts to burst the coffin open. This story reads like it might be true, but once more the victim is unnamed and the careless journalists omitted to provide a source. No mainstream British newspaper reported the case.

In 1904, there was a sensational story emanating from the Vienna correspondent of the *Daily Express*: Helena Fritsch, the young daughter of a wealthy farmer in Egerskeg, Hungary, was buried with great pomp, with a number of valuable rings on her fingers. The evening of the same day, the graveyard sexton heard a knock at his window: he was horrified to find that it was the girl he had helped to bury. It turned out that two thieves had dug down to the coffin and cut three of her fingers off to steal her rings; the pain had roused her from her death-like cataleptic trance, and she had climbed out of her coffin and rejoined the rest of humanity. But although the *IPN* honoured Helena Fritsch by clearing the front page, there are serious doubts whether she ever existed at all; the legend of the 'Lady with the Ring' who is revived by grave robbers has been told and retold, with different names for the protagonists, since the fifteenth century.

THE ILLUSTRATED POLICE NEWS

LAW COURTS.
AND WEEKLY RECORD
ESTABLISHED 1864

No. 2099. [REGISTERED AT THE G.P.O. AS A NEWSPAPER] SATURDAY, MAY 7, 1904. Price One Penny

SHE SAW TWO MEN CLIMBING UP A LADDER.

THE SEXTON SAW THE FACE OF THE GIRL HE HAD BURIED.

A YOUNG GIRL'S RESURRECTION.

BURIED ALIVE, SHE IS BROUGHT TO LIFE BY ROBBERS CUTTING THE RINGS OFF HER FINGERS.

A retelling of the legend of the 'Lady with the Ring', from the *IPN*, 7 May 1904.

In Victorian Britain, the establishment and the medical profession stood united in condemning the continental obsession with the risk of waking up in a coffin underground. As a result, the mainstream British newspaper press published very little about the uncertainty of the signs of death and the danger of premature interment. But as we have seen, the *IPN* avidly reproduced a vast array of newspaper stories about people either being buried alive or narrowly escaping this dire fate. One reason for this may well be that someone on the editorial staff of the *IPN* (most probably George Purkess himself) had a genuine fear of premature interment. It might also be that they were attracted by the sheer horror value of the stories and the potential for lurid illustrations, particularly since no attempt was made to agitate in favour of burial reform or to criticise the currently used criteria for declaring people dead. Although the *IPN* blithely concluded that hundreds of people were buried alive each year, no attempt was made to comment on the reasons for this, or to suggest a remedy.

The Scottish Giant, 1878

In my book *The Two-headed Boy, and other Medical Marvels*, later re-issued in the UK as *Freaks*, I described the life and times of Daniel Lambert, a native of Leicester who weighed not less than fifty-two stone. When he exhibited himself for money in London in 1806, he was acknowledged as the heaviest man ever seen in Britain. The story of the Leicester colossus has since been regurgitated by several plagiarists, on the internet and elsewhere, and has also reached Wikipedia. In contrast, much less is known about the first man in Britain to challenge Lambert's weight record, the publican William Campbell, but thanks to the *IPN*, I am now able to remedy that state of affairs.

William Campbell was born in Glasgow in 1856. His father was tall but of ordinary weight and build; his mother was short and quite thin. He was one of seven siblings. But whereas his brothers and sisters were of normal proportions, William's weight increased in an alarming manner: at the age of just ten, he weighed eighteen stone. He trained to become a printer, but his extreme obesity – upwards of forty stone already in his late teens – rendered him incapable of finding paid employment. In September 1875, he married Polly, the daughter of Burnley photographer John Kelly. In November 1877, they took up the lease of the Duke of Wellington public house at High Bridge in Newcastle.

In February 1878, the Newcastle correspondent of the *Lancet* visited William Campbell, who was now claiming to be the heaviest man in Britain, weighing more than fifty-two stone. He was six feet, eight inches tall, and measured ninety-six inches round the shoulders, round the waist eighty-five inches, and round the calf thirty-five inches. Although he was not yet twenty-two years old, his general health was far from good; he suffered from a 'cold' and an erysipelatous infection of one of his huge legs. Although he only admitted a 'moderate' consumption of alcoholic beverages, he smoked like a chimney, and his heartbeat was weak and

WILLIAM CAMPBELL THE SCOTTISH GIAN'

William Campbell, the Scottish Giant; like the following two, this image is from the *IPN*, 8 June 1878.

irregular. The Newcastle doctor thought Campbell's occupation and habits were scarcely conducive to health and longevity, even though they might increase his weight and popularity.

In March 1878, William Campbell went on exhibition at the Egyptian Hall in London as 'Her Majesty's Largest Subject, The Heaviest Man in the World'. The freak-show was open from twelve until four in the afternoons, and from seven until nine in the evening. He appeared in Highland costume, and appeared both jovial and intelligent. He had a large smile and a broad accent, and dressed in very broad cloth. A facetious author in *Funny Folks* magazine hoped he would emerge from Egyptian Hall worth his weight in gold. When interviewed by a journalist from the *Era* newspaper, Campbell said he had little liking for show business, but since he was now incapable of locomotion, there was nothing else for him. He also cracked a few jokes, however, saying that he should be considered a public benefactor for having tested so many coach springs, to make sure they were fit for service. He also told the story of a very diminutive friend of his, who had been rebuffed with the words 'All one charge, big or little' when he asked a tailor for a reduction in the price for a suit. The little man then ordered two suits, one for himself, and one for his friend William Campbell!

William Campbell remained in London throughout March and April, before exhibiting himself at the Paris Exposition. In May, after returning

GETTING THE COFFIN OUT OF WINDOW

Right: The wall of the house is demolished to enable the Giant's coffin to be removed.

Below: William Campbell's coffin is lowered onto the hearse.

A GIANTS FUNERAL—NEWCASTLE ON TYNE—LOWERING THE BODY

to Newcastle, he fell seriously ill; he expired on 26 May, in his bedroom at the Duke of Wellington public house, from erysipelas and congestion of the lungs according to his death certificate. There were obituaries in several newspapers, but the *IPN* went one better: would it not be *funny* to reproduce a drawing of Campbell in Highland dress, and some illustrations of his funeral. Without any piety towards the family of the deceased, some lugubrious drawings were produced by the *IPN*'s artists.

When the time had come for the Scottish Giant's funeral, the High Bridge area was completely thronged by curiosity-seekers who wanted to see the immense coffin. After the window had been removed, and part of the wall demolished, it was hoisted up to the bedroom, where a number of strong men put Campbell's remains into it. Using a trolley, the coffin, now weighing nearly a ton, was carefully deposited onto the hearse. The procession started just after half-past two in the afternoon: first came the Buffalo Band, playing 'Dead March in Saul', then a hundred members of the Buffalo Society, some kind of down-market Freemasonry of which Campbell had been a prominent member. The hearse was followed by five mourning coaches and a throng of mourners on foot. The windows and roofs of the houses along the route were crowded by spectators, some of whom had even climbed Gray's monument to see this bizarre funeral cortege. In Jesmond cemetery, more than two thousand people had assembled, with an equal number standing in the road outside. After the coffin had been gingerly lowered into the grave, the vicar of Newcastle read the burial service. The Duke of Wellington public house was repaired after William Campbell's coffin had been taken out; it appears as if it is still standing today, at No. 18 High Bridge. According to an internet account, which I wish I had remembered to verify at my latest visit to the Newcastle watering-holes, the house has a plaque commemorating the Scottish Giant.

Whereas Daniel Lambert was weighed several times, the allegation that William Campbell was more than fifty-two stone in weight seems to rely only on his own testimony. Whether this estimate was correct, and whether he was really heavier than Lambert, remains entirely unclear. Otherwise, it would appear as if the Leicester phenomenon remained unchallenged well into very recent times. In 1905, the heaviest Briton alive weighed just forty-four stone, and in 1980, Lambert's record still stood. But since that time, an epidemic of obesity has struck the world. Peter Yarnall, of East Ham, was said to have weighed fifty-eight stone when he died in 1984. Christopher McGarva, from Sleaford in Lincolnshire, was estimated to weigh sixty-five stone when he expired in 2005. Football supporter Barry Austin, of Birmingham, was alleged to weigh sixty-five stone in 2009. In October the same year, Paul Mason, of Ipswich, weighed in at seventy stone when transported to hospital in a specially strengthened ambulance.

Marian, the Giant Amazon Queen, 1882

Marian Wedde was born on 31 January 1866, in the village of Benkendorf in Thüringen, Germany. Her parents were ordinary German country people, the father working as a fireman at a large distillery for spirits; she had nine brothers and sisters, all of normal stature, but from an early age, Marian grew to be extremely tall. A special stool had to be manufactured for her use at school. To prevent her head bumping into the low ceilings of the farmhouse, she had to walk with a pronounced stoop. Once, she fell down heavily and hurt her ankle, an injury leading to permanent lameness. In 1882, she was 'discovered' by the German impresario Herr Kopf, and exhibited for money in Berlin, Hamburg and other cities. In July 1882, she was taken to London, where the operetta *Babil and Bijou* at the Alhambra Theatre, Leicester Square, had a part of an Amazon Queen purposely written for a gigantic actress.

Marian spoke no English, but this did not matter, since her role in the play was a silent one. Dressed in an azure tunic and a silver cuirass, she walked heavily about on stage, to the audible admiration from the audience. A man of over six feet in height could easily walk erect under her outstretched arm. Although quite heavy-featured, she was not bad-looking: the theatrical critic George Augustus Sala even wrote that, 'Notwithstanding her colossal height and build, she is very well proportioned, and she is decidedly handsome, possessing as she does the true pre-Raphaelite maxillary angle.' Her English impresario, Mr William Holland, of the Alhambra Theatre, kept pointing out to the journalists that since Marian was only sixteen years old, she was still growing.

Marian soon became one of the leading human curiosities in London. She was depicted in the *IPN*, along with her manager William Holland, and her portrait appeared on all the theatre posters for *Babil and Bijou*. One of the few people who disapproved of her was the theatrical critic Clement Scott, who wrote:

> Suppose it had been suggested to me that good music would be put on one side, good singers cold-shouldered, beautiful ballets made a second consideration, our lovely English women rendered of no account, singing, acting, decoration, spectacle, art, all made subordinate to one abnormal monster - well, I should have laughed the Barnum to scorn who had such faith in monstrosities and the eccentricity of the English public. But, as it turns out, I should have been extremely wrong. Mr William Holland, of the Alhambra Theatre, has proved that at any rate. He has discovered in Germany a giantess who, massive, awkward, and unwieldy as she is, has managed to draw more people to the Alhambra Theatre than have ever before been known to assemble there at this time of year ... No one talks of anything else but Mr. Holland's

THE GIANTESS AT THE ALHAMBRA THEATRE.

Marian, the Giantess at the Alhambra Theatre, from the *IPN*, 29 July 1882.

The Alhambra Theatre in Leicester Square, from an old postcard.

giantess, with her amiable inexpressive face, her clumsy gait, and her speechless look of dismay. It does not amuse me to hear that she is still growing; I only pity the fate of the poor girl so cruelly ill-used by Nature.

Marian carried on acting the part of the Amazon Queen in *Babil and Bijou* throughout July and August 1882. In late August, she held two receptions at the Crystal Palace, in front of an admiring crowd. The popular operetta carried on playing throughout the remainder of 1882, with the giantess taking part in every performance. On 3 December, she attended a party at Marlborough House, at the invitation of the Prince and Princess of Wales. The jocular Prince gave the young giantess a glass of champagne, and although she was normally a strict teetotaller, she emptied it by Royal command. On 16 December, the *Morning Post* carried the following advertisement: 'Wanted, a respectable young man to accompany Marian, the Giant Amazon Queen, on her tour through the provinces; must make himself agreeable; liveries found. Apply to Mr W. Holland at the Alhambra.'

Marian's provincial tour began at the Trade's Hall in Glasgow on 1 January 1883. She wished the audience a 'Happy New Year' in a strong German accent. A *Glasgow Herald* journalist found her handsome and agreeable, although her hands and feet were of an enormous size. Mr Holland introduced her on stage, describing how she had been 'discovered' in Germany and complimenting her for her healthy appetite. Marian remained in Glasgow for nearly a month before travelling on to Dundee and Aberdeen. In February, she was exhibited at the Newcastle Town Hall; in March, at the Cutlers' Hall in Sheffield. A journalist from the *Sheffield & Rotherham Independent* thought her good-looking and well proportioned, and most pleasant in conversation; during her six-month stay in London, her stature had increased by four inches. In May, Marian was at Reynolds' Waxworks in Liverpool, where she was joined by Herr Brustad, a giant who had just returned from Barnum's circus in America, and by the midgets 'Colonel Ulpta' and 'Major Tiny Tim'. Colonel Ulpta cracked jokes like a champion and sang various comical songs; when he introduced Marian and her fellow performers to the gawping Liverpudlians, he of course pointed out that she was still growing.

After leaving Liverpool in late May 1883, nothing was heard of Marian in the English papers for several months; there were rumours that she had been taken back to Germany to be exhibited for money, or that her health was failing. Unfortunately, the latter rumour turned out to be the truth: Marian died in Berlin on 22 January 1884, just before her eighteenth birthday. The catchphrase 'she is still growing' was repeated even in her newspaper obituary, and it was added that her death had been somewhat unexpected, and that she had been under engagement to proceed to America. Poor Marian was finally free from the people who had exploited her; she would be spared the heartless stares from the American sideshow 'rubes'; she had reached her final height in life and would be growing no more.

Krao, the Missing Link, 1883

In January 1883, the Royal Aquarium advertised a novel attraction for the curious: the hairy little girl Krao, who had just arrived from Laos. Mr G. A. Farini, her manager, presented her as the 'missing link' between human and ape, and the living proof of Darwin's theory of evolution. He claimed that the intrepid German explorer Carl Bock had also captured Krao's parents, and that all three belonged to a hairy tribe of people living in the interior of Laos. Her father's body had been completely covered with a thick hairy coat, like that of an anthropoid ape. His long arms and rounded belly added further to his simian appearance. He had been incapable of speech when caught, Herr Bock claimed, but on board ship, he had been able to utter a few words in Malay. The mother was, for reasons unexplained, detained at Bangkok by the Siamese Government, but these authorities apparently had no objections to six-year-old Krao being taken from her parents and transported to the other side of the globe.

The London journalists were treated to a special showing of the Missing Link, or Human Monkey. Some of them were taken in by Farini's banter about Krao's father having a face resembling that of a Skye terrier and her entire tribe being hairy, but others found the little girl perfectly normal apart from her hairy growth. Krao was interested in a gentleman's shiny clock, and she pointed out a lady who had previously shown her kindness with the impromptu cry of 'Look, papa!' to Mr Farini. The correspondent of the *IPN* was amazed that the little girl possessed 'hirsute developments such as probably were never seen on human being since the days of Esau'. She was playful and good-natured and politely said 'Good-bye!' to the journalists when they left her. Krao was soon the shining star of the Royal Aquarium, completely outclassing its other performers, including Professor Mark's Dogs, the American Knockabouts and John Cooper's Trained Lions. The drawing in the *IPN* shows a rather bored-looking Krao sitting on stage playing with her toys, ignoring the audience gawping at her.

In *Nature* magazine, Krao was described by the anthropologist Dr A. H. Keane, who was one of the many Darwinists searching for the 'missing link' between human and ape. Both Africa and Asia were given attention by the zealous evolutionists, who were searching for atavistic signs, like tails or abnormal hairiness, in what they termed inferior races of mankind. Dr Keane had previously published a paper on the Ainu tribe in Ezo and Sakhalin, and postulated the existence of a primitive hairy race in Further India. These preconceived notions made him a willing

Krao being exhibited,
from the *IPN*,
13 January 1883.

dupe to the showman's spiel. With rapt attention, he examined little Krao, who had by then been in London for ten weeks. She had acquired several English words, which she used intelligently, and Dr Keane had to conclude that her intellect was that of a normal human child. Her entire body had a coat of rather thick, black hair, but its growth was nowhere close enough to conceal the skin. She was remarkably supple and agile, and Dr Keane was interested to note that her feet had particularly long toes, with which she could actually grasp objects, and that her hands were so flexible that they could bend quite back over the wrists. He could detect no simian characteristics in the shape of her face, although the showman assured him that she used to stuff food into her cheeks just like a monkey, and that her lips could protrude so far as to give her 'quite a chimpanzee look'. She was given to terrible outbursts of rage when denied something, Mr Farini said, and the only thing that could suppress her unruly behaviour was the threat that she would be sent back to her own people. With these observations in mind, Dr Keane concluded that Krao was the living proof of a hairy race in Laos, and thus a phenomenon of exceptional scientific importance.

Krao remained in London until late July 1883, when she travelled to Liverpool, and then on to Dublin in September. In 1884 and 1885, Krao toured Germany and Austria. She was exhibited at the Frankfurt Zoological Gardens, and the usual ostentatious advertising ensured a record audience: the zoo was so crowded that a twentieth-century German writer pronounced these shows the most memorable in its 150-year history. On the handbills and posters, a distinctly simian-looking Krao was portrayed dressed in a loin-cloth only; her hairy growth was exaggerated, and she stood grasping the branch of a tree in front of a jungle background. Several medical men examined her, among them the German dentist Julius Parreidt. He was interested to note that, unlike many other hairy people, Krao did not have a diminished number of teeth. In 1885, a certain Herr Bastian could announce that the explorer Bock's dramatic account of how Krao had been captured with her 'wild' family was nothing but a pack of lies; in fact, she had been born in Bangkok, the child of two normal parents, who were both still living! In 1886, Krao and Mr Farini came to Paris. Here, she was examined by the French anthropologist Dr Fauvelle, who was as eager as Dr Keane in his search for her supposed primitive and ape-like characteristics. Krao was lively and agreeable throughout the interview, and did not object to being examined. Apart from her hairy growth, Dr Fauvelle noted that her ears were rather large, that her nose was flat, and her joints very supple and flexible; all these observations were given a sinister interpretation. The impresario, always eager to make his charge appear even more interesting, assured him that she had thirteen ribs and the same number of thoracic vertebrae, that she had double rows of teeth, and that her behaviour was often quite ape-like. In all earnestness, Dr Fauvelle wrote that he unfortunately been unable to assess the intelligence of this strange 'ape-girl', since her command of the English language was far superior to his own!

Krao spent all her life in show business. Throughout the 1890s, she toured Europe with her manager Mr Farini, who had become her adopted father, and her English governess. In 1893, a certain Herr Maass saw the now seventeen-year-old Krao being exhibited in Berlin. The prudish German considered her short dress somewhat risqué, although not unbecoming. She was quite a young lady, he wrote, and her manner was decent and friendly. It was clear to him that all the stories about her supposed ape-like characteristics were just inventions to make her even more interesting to the gullible public. Krao again toured Britain in 1899, with a lengthy stay at the Panopticon in Cardiff, where she became quite a favourite. Krao later became one of the stars of Ringling Bros. and Barnum & Bailey's circus in the United States. One would not have supposed that a young girl who spent her adolescent years being exhibited as 'The Human Monkey' in various zoos and monster-museums would grow up to be a harmonious and well-adjusted individual, but it is claimed that Krao became one of the most popular 'old troupers' of the circus. She was an educated, well-read woman who spoke many languages. Krao died in New York, in 1926.

The Birmingham Midget, 1884

Dysfunctional families, who neglect and mistreat their children, are a daily feature in the newspapers. A dismal tale from the *IPN* would suggest that this is far from a modern phenomenon, however.

In early July 1884, Mrs Emma Evans, the wife of a Birmingham mechanic, gave birth to a most extraordinary child, less than nine inches long and weighing less than ten ounces but still perfectly formed. Since all the neighbours thronged to see little Lilly Evans, the Birmingham Midget, it did not take long for her parents to realise that they were on to a good thing. After the Midget had been rented to a showman for 30s a week, Mr Evans downed his tools and descended into an alcoholic daze. When Emma Evans accompanied the Midget on tour, she brought a knapsack of gin bottles with her wherever she went. On 17 August, the Midget fell ill with convulsions. She was taken out for a ride, in the vain hope that such an experience would cause the tiny creature to rally, but the Birmingham Midget expired the next day.

Emma Evans now tried to make a deal with the showman, or perhaps a doctor keen on collecting curiosities, to sell the tiny corpse. An auction was started, with several interested bidders, but these macabre proceedings were halted by Mr Weekes, the deputy coroner for Birmingham, who held an inquest on the Midget on 21 August. When questioned by the stern Mr Weekes, Emma Evans denied ever being drunk, although she admitted keeping the Midget awake for exhibition purposes. A woman who had made an elaborate dress for the Midget testified that poor Lilly had been exhibited throughout the day, with the exception of dinner and teatime. She had suckled the mother when the latter was sober, and had been fed 'scalded biscuits' when that was not the case.

'But was she not nearly always drunk?'

'Yes.' [sensation in court]

The verdict of the deputy coroner was that Lilly Evans had died due to the neglect of the mother, and the rigours of being exhibited for money. He treated Emma Evans to a severe tongue-lashing, adding that she had narrowly escaped prosecution for manslaughter.

But the 'dysfunctional' Emma Evans was not done yet. Since she freely exhibited the corpse to any person giving her a tip, the house where she lodged, in Francis Street, was thronged with the curious. On 24 August, the undertakers put the Birmingham Midget in her tiny coffin, and the procession to Warstone Lane Cemetery could begin. Such was the crowd attending this singular funeral that Francis Street was impassable for fifteen minutes. Not trusting the mother's promise that the remains of the Midget would not be sold to the showman, the police halted the

FUNERAL OF THE BIRMINGHAM MIDGET

The funeral of the Birmingham Midget, from *IPN*, 6 September 1884.

procession midway and opened the coffin, to reveal the tiny corpse within. The detestable Emma Evans was hissed and yelled at by the mob and would have been lynched had the police not protected her. When the undertaker grasped the tiny coffin and put it underneath his coat, as depicted by the *IPN* artist, there was a loud yell of laughter from the mob, a dismal farewell to the unfortunate Birmingham Midget.

The Strange Death of the Earl of Lauderdale, 1884

The Earldom of Lauderdale, created in 1624, is one of Scotland's most distinguished titles. The Earl of Lauderdale is the hereditary clan chief of Clan Maitland, and the bearer of the National Flag of Scotland. But after a number of elderly Earls had died childless in the mid-nineteenth century, the title was in serious danger of becoming extinct. At the death of James Maitland, the ninth Earl, in 1860, he was succeeded by his elderly brother, Admiral Sir Anthony Maitland. The next in line to inherit was Admiral Sir Thomas Maitland, another childless old gentleman. It was speculated in the newspapers that perhaps the title would once be inherited by Charles Maitland, the great-great-grandson of the second son of the sixth Earl. The son of an eccentric clergyman, this individual was living in very humble circumstances. Having served as an army soldier for a while, he now made his living as a goods guard on the Exeter railway.

And indeed, when the old Admiral expired in 1878, the obscure Charles Maitland, by this time fifty-six years of age, was in a position to remove his humble railwayman's cap, replace it with an elegant tall hat, and take possession of the family seat at Thirlestane Castle. One might have expected the railway guard turned twelfth Earl of Lauderdale to have led a jolly life, wining, dining and partying to excess to celebrate his elevation to the peerage. But Charles Maitland was a gloomy, morose character, who shunned company and became a recluse. He made the news in 1879 when he announced that he no longer wished to belong to the Conservative Association, not because he disagreed with the principles of Toryism but because he did not want to belong to any political party. His only other newsworthy actions were that he allowed his tenants to hunt rabbits and hares on his estate, and that he once went to the theatre in Edinburgh.

What, I hear the reader exclaim, is this obscure Scottish peer doing in the *IPN*? A railway guard becoming an Earl might be *news*, but to qualify for the *Illustrated Police News*, he would have to attend the House of Lords dressed in his railwayman's uniform, shoot at his tenants poaching for rabbits, or leap headlong into the orchestra pit of an Edinburgh theatre, shouting 'Hooray for Auld Scotland!' But although the *life* of the twelfth Earl of Lauderdale had been unspectacular, his *death* would

LORD LAUDERDALE STRUCK BY LIGHTNING

The Earl of Lauderdale is struck by lightning, from the *IPN*, 23 August 1884.

be a dramatic one. In early August 1884, Scotland was struck by some tremendous thunderstorms. Not heeding the old adage that it is wise to stay indoors under such circumstances, the Earl of Lauderdale made his way across the Braidshaw Rigg on his estate, accompanied by some keepers. All of a sudden, there was a tremendous flash of lightning, completely blinding the keepers. They could perceive that the Earl had been struck by lightning, and that his pony had been killed. The Earl was carried to a farmhouse nearby, where he recovered consciousness and said a few words. It was considered curious that the lightning strike had fused his watch and chain. A few hours later, the Earl became comatose and died.

'An Earl killed by Lightning!' was *Illustrated Police* news. With a crude illustration of the luckless peer collapsing to the ground, the *IPN* reported that the former railway guard had been of somewhat eccentric habits, and that he had shrunk from going into society. Since the twelfth Earl was childless, the title was inherited by a cousin, Major Frederick Henry Maitland of Bombay. Since that time, the title has been inherited in a more direct line, with railway guards playing no part whatsoever; the Earldom of Lauderdale is still extant today.

Elizabeth Lyska, the Russian Giantess, 1889

Elisaveta Philipovna Luska, whose name was later anglicized to Elizabeth Lyska, was born on 16 September 1877, the daughter of poor peasants in the province of Kharkov in south-western Russia. She was the fourth of seven children, all of them seemingly healthy and normal. But from the age of four, Elizabeth began growing at an alarming rate. The local doctors were completely nonplussed, predicting that she might become a veritable giantess.

After the death of Elizabeth's father, the Lyska family faced poverty. In 1888, they began exhibiting Elizabeth for money, first at local fairs and markets, but later at theatres in Berlin, Vienna and other major cities. In late 1889, when Elizabeth was taken to London for exhibition at the Westminster Aquarium, she was six feet eight inches in height, and one of the tallest women in Europe. In spite of her size, she was still very childish, and delighted in playing with dolls and reading illustrated children's books in her own language. Although her uncle had been allowed to accompany her to London, she missed her mother very much.

When seen by an *IPN* journalist in November 1889, Elizabeth Lyska seemed in good health and spirits. Her uncle, a rotund Russian of ordinary height, demonstrated a bundle of documents proving her age and parentage. In Vienna, she had been admired by the Emperor and Empress, and in Berlin, she had been examined by the celebrated Professor Rudolf Virchow. The uncle took care to demonstrate Elizabeth's enormous hands and feet, which were much larger than his own. He told a story of how she had once been teased by a boorish young peasant when exhibited in her native land; without warning, the giantess had struck him a mighty blow with her open hand, knocking him senseless.

The original deal between the showmen and the Lyska family had been that Elizabeth should return home after one year of touring, and there is reason to believe that this agreement was honoured. But in 1891, Elizabeth was back in Britain, touring the countryside. A journalist from Frank Leslie's *Popular Monthly*, who met her in Winchester, could report that the now fourteen-year-old Elizabeth was nearly seven feet tall. In 1893, the Russian Giantess was back at the Westminster Aquarium, being exhibited together with the dwarf 'Princess Topaze'. She was now seven feet six inches tall, and strong and vigorous-looking. Her four years in show business had not induced her to learn any onstage tricks, but she watched with interest when Princess Topaze danced and performed with her thought-reading dog. After spending much of 1893 in London, Elizabeth Lyska returned to the continent. In April 1896, she was performing in St Petersburg, and it was planned that she would visit the United States in the summer. This never happened, however, since Elizabeth Lyska fell dangerously ill; she died quietly back in her home village later in 1896.

The question of what was wrong with Elizabeth Lyska is easy to answer: just like the aforementioned Marian Wedde, she must have suffered from gigantism caused by a pituitary adenoma overproducing

Elizabeth Lyska, the Russian Giantess, from the *IPN*, 23 November 1889.

growth hormone. Individuals with pituitary gigantism usually have enormous hands and feet, as a result of overgrowth of the soft tissue. It is only in the story-books that giants are stupid: another historical example, the celebrated 'Swedish Giant' Daniel Cajanus, was an educated man who spoke at least three languages and became a published poet. Elizabeth

Lyska did not share his linguistic ambitions, but this may well have been a result of the showmen keeping her isolated in between shows, to facilitate her exploitation. Apart from an article at the TallestMan.com website, and various other online scraps, this article is the only memorial to this little-known giantess.

Barnum's Freaks in 1897

Phineas Taylor Barnum, the great American showman, was born in 1810. His career began with a number of rather distasteful pranks, like the exhibition of Joice Heth, a blind woman said to be 160 years old and the nurse of George Washington; the Feejee Mermaid, made from the head and torso of a dried monkey and the rear part from a large fish; and the celebrated midget 'General Tom Thumb'. He stockpiled his curiosities, both human and animal, at his American Museum in New York, but in 1865, the museum burnt to the ground. After another museum had also been ravaged by fire in 1868, Barnum's collection had been severely depleted, and he decided to start a new career. A clever, business-minded man, he soon was the owner of P. T. Barnum's Travelling World's Fair, a large circus that toured the United States. In 1881, he joined forces with another circus magnate, James Bailey, to form Barnum & Bailey's Greatest Show on Earth, a grand three-ring circus that outshone anything in the American entertainment world. It employed 370 circus performers, and had a large menagerie of elephants, horses, camels and other animals. Barnum was still fond of various newsworthy business deals, like purchasing the famous elephant Jumbo from the Zoological Society of London in 1882. Towards the end of his life, he became something of a philanthropist, settling down in Bridgeport, Connecticut, and supporting Tufts University and various other charitable causes. In spite of the odium caused by the purchase of Jumbo, P. T. Barnum was something of an Anglophile, and one of the high points in his career came in 1889, when his circus performed at Olympia in London.

P. T. Barnum suffered a stroke in 1890, and died the following year. Although the great showman was now gone, Barnum & Bailey's Greatest Show on Earth carried on without interruption, ably led by James Bailey and his colleagues. They found it profitable to visit London again in 1897, bringing all the performers, and a formidable menagerie of animals, with them to Olympia. The Greatest Show on Earth also employed a large sideshow, in which various 'freaks' were exhibited; some of them had been with the circus for decades. When the sideshow was featured by the *IPN* in 1897, some of the most celebrated performers were depicted. Most famous of them was our old friend Jo-Jo, the Dog-Faced Man, who had toured with Barnum since he was a youngster back in 1884. He was then called

Barnum's Freaks, from the *IPN*, 18 December 1897.

'The Russian Dog-Faced Boy' and used to bark and growl at the audience. As we know, his real name was Fedor Jeftichejev, and he was a native of the province of Kostroma in Russia. Already back in 1873 and 1874, he had been exhibited for money in Belgium, France and England, together with his equally hirsute father Andrian; they both suffered from an inherited form of excessive hairiness called hypertrichosis congenital lanuginosa.

By 1897, Jo-Jo was a seasoned performer: the *IPN* journalist wrote that 'his good-humoured face is covered with long silky hair, giving him the appearance of a Skye terrier'. His heart was not broken when one of the sideshow 'rubes' asked him whether he had mislaid his razor, or inquired if he had paid the dog-tax, for the thousandth time. He was a great success when the circus went on to tour France in 1901 and 1902, going through his usual act on stage in front of the astonished Frenchmen. Jo-Jo died from pneumonia when the circus toured Greece in January 1904.

The other performers in the picture are also worthy of a short discourse. The 'Skeleton Dude' was the abnormally thin James W. Coffey, who was born in 1852 and began his career of exhibition in the Chicago dime museums in 1884. He joined Barnum & Bailey's Greatest Show on Earth in the 1890s, becoming a well-known personage in his elegant suit of clothes, with a monocle, long moustaches and a cigarette. He used to say that he would never marry, since 'most women don't like their Coffey thin', but he did find the woman of his dreams in the late 1890s and sired a healthy child. He then fell on evil times, being exhibited in various dime museums and taking up palmistry with little success; the last we know about him is that he was taken care of by the city of Burlington, New Jersey. The 'Man with Two Bodies' is the Indian Laloo, who had a headless parasitic twin growing from underneath his sternum. He was otherwise completely healthy, and got married in 1894. While performing with another circus in Mexico, he died in a train accident in 1905. The 'Half-Man' is Eli Bowen, a veteran performer at the Greatest Show on Earth. Due to a birth defect known as phocomelia, he entirely lacked legs, but had a pair of feet protruding from his pelvis. Having learnt, from an early age, to use his arms and shoulders to compensate for his lack of legs, Bowen became a noted acrobat, performing with many circuses. He was sometimes teamed with the 'Armless Man' Charles Tripp, and there is a famous photograph with Bowen steering a tandem bicycle, with Tripp sitting behind pedalling the machine. Bowen died in 1924, aged seventy-nine; Tripp lived on until 1939, when he was eighty-four years old. There were many Tattooed Men and Ladies active in the sideshow business at this time, and the two depicted among Barnum's freaks were named as Frank and Annie Howard. Finally, there was 'Miss Annie Jones, the amicable and accomplished bearded lady, whose glossy black hair reaches to her ankles'. She was a veteran performer with the Greatest Show on Earth, having been exhibited for money since she was a child.

Machnow the Giant, 1905

Feodor Machnow was born in 1878, in the village of Kasciuki near Vitebsk in what is today Belarus. After his mother had died in childbirth, he was raised by his grandparents. His father later remarried and took Feodor back; in his second marriage, he sired three children of normal size. Not much is known about Machnow's early years, except that already as a schoolboy he grew to be very tall. In 1902, when he was twenty-four years old, he married the local schoolmistress Efrosinja Lebedeva, and soon was the father of a healthy young daughter. A local impresario made plans to have the seven-foot-ten-inch giant exhibited for money: in 1902, Machnow went to Moscow, and in 1903 and 1904, he was exhibited in Berlin and Paris to great acclaim. His management exaggerated his height, claiming that he was nine feet eight inches tall, and they made him dress in a Cossack outfit, with high boots, an embroidered greatcoat, and a tall fur hat.

In early February 1905, Feodor Machnow and his manager Oscar Bollinger travelled from Berlin to London in a specially ordered saloon. The journey was not a particularly pleasant one, since due to his height and bulk the giant had to travel in a reclining position on both land and sea. His wife and child travelled with him. He was contracted to be exhibited at the Hippodrome, and the management of this establishment had hired a very large carriage to pick the giant up at Victoria Station. There was much consternation when Machnow stepped out into the Strand, to be measured for a dress suit at a tailor's shop: it took fifteen yards of double-width cloth, five times more than for an ordinary man. When Machnow wanted some refreshments after being measured, he was given a jug containing five pints of milk, in which were beaten up thirty-three eggs; the thirsty giant drank the cholesterol-rich contents of this jug with audible satisfaction. Machnow was a great success at the Hippodrome, where he was greeted by full houses. The Prince and Princess of Wales came to see him on 6 March. When Machnow was taken to Brighton in a motor car, he was insured for £5,000. He went in a twenty-four hp Napier, and his wife followed in a ten hp de Dion. The giant enjoyed his ride, and he drank quantities of hot milk and port wine, although he worried about his wife and child, and refused to take any food in their absence.

Machnow was somewhat feeble-minded, and his linguistic ability was limited to the Russian dialect spoken in his native village, and a few words of German. His wife supervised the giant's interactions with the outside world, but he could only communicate through a Russian interpreter. He lived at the Hippodrome, something that was cheap and convenient for the management, who did not want any person to see the giant for free. Picture postcards of the 'Hippodrome Giant' enjoyed excellent sales. One of them had the giant's menu on the reverse: he breakfasted at 9.00 a.m., drinking two pints of milk and a pint of tea, and eating sixteen hard-boiled eggs and six to eight small loaves and butter. Luncheon was served at 12.00 noon: he ate two to three pounds of meat and five pounds of potatoes, and drank

Right: The Hippodrome, from an old postcard.

Below: A feature on Feodor Machnow, from the *IPN*, 18 February 1905.

THE GIANT'S BOOT COMPARED WITH AN ORDINARY MAN'S

GOLD RING WORN BY THE GIANT (ACTUAL SIZE)

MACHNOW, THE RUSSIAN GIANT.

MACHNOW'S HAND & AN ORDINARY MAN'S

SHAKING HANDS WITH THE AUDIENCE AT THE LONDON HIPPODROME.

two pints of beer. Dinner was served at 5.00 p.m.: a large bowl of soup, three to five pounds of meat, fowl, fish and vegetables, three pounds of bread, and three pints of beer. Supper was at 9 p.m.: two pints of tea, ten to fifteen eggs, and bread and butter. Before and after each performance on stage, he drank three pints of strong broth. This unwholesome and calorie-rich diet made sure that Machnow was soon as sturdy as he was tall: he steadily increased in weight, and soon weighed in at 365 lbs.

Feodor Machnow remained at the London Hippodrome at least until April 1905. He was exhibited in Paris in June the same year, and then went on to Belgium, Holland and Italy. There is a story that while in Rome, Machnow was received in audience by the Pope, who gave the giant's pretty little daughter a gold cross on a chain. In March 1906 the giant was exhibited in Cardiff, and the following month he was back in London. Machnow had been seen by an agent of William Hammerstein's music hall in New York, where a plethora of human and animal performers were being exhibited. The giant's management was approached with an offer, and it was agreed that Machnow should cross the Atlantic in June 1906, when his tour of France and Britain had been completed. It was arranged that on 4 June, the giant would embark the liner *Pretoria* for New York. Machnow was transported to the Prince of Wales dock in Dover, but when it was explained to him that he was about to cross the Atlantic, he refused to leave the carriage, since he was very fearful of the sea. In spite of the tearful entreaties of his wife, he refused to budge. His management team then called for the service of twenty sailors, and the giant was forcibly pulled out of the carriage and carried on board the liner! Machnow had an unhappy time on board ship, since everything was too small for him, and since he suffered badly from sea-sickness. He slept on a number of mattresses on the floor of the stewards' cabin. Since the other passengers protested against dining in the same room as the giant, he ate alone. When the ship arrived at Ellis Island, Machnow was detained by the immigration authorities, since some mean-spirited person in Newcastle had written an anonymous letter stating that the giant was weak-minded, and that he had been compelled to cross the seas against his will. But Hammerstein had a tame doctor in readiness to vouch for Machnow's sanity, and the giant and his wife and children were set at large in New York.

In July 1906, William Hammerstein arranged a publicity stunt for his music hall: the giant Machnow should be taken for a ride in an automobile to Central Park, where he would take a walk and meet some of his admirers. A band was playing in Central Park, but the music stopped when the giant stepped out of the automobile. A crowd of people soon formed around him, and the giant greeted some small children, who were quite frightened by this towering colossus. When he wanted to shake the hand of a timid old lady, she collapsed from fright on a bench. A number of policemen made an appearance, accusing Mr Hammerstein and Machnow of causing a crowd, and calling for the people to disperse. Hammerstein was forced to sign a bail bond by an officious police sergeant, but when the giant was asked to sign it, he refused to do so. The timid Machnow had been frightened by the policemen shouting and blowing their whistles, and he had got it into his head that if he would sign the bail bond, he would be signing away his children, and he would rather die in a dungeon than do that. The police sergeant then arrested the giant and took him to the police station in their patrol wagon. Machnow's wife, who was also arrested, wept and cried, but the giant did not budge. In the end, the wife, who was the only person who could communicate with the muddled giant, said that if he would not sign the document, he would surely die in the cells, and then the American doctors would steal his remains and mount his skeleton in a private museum. This prospect frightened the giant so much that he agreed to sign the bail bond, and he was free to go, returning to the music hall in the automobile, and being greatly relieved that his children had not been taken away from him.

William Hammerstein also arranged for the giant Machnow, who had previously met the German chancellor, the Prince of Wales and the Pope, to be taken to Washington to meet President Theodore Roosevelt. The simple-minded giant found it hard to believe that the President really lived in the White House, since there were no soldiers there. An interpreter was present, and Machnow addressed Mr Roosevelt as 'King and Emperor of all the Peoples of the World'. He wanted to kiss the President's hand, but

German and French postcards of Machnow the Giant.

Two postcards of Machnow at the Hippodrome.

"GIANT MACHNOW," 25.2.05.
At London Hippodrome, with his Humber Car.

The following is his food for one day : —

BREAKFAST, 9 a.m.—One to two quarts of milk or tea, sixteen hard-boiled eggs, six to eight small loaves and butter.

LUNCHEON, 12 mid-day.—Two to three pounds of meat, five pounds of potatoes, one quart of beer.

DINNER, 5 p.m.—Soup, three to five pounds of meat, fowl, fish, vegetables, potatoes, three pounds of bread, one to two quarts of beer.

SUPPER, 9 p.m.—Ten to fifteen eggs, with bread and butter and one quart of tea.

Before and after each Performance three pints of OXO.

A postcard showing Machnow and his car in front of the Hippodrome, with the giant's daily menu on the back.

this was not allowed. As the giant was transported back to the railway station, his wife threw a tantrum, since she did not believe that the man with the eye-glasses they had just met was really the President, since he was not surrounded by soldiers, and since his portrait was not on the money. They had been fooled, she exclaimed, and she demanded to return to New York straight away.

Machnow remained in New York for several months to come, being exhibited at Hammerstein's music hall, before making a tour of the provinces. There were many newspaper articles about him, and some of the reporters were allowed to interview Machnow through an interpreter. They found him childish and simple-minded, and wholly reliant on his wife for interactions with the world. The giant had little strength and very little courage, and the only areas where he showed talent were in eating and in smoking cigarettes. In spite of being surrounded by various American delicacies, he stuck to a simple and rustic diet of meat, potatoes, lard and cabbages, with plentiful helpings of eggs with every meal. He used to smoke eighty strong Russian cigarettes each day. He was meek and vacillating, and as long he had a good supply of food and cigarettes, his wife could boss him about at will. Machnow's greatest fear was that the American doctors would murder him, to exhibit his skeleton. While he was in New York, a certain Dr Carleton Simon had offered $1,000 for Machnow's brain, since he wanted to examine the pituitary gland for abnormalities, and the fearful giant imagined that the medical man would kidnap him to saw his cranium open and take out the brain.

Fearing the American doctors, Machnow left the United States and returned to his home in Russia. He had been allowed to keep a proportion of the earnings from his long tour, enough for him to buy much land near his native village: he was now a peasant no longer, but an independent landowner. The stalwart Oscar Bollinger persuaded him to return to Britain in June 1908, for another stint at the London Hippodrome, followed by a long tour of the provinces, appearing in Burnley, Nottingham, Sheffield, Manchester and Birmingham. The giant's wife and two children, a boy and a girl, were with him throughout this tour. His unwholesome diet made sure that he was slowly but steadily increasing in weight; his even more pernicious smoking habits led to attacks of bronchitis with incessant coughing. The ailing giant returned to his home country with his wife and children. He suffered from circulatory problems in his huge feet, and from chronic bronchitis that eventually led to his death, from pneumonia, in 1912. His wife made sure that a fine gravestone was erected to celebrate the giant and his unique career; it is still standing today.

The reason for Machnow's abnormal growth is the same as for Marian Wedde and Elizabeth Lyska: a pituitary adenoma causing the overproduction of growth hormone. A key question is of course how tall Machnow really was. In 1903, he was stated to be ten feet six inches tall, in London in 1905 nine feet eight inches, and in America in 1906 nine feet two inches. An internet website celebrating the giant claimed that he was nine feet six inches (285 cm) in height and thus the tallest person to have walked the earth. The objection is, however, that giants on show have always exaggerated their heights. Daniel Cajanus, the 'Swedish Giant' (1704–1749), used to claim that he was eight feet four inches in height, whereas in reality he was seven feet eight, and the 'Irish Giant' Charles Byrne (1761–1783) also claimed that he was eight feet four inches in height, although he was 'only' seven feet ten. In the photographs of Feodor Machnow, care was always taken to make sure that the giant was wearing a tall hat or an enormous fur cap, and that he was surrounded by very short people. According to the American newspapers, Machnow's wife was five feet four inches in height, and analysis of four photographs where she is depicted next to her gigantic husband would indicate that Machnow was around seven feet eight inches tall, and definitely no taller than seven feet ten, the height given for him in his Wikipedia entry. Thus, although Machnow was definitely a true acromegalic giant, he was far from one of the extremes, and there is no question of him challenging the height of the world's tallest man Robert Pershing Wadlow, who stood eight feet eleven inches in his socks.

3

Hermits and Misers

A North Wales Hermit and His Menagerie, 1869

For many years, a hermit named Evan Gwynn resided in the obscure village of Brocklyn, North Wales. He was a morose and moody old man, very dirty in his habits, and disposed to shun the company of his fellow humans as far as possible. He only emerged from his humble farmhouse, or rather hermitage, once a week, to do his shopping. In 1869, after old Gwynn had not been seen for ten days, local people believed he must have died. After the police had been communicated with, two constables made their way to the hermitage. When they knocked on the door, there was no response.

At length, the constables broke down the front door, made their way along an unlit hallway and entered the front parlour. They were amazed

The hermit Evan Gwynn and his extraordinary menagerie, from the *IPN*, 22 May 1869. The story cannot be verified in the local newspapers, and must be viewed with suspicion.

EXTRAORDINARY SCENE IN THE HOUSE of a HERMIT

to find the hermit sitting in a large armchair, surrounded by numerous cats, dogs and monkeys. One of the latter animals sat chattering on the back of the hermit's chair, gesticulating at the intruders. The cats flew at the policemen, who used their staffs to ward off the half-starved felines.

Evan Gwynn was most cantankerous, demanding to be left alone with his animals. He had been dangerously ill, he said, but was now recovering. All he cared for was the companionship of his animals, since he was weary of the world and at war with all humankind. The kindly policemen were reluctant to leave the feeble old man in such a miserable situation, however; they persuaded him to accept help from a doctor, as well as some nourishment for his emaciated frame. Among the locals, there was much speculation about Gwynn's strange behaviour; it was rumoured that he had been cheated out of a title and estates when still quite young, but this could not be confirmed.

A Welsh Hermit Defended by Rats, 1879

In January 1879, an old man named Joseph Mason was prosecuted for failing to support his wife, and leaving her chargeable to the Aberystwyth union workhouse. It turned out that he had deserted her and become a hermit up in the mountains, miles above the lead mines of Goginan. After the workhouse had appealed to the Llanbadarn Fawr petty sessions, an officer named Jones was sent out to track down the seventy-year-old Mason, described as a former shoemaker. At Goginan, the mountain men

Joseph Mason is defended by his army of rats, from the *IPN*, 11 January 1879. The story originated in the local Welsh papers, and is probably true.

directed Jones toward Mason's humble abode, far up beyond the old mines and the village. After a good deal of searching, he finally found the hermitage, which was in the most miserable condition. Although the locals had warned him not to approach the angry, unpredictable hermit, Jones bravely opened the door. Looking around the gloomy, unlit interior, he could see a heap of turf on the floor of this wretched dwelling, and also some rags that served Mason as a bed. In a corner, he could only just make out the sinister-looking, hunched old hermit glaring at him.

But there was something else: a number of large rats scurrying about; nay, an army of them! Jones stamped his foot to scare the rodents away, but instead they attacked him with the greatest audacity, leaping up and biting at his trousers. Having received the shock of his life from the furious rodents, Jones was put to headlong fright. According to the Welsh mountain men, the old hermit had 'tamed and trained his strange companions during his sojourn in the mountains, and encouraged them into his house'. Since Joseph Mason was on the verge of starvation himself, the charge against him was dismissed. It does not seem to have occurred to any person that perhaps he was in need of some help himself, sitting alone in his wretched hermitage above Goginan, with only his rats for company.

The Postman Hermit, 1880

In early May 1880, an elderly man was observed carrying some boards and scaffolding-poles away from a Hammersmith building site. When hailed by a police constable, he dropped the boards and tried to run off, but the

The cabin of the Postman Hermit, with some of his hoard; like the following two, this image is from the *IPN*, 15 May 1880.

constable pursued and captured him. A furtive-looking cove, about sixty years old, he looked like he had seen better days. He was very reluctant to tell the police who he was, or where he lived. The Hammersmith police had ways of making him more talkative, however; after a night in the cells, he gave his name as Lawrence Gilbert, a former postman, who had no address. When the exasperated constables expressed incredulity on the latter point, he offered to show them where he lived.

The police constables were astounded when he led them on a long and meandering walk into the Fulham marshes, where he seemed to know every ditch and footpath. Near the bank of the Thames, opposite Watney's distillery and not far from Wandsworth Bridge, they encountered what seemed almost like a moat, surrounding a very odd-looking cabin. After Gilbert had put a hidden drawbridge over the moat, and appeased a fierce dog he had left behind to guard his belongings, the police examined the large wooden cabin, which had been erected on poles just above the level of high water. Just outside the hermitage were 200 egg-boxes, some containing worthless rubbish, others silver-plated knives and forks, watches, a collection of books, a dining-room clock, forty tall hats with wigs in proportion, and several post office uniforms. Covered up with tarpaulin, there were a number of sewing machines, furniture, carpets, three wagon-loads of timber, and an enormous quantity of old newspapers and magazines.

The constables were even more amazed when they saw the hermit's hoard inside the cabin. There were sixty large mailbags, all of them full of undelivered letters, and a quantity of parcels and packages. One bag alone contained 2,000 circulars from the controversial politician Sir Charles Dilke, issued but never delivered before the 1874 election. It turned out that

The Hermit's barge.

The hermitage viewed from the Thames.

VIEW FROM THE THAMES.

Lawrence Gilbert had been employed as a letter-carrier by the Post Office from 1862 until pensioned off in 1879, going under the assumed name of John Hatch. Throughout this period, he had stolen thousands of letters, circulars, parcels and newspapers. There were two cheques, one for £360 and the other for £120, and a £5 note, neither of which had been touched by this weird postman hermit. A large quantity of milk bottles found on the premises suggested that Gilbert had been in the habit of refreshing himself with some stolen milk while on his rounds, and that he had jealously hoarded the bottles. A more sinister discovery was a box containing forty old rifles, and a quantity of gunpowder; indicating that the hermit had intended to defend his hoard with every means at his disposal. The fierce dog found guarding the hermitage was handed over to the Dogs' Home at Wandsworth.

Tracking down the antecedents of the 'Postman Hermit on the Banks of the Thames', as the *IPN* called him, the police found that Gilbert had once occupied a house in Marlborough Road, Chelsea, where he had lived in an eccentric manner. He also owned another house, in Hampstead, which he sold for £350. The police presumed that he had once stored his hoard in his Chelsea house, where he had lived for at least forty years. Much of the hoard consisted of objects Gilbert had transferred to his hermitage from this house, bringing it down from Chelsea Bridge using a barge. The Postman Hermit had 'a mania for possession', as the newspapers expressed it, collecting the various items in his 'Fulham Marshes Museum' without regard to profit.

Still, the authorities decided to teach Lawrence Gilbert a hard lesson, to dissuade London's many postmen from similar displays of dishonesty. The Postman Hermit was brought before the Hammersmith Police Court, where he was harshly spoken to by the magistrate, Mr Snell. Part of his hoard was exhibited in court, particularly the cheques and the many letters he had stolen. On 25 May 1880, at the Central Criminal Court, he pleaded guilty to the charge of theft and neglecting to deliver mail entrusted to him, and was sentenced to eighteen months in prison, with hard labour. His later activities cannot be traced.

The Peckham Miser, 1883

In the 1860s and 1870s, a middle-aged man named Henry Davies lived in a large semi-detached house at No. 47 Peckham Grove. His family had moved there some time in the early 1850s, and after his elderly parents had both expired, Henry Davies decided to withdraw from the world and become a hermit. He made a habit of never leaving the house during daytime hours, although he sometimes emerged from its walls after dark to purchase victuals. Since the Peckham Miser, as he was called, took no interest in gardening pursuits, or in maintaining his house, No. 47 Peckham Grove was soon the eyesore of the neighbourhood: its garden became a jungle, and the house very dilapidated.

In 1881, the long-suffering neighbours made a complaint to the Metropolitan Board of Works that the Peckham Grove hermitage was a disgrace to the neighbourhood: it did not have a single whole pane of glass in the front windows. The Peckham Miser received a summons to have his windows repaired, which he reluctantly obeyed: the workmen who entered the house were appalled at the state of the house and the garden. The hermit employed no house-keeper or servant, and he had a strong disdain for cleaning and tidying, and an equally strong reluctance ever to throw anything away; all the rooms were cluttered with junk, and covered in layers of dust. The Miser took an interest in legal actions, and was regularly visited by his solicitor, whom he told that his father had been a wealthy man, and that he got a quarterly allowance of a large amount of money. In 1883, the Miser fell ill with what was diagnosed as kidney disease, meaning that Dr Hentsch, of Southampton Street, Camberwell, also came to call at the hermitage. The house was in a dreadful state, and the Miser quite ill and frail. He told the doctor that he was about sixty years old, although he looked much older. He also volunteered that since his parents had been wealthy people, he had never done a day's work in his life.

Dr Hentsch returned to see Henry Davies a few days later; he suggested that another medical man should be consulted, but the patient said that would be too expensive. When the doctor asked him if he had made a will, he said that he was going to. When the doctor next came to the hermitage, nobody opened the door. Fearing for the worst, he went to the police station, and Sergeant Timbs went with him to No. 47 Peckham Grove. After they had made their way through the overgrown garden, the

Above: Death of the Peckham Miser, and a view of the hermitage, which no longer stands, from the *IPN*, 8 September 1883.

Right: A postcard stamped and posted in 1907, showing old houses in Peckham Grove.

policeman raised a ladder and obtained admission through a back window. He found the Miser lying dead against a dresser, covered with rags. Every room in the house was full of rubbish, and it had not been cleaned for decades. There were piles of documents relating to the Miser's legal actions, one of them a bill for legal costs amounting to £600. The coroner's inquest on Henry Davies returned a verdict of death from natural causes.

A friend of the family wrote a letter to the police superintendent, suggesting that the remains of Henry Davies should be buried in the grave of his parents at Nunhead Cemetery, and this idea was acted upon. It turned out that the Miser actually had a brother alive, but this individual had wanted nothing to do with him, and did not even attend the funeral. In fact, the only mourner was the clerk to the solicitor Davies had employed to supervise his legal actions. He was the sole occupant of the mourning coach following the hearse through the Peckham streets, taking the remains of the Miser to their final resting place.

The Bethnal Green Miser, 1886

Charlotte Granger, an elderly woman, lived in a large house at No. 16 Pleasant Place, Bethnal Green. She was a very wealthy woman, who owned several houses in the City, and not less than sixteen houses in Bethnal Green; she was reputed to hoard gold sovereigns and valuables of every description in her house. As she got older, Charlotte Granger became a hermit, living alone in her large house, which she never left during daytime hours. She never spent sixpence unless she was forced to, and since she never cleaned or repaired her house, it soon became the eyesore of Bethnal Green. In the early 1880s, a complaint was made to the local vestry, regarding the unwholesome smell emanating from the miser's abode. When the sanitary inspector Mr Barrow inspected the premises, every room was in a most filthy condition, and a number of mangy-looking cats and dogs were kept in there, adding to the nauseating smell.

As the 1880s went on, Charlotte Granger's health gradually deteriorated: she suffered badly from the gout, and became an invalid. The state of her

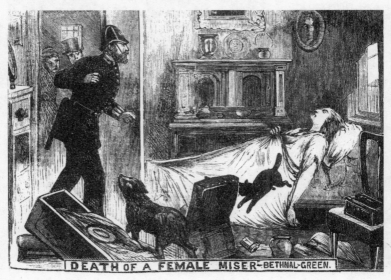

DEATH OF A FEMALE MISER—BETHNAL-GREEN.

The end of the Bethnal Green Miser, from the *IPN*, 2 October 1886.

house did not improve, and Mr Barrow more than once paid her a visit; although the miser had been persuaded to employ two daytime female servants, one of them 'was taken ill through the offensiveness of the place', and the other appears to have shared the lax hygienic belief of her mistress. When Mr Barrow went to see the miser in early September 1886, he found her lying dead on a small couch, in the ground-floor front room. A cat and a dog were sitting in the room.

On 15 September 1886, Mr George Collier, the deputy coroner for East Middlesex, opened an inquest on Charlotte Granger, at the Panther Tavern, Bethnal Green. The significant wealth possessed by the deceased was contrasted to her miserly habits and dismal living conditions. A quantity of gold had been found in the house, as well as half a bushel of twopenny pieces. When Mr Barrow, who had taken possession of the house, searched it together with Mr Thomas Henry Sourbutt, a second cousin of the deceased, they found a quantity of good furniture underneath the dust and dirt. The miser's wardrobe contained some very old-fashioned silk dresses, and six old 'coal-scuttle' bonnets. In a cupboard was some magnificent old china of great value. A newspaper remarked that Charlotte Granger was as popular dead as she had been miserly alive: scores of people daily claimed to be distant relations of hers, to get their hands on part of the miser's hoard.

There was a good deal of newspaper interest when the coroner's inquest on Charlotte Granger was resumed on 21 September. Dr George F. Bates testified that he had been attending the deceased for about ten years, treating her for the gout as well as he could. The miser had denied herself the proper necessities of life, he said, and she had been unable to cook her food properly. She had been struck by a bout of diarrhoea, which led to exhaustion and death. The jury returned a verdict of death from natural causes.

Two Norwood Children Shot By a Hermit, 1898

Allan Neville had worked as a hosier as a young man, but after receiving a small legacy, he decided to withdraw from the world and become a hermit. His house, or rather hermitage, was part of the remains of a crumbling old mansion called Meadow Bank, situated on the Durham Road, mid-way between West Norwood and Streatham Common. This was a very secluded spot, and thus suitable for a hermit who wanted nothing to do with the remainder of humanity. In particular, Allan Neville very much disliked children: he was a convinced paedophobe, who took cover whenever he heard the sound of juvenile voices near his hermitage.

On the afternoon of 30 June 1898, a number of small children had congregated to play in a field adjacent to the hermitage. Nothing happened until quarter-past nine in the evening, when gunfire was heard from the direction of Allan Neville's abode. The children scattered, and some of them ran home to alert their parents. The railway signalman William Dearing was one of these parents, and he seized up his little daughter, who was just three and a half years old, and went in search of the gunman. In the field, he saw an odd-looking man holding a small fowling-piece. When Dearing charged the gunman, he fired his weapon,

HE FIRES AT A FATHER AND CHILD

THE STRUGGLE WITH THE FATHER

EXTRAORDINARY OUTRAGE BY A NORWOOD RECLUSE.
SEVERAL CHILDREN SHOT AT AND WOUNDED.

The hermit tries to gun down the Norwood children, from the *IPN*, 9 July 1898.

wounding both Dearing and the little daughter. William Dearing seized the hermit with hearty goodwill until some other parents, and a police detective, had come to his assistance.

Allan Neville was frog-marched to the local police station, where he was charged with maliciously firing a gun loaded with shot at children, with intent to do them bodily harm. It was fortunate that the hermit only possessed a small-calibre weapon, loaded only with old duck-shot cartridges; if he had possessed a more powerful weapon, much mischief might have been caused. Neither William Dearing nor his daughter were seriously hurt, but a little boy had been shot in the forehead, with one bullet penetrating the skin and causing bloodshed.

When Allan Neville was brought up before the South-Western police court, William Dearing described how the hermit had fired at him. After being apprehended and disarmed, Neville had objected, 'It was a pure accident!' He had himself seen the hermit fire at the children. Albert Henry Dickson testified that his five-year-old son had been wounded in the forehead and face. George Feaner, a young Norwood lad, described how he had been playing cricket in the field when he saw Neville leaving his house, holding a gun, which he levelled and fired at the children. He denied that he had been annoying Neville by throwing stones at his ramshackle hermitage. The prisoner was remanded, and the magistrates offered to accept two sureties of £100 for his appearance. The case attracted a good deal of newspaper attention: 'Extraordinary Outrage at Norwood!' said the headline of *Reynolds's Newspaper*; 'Two Norwood Children shot by a Hermit!' said *Lloyd's Weekly Newspaper* and 'Extraordinary Outrage by a Norwood Recluse!' exclaimed the *IPN*.

On 14 July, Allan Neville was again brought up before the London County Sessions. He was defended by Mr Wheeler, QC, and by Mr De Michele, and pleaded not guilty to unlawfully wounding the children. The prosecution argued that Neville, an eccentric man in good circumstances, had long been annoyed by the children playing in the field at the back of his house. He had written to the police, threatening that unless he received protection from his juvenile tormentors, he would 'introduce a load of shot' into them; the police had though they were dealing with a madman, and ignored him. The signalman Dearing had been a witness to Neville firing his gun at the children, and hitting one of them in the face. The defence argued that Neville had only fired his gun to frighten the children off, and that the gun had not been pointed at them, although a ricochet from the trunk of a tree had led to the little boy being hit. The jury found the prisoner guilty, however, and the Chairman said that although this was a serious case, none of the children had been seriously harmed. He did not want to degrade the prisoner with a term of imprisonment, as he expressed it, but Neville was fined £50 to put an end to his trigger-happy tendencies. This fine appears to have had the desired effect: the Norwood Hermit retired into his hermitage, and never did anything newsworthy again.

4

Ghosts

The Manchester Ghost of 1869

In May and June 1869, there were some very strange goings-on at the Feathers Hotel, situated in London Road, in the middle of central Manchester. For six weeks, there were regular ghostly disturbances, reported both by the guests and the hotel staff: dismal groans were heard at night, as well as the sound of ghostly footsteps, and above all the ringing of all the bells in the hotel. When the weary waiters went to sleep, they were disturbed sometimes by a solitary tinkle, sometimes by a loud peal of all the hotel's fourteen bells. After a few weeks of this torment, ghost hysteria broke out: the hotel staff became convinced the place was haunted, and some of them were reduced to nervous wrecks, losing much sleep waiting for the next ghostly tinkle from the bells. Some nights, they kept a strict watch for many hours, without any spooky sounds or other manifestations of the ghost, but as soon as the tired waiters, pot-boys and kitchen-maids went to bed, the bells started to ring again.

At first the landlord of the Feathers pooh-poohed the idea of his hotel being haunted, but after the ghost hysteria had spread like wildfire among all members of his staff, he called in a reputable firm of bell-hangers. They rearranged the wires and muffled the bells, assuring the landlord that the problem was solved. And for a while, it seemed as if the Manchester Ghost had been laid to rest: for six nights after the repairs, the tired, nervous domestics enjoyed the uncommon luxury of full nights of sleep. But the mischievous spectre was soon up to its old fun again: the bells kept ringing throughout the night, at regular intervals, and the long-suffering landlord finally called in the police. A 'special detective' was stationed at the hotel, and this Victorian ghostbuster had assistance from several uniformed constables. They thought it very queer that a ghost would haunt a major hotel at one of the busiest streets in central Manchester, right opposite the London Road Station (today Manchester Piccadilly). Late one evening,

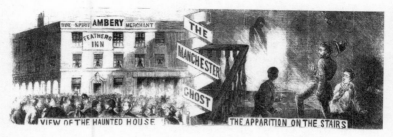

VIEW OF THE HAUNTED HOUSE · THE APPARITION ON THE STAIRS

To the left, the haunted hotel; to the right, the Manchester Ghost frightening the police constable and the two boys. From the *IPN*, 12 June 1869.

one of these policemen, and two boys, heard spooky noises from the hotel's top floor. When they went up to investigate, they saw what they called 'an indescribable presence' on the top of the stairs: two days later, they were still in a state of nervous prostration, and unable to give any account of the sinister spectre's appearance and disappearance.

The ringing of the bells went on for several more weeks, testing the already severely jarred nerves of the Feathers' domestics. The cook resigned her comfortable position, preferring poverty to being under the same roof as the Manchester Ghost. Later, there was a newspaper report that she had suffered a dangerous nervous collapse, and was in bed seriously ill. By mid-June, the hotel was nightly crowded by hundreds of people, excited by curiosity about the ghost, and thirsty for information about the spectre. They were also thirsty for beer, wine and spirits, to the great profit of the landlord, who was said to welcome his singular guest, and hope that the ghost was in for a long stay at his hotel. Hundreds of people also thronged the streets and lanes outside the hotel, anxious to hear the latest news, and to see the ghost or hear the bells ring. Quite a force of detectives and police constables were investigating the mystery.

'Whatever else may be thought of it, this revival of the Cock Lane spirit has been and continues most successful as a sensation in drawing crowded houses,' the *IPN* somewhat laboriously summarized as to the progress of the Manchester ghost hunt. The ending of the story is unfortunately not recorded, even in any local newspaper. Thus, the identity of the ghostly figure in the stairway remains a mystery, as does the persistent ringing of the bells. In some other Victorian poltergeist cases, with ringing of the bells and ghostly bumps in the night, the culprit has been found to be some mischievous domestic, who wanted to frighten his or her colleagues. Perhaps in this particular case, the landlord himself, or some accomplice, might also be among the suspects, since he was the only person actually making a profit from the ghost story.

The Feathers Hotel was a relatively old building, operating under the same name at least since 1850. With time, it acquired quite a bad reputation, and seems to have housed a low clientele. According to the *Manchester Times* of 12 September 1885, the magistrates declined to renew the license of the landlord of the Feathers to keep a public house, since he had been convicted of harbouring women of ill-fame. There is no mention of the tavern operating under its original name subsequent to that calamity, and the building is no longer standing today.

The Jumping Ghost of Peckham, 1871

In 1871 and 1872, a series of ghost scares occurred in Peckham and its vicinity. In November and December 1871, a 'ghost' had been breaking windows at night, but this vandalism ceased after the arrest of a foreigner with a catapult. In April and May 1872, there was another window-breaking epidemic, which was blamed on a thirteen-year-old girl named Nott, who was caught red-handed and severely fined the month after.

On October the same year, there were several sightings of a figure dressed in white, who prowled the Peckham lanes, frightening women by making spooky noises, or grabbing them from behind. Quite a few people saw the ghost, which was described as very tall, between six and eight feet depending on the witnesses' level of intoxication, and with a most forbidding countenance. Some accredited the ghost with horns, others were certain it had luminous breath; yet others believed it had boots fitted with springs, enabling it to leap like Spring-Heeled Jack. The ghost screamed and gibbered in a weird, penetrating voice; it jumped high fences, and ran at near-superhuman speed. In early November, the two daughters of Dr Carver, headmaster of Dulwich College, were so badly frightened by the ghost that several days later, the youngest had not fully recovered.

A vigilante Anti-Ghost Fund was established, and the ghost was burnt in effigy by the local inhabitants. Nevertheless, there were several new sightings of the figure in white, and many reports of windows being broken. Some people were convinced they were dealing with a proper ghost; many believed some prankster was at work; some rationalists thought it was just some weird mass hysteria. On 27 November, a lad named Arthur Ridgway was carrying home a stone flask containing half a gallon of beer. A figure dressed in dark sneaked up to him, spread his arms to reveal a white suit, and uttered 'some dismal cries'. Terrified, Ridgway dropped his beer and ran home. The very same evening, thirteen-year-old Matilda Ayers was also confronted by the ghost: the strange being spread its arms, uttered some strange sounds, and greatly alarmed her.

There was quite an outcry in Peckham, with people milling about looking for the ghost. A group of workmen turned vigilantes decided to catch the man frightening the children. They saw an odd-looking

THE APPEARANCE OF ANOTHER GHOST

The Jumping Ghost of Peckham attacks; from the *IPN*, 28 December 1872.

cove nearby, throwing peas at the shutters just like the ghost had been supposed to have done. They pursued him to a house, where he was later taken into custody by a police constable. The suspect turned out to be the homeless, unemployed Joseph Munday, described as a singular-looking man wearing a large curly wig. A number of peas were found in his pockets; he said he had bought them to eat. He had no explanation for the strange garb he was wearing, with 'a white slop' inside a dark cloak. The lad Ridgway and the girl Ayers both identified him as the 'ghost' they had seen, and since the destitute Munday was unable to find bail, he was sentenced to six months in jail.

When Munday was carted off to prison on 7 December, calm was restored to Peckham and its environs. But ten days later, a man named James Sanson, driving a cart outside Bury in Lancashire, far away from Peckham, was dismayed to see a tall white figure approaching his vehicle. According to the *IPN*, the ghost 'twisted itself about and performed a number of antics fearful to witness; it shrieked and gibbered at once discordant and appalling'. Although Sanson whipped up his horses, the ghost kept up with him for several minutes, before it disappeared with a final wild shriek. Was this the original Peckham Ghost, or rather ghost impersonator, enjoying another of his pranks after finding Peckham too hot for him after the arrest of the copycat Munday?

The Haunted Murder House Near Chard, 1879

In 1879, one of the veteran inhabitants of the tiny village of Knowle St Giles, situated between Chard and Ilminster in Somerset, was the eighty-three-year-old farm labourer Samuel Churchill. In spite of his age, he was still working on various farms, cutting hedges and tending pigs and poultry. Samuel Churchill had been married once before, but his wife had died twenty-five years earlier; they had a daughter named June who had married the labourer George England. After Samuel's first wife had died, he had employed a much younger woman named Katherine Walden as house-keeper, and they had an illegitimate son named Samuel, before Katherine finally managed to persuade the stubborn old man to make an honest woman of her in 1871. They lived together in a small cottage, along with the adult son Samuel. Katherine's mother, a cantankerous old woman who was nearly deaf and blind, also lived with them.

Samuel and Katherine Churchill never got on particularly well, however. They quarrelled at regular intervals, and these altercations sometimes ended in blows. Old Samuel was still hale and hearty, but Katherine was a strong, forceful woman with a furious temper. Since she worked as a laundrywoman, and in the fields, she was sturdy and muscular. It was well known in the neighbourhood that Samuel and his wife fought frequently and angrily. Samuel's daughter June England disliked her overbearing stepmother, and often said that one day, this wicked woman would bully her dotard husband into making a will leaving all his money to the bastard son Samuel. Katherine was equally fearful that June would persuade old Samuel to cut her illegitimate son out of the will. In 1877, Katherine and

The murder near Chard, from the *IPN*, 29 March 1879.

THE ALLEGED MURDER NEAR CHARD.

Fore Street, Chard, from an old postcard. The inquest on Samuel Churchill was held at the George Hotel [which still stands], a few houses down the left side of the street.

young Samuel had set upon the old man when he was returning from Ilminster Fair: they had beaten him up and torn the shirt off his back. Old Samuel had sought refuge with the Englishes, complaining of the harsh treatment to which he had been subjected, but the wily Katherine had later persuaded him to return home.

On 4 March 1879, George English was called to Samuel Churchill's cottage, after word had spread that there had been an accident. He found old Samuel dead in the fireplace, his body much burnt and charred. Sharing his wife's low opinion of Katherine, George English immediately suspected that she had murdered the old man. He saw her lurking in the bedroom, and remarked that this was a bad business, and the sinister woman agreed. She said that old Samuel had been suffering from fainting fits, and that he must have fallen into the fire when she was out. When she came back home, she had tried to pour water on him, but he was already dead. A police constable and a doctor came to the cottage, and although old Samuel's body was very badly burnt, they found marks of blows to the face, head and hands. A blood-stained bill-hook matching these injuries was found hidden on the premises. When Katherine was taken away by the police, she turned to her son Samuel and said, 'See to the will, and mind they don't cheat you out of the money!'

When Katherine Churchill was on trial for murder at the Taunton Assizes, before Baron Huddleston, the doctor and the two Englishes gave damning evidence against her. George English added that a few weeks before the murder, he had heard old Samuel threaten to cut his illegitimate son out of the will. As for young Samuel himself, he was fortunate to possess a cast-iron alibi: at the time of the murder, he had been at work at a farm nearby, with a number of other labouring men. A young servant girl, Eliza Barrow, had an important story to tell. She had been walking past Samuel Churchill's cottage when she heard an outcry of 'Murder!' and saw a woman attack an old man. She ran to her master's house, suggesting that perhaps he ought to go to the Churchill cottage

THE HAUNTED COTTAGE NEAR CHARD.

The ghosts frighten the inhabitants of the murder cottage, from the *IPN*, 20 December 1879.

to make sure that all was well, but he just laughed, saying that the two Churchills were notorious for their fighting and quarrelling. In the end, Katherine Churchill was found guilty of murder and sentenced to death. The usual squeamishness with regard to hanging women did not apply to such a hardened wretch, who had beaten her elderly husband to death for reasons of greed of gain, and she was executed within the precincts of Taunton Gaol on 26 May.

In December 1879, the following short but sinister account was published in the *IPN*, quoted from a Plymouth newspaper:

In March last an old man named Churchill was murdered in a cottage near Chard. For some time after the execution the building remained uninhabited, but at length it was let to a labourer and his family, but the incomers soon found they could obtain no rest. They state that the murderess, 'Kitty', has been frequently seen to glide about the premises in ghostly attire, and that old Churchill has been distinctly observed to look in at the window, with hideous countenance. This added to the appearance of blood on the floor of the room in which the tragedy was enacted, supernatural movements amongst the furniture and other articles, and unearthly noises in the immediate vicinity of the cottage, so unsettled the occupants that they at last abandoned the dwelling, which is now regarded as 'haunted'.

It is a pity that nothing is known about the later fate of this extraordinary haunted murder cottage near Chard: does it still exist today, and are these formidable ghosts, worthy of the Amityville House of Horrors, still active on the premises?

The Ghost of Berkeley Square, 1879

Berkeley Square is one of the most historic garden squares in the City of Westminster. It was laid out in the mid-eighteenth century by the architect William Kent: the building of the tall, quality terraced houses continued apace, and Berkeley Square soon became one of the most sought-after residential squares in London. The eastern and southern sides of Berkeley Square have suffered badly from the Developer, with unsightly modern blocks and hotels dominating the square, but a number of original Georgian houses remain in the southern part of the western terrace.

In 1879, there was a sensational article in *Mayfair* magazine, concerning one of London's most notorious haunted houses, situated at Berkeley Square. Long abandoned due to the persistent haunting, the house presented a woeful appearance to the world: it had not seen a lick of paint for decades, and the area was full of rubbish and thrown-away handbills. The *Mayfair* journalist claimed that a girl had once been staying in the ghost room of the haunted house: the following morning, she was found stark raving mad and never recovered. A gentleman, who was a disbeliever in ghosts, demanded to stay the night in the haunted room; he was found dead in the middle of the floor, after having frantically but vainly rung the bell for succour from some supernatural menace.

A postcard stamped and posted in 1905, showing the south-western corner of Berkeley Square; No. 50 is the second house from the left.

THE GHOST OF BERKELEY SQUARE.

The Ghost of Berkeley Square, from the *IPN*, 23 December 1874.

THE " HAUNTED HOUSE," BERKELEY SQUARE

The haunted house at Berkeley Square, from Charles G. Harper's *Haunted Houses*.

There was much interest in London's spectral world in the 1870s, and the story of this extraordinary haunted house spread far and wide in the newspapers. It was no secret in the neighbourhood that the ghost house was No. 50 Berkeley Square, since this house, situated near the southern extreme of the western terrace, was of very neglected and dilapidated appearance. The correspondents at *Notes & Queries*, a weekly magazine devoted to antiquarian pursuits, took an immediate interest in this singular Mayfair ghost story. The sceptics made sneering noises, saying that they would not believe in the Ghost of Berkeley Square until the lunacy documents for the girl, and the police investigation of the death of the gentleman, had been made public. The pro-ghost lobby soon made headway in the debate, however, by pointing out that the house's reputation for being haunted had been established at least as early as 1872, thus seven years before the *Mayfair* article.

As the *Notes & Queries* correspondents pondered the history of No. 50 Berkeley Square, they found that from 1770 until 1827, the house had been home to Prime Minister George Canning. It was later purchased by Lord Curzon, and inhabited by his daughter, the Hon. Miss Elizabeth Curzon, who died in the house in 1859. During her residence, the house appears to have been free of ghosts. Her former manservant George Vincent, who had since become Head Porter at Brasenose College, Oxford, wrote to inform the *Notes & Queries* correspondents: 'I entered the house, 50, Berkeley Square, London, on March 20, 1851, in the service of the late Miss Curzon, who died in May, 1859. During the nine years I was in the house, and I have been in it at all hours alone, I saw no greater ghost than myself.'

The *Notes & Queries* ghost hunters found that not long after the death of Miss Curzon, the lease of No. 50 Berkeley Square had been purchased by a certain Mr Myers, who was supposed to be very eccentric. There was a story that he had once been engaged to be married, but only to be jilted in the very last minute. This dismal experience made him into a recluse, who never left the house, or maintained it in any way. According to Lord de la Zouche, the nephew of Miss Curzon, the house was reputed to be haunted already in 1863 or 1864. A correspondent to *Notes & Queries* stated that during the years the 'eccentric gentleman' inhabited No. 50 Berkeley Square, soap, paint or whitewash was never used. He was occasionally visited by a sister, and had two resident maidservants in the house. By degree began the ghost stories – 'insanity', 'murder', 'walls saturated with electric horror' etc. After the 'eccentric gentleman' had died, his sister sent in an estate agent to see whether it would be worthwhile to put the house in order for the remainder of the lease. He found the house in hideous disrepair, and asked the maidservants if they had ever seen any ghosts; the answer was 'We never seed any!'

In December 1880, another correspondent to *Notes & Queries* could report that No. 50 Berkeley Square had just been repainted and made ready for another tenant. This tenant may well have been a certain Major Du Pré, who was later stated to have lived in the house with his wife, albeit not for very long. In June 1884, it was reported that Lord Selkirk had just taken No. 50 Berkeley Square; in 1915, the *Daily Mirror* stated that Lady Selkirk was still living there in peace and comfort; according to a 1924 account, the elderly noblewoman had died in the house, undisturbed by any ghost. In 1928, the haunted house was inhabited by Sir Philip Grey-Egerton, Bart. From 1938 until 2015, No. 50 Berkeley Square has been the headquarters of Maggs Bros, antiquarian booksellers, who have reported that there were no indications that the house was haunted during their tenure; I visited this elegant upmarket bookshop back in 1999 to purchase an old French book about premature burials, having a good look at the house but not seeing trace of any ghost.

Elliott O'Donnell was a celebrated ghost-hunter of the 1920s and 1930s, who wrote copiously on various aspects of the supernatural. A highly strung, nervous Irishman, he could literally see ghosts everywhere, even when there were none. Elliott O'Donnell could of course not stay away from the Ghost of Berkeley Square; these two were made for one another, and O'Donnell many times discussed the celebrated London spook. In a 1908 lecture, he mentioned two versions of the haunting at No. 50 Berkeley Square, leaving it to the audience to decide which one to believe. According to one story, every person who stayed in a certain room at No. 50 at a certain time died of fright. About the year 1880, a reckless major, who cared little for ghosts, decided to spend the night in the haunted room. In the dead of night, a revolver shot was heard from the room. The major was found in bed, stone dead from fright, and clutching a smoking revolver. According to the second version, two sailors took refuge in the haunted house one night. There was a dull thud at the door, through which came a shapeless creature of so horrifying an aspect that one sailor died from fright, on the spot; the other sailor was found wandering about the basement, a raving lunatic.

In his 1923 book *Ghosts Helpful and Harmful*, Elliott O'Donnell put the malignant Berkeley Square spook firmly in the 'Harmful' category. He quoted the original article about the girl who went mad and the gentleman found dead in the house after vainly ringing for help. Although it was fashionable among his rationalist contemporaries to scoff at London's historic ghost stories, Elliott O'Donnell declared himself a firm believer in the Ghost of Berkeley Square. A lady had told him that a certain 'Captain B.' had once come to stay at No. 50 Berkeley Square, where his fiancée and her family lived. Rather recklessly, considering the fearsome reputation of the haunted room, he decided to spend the night in there. At twelve o'clock, and on each succeeding hour, he would ring the bell once if all was well, and twice if he needed assistance. The fiancée and her family would be sitting in the hall to reply to his signals. At midnight and at one, the bell sounded only once, but at two o'clock, it rang twice. The fiancée and her family ran up the stairs, but as they gained the landing, a solitary revolver shot was heard. As they burst open the door to the haunted room, they discovered Captain B. sitting bolt upright in the bed, holding a still smoking revolver. He was stone dead from fright, and the expression on his face was so terrible that no person could look at it twice.

As some light relief after these horrors, Elliott O'Donnell then told the story of the two cockney sailors Bert and Charlie, who decided to enter the empty house at No. 50 Berkeley Square after being stranded in Mayfair without a penny. But the Ghost of Berkeley Square did not approve of these two uninvited guests, and it decided to give them a proper fright. In the middle of the night, the two sailors heard muffled footsteps walking up the stairs, and the door slowly opened. Outside stood a tall, shadowy spectre that resembled nothing human or animal. The terrified Bert ran to the window and slid down the water-pipe, but Charlie was found the following day, wandering round Berkeley Square in an insane condition. Bert eventually managed to tell the tale, and it was reported to Elliott O'Donnell's aunt, the wife of Colonel John Vise O'Donnell, a very truthful lady who had first-hand authority for it. The ghost was clearly an elemental spirit, O'Donnell pontificated, possibly attracted to the house by a crime or series of crimes committed on the spot, or else by a pool of stagnant water that once stood on the site.

In his 1933 book *Ghosts of London*, Elliott O'Donnell wrote that when he had visited London as a schoolboy in the early 1890s, he soon made his way to No. 50 Berkeley Square, to admire London's most haunted house. Although the late Lord Curzon of Kedleston had told him that the house was in fact not haunted, O'Donnell remained unconvinced. He retold the *Mayfair* story, which he this time dated correctly to 1879, and then gave a lengthy account, with much invented cockney dialogue, of the two sailors Bill and Mick who entered the empty house at No. 50 Berkeley Square. After hearing the ghostly footsteps approaching, and seeing the intensely horrible shape in the doorway, Mick jumped headlong from a rear window into the back yard and broke his neck, but Bill ran away and told a police constable about the haunting.

As late as 1956, Elliott O'Donnell retold the Berkeley Square ghost story in his book *Phantoms of the Night*. Various attempts had been made to discount the haunting, by claiming that the story had been invented by a caretaker who did not want the house to be rented out. Another story was that the house had once been inhabited by a very eccentric recluse and misogynist, who inhabited only one room of No. 50 Berkeley Square, and allowed the other rooms to go to wrack and ruin. He used to wander about the house at night, with a lighted candle in his hand, and this led to the report that the house was haunted. Elliott O'Donnell remained a firm believer in the Berkeley Square ghost, however, and he again quoted the story of the sailors Bill and Mick, stranded on central London at some time in the 1870s. This time, the ending is that after encountering the Ghost of Berkeley Square, Mick leapt headlong from a front window into the deep area, and broke his neck, whereas Bill was found on the pavement in a swoon.

There is no question, for a close student of Elliott O'Donnell's Edinburgh ghost stories, that this once-famous ghost-hunter was something of a bounder, who made up many of his spooky tales. A study of his writings on the Ghost of Berkeley Square does not change that impression in the slightest. Neither the foolhardy major turned captain nor the two protean house-invading sailors have any part to play in the original records of the haunted house in Berkeley Square, and it must be suspected that O'Donnell invented these yarns to make his ghost stories more interesting. The damage done by Elliott O'Donnell's many rehashes of the Berkeley Square ghost story has been permanent, since a number of internet plagiarists have swallowed his yarns hook, line and sinker. The military officer may well have died from fright in O'Donnell's yarn, and one of the sailors may well have leapt headlong through a window, but both are alive and well on the internet, in a multitude of versions.

In 1907, the ghost hunter Charles Harper wrote that according to his friend Mr Stuart Wortley, the secret of the house was that Mr Du Pré, of Wilton Park, had shut his insane brother in one of the rooms; the lunatic's strange groans and cries had given the house its sinister reputation. In 1928, a correspondent to the *Daily Mirror* corroborated this yarn, which has since been 'improved' further on the internet: it was an unnamed young man who was kept prisoner in the house, fed through a hole in the door, until he went mad and died. The *Grey Ghost Book* added that according to Mr Ralph Nevill, a relation of the elusive Mr Myers, the haunting dated back to the eighteenth century; the house was also haunted by a child who had been tortured to death in the nursery, and by a man who had gone mad waiting for ghostly messages to appear on the walls. The celebrated ghost hunter Harry Price discussed the 'Electric Horror' of Berkeley Square at length, hoping that if the poltergeists on the premises were up to any further mischief, Maggs Bros. would send for him to investigate.

R. Thurston Hopkins, another authority on the spectral world, quoted Elliott O' Donnell's story of the two sailors at length, and added a ghost of his own: when a certain Mr Bentley had inhabited the house, his eldest daughter's boyfriend had been frightened to death in the haunted room after first taking a shot at the 'Nameless Horror' of Berkeley Square with his army pistol. In 1985, Richard Whittington-Egan again discussed the

Ghost of Berkeley Square, quoting O'Donnell's yarns but maintaining a healthy sceptical attitude. The same cannot be said for the present-day internet chroniclers of London's ghosts, who regurgitate garbled versions of Elliott O'Donnell's tales from Berkeley Square with enthusiasm. Another room in this house of horrors was haunted by the ghost of a little girl who had been murdered by a sadistic servant, yet another by the spirit of a young woman who had thrown herself from a top floor window after being abused by her wicked uncle. A large number of people had died from fright after encountering this formidable army of ghosts, from the time of George Canning until the present era. Clearly the time had come to shed some new light on this extraordinary house, the most haunted in London according to its sensationalist Wikipedia entry.

It is curious that in 1876, before the debate on the Ghost of Berkeley Square, the *IPN* repeated a newspaper story claiming that it was the ghost of the daughter of the celebrated murderess Sarah Metyard, active in the 1750s. Sarah Metyard was a Mayfair harridan who kept a small knitting factory in Bruton Street, not far from Berkeley Square, staffed with half-starved parish apprentice girls. She beat and flogged the girls for every misdemeanour, and one of them, Anne Naylor, died after being on the receiving end of a brutal beating. Sarah Metyard and her daughter dismembered the corpse and burnt some body parts, throwing the remainder of the body into an open sewer. When Anne Naylor's sister suspected that she had been done away with, the two Metyards murdered her as well, and got rid of the body in the same manner. Four years went by, with the Bruton Street murderess flourishing, but then Sally the daughter informed on her mother after being ill-treated herself. Both mother and daughter were hanged and then dissected at Surgeon's Hall. The 1876 newspaper story has Sally Metyard going into service in the house at Berkeley Square, and then haunting the premises after having perished on the scaffold, but in real life, she was living in sin with an admirer at the time she informed on her mother.

Making use of the relevant Post Office directories, it was not difficult to make a list of the inhabitants of No. 50 Berkeley Square. The earliest directory is that of 1842, and we see that after the death of the Hon. Miss Curzon in 1859, the house was not listed until 1882, when it is stated to be 'unoccupied'. Clearly, at a time when most householders in salubrious parts of London felt proud to be listed in the directories, the elusive Mr Myers preferred anonymity. After the 'haunted' years, there was a brief interregnum when Miss Myers was listed as the householder, before the Earl and Countess of Selkirk helped No. 50 Berkeley Square back to respectability during their lengthy residence. No 'Mr Bentley' is ever listed as the householder, so the tale of R. Thurston Hopkins must be a falsification. Nor is Major Du Pré on the list of householders, casting doubt upon his involvement with the haunted house; we also know that the house was reputed to be haunted long before his alleged tenure some time in the early 1880s. Moreover, although Colonel William Baring Du Pré had two brothers, both Major Francis James Du Pré and Captain Charles Hinton Du Pré were fully sane, showing no predilection for chewing the carpets and foaming at the mouth in a locked garret in Berkeley Square.

The next mystery to address is that of the 'eccentric gentleman' Mr Myers. In her *Reminiscences*, Lady Dorothy Nevill claims that a certain Mr Myers married her kinswoman Lady Mary Nevill, and that their offspring were the key players in the Berkeley Square mystery. Some research shows that this statement is nothing but the truth: on 2 January 1802, the East India Company clerk Thomas Myers married Lady Mary Catherine Nevill, the daughter of the second Earl of Abergavenny. Thomas Myers was born in 1764, the son of the Revd Thomas Myers and his wife Anne Wordsworth. He was a clever, industrious man who sought patrimony to enter the House of Commons, but the Earl of Abergavenny did not like him; the snobbish nobleman thought his daughter had married beneath herself, and wanted nothing to do with Myers and his family. Before the premature death of Lady Mary in 1807, aged just twenty-four, she had given birth to two children, Thomas and Mary Myers. Thomas Myers Sr served as a MP for Yarmouth from 1810 until 1812, before sinking back into obscurity. He died in 1835, leaving a handsome fortune to his two children. Mary Myers became an old maid: a quaint old-world figure, of a very retiring disposition, she was well known to Lady Dorothy Nevill, and told the memoir-writing noblewoman many stories about the haunted house at No. 50 Berkeley Square

Miss Myers used to say that her brother was very eccentric, to a degree that bordered upon lunacy. Once, he had taken the house at No. 50 Berkeley Square, with the intention of living there together with his wife, for at the time he was engaged to be married. He furnished the house, and made every preparation to receive his bride in there, but a few days before the wedding, she jilted him for another man. Poor Mr Myers became even more deranged after this incident: he entrenched himself at No. 50 Berkeley Square and never went out of the house. He kept two live-in domestics, but he made no exertions to keep the house in order, and it soon became very dilapidated. There is nothing to suggest that Thomas Myers Jr ever left No. 50 Berkeley Square: he remained at the house until the end, remaining in his bedroom during daytime hours, but sometimes taking a stroll through the empty rooms at night. In 1873, he was prosecuted at the Marlborough Street Police Court for neglecting to pay taxes that were due, and a warrant was issued against him. His death certificate says: 'Thirtieth November 1874, 50 Berkeley Square, Thomas Myers, Male, 71 Years, Gentleman, Paralysis agitanus, Diseased heart certified, Jane Long present at the Death.' 'Paralysis agitans' [so spelt] is an archaic term for Parkinson's disease, and it is understandable that an individual afflicted with this disagreeable, and at the time quite untreatable, disorder would be inclined to stay indoors. Thomas Myers Jr was clearly a 'gentleman' without professional occupation, probably as a result of a substantial inheritance from his father. Jane Long, the witness on his death certificate, may well have been one of his maidservants.

To my mind, there is no doubt that the legend of the haunting of No. 50 Berkeley Square is linked to the very untidy and dilapidated look of the house during the residence of Thomas Myers. In elegant Berkeley Square, the house stood out like a sore thumb, and this set the tongues wagging: although the ailing Myers was still living there, there were rumours that the house had been deserted due to the persistent haunting. It is not uncommon that houses notorious for their neglected appearance are believed to be shunned because a notorious murder took place there, but not a single house in Berkeley Square is included among the Murder Houses of London. Alternatively, the dilapidated look of the house might inspire a 'Miss Havisham' or 'Dirty Dick' legend about some tragic recluse who had once been crossed in love. One example is Nathaniel Bentley's old house in Leadenhall Street, another a similarly neglected house at No. 19 Queen's Gate, Kensington. Richard Whittington-Egan once investigated a Liverpool legend about a badly maintained house at No. 1 Mulgrave Street, reputed to have been the home of a 'Miss Havisham' character; the truth turned out to be that it had been deserted for many years after its owner had died in 1906, since his maiden sister thought it harboured too many painful memories.

What is the source of the original Berkeley Square ghost story? According to an account in the *Notes & Queries*, there was suspicious resemblance between the Berkeley Square ghost story and a spooky tale published in a collection called *Twilight Stories*, or perhaps *Tales for Christmas Eve*. It turns out that this anthology is the work of the once-famous literary lady Rhoda Broughton, and that it contains a ghost story entitled 'The Truth, the Whole Truth, and Nothing but the Truth', originally published in *Temple Bar* magazine in February 1868; this story is virtually identical to that of the Berkeley Square ghost, except that the insane housemaid is taken to the doctor's home instead of to the hospital. When a correspondent to *Notes & Queries* wrote to Rhoda Broughton, asking if she had based her story on the Berkeley Square haunting, her reply was that she had in fact heard it from informants in the country. Thus it would seem as if life imitated art rather than the other way around: the wagging tongues of Mayfair transposed the *elementa* of Rhoda Broughton's ghost story to the dilapidated house inhabited by the ailing recluse Thomas Myers in Berkeley Square.

The story of the Ghost of Berkeley Square is really a cautionary tale about internet historiography: the online repositories are full of imaginative disinformation about the spectres of No. 50, with various charlatans 'improving on' the bogus ghost stories of Elliott O'Donnell. The sad tale of a hermitical outcast from society, crippled by Parkinson's disease, has spawned the conjuration of a dozen formidable spectres, flitting round the dilapidated rooms at No. 50 Berkeley Square, ready for any mischief. In blissful olden times, before the internet, foolish and credulous people tended to believe whatever they had read in a book; today, they are instead lured into gullibility by various online fantasies, based upon decades of piling untruth upon exaggeration. The malevolent poltergeists of No. 50 have attained internet immortality, and they are clearly looking forward to a long and eventful existence on the margins of London history; in present-day Mayfair spectral lore, common sense is disregarded and History's Muse ignored; in the ghostly internet gloom, no nightingale sings at Berkeley Square.

The Mystery of Sarah Duckett, 1881

In late September 1881, the farmer Bill Roberts was walking home to his house near Church Stretton, Shropshire. It was a dark and cloudy night, the moon flitting in and out of the clouds being the only light for the sturdy countryman making his way through the narrow roads and paths. Suddenly, he saw the figure of a woman dressed in white standing nearby. He recognized her as Sarah Duckett, a spinster who had disappeared from the neighbourhood several years earlier. He was about to speak to her when she slowly glided away from him, and disappeared down the shaft of an old mine called the Copper Hole. Bill Roberts had seen a ghost!

The Shropshire Ghost frightens Bill Roberts, from the *IPN*, 15 October 1881.

Having received the fright of his life, Roberts alerted all his friends and neighbours. Surely there must have been foul play when Sarah Duckett disappeared, he reasoned, and surely her dead body must have been dumped down the Copper Hole. It turned out that Sarah Duckett had gone to Australia about seven years earlier, returning eighteen months later. It was gossiped that, by one stratagem or other, she had earned a good deal of money down in the Antipodes. The last time Sarah Duckett had been seen alive was at the Church Stretton railway station, from whence she had been walking up Haze Road. The murderer must have been waiting for her up there, Roberts deduced. He and his friends decided to empty the Copper Hole to find Sarah Duckett's skeleton, and lay the ghost to rest.

There was widespread newspaper interest in the Shropshire Ghost and the excavation of the Copper Hole. *Reynolds's Newspaper* could report that every day, the old mine was visited by hundreds of people. The place resembled a country fair. Three respectable ladies had recently seen the ghost, and identified it as Sarah Duckett. A team of twenty people, led by Roberts, were making good progress emptying the deep mine shaft. The *IPN* could of course not stay away from this remarkable ghost story. With an illustration of how the Shropshire Ghost frightened Bill Roberts, it reported that all the locals were convinced that Sarah Duckett had been murdered, and that the solution lay at the bottom of the now nearly empty mine shaft.

When, after more than three weeks of hard work, the Copper Hole had been excavated without any human remains being found, a local dignitary received an anonymous letter: 'You will fail to find the body of Sarah Duckett in the Copper Hole; look in the cellar of the Toll Bar, examine the part nearest the road, in the left hand corner.'

Bill Roberts and his workforce promptly followed this recommendation, but after they had been digging for a week, another anonymous letter was received, purportedly from Sarah Duckett herself! She was amazed to see all this fuss on her behalf, she wrote, since she was happily married, and living in Martley, Worcestershire! Roberts and his men put down their spades with consternation, but inquiries demonstrated that the letter was a hoax. The workmen renewed their digging, egged on by several more sightings of the ghost.

After the ghost hysteria had reigned supreme in Church Stretton for more than a month, another local dignitary wrote to the registrars of Worcestershire, saying that he had spoken to the relatives of Sarah Duckett, who believed that she had died in Worcestershire in 1876. Indeed, it turned out that Sarah Duckett, aged forty-five, a domestic servant, had expired at the Worcester Infirmary in June 1876. But when Roberts and the other ghost-hunters were told about these matters, they stubbornly shook their heads. Had they not seen the ghost of Sarah Duckett themselves? Surely,

THE GHOST OF SARAH DUCKETT - SHROPSHIRE

The ghost of Sarah Duckett appears again, from the *IPN*, 25 November 1882.

there must have been some mysterious conspiracy, with another woman being buried in Worcester to cover up the hideous murder of poor Sarah Duckett, and the theft of her Australian fortune.

Although there were no further sightings of the ghost for many months, Roberts and his friends kept murmuring about the mysterious fate of Sarah Duckett. In November 1882, a young countryman was drinking at a public house in Church Stretton. When the ghost was mentioned in conversation, he laughed aloud and ridiculed it. But when walking home, he saw a woman following him. He several times stopped to let her pass him, but she did not. Finally, he stood still and waited for her to come up to him. When she glided up to him, he could see that she was all dressed in white, and that she was holding her bonnet out to him. It was the ghost!

Nearly delirious with fright, the young man ran home to the farm where he was working. Since then, the *IPN* reported, an old man had fainted dead away when accosted by the ghost of Sarah Duckett, a youth on horseback had been severely frightened, and an old lady seeing the ghost through her parlour window had received 'a serious injury to her nervous system'. Many people around Church Stretton were once more murmuring that Sarah Duckett's ghost was on the prowl. A more likely theory is that some local prankster dressed up as a ghost to have fun frightening some of the gullible locals, and that the same individual had a hand in sending the various anonymous letters.

The Hackney Ghost, 1895

In the summer of 1895, there were rumours of some very queer goings-on in the churchyard of St John's, Hackney. A figure dressed in white had been seen in the churchyard by at least a dozen witnesses; more than once, it had caused women to faint, by the simple expedient of sneaking up to them and uttering that outcry thought to be favoured by the spiritual world – 'Boo!' There was a quaint gravestone in the churchyard, depicting three boys playing cards at a table. It was rumoured that one of these boys, who had been losing heavily, had exclaimed, 'May God strike me dead if I do not win this game!' He lost, stood up to leave the table, and dropped dead! Had he returned as the Hackney Ghost?

In August 1895, many local inhabitants were too fearful to venture anywhere near the churchyard at night. But the gangs of young Hackney roughs were not as easily scared: they suspected that some prankster was amusing himself by frightening the local women. They armed themselves with sticks and bludgeons, brought with them lanterns and candles, and marched to the churchyard to lay the ghost to rest. The word went round the neighbourhood and a veritable panic resulted: more than six thousand people invaded the Hackney churchyard, looking for the ghost.

The mob climbed the railings, clambering over graves and gravestones to reach the rear of the church, where the ghost was believed to manifest itself. They waited until midnight, but no ghost turned up. Some jokers instead began to improvise: by giving 'unearthly cries' they caused part of the mob to stampede, and some sheets of newspaper dropped down from the branches of a tree had a similar effect. According to *Lloyd's Weekly Newspaper*, several people were injured during these stampedes, and the damage done to the graves was very great. After a number of people had their pockets picked, some police constables arrived, but they were powerless against the

The hunt for the Hackney Ghost; from the *IPN*, 31 August 1895.

frenzied mob. Reinforcements were called for, but not even a force of fifty constables was capable of restoring order. The next evening, the churchyard was again under siege from intrepid ghost hunters, but the combined effect of a thunderstorm and the presence of forty constables kept them quiet. The Hackney Ghost was never seen or heard of again.

The Fairwater Mystery, 1896

On 10 July 1896, a pistol shot rang out in a lonely back road just outside the village of Fairwater, near Cardiff, and a loud scream was heard. A traveller saw a man hurrying away from the direction of the scream; this individual 'wished him a gruff good-night'. Later, the traveller saw the body of a man lying on the side of the road. He had been shot about 100 yards behind, but had not died outright, instead running in terror up the road, spouting blood as he went. Both men and women fainted at the ghastly sight.

The murdered man turned out to be the thirty-three-year-old workman David Thomas, who was married with two children and lived in a cottage near Ely. He had never been involved in anything illegal. A few months earlier, he had been employed as a carpenter by Lord Windsor at St Fagan's Castle, and seemed to like his new job. The evening Thomas was shot dead, he had gone to the local to have a few pints, and people had seen him start walking home at a brisk pace.

There were several more or less far-fetched theories about the Fairwater Mystery, as it was called. Firstly, it was suspected that one of the unsuccessful applicants for the St Fagan's position had killed him as revenge. But after it had been discovered that Thomas had actually been earning less than the recommended union wage, it was instead suspected that the carpenter's trade union had murdered him, in order to set an example about such matters.

The South Wales Police made little headway with this mysterious crime. After a while, they seem to have adopted the principle that if there are no suspects closer to home, then look for a dodgy Irishman. But although a drunken Irish sailor, and later also a dodgy Dublin shoemaker, were said to have closely resembled the description of the murderer given by the solitary witness, both of them turned out to have an alibi. The only casualty was the shoemaker's landlady, who was said to have lost her reason when the police came and arrested her lodger. The Cardiff *Evening Express* roundly criticized the police for their lack of initiative, and offered a £50 reward for the apprehension of the murderer. Not unreasonably, the newspaper demanded that Scotland Yard was called in, but this never seems to have happened.

Some journalists from the *Western Mail* instead made use an approach not unfamiliar to aficionados of modern American crime drama: they got hold of a psychic detective. At a Cardiff séance, a young lady medium had recently gone into a state of trance, with a strange convulsion, and hissed out 'I – WILL – have – my – revenge!' When the interlocutor asked 'Who are you, friend?' the spirit answered 'David Thomas. I – was – shot!'

This was good enough for the journalists, particularly since the girl was young and not bad-looking. They decided to bring her to the murder scene, to see what would happen. And they were not disappointed. The histrionic girl first claimed to see the murderer approaching, describing him in some detail. She then screamed and moaned in agony, reliving the murder scene, and clasping her back in intense agony, as if she had just been shot. After she had collapsed, David Thomas's spirit returned, demanding revenge, and actually naming his murderer. After reviving, the hysterical medium rushed round the murder scene, screaming 'Look, look! Look at the blood!' Before the journalists were able to drag her away, she yelled 'He is there!' Asked who she meant, she pointed into empty space and screamed, 'The ghost!'

This unedifying scene would not have been out of place in the 'Cartman's Incredible Gift' episode of the amusing *South Park* animated series. The *Western Mail* journalists wrote a full-length feature about the experiences of their psychic detective, which was of course later reproduced, with an illustration, by the sensational *IPN*. The police do

A SPIRIT MEDIUM SEES A MURDERED MAN'S GHOST.

'I see him! The ghost!' From the *IPN*, 22 August 1896.

not appear to have taken it seriously, which is probably good; what if one of the Cardiff detectives had been a late nineteenth-century equivalent of his foolish *South Park* colleague, and what if the name of one of the arrested Irishmen had matched that given by the medium?

The Fairwater Mystery is still unsolved. One might speculate that an enemy of David Thomas, perhaps enraged that he was an unemployed pauper when Thomas had found security at St Fagan's, had been lying in wait for him outside the pub, but there are no clues to the identity of the murderer.

The Plumstead Ghost, 1897

In October 1897, many people saw a ghost flitting about near St James's Church and school, Plumstead. Sensitive little girls had fainted dead away when the white spectre approached them; some were still in bed, said the *Daily News*, suffering from nervous exhaustion. A timid schoolmaster had been frightened out of his wits when the Plumstead Ghost suddenly grabbed hold of him from behind and shouted 'Boo-hah!' at the top of its voice. An old couple visiting the churchyard received a similar shock when the ghost hailed them from a tree, making use of the same uncouth outcry.

When another schoolmaster was taking an evening walk, he heard rustling in the hedges nearby, and a shout of 'Boo-hah!' He had brought with him a large Newfoundland dog, which he set on the spectre. Since the master distinctly heard the ghost give a yelp when the dog's fangs made contact with its buttocks, he became convinced that the Plumstead Ghost was flesh and blood. He spoke to both masters and schoolboys, asking them not to be fearful, but to teach the ghost a hard lesson if they came across it.

The rowdy schoolboys decided to do just that. One evening, after scouts had reported that the ghost was at large, a troop of schoolboys, a hundred strong, stormed the churchyard. Shouting and yahooing, they pelted the ghost with stones, but without scoring any hits on the absconding spectre. Instead, their missiles broke some valuable stained glass. Pursued by the Newfoundland dog, which had belatedly been brought into the action, the ghost was seen to disappear into the hedges.

Since the schoolboys had been so very rowdy, the police arrested two of the ringleaders and brought them to Woolwich, but after the masters had explained the extraordinary circumstances of their riot, they were both discharged. The evening after, the Plumstead Ghost was seen in the grounds of Mr J. R. Jolly, JP. Arrayed in white attire, and wearing some kind of grotesque mask, the spectre was sitting in a tree, shouting its usual 'Boo-hah!' to frighten some female domestics. Mr Jolly was not at all amused: he sent for the police and the ghost was arrested. It turned out that the spectre's white garb had been torn, and his buttocks badly bruised, from his two encounters with the fierce Newfoundland dog.

He turned out to be a local engineer, whose mind had become unhinged after he had lost a good deal of money in litigation. The friends of this unbalanced engineer made sure he was put under restraint in an asylum, and the Plumstead Ghost was laid to rest.

A GHOST APPEARS NEAR WOOLWICH.
SCHOOLBOYS ENJOY THE SPORT OF PELTING IT.

The Plumstead Ghost pelted by schoolboys; from the *IPN*, 6 November 1897.

The Fighting Ghost of Tondu, 1904

Today, Tondu is an obscure Welsh village, situated on the Bridgend to Maesteg railway line, three miles north of Bridgend. It enjoyed a considerable industrial boom in Victorian times, with large ironworks and collieries, as well as becoming a railway junction for the coal trains. Its fortune and prosperity seem to have been waning already in 1904, when Tondu acquired one of its most sinister inhabitants ever. For some time, there had been talk of the disused colliery at Ynisawdre being haunted. On an early September morning in 1904, some workmen saw a tall spectre, shrouded in white, in the neighbourhood of Felinfach. When the ghost glided towards them with a drawn-out 'Booh!', its great black sockets that took the place of eyes fixed straight ahead, all twelve sturdy Welsh miners took to their heels. When they finally dared to look back, the ghost had disappeared.

Not long after, another Welshman was taking a midnight walk down the lonely, narrow road adjoining the deserted buildings and coke ovens of the abandoned Ynisawdre colliery. At the far end of a tunnel he was astonished to see a tall, cadaverous figure waiting for him, all shrouded in white. The head resembled a skull covered with wrinkled parchment; the eyes were hollow sockets, with a cavernous glow. Suddenly, the ghost ran up to the terrified Welshman, its long arms outstretched. It grasped

IT SWIFTLY GLIDED TOWARDS HIM.

WORKMEN WERE SCARED BY IT

'Booh!' The Fighting Ghost of Tondu on the charge, from the *IPN*, 17 September 1904.

him with hearty goodwill, with such a vice-like grip that he could hardly breathe. When he tried to grapple with this singular ghost, his hands met just thin air. Having toppled its opponent over, the Fighting Ghost of Tondu glided off with a hollow laugh.

'A Ghostly Reign of Terror in Glamorganshire' exclaimed the headline of the *South Wales Echo*. Village ghosts were not unknown in this part of Wales, but they used to be timid and unadventurous, behaving with becoming decorum and keeping a safe distance from human beings. Although this novel spectre was draped in white, the proper attire for any self-respecting ghost, and made use of the equally orthodox outcry 'Booh!', it seemed much more combative, putting twelve strong men to flight, and then successfully wrestling another. A servant girl had recently seen the Fighting Ghost stalking the ruins of the abandoned colliery at Ynisawdre, uttering dismal groans and waving its arms about. The women and children of Tondu were kept indoors after nightfall, and bands of stalwart men, armed with bludgeons and pitchforks, patrolled the country roads to stop the Fighting Ghost. The *Daily Mail*, which took an interest in the pugnacious Welsh spook, predicted that the desperate midnight encounter in Tondu would pass into local history: 'Watchers, well-armed, are still searching for the apparition, but since the experience of the stalwart villager of the catch-as-catch-can tactics of the unearthly wrestler, people have been wary.' Two people out looking for the Fighting Ghost had heard the sound of spectral galloping horses, as if the Welsh spectre was taking exercise on horseback, and the ghost stories in the district were multiplying.

It would appear as if the short career of the Fighting Ghost of Tondu ended in late September 1904, after it had been immortalized in the *IPN* and other publications. Its origin is likely to have been the same as those of other 'suburban' or 'village' spectres (ignoring the sad fate of the Hammersmith Ghost of 1814, who was shot dead by an armed ghost-hunter): some prankster amused himself through dressing up as a ghost and frightening timid and superstitious people in the neighbourhood. Although the annals of the *IPN* provide several instances of 'suburban ghosts' being caught, beaten up, or mauled by fierce dogs, the Fighting Ghost of Tondu seems to have been spared such indignities; there is no mention of its activities after September 1904.

5

Dogs

Newfoundland Dogs to the Rescue!

Throughout Victorian times, Newfoundland dogs were very highly regarded, mainly due to their ability to save human lives during shipwrecks or bathing accidents. The struggle between life and death, with the helpless human in the hands of the hostile elements when a compassionate brute creature takes his side and brings him to safety, was a subject that fascinated the Victorians. Heroic Newfoundland dogs were depicted in schoolbooks, on popular engravings, and in books on natural history. These dogs were considered not just brave and altruistic, but also extremely intelligent. A large proportion of the anecdotes of dogs told and re-told by the early Victorian dog-fanciers were related to the extraordinary sagacity of the Newfoundland. To the sentimental Victorian naturalist, these dogs were not just superior to all other members of the canine tribe, but also more admirable than non-human primates. Apes and monkeys were viewed with suspicion at this time: did these filthy monkeys not hide their nuts in an unmentionable place, and did the great apes not have lurid designs on white women?

In Victorian collections of dog stories, and children's books and magazines, wise and altruistic Newfoundland dogs make use of their superior intellects to protect children, catch thieves, and rescue people from various calamities. If an imprudent child is in danger from drowning, fire, or falling down a precipice, a sagacious Newfoundland dog is never far away. If burglars or robbers are up to mischief, the watchful Newfoundland drives them away. The cult of the Newfoundland dog in popular culture reigned supreme throughout the nineteenth century, not just in Britain but in most European countries, even those where Newfoundland dogs were extremely scarce, like Sweden. Some authors have suspected that this cult rests on far from solid foundations. Some of the unreferenced old yarns about super-intelligent Newfoundland dogs read more or less like fairy tales; were they equally devoid of factual foundation?

So, how many *true* stories of sagacious and lifesaving Newfoundlands are there? The answer has to be: certainly very many! These dogs have a powerful instinct to retrieve objects from the water, and to save people struggling to swim, and they were several times featured in the columns of the *IPN*. In July 1868, Mrs Jane Titherleigh, the wife of a Hull ironmaster, was taking a cruise with her little son in a small sailing boat when the son suddenly fell overboard. Consternation ruled among the humans on board, since they were all indifferent swimmers, but a Newfoundland dog leapt overboard without being prompted in any way, swam up to the young lad, and dragged him back to the vessel. The boy was none the worse for his ducking, but Mrs Titherleigh fell into hysterics.

In February 1872, some watchmen on duty at Sable Island, off Nova Scotia, saw a large Newfoundland dog come walking up to them. Although the dog seemed quite exhausted, it whined as if it wanted them to follow it. The Newfoundland dog led the men to the shore, but it was becoming very dark. One of the watchmen got the idea to let the dog hold a lantern in its mouth to guide them, and the dog willingly obliged. The Newfoundland dog led them to a woman and a child, both half dead from privations. It was the wife and daughter of Captain Fletcher, of the Liverpool barque *Lilly Parker*, which had been shipwrecked nearby. When the ship had sunk, Mrs Fletcher had hung on to her little daughter with one hand, and to the Newfoundland dog's collar with the other. After the powerful dog had dragged them ashore, the sagacious animal had spontaneously gone to look for help.

WONDERFUL SAGACITY OF A DOG

A sagacious Newfoundland saves a child from drowning, from the *IPN*, 4 July 1868. Note the swooning Mrs Titherleigh in the background.

The clever Newfoundland saving Mrs Fletcher and her daughter, from the *IPN*, 30 March 1872.

In June 1875, some children were sitting on the Thames embankment near Waterloo. A gust of wind suddenly blew a little girl into the river, where she could be seen to be struggling. A gentleman passing by unleashed his Newfoundland dog, appropriately named 'Ready', and made the dog aware of the girl's situation. Without further prompting, the dog leapt into Thames, seized the girl by the collar of her cape, and swam to the stairs nearby.

In June 1896, some children were playing on the tram lines near Daubhill Mill, Bolton. They were watched by a Newfoundland bitch named 'Princess May', lying down in front of the door of her master's house. But when the tram-car approached at a brisk pace, one of the children fell down in front of it. The driver desperately tried to rein in the horses, and people shouted with alarm, but Princess May dashed across the road, grabbed the three-year-old boy by his frock, and pulled him to safety. When some journalists were incredulous of this novel instance of Newfoundland dog sagacity, they were taken to task by Mr Fred. Lomax, the secretary of the Bolton and District Humane Society, who had carefully collected witness testimony of the rescue. He, too, had initially doubted this extraordinary story, but four witnesses unanimously stated that Princess May had acted independently, and that she had been clearly seen to drag the boy to safety before any human rescuer could reach him.

The boy himself, the three-year-old son of Mr T. Hurst, of No. 10 Stainsbury Street, Daubhill, was tracked down by Mr Lomax, as was Mr T. Baxendale, of No. 18 Oak Street, who had run to pick up the child when the dog came bounding up to carry it out of danger. Princess May herself was a sturdy black Newfoundland bitch, the property of Mr J. H. Edge, of Daubhill. He told a journalist that his dog had once won a prize at a dog show in Dublin; she was very fond of children, and a good swimmer and plunger. The Newfoundland dog which used to walk in front of the local Artillery Band was the brother of this splendid animal. In November, Princess May appeared at a Humane Society presentation ceremony at Bolton Town Hall, along with eleven humans who had performed various heroics. Lord Stanley MP and the Mayor of Bolton presented them with a silver medal each; the dog also received a silver collar to be able to wear hers in a becoming manner. The next month, Princess May was the guest of honour at a grand dog show in London, walking round the ring to show off her collar and medal.

In my book *Those Amazing Newfoundland Dogs*, I have collected twelve primary newspaper accounts of Newfoundland dogs being ordered by their masters to leap into the water and rescue a drowning person. Furthermore, there are not less than eighteen newspaper stories of these dogs spontaneously plunging into the water to go to the rescue, without any command. The majority of these accounts provide the place, the name of the person rescued, and sometimes even the name of the dog and its owner. Most of these accounts were published in good-quality newspapers, and published by more than one version, by different journalists, providing additional credibility. There are also four primary newspaper accounts of Newfoundland dogs either swimming to shore from a ship carrying a rope, or swimming from shore with a rope to a stricken vessel.

A Newfoundland dog saves a child from drowning in the Thames, from the *IPN*, 8 September 1883.

Already the dog author Rawdon Lee found it peculiar that so many early Victorian authors extolled the superior intellect of the Newfoundland dog; in his opinion, they were much like other dogs. He has had support from Professor Stanley Coren's influential *The Intelligence of Dogs*, which ranks the Newfoundland as number thirty-four out of seventy-eight breeds, with regard to obedience and working intelligence. The Victorian dog fanciers would have considered this an insult to their sagacious breed. Nor have some of the present-day Newfoundland dog enthusiasts appreciated Professor Coren's ranking of their breed, objecting that intelligence does not equal obedience. They have pointed out that although the Newfoundland is hampered by its independent nature and short attention span, the dogs are definitely more clever than most large breeds, particularly with regard to problem solving. An anecdote in Professor Coren's book would support their case: a tired Newfoundland bitch was annoyed by a yapping little Maltese terrier wanting to play. In the end, the great black dog seized the little terrier by the scruff of the neck and walked out to the bathroom. Here she deposited it into a large, empty bathtub, where it was securely confined, before contentedly returning and settling down to sleep. This not only shows a very good example of creative action in dogs, but also that the old stories of sagacious Newfoundlands ducking annoying little dogs in ponds or ditches are likely to be true.

Professor Coren also has a very low opinion of the Newfoundland as a watchdog. In my opinion, this is true for most bitches, and also many male dogs, due to their placid and friendly nature, and lack of suspicion towards strangers. Any burglar who takes on a large and alert Newfoundland male used to guarding his territory, and being protective of the other members of the household, may well be mistaken to rely too much on the Professor's advice, however. It is curious to note that many of the early Newfoundland dogs in Britain, Lord Byron's Boatswain prominent among them, were known for their pugnacious nature. According to many sources, they were also excellent watchdogs: vigilant and wary of strangers. *The Times* newspaper provides many examples of burglars emerging second best from encounters with fierce Newfoundland dogs, and even reports of smugglers and thieves themselves keeping Newfoundlands to set on the police and customs officers.

To analyse the problem of the changing Newfoundland, it is it important to take into account the work of Professor Jasper Rine and co-workers, with regard to canine genetics. A Border collie is a very intelligent dog, concentrated and intense; it has a strong herding instinct: crouching and 'giving eye' when it sees some recalcitrant sheep, or sometimes even a human being it considers to require some herding. The present-day Newfoundland is friendly and easy-going, has webbed feet and loves water, and holds its tail high. Rine and his colleagues cross-bred a male

A Newfoundland dog saves the boy James Alford from falling down a precipice, from the *IPN*, 18 November 1876.

A CHILD SAVED BY A DOG-ASTOUNDING ESCAPE

Border collie with a Newfoundland bitch; the union of this mismatched couple produced seven healthy puppies, which were in turn bred with each other, resulting in a third generation of twenty-three 'grandchildren'. These dogs exhibited a seemingly quite random combination of 'Border collie' and 'Newfoundland' traits: for example, one of the dogs might be very intelligent but also friendly, holding its tail high but hating water, and possessing the herding instinct to 'give eye'. It is important that the typical traits of these dogs appear to be inherited separately.

With these arguments in mind, let us return to the early Newfoundland dogs. These dogs were selectively bred to have webbed feet and a talent for water work, but also to be intelligent and altruistic, with a strong instinct to rescue some person falling into the water. The dogs should also be watchful and wary of strangers, unafraid to 'have a scrap', and ready to defend their masters. Unlike the sheepdogs, mainly trained to follow the signals of their masters, the working Newfoundlands were bred to take initiatives of their own; it would not do if the ship's dog stood waiting for orders when a net full of fish was lost, or a sailor drowned. Understandably, these remarkable dogs were widely admired in Georgian and Victorian Britain. The stories of Newfoundland sagacity recounted in this book are only the tip of the iceberg; there is no wonder these amazing dogs were so widely featured in magazines, children's books and books of anecdotes on natural history. We will never know what genetic event triggered the development of these remarkably intelligent early Newfoundland dogs.

A recent study aimed to determine whether dogs would seek help from a bystander if their owner feigned a heart attack, or pretended to be trapped underneath a falling bookcase; they did not. There is a marked contrast between these very Ordinary Dogs standing by uselessly when their owner was in trouble, and the heroics of the Newfoundlands described earlier in this chapter; for example, the extraordinary Princess May not just sensing danger to the child on the tram line, but taking appropriate action with commendable alacrity. There was clearly something special about the Newfoundland dogs in those days, something that set them apart from other breeds of dog.

With time, the Newfoundland dog fanciers valued different qualities in their dogs, and adapted their breeding accordingly. For example, since they were not used as watchdogs, there was no need for them to be watchful and wary of strangers; in recent times, the dogs have become increasingly placid and friendly, not just to their owners, but to everyone else. A calm and stolid temperament, great size and solid black fur were considered as valuable characteristics, whereas the spirit and watchfulness formerly exhibited by the dogs was no longer appreciated. It would appear as if selective breeding in the last 150 years has led to the Newfoundland dogs losing a good deal of their pugnacity and guarding instinct along the way – and also some of the intelligence for which these amazing dogs were once rightly admired.

A Famous Detective's Life Saved by a Dog

Detective Chief Inspector Nathaniel Druscovitch for many years kept a large black-and-white Newfoundland dog named 'Blackbeard', which had come into his possession in quite a singular manner. Druscovitch was considered one of the foremost brains of Scotland Yard, and was promoted to Chief Inspector in 1870, at the age of just twenty-nine. His excellent linguistic skills made sure that he was often made use of in negotiations with foreign police services, and in matters concerning the extradition of criminals who had sought refuge abroad. Druscovitch, who was a small, wiry man, had once tracked down a noted coiner named Ambrose Jackson to a dilapidated house in Battersea. Fearful that the coiner would make his escape, he decided to arrest him single-handedly, since help was not immediately at hand. But the tall and sturdy coiner was armed with a large knife, and after a desperate struggle, he seized hold of Druscovitch with a hearty goodwill, and aimed a lethal stab at his heart. But then the door burst open, and a large Newfoundland dog leapt into the room. It seized hold of the desperado with its powerful jaws, and Druscovitch managed to disarm and handcuff him. It was Blackbeard, the landlord's dog, who had heard the detective's shouts for assistance,

Inspector Druscovitch is saved by the Newfoundland dog 'Blackbeard', from the *IPN*, 8 May 1897.

and taken action to rescue him. Druscovitch bought the dog and gave him a home in his house; when Blackbeard died after many years, he was buried in the long garden behind the house, with a tombstone reading, 'He saved my life.'

Nathaniel Druscovitch was not just a dog-loving crime-fighter, but a somewhat disreputable character who was disappointed by his low salary at Scotland Yard. Together with Chief Inspector William Palmer and Inspector John Meiklejohn, he started taking bribes from the racecourse swindlers William Kurr and Harry Benson, who had taken £30,000 from the Frenchwoman Madame de Goncourt in a horseracing scam. In 1872, Druscovitch was responsible for handling the extradition negotiations after Marguerite Dixblanc, the Park Lane murderess, had been arrested in Paris. In 1875, Druscovitch and Meiklejohn were investigating the murder of Jane Soper in Borough High Street; the two bent coppers did their very best to inculpate a ruffian named Sheridan Morley for the murder, although the Southwark Police Court was distinctly unimpressed with their lack of hard evidence against him. Had Morley in some way got into the way of Kurr or Benson, and had they instructed their bent coppers to frame him for the murder of Jane Soper, or did Druscovitch and Meiklejohn deliberately set out to fabricate a 'solution' to the murder, to forward their own careers and cover up the taking of bribes?

Tipped off by their bent coppers, the two swindlers William Kurr and Harry Benson kept one step ahead of the police throughout most of the

1870s. But in the end, the three crooked detectives got their well-merited come-uppance. Druscovitch, Palmer and Meiklejohn were all convicted of taking bribes in 1877, sentenced to two years' imprisonment each, and dismissed from the police force. This time, there was no Newfoundland dog to save Nathaniel Druscovitch, and he felt his disgrace keenly. After being released from prison, he tried to establish himself as a private inquiry agent, but not with much success; he died from tuberculosis in 1881, aged just thirty-nine. Ex-Inspector Meiklejohn survived for many years after his disgrace, a shabbily dressed and gloomy-looking old man, who left his usual haunts in Fleet Street and the Strand shortly before the outbreak of the Great War.

A Dog as Witness

The earliest cutting in an *IPN* file on animal antics in court is from 1871: Mr Samuel Bowden, landlord of the King's Arms tavern in Blackman Street, Borough, had lost a valuable performing dog, which had later been found as the property of the young labouring man Charles Carr. When Carr was summoned before the Southwark police court, the dog was also present in court. Carr said that he had purchased the dog in Peckham three months ago, but since he had been a regular at the King's Arms, there was suspicion that he had stolen the animal from Mr Bowden's servant. To prove that the dog was his, Mr Bowden made it show off one of its tricks in court. He placed an old straw hat on the dog's head, and a pair of spectacles on its nose, and the dog immediately sat up on its haunches. Mr Bowden then placed a pipe in its mouth, and the solemn manner in which the dog sat up caused roars of laughter in court. The magistrate declared himself satisfied that the dog belonged to Mr Bowden, and cautioned Carr as to his future dealings in dogs.

In November 1878, a certain William Needham appeared in court to answer a summons taken out against him by 'Professor' Moffat, an instructor of performing animals, for detaining a black-and-tan terrier dog. Moffat claimed that this valuable dog, whose artist's name was 'Soot', had been lost nine months earlier, but he had later seen it in the company of the defendant, and claimed it as his own. Needham declared that the dog was his, however, and refused to part with it. This time, the dog was entirely unwilling to perform any tricks in court, something that of course led to suspicion. With a flourish, the 'Professor' instead opened a large bag he had brought with him, and produced a large black cat named 'Jim': this animal was a performing cat of great repute, he declared, and the partner of the dog Soot. On its master's command, the performing cat frisked and gambolled, swung round in a trapeze, and mewed loudly when its name was called. There was considerable hilarity in court at this

A performing cat in court, from the *IPN*, 23 November 1878.

unprecedented display of feline docility, but it did nothing to convince the magistrate that the dog belonged to Moffat. In the end, the summons was dismissed, since in spite of the display with the cat, the magistrate did not think the complainant had made out his title to the dog.

In spite of the unsatisfactory display of the terrier Soot, a dog appeared as a witness in the Hammersmith police court in September the very next year. A lad named Frederick William Hoare had summoned Mr Theodore Gordon, of Godolphin Road, Shepherd's Bush, for allowing a ferocious dog to be at large unmuzzled. When he had been passing Shepherd's Bush Common, a large dog had rushed from underneath one of the seats and bit his leg. He had a mark on his leg, and four holes in his trousers. The magistrate Mr Paget inquired for the dog, and Mr Read, who defended, ushered it into the police court. It was a large, benign-looking dog, which ran up to the bench and jumped up to the magistrate in a friendly manner before seating itself on one of the chairs. Mr Read said that he could call witnesses who would give the animal a good character as a quiet, peaceable dog. When Mrs Gordon had been seated on the green, with the dog playing nearby, the complainant and another lad had come along, swinging their arms and snapping their fingers in an obnoxious manner, and giving the dog an invitation to join them in their little fun. The bonhomous Mr Paget reproached the defendant, and said that a dog of this size should not be allowed to be at large in a place used for the recreation of children, and that it should be kept under proper control.

A DOG CALLED AS A WITNESS.

A DOG AS WITNESS

Above: The canine witness at Hammersmith, from the *IPN*, 27 September 1879.

Left: The Saddleworth dog in court, from the *IPN*, 30 October 1880.

He dismissed the summons, however, since it could not be said that it was a dangerous dog, and the canine witness walked free as a result.

The next year, another dog was in court, this time at the Saddleworth Petty Sessions. A man named John Torkington was charged with stealing a dog, value of £5, from one Hosea Hill. Torkington said that the dog knew him well, and was very fond of him; he had tried to send it away, but it would not go away. The large, sturdy dog appeared in court, and when the prisoner called it, the animal jumped up at him, wagging its tail merrily. This display of canine affection, as well as other evidence, persuaded the court that Torkington was innocent, and he left the Saddleworth Petty Sessions with the dog.

The final cutting in this file is from the *IPN* of 19 March 1904, and concerns a murder trial in America. An American showman and his wife stood accused of having murdered their partner, to gain sole control of a travelling menagerie and waxworks show. A bloodstained axe had been found, and it was suspected that a large performing monkey had been an eyewitness to the murder. As the showman and his wife stood in the dock, this monkey was brought into court. The moment he saw the two prisoners, he flew at them savagely, and this convinced the court of their guilt: the man was sentenced to death, and the woman to penal servitude. It attracts suspicion that neither of the suspects is named, and that it is not stated where the trial took place. Such monkey-business in court appears undignified in the extreme, and to swear away a man's life on that kind of evidence would be quite unthinkable even in the American Deep South. Most probably, the tall tale of the monkey in court originated as a 'from our Foreign Correspondent' newspaper falsification, intended to adorn the pages of some disreputable Sunday newspaper.

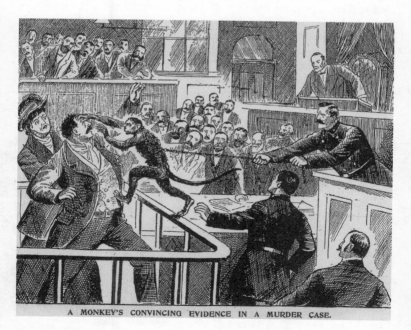

A MONKEY'S CONVINCING EVIDENCE IN A MURDER CASE.

A monkey appears in court, from the *IPN*, 19 March 1904.

The Sagacity of the Dog, 1872

The *IPN* journalists had a distinct fondness for reporting stories about dogs and their doings. In their somewhat biased minds, there were good dogs, who rescued drowning people, captured burglars, and gave the alarm when there was a fire; then there were bad dogs, who worried sheep, stole meat from butcher's shops, and bit people in the buttocks. In December 1872, a time when there was a shortage of murder and mayhem to report, the *IPN* made use of a series of articles just published in the *Daily Telegraph* for a feature on 'The Sagacity of the Dog – Reason or Instinct?'

The main story concerned the dog trainer M. Léonard and his dominoes-playing dogs. Already the great Munito, a performing poodle who had been at large in London as early as 1817, had been an excellent player of dominoes, and M. Léonard's dogs were equally well educated. The dog sat down on a chair by the dominoes table, and the newspaper writer and M. Léonard seated themselves opposite. Six dominoes were put before the dog, and the same number in front of the writer. They both played in a conventional manner, the dog taking the pieces and putting them in their correct position, until the writer deliberately played a wrong number. The dog looked surprised, stared very earnestly at the writer, growled, and then barked angrily. Finding that no notice was made of his remonstrance, he pushed away the wrong domino with his nose, and took a suitable one from his own pieces and put it there instead. The writer then played correctly, but the shrewd dog won the game. It was considered impossible, the newspaper writer stated, that M. Léonard could in any way have guided the dog, but most probably, this is exactly what happened: dogs are very clever when it comes to reacting to hidden cues.

The Sagacity of the Dog, from the *IPN*, 27 December 1884.

The next correspondent to the *Daily Telegraph* described how he had visited the Beach Mansion Hotel in Southsea, where the manager had a large greyhound. 'That is a fine dog!' he had exclaimed, and the manager had replied, 'Yes, and a most remarkable one!' Last winter, a poor dog had come every day to their street door, and the charitable greyhound had always given him something to eat, either from its own food or from bread or meat it had picked up from the larder; the greyhound had laid the food in front of his poor brother dog, licked his nose, and walked away with obvious satisfaction. A tall story indeed, and scarcely to be believed, although the writer put emphasis on the charity and 'brotherly kindness' of the canine tribe. The next story came from a surgeon in Leeds, who had found a lame dog in the street, and dressed its broken leg. He had kept the dog indoors for two days, but even when set at liberty, the grateful street mongrel kept coming back for the dressings to be changed each morning. After the sagacious dog had been cured, it brought back two other lame street dogs, pointing them out as worthy objects for the surgeon's attentions!

Not long ago, a dog in Ramsgate had rescued a family from great danger by seizing hold of a night-watchman's coat to bring him to the Railway Tavern, which was on fire. Indeed, the idea of Man as the only reasoning being would have been challenged if dogs had possessed the power of speech: limited by the anatomy of their voice-boxes to barking, growling and whining, these animals were prevented from showing off their formidable intellects. The philosopher Leibniz was quoted concerning a dog that had been taught to pronounce thirty words, and as I have shown in my book *Amazing Dogs*, some of these animals have a talent for mimicking the human voice, with Don the Speaking Dog becoming a favourite performer in the Berlin and New York music halls in the years prior to the Great War. The *IPN* provided a large engraving showing a number of these sagacious canines showing off their various skills.

The Rat-Killing Monkey of Manchester, 1880

In Victorian times, the 'sport' of ratting enjoyed considerable popularity. In this sleazy pastime, a number of rats were put into a rat-pit, and then an angry terrier dog was released. Bets were made how many rats the dog could kill within a certain amount of time, or how long it would take for the animal to kill twenty or a hundred rats.

It would appear as if ratting originated as a form of eighteenth-century dog trials, where the killing instinct of young terriers was tested by giving them a few rats to kill. With time, the sport spread to London and other cities. Instead of just being dog trials, the ratting matches became

A ratting scene.

increasingly competitive, with a higher amount of rats put into the pit, and a good deal of betting going on. A dog owner might announce in the newspapers that his animal was capable of killing a certain number of rats in a certain amount of time – say, twenty rats in five minutes – and bets were matched whether the dog would be capable of this feat. After a sack of live rats had been emptied into the pit, the dog was let loose on its path of destruction. The best dogs dispatched each rodent with a swift bite, without worrying at it or carrying it around, before attacking the next rat. The rats scurried around as well as they could, sometimes piling up in the corner of the rat-pit as if to seek protection, at other times desperately fighting for their lives.

Already in the early 1800s, there were several rat-pits in London, the most famous of which was the Westminster Pit, located in Duck Lane, Orchard Street. In the 1820s, this sleazy establishment became the catalyst of the growth of London ratting, thanks to 'Billy the Raticide', the most famous ratting dog ever. Billy was a muscular dog of twenty-six pounds weight, mostly white in colour, with strong jaws and a fierce glare in his eye. He had set a record already in 1820, by killing twenty rats in seventy-one seconds, at the cost of being deprived of one of his own eyes by one of the infuriated rodents. In September 1822, Billy was wagered, for twenty sovereigns, to kill a hundred rats in less than twelve minutes. Since ratting of this magnitude had rarely been seen before, the Westminster Pit was completely full. The audience, nearly two thousand strong, laid many

The Great 100-Rat Match.

The Great 100-Rat Match.

hundreds of pounds on the outcome of the match. There was a huge cheer when Mr Dew brought the squirming, growling Billy down to the pit, and another when a huge sack of large sewer rats was carried into the arena. The gentlemen puffed hard at their cigars to escape the pungent smell of the rodents, and tankards of beer were liberally swigged from. There was a roar as the umpire and timekeeper checked their watches, and Billy was set free. To the delight of his supporters, the fierce little dog dispatched all hundred rats in eight minutes, forty-five seconds, a new world record.

There could be serious grudge matches when two ambitious dog fanciers or rat-pit proprietors matched their best dogs against each other. Syndicates were formed to back the dogs, hundreds of pounds were betted, and crowds gathered in their thousands to back their favourites. The beer and the excitement sometimes got the better of the audience, and serious fights could break out. When a celebrated provincial ratting dog challenged one of the London stars, the atmosphere might resemble that of a present-day football game between a London club and an out-of-town rival. In 1848, the London dog 'Jack' was carried round the streets in a drunken procession after beating the Southampton bitch 'Beauty' by 106 rats to 100 in a fiercely contested encounter. In another epic ratting match, the Manchester bitch 'Miss Lily', under eight pounds in weight, was wagered to kill a hundred large barn rats. After a frenzied effort, she narrowly lost by one minute, forty seconds; still, the London sportsmen gave her a standing ovation.

The Godfather of the London Ratting Fancy was Jemmy Shaw, a dog-fancier and publican who kept his rat-pit at the Blue Anchor, Bunhill Row, St Luke's. Jemmy was proud of his little dog 'Tiny', only five and a half pounds in weight, since this fierce little terrier had once won him a large bet by killing two hundred rats in less than an hour. By the 1840s, the ratting matches were governed by a strict system of rules, constructed to ensure fairness for the dog-owners, and fair play for the betting fraternity. There was always a match umpire, and a time-keeper as well. The dog's second was strictly forbidden to interfere with the gory proceedings in the pit, except to cheer the animal on with gestures and verbal commands. He was also allowed to take the dog out of the pit, if he felt it needed rest or refreshments, and to blow on the rats, when they had piled up in the pit corner, in order to disperse them. After some distressing incidents involving frenzied sewer rats running up the handler's legs and inflicting very painful bites, the dog handlers made it a habit of wearing their trousers tied to their boots.

A sample of the rats were closely examined before the match, to rule out that they had been drugged with laudanum beforehand to make the dog's task easier. A dog could be disqualified for a false pick-up, or for

Ratting in the Haymarket, from the *IPN*, 24 December 1870.

jumping out of the pit. A badly trained dog worrying the rat after killing it, or carrying it proudly around the pit, brought a volley of oaths from its backers. A tricky question was what to do if some of the rats had been shamming dead. In a fifty-rat match, three rats, and three rats only, were allowed to 'come to life' after time had been called and the dog lifted out of the pit. The opposite party was allowed to make an appeal by calling out 'That 'un 'baint dead, guv'nor!' and pointing at the rodent in question. The umpire would then put the rat within a chalked circle on his table, and strike its tail three times with a metal rod; if the rat managed to crawl out of the circle, it was 'alive', otherwise it counted as 'dead'.

Supplying rats for London's seventy rat-pits was an industry of its own. If we assume that these establishments were each open twice a week, and that two hundred rats were destroyed at each session, this would imply that the rat-pits of London alone would require four thousand rats each day. The rodents were supplied by a network of rat-catchers, who scavenged for live rats in warehouses, hedges and ditches, and often in the sewers as well. Jemmy Shaw, who boasted that he never had less than two thousand rats on the premises, had a number of rat-catcher families dependent on him. He bought between three and seven hundred rats each week, paying two or three pence for large, well-fed specimens. Jemmy kept his rats well fed on good barley meal, not from kindness of heart but to keep them from eating each other. In spite of the relatively decent rewards, rat-catching does not appear to have been a very amusing line of work. Henry Mayhew once spoke to one of the rat-catchers, who gave a graphic demonstration what it felt like to have your finger bitten to the bone by a large sewer rat, and showed the best technique to pull out a rat's teeth that had broken off inside a bite wound.

The long-time aim for Jemmy Shaw and other Victorian dog-fanciers was of course to find a dog capable of matching the exploits of Billy the Raticide. During the 1840s and 1850s, there were several attempts at beating Billy's epic hundred-rat record, but none was successful. But in 1861, Jemmy Shaw's black-and-tan Bull and Terrier Jacko was spoken of as a future star in the London rat-pits. Jacko destroyed sixty rats in two minutes, forty-two seconds, with a killing time of just 2.7 seconds per rat. In 1862, Jacko beat Billy's record, killing a hundred rats in just five minutes, twenty-eight seconds. There have been claims from various 'experts' alleging that the exertions of Billy, or Jacko, or both, had been aided by some person drugging the rats beforehand. But as we have seen, there were safeguards against such skullduggery, and the matches took place before numerous and critical spectators; had the rats been drugged, they would surely have detected it. The crowning touch of Jacko's career was the famous thousand-rat match of 1862, in which Jemmy's

The amazing Ratting Monkey, from the *IPN*, 4 September 1880. Note the expression on the dog's face in the background.

famous dog killed a hundred rats once weekly for ten consecutive weeks, destroying the total of a thousand rodents in less than a hundred minutes. Jacko was still alive in 1866, when he and Jemmy were guests of honour at the Crystal Palace dog show; between 1861 and 1866, Jacko had won three hundred matches, and destroyed eight thousand rats. Just like Billy, Jacko was stuffed after death; his record still stands today.

There was turmoil among the Manchester Ratting Fancy after an unprecedented match in 1880. In Hollingwood, Mr Benson's fox terrier 'Turk' was matched against Mr Lewis's monkey for £5, in a twelve-rat match. Since the monkey was an unknown quantity, and the dog a formidable ratter, Turk was the favourite, although much betting took place on either side. After the dog had killed the twelve rats in very good time, the monkey was put into the rat-pit. Mr Lewis handed it a hammer, which the clever primate made good use of, bashing the rodents' heads in with alacrity and winning the match with time to spare. As the *IPN* expressed it, 'One may talk about a dog being quick at rat-killing, but he is really not in it with the monkey and his hammer. Had the monkey been left in the ring for much longer one would not have told his victims had ever been rats at all – he was for leaving them in all shapes.' Several months later, it was still debated whether the rules of ratting should be amended to exclude monkeys wielding blunt instruments.

Lady Florence Dixie and Hubert the St Bernard Dog, 1883

The author and traveller Lady Florence Dixie was an eccentric society figure in the 1880s and 1890s. She was the daughter of the equally dotty Marquess of Queensberry, the defendant in the Oscar Wilde case, and the sister of Lord Alfred Douglas. She married the wealthy alcoholic Sir Beaumont Dixie in 1875 and took him with her on long journeys to Africa and South America, in vain attempts to sober him up. In early 1883, when they were back in England, Lady Florence unwisely decided to meddle in Irish politics, condemning the Fenians with great vehemence. After she had allegedly received several death threats from the enraged sons of Erin, Sir Beaumont decided to purchase a large St Bernard dog, named 'Hubert', to serve as his wife's bodyguard.

On 17 March 1883, Lady Florence Dixie came running up to the Fishery, their elegant Regency house near Windsor. Two men dressed as women had suddenly attacked her, she breathlessly explained, flinging her to the ground and attempting to stab her three times! When she screamed for help, the villains stuffed earth into her mouth and knocked her on the head. Her fate would have been a dreadful one indeed, had not the faithful Hubert come bounding up to pull away the man with the knife!

'I owe my life to this Mount Saint Bernard dog!' Lady Florence exclaimed when giving interviews to the journalists. She and Hubert were the celebrities of the day, particularly in the anti-Irish press: attempting to murder a defenceless woman was considered just the thing to expect from these dastardly Fenians. Hubert became the most famous dog in Britain. He was praised in the newspapers for his heroism, and the *IPN* published his portrait. A gentleman sent Hubert a silver-studded collar, and many people sent him bones, beefsteaks and other treats.

The sensational attack on Lady Florence Dixie, and the dog Hubert drawn from life, from the *IPN*, 31 March 1883.

A wealthy American who offered to purchase Hubert, and a showman who wanted to exhibit the hero dog in a music hall, were both turned down by the snobbish Lady Florence, although she consented to Hubert becoming the special invited guest at a dog show in Durham, where he was awarded first prize. The crowning touch in Hubert's meteoric career as a four-legged celebrity came when, as a newspaper expressed it: 'To-day, Hubert, the dog to whose courage and devotion Lady Florence attributes the preservation of her life, was photographed by Mr Snooks, of Windsor, and an autographed copy was sent to H.M. the Queen.' Unless this paragon of canine virtue had added handwriting to his accomplishments, it was probably Lady Florence who supplied the autograph, however.

But after the police had begun to investigate the mysterious incident at the Fishery, there were serious doubts whether there had been any attack at all. Nobody had seen the two assassins in drag; had they used some magic spell to return to Ireland, or had Hubert eaten them? Lady Florence's dress was not dirty, and her injuries were very superficial. Nor had any of the several people near the Fishery gardens heard Lady Florence scream, as she claimed to have done. If a St Bernard dog is approached by threatening strangers, it is natural for the animal to bark, but nobody had heard Hubert utter a single yelp. And the booming bark of a fully grown St Bernard male would carry for half a mile at least, in quiet Victorian times. After it turned out that an Eton master had actually seen Lady Florence return to the Fishery, looking quite unhurt, the newspaper opinion quickly changed. Although several gentlemen objected that it was caddish to doubt the word of a noble lady, and although the *British Medical Journal* suggested that Lady Florence might have suffered from hallucinations, the eccentric lady and her silent four-legged accomplice both became laughing-stocks. It was even suggested that she had been drunk at the time, since she was known to share her husband's predilection for the bottle; the witty Countess of Antrim had once called her and her husband 'Sir Always and Lady Sometimes Tipsy'!

Several ribald poems were written to ridicule Lady Florence, with verses like:

Lady Florence, Lady Florence, when you cried aloud for help,
And when your faithful hound proclaimed his presence with a yelp –
Why did no one hear you, in your own or neighbour's grounds?
The public to your ladyship this problem now propounds.

Lady Florence, Lady Florence, that such want of faith should be!
The public will not presently believe the things they see.
But when you next adventures of this kind should have to tell,
Please arrange to have some witnesses upon the scene as well!

Hubert also received his fair share of ridicule. A letter to *Punch*, allegedly from the dog 'Toby', suggested that the two villains must have crammed dirt down Hubert's throat to prevent him from barking. Toby called on the Dog of Crime to end his silence on this mysterious matter, and to answer those who doubted the heroism of the St Bernard dogs, were it carrying half-frozen children to the monastery, or fighting armed assassins. *Funny Folks* published an amusing poem, allegedly written by someone who had seen Hubert at the Warwick dog show, beginning with:

> So thou art Hubert, canine stout,
> > Whose teeth – good gracious, what a row! –
> Put banded murderers to rout.
> > (At least we're told that this was so.)
> That massive throat bayed noble rage
> > As at the dastard pair you flew,
> Just like a dog upon the stage!
> > (That is, if what's been said is true.)

Lady Florence Dixie's career took quite some time to recover after this disastrous ending to the 'Windsor mystery' of 1883. She published several more books, and became known as a proponent for equality between the sexes, rational female dress, and various kinds of medical faddism and quackery. When she expired in 1905, those who shared her views wrote approving obituaries. Sir Beaumont said that he was heartbroken, but a few months later he married a barmaid.

And what about that canine prodigy, Hubert the St Bernard dog? It is sad to say that he sunk back into obscurity, fading away like a shooting star that once had lit up the firmament, or some luckless Big Brother contestant trudging back to his job stacking shelves in the supermarket.

A Welsh Greyfriars Bobby, 1895

In the annals of canine faithfulness, the little Edinburgh terrier Greyfriars Bobby has long held an exalted position. This extraordinary dog was supposed to have kept vigil at his master's grave from 1858 until 1872, spending a total of fourteen years mourning at the Greyfriars cemetery in the Edinburgh Old Town. In 1873, a monument was erected outside Greyfriars to celebrate this faithful dog; it is still standing today, along with gravestones for Bobby and his presumed master inside the cemetery. Bobby is today Scotland's most famous dog, and his value for the Edinburgh tourist board must be very considerable indeed. For every visitor coming to see Greyfriars and its historic churchyard, there are ten who have come merely to see Bobby's grave and to worship in front of the iconic dog monument. Tourists from all over the world come to admire Edinburgh's canine saint, many of them weeping profusely when they hear the pathetic story.

But in real life, there is no truth to the legend of Saint Bobby, except that there really was a resident dog at Greyfriars from around 1860 until 1872. An elderly terrier mongrel, it made itself useful ratting in the church, and chasing away the cemetery cats. In 1867, the *Scotsman* and other newspapers published the story of Bobby's presumed vigil at his master's grave, and just like Lord Byron, the cemetery dog woke up one day and found himself famous. Many people came to Greyfriars to see this canine prodigy, although they were sometimes disappointed that instead of lying on the grave mourning his master, Bobby was ratting in the church, or out visiting his friends living near the cemetery. The verger James Brown sold cabinet card photographs of Bobby to these visitors, and the restaurant owner John Traill, who gave Bobby luncheon each day at the sound of the one o'clock gun, got much custom from people who wanted to see the famous dog.

Both Brown and Traill knew that Bobby was not keeping vigil on any grave, and that he came and went as it suited him, but they were impressed with the steady flow of cash from the visitors to Greyfriars. When the elderly Bobby died later in 1867, they recruited a replacement cemetery dog who held court at Greyfriars until his death in 1872. As a journalist 'in the know' put it, the old dog was soon 'honoured to death', and 'transformed into the similitude of a pure Skye terrier.' In the original legend, Bobby's master had been a poor old man from Edinburgh named Grey, but this was soon 'improved': the master had been a Pentland farmer named 'Auld Jock', or, in the latest version of the tale, an Edinburgh police constable. Supported by the Edinburgh pro-Bobby zealots, the spectral 'Constable John Grey' still patrols the Edinburgh streets with his tiny police dog.

The *IPN* stayed well clear from the cult of Greyfriars Bobby, and the Edinburgh cemetery dog was never featured in this newspaper. But instead, some more truthful stories of faithful dogs occasionally made an appearance. In 1894, a Southend gentleman had left the boarding-house where he had been staying, to take a walk with his dog, but this was the last that was ever seen of him. His dog was later found at the pier-head, howling dismally; since it was dripping wet, it was presumed that its master had committed suicide by leaping into the sea from the pier-head, and that the dog had jumped after him. The gentleman had sent suicide notes to his wife, from whom he was living apart, and to his business partner; his relatives offered a reward of £10 for the recovery of his body, as the poor dog kept vigil at the pier-head, waiting for its master to rise up from the sea.

A·Faithful·Friend

The mourning dog in Southend, from the *IPN*, 3 March 1894.

A·FAITHFUL·DOG.

The Welsh Greyfriars Bobby, from the *IPN*, 28 December 1895.

In December 1895, the Welsh shepherd Daniel Thorp perished in an attempt to cross the Mardy Mountain during a snowstorm. When his body was discovered several days later, his faithful sheepdog was keeping vigil by the body. This is one of several instances of a dog remaining with the body of its master for some considerable time: at the Derwent Dam in Derbyshire, the heroic sheepdog Tip kept vigil by her dead master for fifteen weeks. It is the nature of the dog to remain with the pack leader, whether four- or two-legged, in such a situation. In contrast, it is not logical behaviour for a dog to rest upon its dead master's grave. Firstly, a dog has no clear concept of death, or ability to connect the once-living master with the flesh buried in the coffin. Secondly, one of the primary instincts in a healthy dog is that of self-preservation: it would make no sense for the dog to pine to death lying on the grave, instead of getting on with life.

The Dog of Valencia, 1906

In 1906, there was a newspaper story emanating from Valencia in Spain, to the effect that a wealthy gentleman from this town had been murdered while he was out walking his dog. The large, sturdy dog was the only witness. It led its master's son and two police constables to the place where the murderer had buried his victim, and the body was unearthed. The constables later went into a tavern to have a drink, accompanied by the sagacious dog. They were astounded when the animal flew at the throat of one of the other drinkers at the tavern – it was of course the murderer, who had been recognised by the faithful animal. After the villain had been forced to confess, he was arrested by the policemen.

'Cor blimey!' I can hear the reader exclaim. 'That was one hell of a dog!' But perhaps there are one or two who have heard the story before? The truth is that from classical antiquity, there are several versions of a legend of a man being murdered by jealous enemies, with his dog as the only witness. In his *Scripta Moralia*, Plutarch wrote of King Pyrrhus of Epirus, who saw a dog that had kept vigil over its murdered master's corpse for three days without access to food. The King made sure the man was decently buried, and took care of the faithful dog. At an army review, the dog started barking at two soldiers, and they promptly confessed to the murder. When Hesiod, called the Wise, was murdered, his faithful dog brought to justice the sons of Ganyctor of Naupactus, who had murdered him.

When an officer named Hecati was murdered in Antioch, his dog was the only witness. According to St Ambrose's *Hexaëmeron*, the sagacious canine later identified the murderer, and grasped him with its powerful jaws until he confessed. Another legend told of a certain Sir Roger, a knight at the court of the King of Aragon, who was mortally wounded and left to die by his enemy Sir Mardock. Roger's faithful greyhound remained with

The Dog of Valencia, from the *IPN*, 18 August 1906.

him until he died, and then it scraped a pit for his body and covered it with grass and leaves. After keeping vigil over Roger's remains for seven years, the gaunt dog went to the King's palace on Christmas Day, where it was recognised and given a meal. Cheered by such festive generosity, the dog returned, but this time it encountered the hated Mardock, whom the faithful animal promptly dispatched. The greyhound then led the King's soldiers to Roger's grave. His remains were dug up and given a proper burial in consecrated grounds. A proper monument was erected, at the foot of which the faithful dog soon after expired.

Giraldus Cambrensis adds another dramatic development to the legend, namely that after the dog had detected its master's murderer, it was allowed to fight a judicial duel against this miscreant. This twelfth-century *chanson de geste* of 'La Reine Sibile' took place at the court of Charlemagne, but it reoccurs in the legend of the Dog of Montargis, set in 1371 during the reign of Charles V of France. When the officer Aubry de Montdidier is passing through the forest of Bondy near Montargis, he is attacked by two jealous enemies, the Chevaliers Landry and Macaire. He is defended by his large greyhound, but Macaire is able to dispatch Aubry when the dog is busy biting the other villain. The Dog of Montargis kept vigil over Aubry's body until hunger forced it to come into town. When it saw Landry and Macaire, it growled and tried to attack them. This made the King suspicious that these two had murdered Aubry, and the dog was allowed to prove its accusation like a gentleman, in a judicial duel.

One version has the duel between Macaire and the Dog of Montargis take place at Charles V's court in Montargis, and another places it at 'L'Île Notre-Dame' in Paris. Both agree that a plentiful company of ladies and gentlemen were present at the arena to cheer the combatants on. The distribution of arms for this strange duel was distinctly unfair: the sturdy Macaire was provided with a large shield, with which to ward off the dog's attacks, and a long cudgel, with which to belabour it. The Dog of Montargis was given only a large barrel, in which to take cover against the Chevalier's assault. But the faithful dog eschewed such defeatism, and went for Macaire's throat like a bullet. The Chevalier was forced to confess his crime, and he was later executed as a murderer. The tale of the Dog of Montargis was long believed to be historical, but competent antiquaries have disproved it as one of several versions of a long-lived ancient myth. The Dog of Montargis is immortalised in a dramatic bronze sculpture of the duel, by Gustave Debrie, situated in front of the Girodet museum in central Montargis.

In Paris, the drama *Le Chien de Montargis, ou la Forêt de Bondy* premiered in 1814, and had an uninterrupted run in until 1834. Translated into English as *The Dog of Montargis, or the Forest of Bondy*, and staged at the King's Theatre, it was to remain the staple item for canine thespians for many years. In a remote forest, the officer Aubry is murderously attacked by two enemies, Macaire and Landri. He is valiantly defended by his large dog Dragon, but when the faithful animal is kept occupied by Landri, the second villain gives Aubry the fatal wound. Later, an innocent deaf-mute simpleton is 'framed' for the murder, but Dragon saves him by producing a sash he has torn off Macaire's uniform. Each time Dragon sees the murderers, he growls and tries to attack them. The King gives the brave dog the right to trial by battle, and after a long and gory fight, the defeated Macaire confesses the murder. This scene introduced the trick of 'taking the seize', in which the acting dog leaps up onto the villain and seizes him by the throat. The actor playing the villain had to wear protective padding round his neck, and yell 'Take off the dog!' once he was brought down. With its racy plot and exciting fight scenes, *The Dog of Montargis* would remain a staple item of dog drama for decades to come. In spite of this, the play did not always come off as planned; it is recorded that once, the friendly acting dog stood watching the audience and wagging his tail, instead of 'taking the seize'. The infuriated villain desperately tried to induce him to attack; in the end, he had to fly at the placid dog himself and lift the animal up to his throat.

Thus the story of the Dog of Valencia is nothing but a re-working of an ancient but powerful myth of canine sagacity and loyalty. Since the *IPN* had featured the original Montargis story in 1874 and 1882, it is surprising that the experienced journalists swallowed such an unreliable foreign yarn whole, and honoured it with a full-page illustration.

6

Animals

Cats with Nine Lives

As we have seen, the *IPN* had high regard for the canine tribe and its doings: dogs of every description were depicted in its illustrations, from the noble life-saving Newfoundlands to the half-starved, snappish curs infesting the slum streets. In contrast, cats were but rarely featured in this newspaper, although they made an occasional appearance.

In July 1867, a heroic cat made the *Illustrated Police* news. George Amey was an irascible London grocer, who was often at loggerheads with his long-suffering wife Isabella. In early 1867, he left the family home at No. 36 Tottenham Street and moved in with another woman at No. 12 Fitzroy Place. In late June the same year, he made a surprise visit to his

The cat Topsy defends its mistress, from the *IPN*, 6 July 1867.

DREADFUL ASSAULT ON A WIFE. A CAT DEFENDING ITS MISTRESS.

wife, and they soon started quarrelling fiercely. The cad George knocked Isabella down, jumped on her, seized her by the throat and threatened to strangle her. Help came unexpectedly from her large cat Topsy: the infuriated feline made a leap at George, and fastened her claws and teeth into his face. The cruel husband gave a yell of pain, and since he was unable to tear the brave cat away, he had to beg for mercy to have his wife remove the protective animal. At the Marlborough Street police court, he was later sentenced to a month in prison for his brutal assault on his wife. The later careers of husband, wife, and cat remain unrecorded.

Ann Allen was a widow aged upwards of seventy years, living in Birmingham with her elderly cat. In April 1868, the cat broke its leg in some unspecified Midland calamity, and Ann Allen decided to drown it to put it out of its misery. She asked the lad James Spiers to come with her to Belmont Row Bridge, and to carry the cat and a brick. When he asked her if he should throw the animal into the canal, she said that she would do it herself. Tragically, she overbalanced and pitched into the water herself, along with the cat and the brick it was tied to. The lad Spiers raised the alarm, and a boat was promptly launched by some locals, but when Ann Allen's body was recovered four minutes later, she was already dead. The coroner's inquest returned a verdict of Accidental Death, and the ribald tale of the Old Woman Drowned while trying to drown a cat became yet another piece of mid-Victorian sensational news, embellished by a traditional *IPN* illustration.

In 1882, the French showman Joseph Lumeau thought of a novel idea. He recruited a dwarf named Joseph Troublet, who was seventeen years old and barely twenty-five inches tall. The original scheme had been to exhibit the wretched midget in a booth, but Lumeau thought of a more exciting

DROWNING A CAT—DEATH OF AN OLD WOMAN

An old woman drowned while attempting to drown a cat, from the *IPN*, 6 May 1868.

A dwarf killed by cats, from the *IPN*, 12 August 1882.

and innovative scheme. He procured a number of large cats and had them painted with stripes to resemble tigers, and equipped the dwarf with a whip and the dress of a circus animal tamer. Although the poor little fellow had a great aversion to the feline tribe, he was persuaded, by some means or other, to play along, whipping the cats to entice them to attack him. But at a performance at a fair in Beaupré-sur-Saône, things went badly wrong: the cats turned against the 'tamer', and he was literally torn into pieces by the infuriated animals. Aghast at the mischief he had caused, the creature Lumeau absconded, but he was later arrested in Lille and charged with causing the death of the dwarf Joseph through his dangerous idea for a show.

There is no doubt that the tales of the heroic cat back in 1867, and the sad incident of the foolhardy old woman in 1868, were nothing but the truth and contained no exaggeration. They were reported in a number of newspapers, and although decidedly strange even by the standards of the time, contained nothing impossible or exaggerated. In contrast, I initially had my reservations against the story of the Dwarf Killed by Cats, since not only did the story seem too good to be true, but the more unscrupulous Victorian newspapers had no objections to including 'from our foreign correspondent' stories that were wholly invented. There does not appear to have been any place called Beaupré-sur-Saône. It turns out that the story originated in the *Era* newspaper of 5 August 1882, spreading to the *Dundee Courier* and the *IPN*; the arrest of Lumeau was reported in the *New Zealand Herald* of 30 September. Rather disconcertingly, there is also an article in the *Le Petit Cettois* newspaper of 11 August 1882, entitled 'Dévoré par les Chats'; it is sinisterly stated that after the infuriated striped cats were done with him, the luckless dwarf '*n'avait plus figure humaine*'. Unlike the English papers, this article named both the dwarf and the showman, and expressed rightful indignation at the dismal fate of the former of them, and the escape of the other. Cruel and sensational news is not always invented news, and I will leave it to the reader which version to believe: some French penny-a-liner thinking up a very good story to sell to the newspapers, or an inferno of growling, scratching, biting cats, and the luckless dwarf being tormented to death in a bloodbath. Thus a silly newspaper story might become a horror rivalling Poe's flaming orang-utangs, and there are such terrors all around us, if we bother to look for them.

The Trouble with Polar Bears

There is today consensus that polar bears belong in their proper Arctic habitat, and that they have no role to play in circuses and show business. In Victorian times, however, the exhibition of polar bears at menageries and travelling shows was quite widespread. The inherent fierceness and indocility of the animals, and the indifferent approach to security sometimes demonstrated by the showmen involved, more than once led to dramatic situations, picked up with glee by the *IPN*.

In March 1870, Wombwell's Royal Menagerie was performing at Glasgow. One of the animals on show was a very fine polar bear, said to be the largest in captivity in Britain, and a very morose and savage animal indeed. It was normally fed fish and bread soaked in fish oil, but one day, it got hold of a large shin-bone of beef, intended for one of the tigers. The gluttonous polar bear very much welcomed this change of diet, and after devouring the meat, it attempted to swallow the bone, which got firmly stuck in its throat. An Italian keeper named Lorenzo volunteered to enter the cage and try to help the bear, which showed signs of being suffocated. Mr Fairgrieve, the proprietor of the menagerie, and some other keepers, stood outside the cage, armed with six-barrelled Colt revolvers. When Lorenzo entered the cage, the polar bear made a swipe at him with its forepaw, but it missed and fell to the ground. The brave Lorenzo seized the bear around the neck and tried to pull the bone out of its throat, but: 'His efforts were fruitless, and the howls and terrible rage of the animal were fearful.' Mr Fairgrieve ordered Lorenzo to desist and leave the bear to its fate, but when the Italian released his hold, the bear caught him with its claws and hurled him to the floor. Mr Fairgreave then himself stepped into the cage, and managed to slip a noose round the bear's neck and forepaws. This rope was passed through the top of the cage, and thirty keepers were ordered to haul away. Roaring tremendously, the polar bear was hoisted into mid-air, and Lorenzo was saved. A stout cord was tied to the bone protruding from the bear's muzzle, and it took the strength of four keepers to extract it. The polar bear was then lowered

FEARFUL STRUGGLE WITH A POLAR BEAR

Terrible struggle with a polar bear, from the *IPN*, 12 March 1870.

to the floor of the cage, and water was poured onto it. The valuable animal recovered from its ordeal without harm or injury, and so did Lorenzo, in spite of a number of deep flesh wounds from the bear's claws. Mr Fairgrieve received an ovation from those present for his admirable coolness and bravery.

In January 1876, a member of the ursine tribe was again up to mischief, this time at Lime Street station in Liverpool. The animal belonged to a menagerie, who had just imported it from abroad. The polar bear had travelled inside a large barrel, which fell down from a hand-truck, giving the bear the chance of escape. It seized hold of a lady named Mrs Montgomery, so that her breath was quite taken away, but the animal was promptly subdued by a troop of railwaymen, and Mrs Montgomery suffered no broken bones. She still took the North-Western Railway Company to court, however, claiming to suffer painful nervous and physical sensations ever since being caught in the bear-hug. She was awarded £60 compensation, and the railway company was told to improve its routines with regard to the transportation of dangerous wild animals; since Mrs Montgomery had been wearing a sealskin jacket, it was presumed that the polar bear had been reminded of its Arctic seal-hunting exploits back in happier days.

A LADY HUGGED BY A POLAR BEAR.

A lady hugged by a polar bear, from the *IPN*, 22 January 1876.

In November 1878, another polar bear was on the prowl in Dundee. A certain Mr Woods had imported two polar bears from the Davis Straits, with intent to exhibit them in a travelling show. The bears had arrived on a whaler, confined to a large cage. But when the cage was lowered in Commercial Street, it fell down and the floor board broke, enabling one of the bears to escape. A large crowd had assembled to see the polar bears, but they ran away in a panic when they saw that one of the animals had escaped. The polar bear ran towards the High Street, scattering the people in its wake. A large dog was set on the bear, and it had nearly caught up with it when the bear suddenly turned round and made a snap at the pursuing dog, with a loud growl. The dog ran away with its tail between its legs. Having almost reached the British Hotel, the bear suddenly and unexpectedly ran inside Mr Jamieson's clothier's shop. The shop-man, and a woman who had taken refuge inside the shop when she saw the polar bear approaching, leapt headlong over the counter to take cover. Fortunately, the bear was distracted when it saw its own reflection in a large mirror, and it emitted terrible roars and bobbed up and down in front of its imagined opponent. Mr Woods and his men stood outside the shop, but no person was brave enough to enter it. A large crowd was congregating, hearing that a polar bear was at large in Dundee. Having surveyed the contents of the shop, and tried to exit through the door that was held fast from outside, the polar bear took refuge underneath the shop counter. Mr Woods and his men now dared to enter the shop, and they fastened a noose round the animal's neck and carried it out of the

Escape of a polar bear at Dundee, from the *IPN*, 23 November 1878.

shop a prisoner, amid the laughter and cheers of the crowd. The story of the polar bear at large in Dundee travelled the world, and in February 2014, it was featured on local television.

Help! My Baby Was Just Taken by a …

The above slightly cryptic headline describes a type of story that was a long-time *IPN* favourite: a little baby is snatched by some threatening, dangerous animal. There is always an illustration depicting the animal running away with the helpless babe dangling from its jaws or talons. What will happen next? You will have to buy the *IPN* to find out!

All right, so you got your copy? Cor Blimey, just look at that one! A baby abducted by a monkey! In the small village of Manxbridge in Somerset, a certain Mr Judcote, a gentleman of private means, kept a large pet monkey named 'Hulch'. Believed to be quite harmless, the beast was allowed to roam wherever it pleased. One day in July 1870, Hulch bounded into a neighbour's garden and snatched a baby from the arms of another child. Gibbering and chattering, the monkey took off with his new companion, climbing an outhouse to get rid of his pursuers. The parents were prostrate with anxiety; what would this filthy animal do with their defenceless little baby? Mr Judcote sent servants to search the grounds for Hulch, carrying various treats to lure the creature from the trees, but they found no trace of the monkey. After spending all day carrying the baby around, Hulch suddenly and unexpectedly came bounding up to some farm labourers and politely handed the baby over to them, as if he had become fed up with this uninteresting toy. The infant was alive and unharmed. The *IPN* leaves it unstated what happened next, except that the parents were said to be equally prostrate with relief when their child was returned to them. Did they insist that Hulch must be chained up, or even destroyed, or did they employ the monkey as a baby-sitter for their infant son to become the Tarzan of Somerset?

In September 1870, the wife of a farmer named Brown, living near Hacketstown in Ireland, went out to milk the cows. She left her little baby inside the house and latched the door. A few minutes later, she heard a servant give a yell, and saw a large sow running out of the house, carrying the baby in its mouth. The frantic mother ran after it into the sty, where she found the mangled remains of her child. At the coroner's inquest, it was concluded that in some strange manner, the sow had been able to unlatch the door, enter the cottage and abduct the baby. It was also commented that the practice of leaving young children unattended was only too prevalent, and could be fraught with fearful consequences.

Later in 1870, a bad year for unattended little children, a little boy named Walter Percival was playing with some other children near

Newtown. All of a sudden, a donkey came galloping up, grabbed Walter by the leg, and made off with him. When Walter screamed for assistance, his father and uncle, who had been playing in a football match nearby, came running up. They stopped the donkey and belaboured it with sticks

A CHILD STOLEN BY A MONKEY.

'Hulch' abducts the future Somerset Tarzan, from the *IPN*, 9 July 1870.

A CHILD KILLED BY A PIC

Above: 'Stop the pig! Stop the pig!' From the *IPN*, 17 September 1870.

Left: 'Stop the donkey, boys!' From the *IPN*, 19 November 1870.

CHILD KILLED BY A DONKEY

until it dropped little Walter, who was brought home and put to bed. The strange behaviour of the donkey was much marvelled at. Since the beast had recently been worried and bitten by a strange dog, it was suspected that it might have been suffering from hydrophobia. Little Walter seemed to rally for a while, but his wounds were considerable; the little sufferer fell into a state of insensibility and expired the following day. What happened to the dog and the donkey was not recorded.

In June 1880, the Oxford housewife Mrs Emma Olds saw her large spaniel dog run out of an outbuilding, carrying something in its mouth. 'There goes the dog,' she said placidly. The dog ran out into the street, where there was a great outcry, since the animal was carrying the body of an infant dangling from its jaws. Screaming and yelling with horror and revulsion, the Oxford townspeople desperately pursued the dog, but it disappeared into an alley. When Mrs Olds' spaniel was found, it seemed very well fed, and next to it was a round object, the head of the baby. The dog had shared its meal with some other disreputable-looking street mongrels. The curs would have been in immediate danger of being lynched, had Mr Olds and a certain Mr Jelfs not been able to explain the circumstances. In an outbuilding to the Three Pigeons public house, near where the Oldses lived, an inquest had been held on the body of an infant found drowned in the Oxford and Birmingham Canal. The jurymen had adjourned the inquest to have a drink at the pub, since the dead baby was 'high' and smelt very badly. Although a pig-trough had been put over the little corpse, the hungry dog must have shoved it out of the

BODY OF A CHILD EATEN BY A DOG AT BANBURY

'You naughty doggies!' From the *IPN*, 12 June 1880.

way, stolen the corpse, and ran off with it. It is not known if the careless jurymen were content with putting the infant's head on a plate, to have it staring accusingly at them when the inquest was resumed, or whether they brought the dog along to 'represent' the rest of the child.

'Disgusting!' I can hear the reader exclaim. 'Can it get any worse?' Well, this is the *IPN*, so it certainly can – 'Help! My baby was just taken by – an enormous eagle!'

A Child Carried Off by an Eagle!

The notion that eagles were capable of abducting children goes back to ancient times, as evidenced by the legend of Zeus and Ganymede. Several seventeenth-century instances were reported from Scotland, England and Norway. In some of these early cases, the child is devoured at the eagle's nest. In other instances, it is taken to the eyrie unhurt, to be saved by its brave parents, who climb a precipice and shoot the eagle dead. In yet another version, the little boy [or girl] is actually nurtured by the philanthropic bird; when later accidentally found in the eagle's nest, he [or she] is adopted by some local magnate, and later becomes a famous chieftain [or wise woman]. The crest of the Earl of Derby features an eagle and child, to celebrate a legend that one of his forefathers was found in an eagle's nest. There are quite a few Eagle and Child pubs as well, featuring an eagle abduction on their signs.

One of the most famous images from the annals of eagle abductions: the sad fate of five-year-old Marie Delex, said to have been abducted and killed by a golden eagle in the Canton of Vaud, Switzerland.

Animals

In Victorian times, avian abductions were taken quite seriously. What worse fate would there be for a little child than to be carried off in the remorseless talons of an enormous eagle, and then to be torn to pieces and fed to the hungry eaglets in the eyrie? There was a vigorous debate in the scholarly journals whether a golden eagle was really capable of lifting a twenty-pound child from the ground, but in the schoolbooks and the works on popular zoology, there was no doubt that these monstrous birds could snatch even older children away at will. To keep the children safe, the eagles must be made extinct, it was reasoned. The epicentre of this eagle-mania was in Norway, where the country people were very fearful of avian abductions, and where horrid stories of children being snatched and their skeletons recovered from eagle's nests abounded. There are also a surprising amount of eagle abduction stories in various American newspapers, including the *New York Times*.

The earliest child-snatching eagle to make an appearance in the *IPN* is from August 1869: several French newspapers could report that near Mount St Gotthard, a little boy between three and four years of age had been taken by an eagle. The boy's father, a carpenter named Fonari, who had been repairing a house nearby when the eagle struck, pursued the bird up into the Alps, armed with a hatchet. He managed to strike the bird some heavy blows, inducing it to descend, and then seized hold of the child, which was not injured in any way but the agony of its mother, who had witnessed the conflict from the base of the mountain, is easier to imagine than describe.

A frenzied father pursues an enormous eagle that has taken his little son, from the *IPN*, 7 August 1869.

In April 1880, a three-year-old child was sitting on a stile feeding chickens in Pearson County, North Carolina. A large eagle suddenly swooped down on the chickens, scattering them in all directions. As the child ran off, the eagle made a second swoop, and caught the child in its talons. It attempted to fly off, but the child was too heavy, and it only managed to fly a short distance. The eagle's talons were so entangled in the child's clothes that it could not get free, making it easy for the child's father to kill it. The child had some deep scratches, but survived its ordeal. This story may well be true, but the *IPN* illustration is grossly exaggerated, with an enormous eagle soaring aloft with the child dangling from its talons.

Animals attacked or abducted by eagles were considered newsworthy enough to be included in the *IPN*: a cat, a stag and a fox. In March 1889, it was reported that in Somerset, an eagle had swooped down and abducted a small rough terrier dog. Worse was to some in August 1898: in Ungheni, Romania, a peasant woman who was shearing maize had brought with her a little child, which was sleeping on the straw. All of a sudden, an enormous eagle swooped down and carried it off.

In May 1904, the eighteen-month-old daughter of a Sutherlandshire crofter disappeared from the family cottage, situated a mile away from Invershin station, on the Highland Railway. At first, it was thought that she had been taken by gipsies, but a gamekeeper found the mangled remains of the child in a crevice in the mountains. Both eyes were missing, and the

The American child-snatching eagle, from the *IPN*, 1 May 1880.

Little 'Greyfriars Bobby' is taken for a ride by an eagle, from the *IPN*, 23 March 1889.

The Romanian child-snatching eagle, from the *IPN*, 13 August 1898.

body showed signs of having been fed from by birds. It was immediately presumed that an eagle had swooped down and taken the child, and the story was reported in the *Daily Express* and other mainstream newspapers. Two years earlier, an eagle had attacked and killed a deer in Sutherlandshire, and fed from its body until keepers drove it off, but it was fifty years since these birds had abducted a little child in these parts. The *IPN* cleared the first page and published two thrilling illustrations of the eagle snatching the child away, and the terrible discovery on the crags. But after the coroner's inquest pooh-poohed the idea of an eagle playing any part in the child's abduction, the newspapers lost interest. In 1921, there was again publicity when a child's skeleton was found near Aberdeen; there was speculation that it was a twenty-two-month-old

A child is carried off by an eagle in Sutherlandshire, and its remains are later found in the eagle's nest in the crags, from the *IPN*, 14 May 1904.

child that had disappeared from a croft back in 1914. 'Taken by Eagle?' asked the *Daily Express*, but when there was an inquiry in the Aberdeen Sheriff's Court, several witnesses declared that they had never seen an eagle in the district, and that it would have been possible for a child of that age to have climbed the hillside to reach the spot where the skeleton was found.

After these two Scottish cases of alleged eagle abductions had been disproved, the serious UK newspaper press would have nothing more to do with avian abductions, but the tabloid newspapers, both in Britain and in the United States, kept faith with the marauding eagles, although their stories often came from 'Our Foreign Correspondent' in some faraway land. From about the same time onwards, the ornithologists also parted company with the avian abductions, for good, since experimental research in the 1920s seemed to show that the maximum lifting capacity of a golden eagle was around six or seven pounds. This would mean that if a new-born infant was put on the bird-feeding table, it would be in immediate danger of being taken off by an eagle; older children would be

GRUESOME-DISCOVERY IN AN EAGLES NEST.

The remains of a child are found in an eagle's nest, from the *IPN*, 2 April 1910.

safe from the flying menace, however. This finding led to the old stories of grown children being snatched by eagles being disbelieved as old wives' tales. Ignored by the biologists and fast becoming a 'damned' area of research, the yarns of child-snatching birds of prey found friends among the lovers of zoological anomalies, who reasoned that if ordinary eagles were incapable of lifting a child, this was clearly evidence of the existence of 'thunderbirds' with a wing span similar to that of a small aeroplane.

It was only in Norway that the stubborn country people did not listen to the zoologists: they remained convinced that eagles carried off children at regular intervals. When children disappeared, the eagle was often the first suspect. In 1932, the girl Svanhild Hansen, a native of the outback Norwegian island of Leka, went missing from her home. She was found on a cliff quite some distance away, and claimed to have been abducted by a large eagle. Although she was well-nigh unhurt by her adventure, and although she weighed in excess of thirty-eight pounds, Svanhild the 'Eagle Girl' remained a minor Norwegian celebrity until her death in 2010. The people of Leka were very proud of her, particularly those working in the tourism industry: the eagle kidnap story remains the region's sole claim to fame, and the district coat of arms is adorned with a golden eagle's claw.

There are around eighty newspaper reports of children being carried off [or an abduction attempted] by an eagle [or in a few instances a vulture]. Around half of these are likely to be newspaper canards, and many of the others are misinterpretations of actual happenings. Even the verified finding of a child's remains [or clothes] in an eyrie is not conclusive proof that the child was abducted and killed by the bird, since eagles are carrion eaters. In Norway, the eagle was the paedophile child abductor's greatest friend. Since it is the nature of the eagle to strike hard at its victim with its formidable talons, and to peck at its eyes with its beak, all stories where the abduction victim escapes unharmed or only with scratches must be untrue. The aforementioned weight-lifting experiments for golden eagles have important flaws, and these birds have more than once been recorded to lift jackrabbits, hares (six to seven pounds in weight) and even foxes (eight to twelve pounds in weight). Cats and small dogs have also been preyed upon. There are no reliable instances of heavier prey being abducted, however, and this would indicate that all instances of children heavier than twelve or fourteen pounds being abducted by eagles are false. Eagle behaviour is likely to have changed considerably over time, as a result of natural selection and intense hunting and persecution: shy and wary individuals survived, bold and aggressive ones perished. There might well be some degree of truth in the best-verified nineteenth-century US reports of children being attacked by eagles, however. There are a few true cases of attacks on human beings by eagles affected by 'hunger frenzy', and there are also likely to be a few genuine cases of small infants abducted and killed by eagles. Like being buried alive, the fear of having a child abducted by an eagle is primal and has a perpetual fascination, which still lies dormant in present-day people, as judged by the interest shown in a recent fraudulent Youtube video of an attempted eagle abduction of a small child.

Alas, Poor Jumbo...

Jumbo, Europe's largest elephant, was the pride of London Zoo. In 1882, the American showman P. T. Barnum offered to purchase Jumbo for $10,000, and the Zoological Society of London accepted his offer. But since Jumbo was excessively popular, there was widespread fury at this 'outrageous sale of a national character'. From Queen Victoria down to the lowest guttersnipe, the nation was up in arms against the vulgar Barnum and his henchmen, who were taking poor Jumbo away from his friends in London. But the American would not budge: Jumbo was loaded into a crate and shipped to America on a steamer. The *IPN* commented that 'the singular outburst of affection and regard towards him shown so unmistakably and so tenderly by the great mass of the public has had no parallel in the case of any other animal'.

As the *IPN* had predicted, Jumbo became a nice earner for Barnum; within two weeks, he had paid back the cost of purchasing him and

Jumbo and his keeper
Matthew Scott, drawn
from life in the *IPN*,
4 March 1882.

transporting him to America. At Barnum's circus, Jumbo took precedence over all other performers, whether two- or four-legged. Just like in Britain, the huge elephant became a media celebrity, and was probably the most famous animal of his time. In September 1885, P. T. Barnum's Greatest Show on Earth was visiting St Thomas, Ontario. As the old keeper Matthew Scott was leading Jumbo and another elephant along what he believed to be a disused railway track, a train rapidly approached them. Jumbo was hit hard from behind and expired within a matter of minutes. His death became headline news all over the world, like that of a celebrated monarch or statesman.

Fittingly, there were several conspiracy theories about Jumbo's strange death. One said that Jumbo had drunk much beer and whisky the evening in question, and charged the locomotive head-on in a drunken rage. Another theory stated that Barnum had ordered Jumbo to be assassinated, since the elephant's tremendous flatulence had 'stunk up' the entire circus, and that the train had hit Jumbo's corpse just after the keeper had fired the lethal shot. Both these versions are entirely false, however; eyewitness testimony, as well as the documentation of the injuries on Jumbo's skeleton, indicate that the famous elephant was struck

Jumbo's singular death; a fanciful drawing in the *IPN*, 26 September 1889.

The stuffed Jumbo exhibited, and also some sketches of other, more lively performers; from the *IPN*, 16 November 1889.

from behind. Thus the dramatic *IPN* drawing is quite erroneous, just like another one, from an American paper, which I have reproduced in my 2008 book *Animal Freaks*.

P. T. Barnum was very much aggrieved at the untimely death of his star performer. With typical business-mindedness, he made the best of the situation, ordering Jumbo's skeleton to be mounted, and his hide stuffed by an expert taxidermist. Both versions of Jumbo were brought along when Barnum's Greatest Show on Earth came to London in 1889. The many children who had prayed that Jumbo would soon be restored to his London friends must have been appalled that their prayers had come true in such a dismal manner; the poor elephant had been returned to them in duplicate! The stuffed Jumbo was later given to Tufts University, where it was destroyed by fire in 1975; the skeleton is still at the American Museum of Natural History in New York.

The White Gorilla, 1886

When looking through a large ledger of Victorian cuttings from the *IPN*, I came across a very curious illustrated account of the 'White Gorilla' exhibited at the Royal Aquarium, London, in 1886. It is a generally accepted fact that the only known white (albino) gorilla was the celebrated Snowflake (Floquet de Neu in Catalan), resident at the Barcelona zoological gardens from 1966 until his death in 2003; I can well remember seeing him when I visited Barcelona in 1997. The discovery of another, historical case of an albino gorilla would be quite a zoological sensation. But before asking *Nature* magazine to clear the front page, it seemed prudent to investigate the White Gorilla's career further.

The White Gorilla's first newsworthy action took place in December 1885, when the *Era* newspaper published the following advertisement:

WANTED, all Proprietors of Music Halls, Museums, Circuses, and Menageries to know that Mr Whiteley, Proprietor of Allsop's Waxworks, Liverpool, has purchased a White Gorilla, accompanied by a Black one, which will be exhibited at his Establishment, Lime-street, Liverpool, during the Christmas Holidays.

Note – This is the only White Gorilla ever known. Open to engagements after the Holidays or to be Sold. Price of White one, 250 guineas, and the Black, 85 guineas.

Allsopp's Waxworks was a large establishment, boasting not less than 450 wax effigies and other curious items. When a *Liverpool Mercury* journalist went to see the White Gorilla, he was impressed by the docility of the animal: Mr Whiteley freely allowed his three-year-old son to enter its den. Accepting it as a true white gorilla, he recommended all the curious of Liverpool to see it before it was removed to the Metropolis.

And indeed, it did not take long for Mr Whiteley to accept an offer for the White Gorilla to be exhibited at the Royal Aquarium in London.

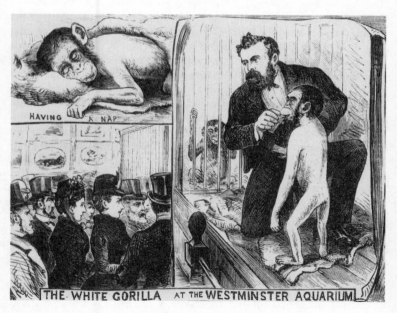

The 'White Gorilla', from the *IPN*, 6 February 1886.

A newspaper advertisement again pronounced it the only one of its kind in the world; indeed, Mr Whiteley offered £100 to any person who could produce its match. A *Standard* journalist who went to see the Gorilla was most impressed with the animal: it was certainly a true gorilla, he wrote, about twenty-six inches tall, and probably aged three or four years. Mr Whiteley had purchased it from South Africa. Its body was pale and nearly hairless, except that the crown of the head was covered with black fur, with a whisker growth down each cheek. The Gorilla was quite tame and affectionate, clasping Mr Whiteley round the neck and kissing him like a child. It answered to the name of 'Bob'. The Gorilla drank thirstily from a tumbler, just like a human being, and had a most intelligent manner. In contrast, the Black Gorilla was quite fierce and angry, and could be handled only by Mr Whiteley. The journalist ended his article with the remarkable words: 'The contrast of the two animals is very great, and as the transformation of negroes into white men has not yet become a recognized fact, so the appearance of a healthy white gorilla which is not an albino, is a mystery in the development of species not yet solvable upon the ordinary hypotheses.'

The *Standard* article was copied or abbreviated into many other newspapers. The White Gorilla was mentioned in the *New York Sun*, the *Chicago Tribune*, and the *Otago Daily Times* in faraway New Zealand. That useful newspaper the *IPN* was the only periodical to feature a drawing of the animal, from life. The zoological correspondent to the *Daily News* accepted the White Gorilla as an albino, blandly commenting that if there were white rabbits and white blackbirds, the gorilla species should be correspondingly afflicted with albinism. A writer in *Moonshine* magazine thought the Gorilla most curious. It seemed quite tame and friendly, although it was sometimes frightened by the drunk and rowdy spectators gawping at it. He suspected that the tumbler the gorilla drank from contained beer, so that the animal 'was just "like a human being" – of the *Aquarium* variety'! A punning writer in the appositely named *Fun* magazine thought the 'ape-pearance' of the White Gorilla most peculiar; Dr Charles Darwin, had he lived, would have thought this specimen the 'ape-x' of zoological discovery.

Thus the White Gorilla ended its four-month innings in the London and provincial press 'not out': no zoologist or newspaper correspondent exposed it as a fraud, and one of them confidently declared it an albino. But from the valuable *IPN* illustration, this could not be possible, since its head is clearly seen to be covered with normal dark hair. Furthermore, the animal looked quite unlike a young gorilla. When I consulted that experienced zoologist Mr Richard Freeman, he at once proclaimed the 'White Gorilla' a young chimpanzee. This was obvious from the shape of its head and the size of its ears. The body and limbs of the animal had been deliberately shaved to expose its pale skin, and the purpose of its elaborate coiffure had been to give it a humanoid appearance. The skin of a chimpanzee varies in colour depending on which part of Africa it comes from, and some of them have pale skin just like a European human. If the animal was unwell, as its remarkable docility might suggest, the skin would appear paler still.

Thus my paper on the 'White Gorilla' ended up in this book rather than in *Nature* magazine. The reason the 'Gorilla' was removed from the Aquarium might well have been that some professional or amateur zoologist had consulted the chapter on 'Apes' in Buffon's *Natural History*, and exposed the 'White Gorilla' as a fraud, but in that case, the newspapers had nothing to say about it. The Aquarium was quite a downmarket establishment, and the people thronging to see the 'Gorilla' were unlikely to have much zoological knowledge. Furthermore, the introduction of popular Darwinism seems to have given people a sense that in the development of species, anything was possible: was this extraordinary 'White Gorilla' not just what some Darwinists had predicted, a 'missing link' between human and great ape?

The last we hear of the 'White Gorilla' was that according to the 'Queer Pets' column in *Young Folks* magazine of June 1886, it was living as a pet in Mr Whiteley's house, together with its unshaved black companion. Whether its remarkable docility had been the result of domestication at an early age, or disease, or the contents of the tumbler it liked to drink from, is anybody's guess. The RSPCA was active and flourishing in 1886, but the riff-raff surrounding the side-show and music-halls of the time had little respect for its teachings: there were some proper scoundrels out there, who exploited animals without any concern for their welfare. It would have served Mr Whiteley right if ten zoologists had come to the Aquarium, each with a shaved chimpanzee on a lead, and demanded a total of £1,000 for possessing other specimens of 'White Gorilla'!

7

Strange Performers

Vincent de Groof, The Flying Man, 1874

In the 1860s and 1870s, the search for man-powered flight was well under way. Intrepid aeronauts invented fantastic-looking flying machines, like *The Bat*, featured by the *IPN* in June 1873. The life expectancy of these pioneers of aviation was generally very short. In Belgium, the shoemaker Vincent de Groof had been active designing ornithopters since the late 1860s. He had tried his inventions out in Brussels, through having them released from a balloon, but after several heavy crashes, and some undignified scenes where the fallen aeronaut was pelted by the mob,

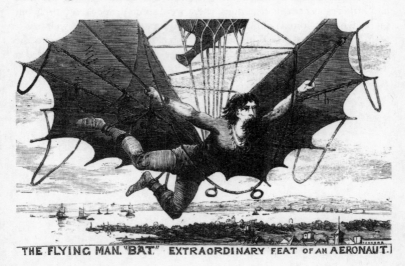

THE FLYING MAN. "BAT" EXTRAORDINARY FEAT OF AN AERONAUT.

The Bat, from the *IPN*, 21 June 1873. Fortunately for the aeronaut, this image is not from life, but from an illustrated pamphlet he had written.

the Belgian authorities forbade such foolhardy escapades. Undaunted, de Groof moved to England, where the accident-prone Belgian became known as 'the Flying Man'.

In June 1874, de Groof's latest ornithopter was ready to be tested. Made from a frame of wood and rattan, with the tail and wings covered with weatherproof silk, it looked like something out of *Donald Duck* magazine. On 29 June, the Flying Man was taken aloft, with his ornithopter dangling from the basket of a balloon manoeuvred by the aeronaut Mr Simmons, and released at the outskirts of London. It is surprising but true that de Groof made it down in one piece: his machine glided down safely and landed in Epping Forest. This unexpected reprieve seems to have put dangerous thoughts into de Groof's head. What if he made a grand descent from Mr Simmons' balloon over central London, to show the world that he was really the Flying Man?

On 9 July, Mr Simmons' balloon made another ascent, this time from Cremorne Gardens, with the ornithopter dangling from its basket. The balloon rose to an altitude of 4,000 feet over the Thames, before descending to 1,000 feet and releasing de Groof's machine. But instead of gliding safely down to the London rooftops, the ornithopter fell like a stone, its wings trapped in an upright position. The contraption landed 'with great violence' in Robert Street, Chelsea. What remained of the wretched aeronaut was taken to Chelsea Infirmary, where he was pronounced dead on arrival. As a contemporary street-ballad poet expressed it:

> On Thursday in health and bloom
> To Cremorne Gardens he bent his way,
> Not thinking that the silent tomb
> So soon would behold his lifeless clay.
> Amid the cheers of thousands he ascended,
> And like lightning he was borne
> But when he to the earth descended,
> The life from him alas was gone.

Madame de Groof fainted dead away when she saw the ornithopter fall, and Mr Simmons the balloonist suffered the same when he saw his colleague plummet to his death. This caused the balloon to swerve dangerously and drift away towards Essex; by the time the smelling-salts had been applied to the swooned aeronaut, his balloon was in serious danger of crash-landing. In the end, the distraught balloonist managed to land on an Essex railway line, just when a train approached! The driver managed to bring the train to a standstill, however, thus preventing further casualties as a result of de Groof's foolhardy experiment.

Vincent de Groof falls to his death, from the *IPN*, 18 July 1874.

Another aeronaut comes to grief, from the *IPN*, 24 August 1895.

Zazel and Zaeo, 1877

In April 1877, the bill-stickers of the Westminster Aquarium were pasting up some mysterious advertisements, containing only the word 'Zazel'. There was much curiosity among the fun-loving Londoners, and at the premiere of Zazel's performance, the Aquarium was completely full. She turned out to be a good-looking, scantily clad teenage girl, who performed a most adventurous trapeze act, and walked the tightrope with the greatest skill. The end of the performance was that Zazel descended into what looked like a large cannon. There was a loud bang and a cloud of smoke, and Zazel flew across the stage, landing safely in a huge net.

Nothing like this 'human cannonball' performance had ever been seen in London, and the newspapers were all full of Zazel's exploits. Backed by several doctors, the Commissioner of the Metropolitan Police wrote to the manager of the Aquarium, querying whether it was right to expose a teenage girl to such a dangerous performance. The manager replied that Zazel had never had any accident, although she had been rehearsing her act for five years. Other doctors certified that her performance was not dangerous as long as the net was fully functional, and that even the cannonball stunt was not an overly severe challenge to female physiology. In fact, the 'cannon' relied on a powerful spring rather than on explosives. The moralists complained that Zazel was not wearing many clothes on stage, but the *IPN* artist, who depicted her in mid-air, did not seem to mind.

Zazel remained at the Aquarium for nearly two years, being paid £125 a week. She was under the management of the impresario Mr Farini, who later took her on a tour of the provinces. In 1879, when performing in Portsmouth, the net broke and Zazel hit the floor hard; she was severely bruised, but resumed her tour a few weeks later, visiting Leeds, Sheffield and Dundee. At this time, a scruffy-looking German named Ernst Richter appeared in London, claiming that Zazel was his daughter Rosa Matilda. Richter had once trained and managed Rosa, he asserted, until the wicked Farini had stolen her away from him. The German tried various legal shenanigans to be reunited with his daughter, but since he was an unattractive-looking fellow, and since Zazel clearly wanted nothing to do with him, he was unsuccessful.

The void left by Zazel's departure from London was filled by another scantily clad female trapeze artist, Adrienne Wieland, alias Zaeo. Her act very much resembled Zazel's, including the use of a catapult in the finale. Although a skilful trapeze artist, Zaeo was somewhat accident-prone. More than once, she injured herself, or fell down hard into the net.

Zazel is fired from a gun, from the *IPN*, 14 April 1877.

The newspapers were full of these incidents, with moralists suggesting that the lacerations to her back from hitting the net could have been prevented had she been decently dressed. Again, the *IPN* and its bawdy-minded artists did not mind at all: a semi-naked, bleeding female body descending through the air was just the right kind of image to sell this particular newspaper.

In 1880, when a circus was performing in Leeds, a strong man caught a projectile supposed to have fired from a cannon. He then offered a reward of £50 to any person in the audience who could repeat this feat. When a local youth accepted the challenge, he was struck hard on the head by the projectile, and was carried out in a coma. This deplorable incident led to the Dangerous Performances Bill being introduced. This bill outlawed obviously dangerous circus and music hall performances, and also curbed the activities of female trapeze artists. Zaeo made an extensive tour of Europe, with considerable success, before returning to Britain in 1890. The Victorian 'moral majority' was outraged at the return of this foreign floozie, flaunting her flesh swinging about in her trapeze, and inspiring lurid thoughts in the minds of innocent youths. Some rather lewd posters for Zaeo had to be censored, because they showed her thighs. Nevertheless, she kept performing throughout the 1890s, touring the countryside extensively. She died in 1906.

After her human cannonball act had become outlawed in Britain, Zazel went to the United States, where she joined Barnum's circus with considerable success, before a back injury sustained during a performance in New Mexico put an end to her career. She married Dr George Starr, the manager of Crystal Palace, and lived on until 1937; a tiny, white-haired old lady who was proud of her adventurous youth.

Accident to Zaeo, from the *IPN*, 8 November 1879.

Zaeo comes to grief again, from the *IPN*, 14 February 1880.

Horsewhipping Salvationists

When Sir Claude Champion de Crespigny, the celebrated sportsman and eccentric, was asked to compile an entry for *Who's Who*, he listed among his hobbies 'horsewhipping salvationists'. This would seem harsh to modern readers, in a world where the Salvation Army exerts a wholesome influence of good: it remains a charitable, somewhat archaic organisation, whose members certainly do not merit horsewhipping or other forms of ill-treatment. But back in the 1880s, when the concept of the Salvation Army was a novel one, it faced widespread and violent opposition. Many

The enraged salvationist George Poulter charges the enemy with his umbrella, from the *IPN*, 3 September 1881.

ordinary working people disapproved of the salvationists, who made a racket marching about in the street with a band. In particular, brewers, publicans and hard-drinking men opposed their message of sobriety, and they did their rabble-rousing best to agitate against the salvationists.

From 1881 onwards, the opposition to the Salvation Army became quite widespread. In the London suburbs and in various country towns, groups of young working men formed 'Skeleton Armies' intended to intimidate the salvationists. Sometimes dressed in elaborate costumes, the Skeletons stood ready when the Salvation Army procession left its barracks: they shouted, swore and played discordant music, before pelting the salvationists with mud and manure. Stealing the battle-flag from the Salvation Army standard-bearer was considered capital good fun among the Skeletons, as well as knocking the caps off the uniformed soldiers, and destroying their musical instruments. Pouring manure over the 'Hallelujah Lasses' in the procession was another speciality. Among ordinary working people, there was support for the Skeletons, and in several instances when these early Salvation Army riots went to court, the magistrates had little sympathy for the assaulted salvationists, stating that they had themselves to blame for making a racket in the street with their musical instruments.

The *IPN* was a working man's newspaper, and it had nothing good to say about the early Salvation Army; instead, it reported the riots with gusto, from a firm pro-Skeleton point of view. In late August 1881, a Salvation Army procession through Wandsworth was pelted with stones

Attack on the standard bearer of the Salvation Army, from the *IPN*, 22 October 1881.

Faith healing by a Salvation Army major,
from the *IPN*, 27 June 1885.

and mud by a number of street roughs. The salvationist George Poulter,
who had been badly pelted with mud by a number of boys, struck out
with his umbrella, hitting the seven-year-old boy William Green hard on
the head, cutting it open. When matters went before the Wandsworth
police court, witnesses testified that the boy Green had not been among
the Skeletons who had annoyed the salvationists; he had been an innocent
bystander, and wholly undeserving of chastisement. Poulter's defence
counsel pointed out that the wheelwright had suffered much provocation,
and that he had struck the blow in a moment of irritation. The magistrate

Attack on the Salvation Army life guards, from the *IPN*, 17 October 1885.

Mr Shiel exclaimed that in his opinion, 'The Salvation Army was a great nuisance. Why could they not go to their devotion quietly, without making a noise in the street.' He fined Poulter ten shillings, and in default ordered him to be imprisoned for seven days.

An attack on the standard-bearer of the Salvation Army in October 1881 was thought capital good fun by the *IPN* and its readers. In January 1882, the Skeleton Army was out in force, attacking a large Salvation Army procession in Sheffield, pelting the salvationists with mud and rotten fruit. In April 1885, a large Salvation Army parade in Bexley was unflatteringly featured, and in June the same year, there was ribald coverage of a faith-healing meeting at the Salvation Army Barracks in Legge Street. Major Pearson, an earnest, elderly salvationist, tried his best to cure various cripples and incurables, but with little success. He 'cured' an old woman with a diseased throat, however, and another who had suffered from weakness and pain; a blind boy remained blind, but a cross-eyed man threw away his glasses and joyously praised the Lord. In October 1885, the Life Guards of the Salvation Army were violently attacked by the Skeletons at Leicester: Commandant Booth was hit by a rotten tomato, and his lieutenant was unhorsed and mistreated. It would take until the late 1890s for this unsavoury epidemic of anti-salvationist activism to abate, and the Skeleton Army to be disbanded.

Two 'hallelujah lasses' being annoyed by some rough types, from the *IPN*, 31 August 1895.

Leona Dare, the Lady with the Iron Jaw, 1888

Susan Adeline Stewart was born in San Francisco in 1854. From an early age, she showed signs of an adventurous disposition, joining forces with the acrobats Thomas and Stewart Hall, who performed as 'The Brothers Dare'. In 1871, she married Thomas Hall and changed her name to Leona Dare. Pretty and vivacious, with long dark hair, she became known as the 'Queen of the Antilles' or 'The Pride of Madrid', although there is nothing to suggest that she possessed any Spanish heritage in the first place. An immediate success in the American acrobatic world, Leona Dare performed as a trapeze artist at Nixon's Amphitheatre in New York, and later joined Joel E. Warner's circus. In August 1872, she introduced a novel routine: suspended from a hot-air balloon, she lifted her husband and partner off the ground, holding his harness in her powerful jaws.

Leona Dare went on to tour Germany and France in 1874 and 1875, becoming quite a success at the Folies-Bergère. Back performing in New York, she quarrelled with her husband and left him in 1876, taking their complicated trapeze apparatus with her. This allowed her to keep performing with another partner, first in Paris and then at the Oxford Music Hall in London. But Thomas Hall tracked her down and took the theatre to court in May 1879 for illicitly using his trapeze. He read his pathetic letters to the fickle Leona aloud in court to gain sympathy. Whereas she had been paid £70 a week, at the Oxford, he was now almost destitute. '£70 a week! Very good pay; a barrister would like to get that!' exclaimed the jovial Mr Justice Denman. When the miserable Hall kept on telling his sob-stories, the bonhomous judge remarked that, 'This was the effect of a man teaching his wife to fly!' But in the end, Hall won his case: the trapeze would be returned to him, or £100 damages in default.

When Leona performed in Vienna, a wealthy banker named Ernest Grunebaum became besotted with her, but she turned down his offer of marriage. After she had suffered a serious back injury, she accepted her Austrian suitor, conveniently 'forgetting' that she was already married. But Leona eventually recovered from her injury and wanted to carry on performing. When she came to Chicago in 1880, her American husband again made himself known, but she managed to divorce him and then married Grunebaum a second time. It is not known what happened to Grunebaum when Miss Leona Dare, as she styled herself, returned to perform in Europe in 1882; no newspaper made any further reference to his existence. When Leona toured Spain in 1884, she was partnered by the young French acrobat M. George. On 22 November that year, they were performing at the Princess Theatre in Valencia. In her trademark finale, when she held the ropes for M. George's trapeze bar in her jaws, Leona 'was seized with a nervous fit' and dropped him. Since safety nets were surplus to requirement in the Hispanic theatrical world at the time, the hapless acrobat hit the floor with a crushing impact. When the terror-struck audience stampeded, several people were crushed and injured. Leona was saved from the trapeze, but M. George died from his injuries.

A disaster of this magnitude would have persuaded most acrobats to keep their feet on terra firma for the foreseeable future, but the daredevil Leona instead thought of a novel stratagem for risking life and limb. She teamed up with the Swiss balloonist Eduardo Spelterini and devised her most dangerous act yet: she would hang on to a trapeze suspended from the balloon only with her teeth, and see Europe's great capitals from a bird's eye perspective! When she came to London in May 1888 and announced her intention to ascend from the Crystal Palace, many Londoners were horrified. This was a most unladylike thing to do, and she should remember the horrid catastrophe that ensued when Mynheer de Groof, the Flying Man, had crashed to death during a similar foolhardy stunt. But Leona made her ascent without complications, rising to a height of five thousand feet above the great crowd. She repeated the performance several times, both in London and in Leicester, once nearly coming to grief when the balloon was carried off by strong winds. Leona and her two assistants went on to perform in Madrid and in Paris, to great acclaim. In October 1889, she was in Bucharest for her final performance together with M. Spelterini.

In 1890, when the now thirty-six-year-old Leona was back performing in Paris, she let go of the trapeze when the balloon was carried off by a gust of wind, and broke her leg. Although she recovered from her injury, she gave up performing a year or two later, and returned to the United States, ending up in Spokane, Washington. A pensioner in the early 1920s, she astounded the local newsmen by showing them her scrapbook of newspaper cuttings in many languages, telling of her past exploits. She died after a brief illness in May 1922, aged sixty-seven.

THE ASCENT OF LEONA DARE FROM A BALOON AT THE C. PALACE

The ascent of Leona Dare from the Crystal Palace, from the *IPN*, 16 June 1888.

Teddy Wick, the Fastest Barber in the West

Edward 'Teddy' Wick was born at Paddington in 1864, the son of a photographer with the same name. The 1881 Census finds him at No. 14 Dungannon Terrace, Fulham, as apprentice to the barber and hairdresser Thomas Mills. In 1884, Teddy Wick married Miss Ellen Keith, the daughter of a labouring man, and settled down at his own barber's shop at No. 418 King's Road, Chelsea. He soon acquired a very good professional reputation: not only was he extremely quick with the razor, but he never cut or grazed any of his clients.

There was an old tradition among the London barbers to hold 'shaving matches' where bets were made that a champion barber would shave a certain number of people in an hour. Fred Gornall, the Lightning Barber of Liverpool, had shaved eighty-two men in an hour back in 1822, but his record had been beaten by Silas Corlett, the Islington Knight of the Razor, who had managed 124 shaves in an hour. In 1887, Teddy Wick made the newspaper headlines after being backed to shave fifty people in an hour for £15 a side; he managed seventy-nine shaves in just less than an hour, and became known as the Champion Barber of London. He was awarded a fine silver cup on which the details of this feat had been engraved.

In November 1889, 'Professor' Teddy Wick won a shaving competition at the Royal Aquarium for £100 a side, beating the Fulham barber Markey. Teddy shaved eleven men in three minutes and thirty seconds, whereas Markey had managed nine in three minutes and thirty-five seconds. The Champion Barber introduced a novel phenomenon at his King's Road barber's shop: his little daughter Nellie, aged only four, would shave five men in twelve minutes. Both Nellie and her younger brother Walter had been instructed by their father since a very early age, and showed considerable promise with the razor, the 'Professor' told a visiting *Pall Mall Gazette* journalist.

By 1893, London had two 'Champion Barbers': Teddy Wick and W. Lloyd of Fulham. They agreed to settle their differences at a grand shaving match at the Imperial Theatre, Royal Aquarium. First, little Miss Nellie, now eight years old, shaved five men in six minutes and forty-two seconds. Then the 'Professor' and his rival took to the stage. After a frenzied effort, Teddy Wick had shaved forty men and Lloyd thirty-one; two men who had been cut were deducted from Lloyd's score, and one man who had been badly shaved from that of the 'Professor'.

Now the Undisputed Champion Barber of London, Teddy Wick joined the ranks of the minor celebrities of the Metropolis. A short, youthful-looking, dapperly dressed cove, the Fastest Barber in the West of London lost no opportunity to give a newspaper interview. One wall in his barber's shop was covered with autographed photographs of his clients: peers, politicians, actors and magnates of every description. Teddy Wick

The Champion Shaver, from the *IPN*, 22 October 1887.

The Shaving Match at the Royal Aquarium, from the *IPN*, 12 November 1887.

went on to tour the music halls showing off his skills, and once took part in a Lion Wager, shaving the lion-tamer in a cage full of lions. Both men left the cage alive, but the following day, the lion-tamer was mauled to death by his beasts.

The 1901 Census finds Teddy Wick in a barber's shop at No. 74 George Street, Camberwell, with a new wife named Daisy and five children from his first marriage. Nellie, who was now sixteen years old, was one of his two assistants. At the time of the 1911 Census, Teddy Wick was at No. 47 Euston Road, King's Cross, with his wife and a six-year-old son named Archibald. 'Professor' Teddy Wick, the Fastest Barber in the West, died in October 1938 aged seventy-four, from carcinoma of the stomach according to his death certificate.

Tragic Death of a Parachutist, 1889

Just imagine the scene. Park van Tassel, the intrepid American aeronaut, makes an ascent from Honolulu in front of a cheering crowd. But ominously, the balloon is beginning to drift seaward. Unable to control the craft, van Tassel leaps from the balloon and opens his parachute, but as he slowly descends, there is something waiting for him down there... People trying to rescue van Tassel are appalled to see the sharks grab the unfortunate aeronaut, tearing him to pieces.

'Professor' Park van Tassel was a Albuquerque showman and bartender who took an interest in ballooning from 1879 onwards. He was more than a little accident-prone, often crash-landing and injuring himself. Sometimes, he was booed by the mob for 'chickening out' when his balloon refused to take to the air altogether. Once, a spectator was knocked out cold by the ballast the careless Professor threw from the balloon. Another time, van Tassel was himself beaten up by a friend of his after making an injudicious remark about his girlfriend, and put in hospital before the balloon ascent could even be contemplated. Plans for two San Francisco youngsters to have a 'balloon marriage' in van Tassel's craft in 1884 had to be inhibited because no priest or justice of the peace could be persuaded to take a ride with the accident-prone aeronaut. In 1887, a Los Angeles ascent had to be cancelled because of sabotage: 'somebody had been monkeying with the pipe', as the Professor himself expressed it.

There were several cabinet cards depicting the daredevil van Tassel: a sturdy, muscular man with a large handle-bar moustache. Some time in the 1880s, he married his wife Jeanette. A tall, handsome blonde, she was a daredevil just like her husband, making several successful balloon ascents. She was the first woman in the United States to perform a parachute jump. But as we know, it looked very much like Mrs van Tassel had become a widow in November 1889, when the *New York Times* reported that the Professor had been killed by sharks off Honolulu, under the singular circumstances outlined above. But fortunately for the aeronaut and his wife, it turned out that the news of his death had been very much exaggerated. There had actually been two men in the balloon, and although the Professor's helper Joe Lawrence had been eaten by the

TRAGIC DEATH OF A PARACHUTIST.

Tragic death of a parachutist, from the *IPN*, 14 December 1889.

sharks, the indestructible van Tassel had successfully kept afloat and evaded the marauding sharks, to be rescued by a local boat crew. Most people would have remained on dry land for good after such a narrow escape, particularly since van Tassel had very nearly been killed earlier the same year, when his legs had got entangled in the balloon support lines after part of his parachute had opened.

But the American adventurer sought pastures new in the Antipodes, together with a troupe of performers showing off gymnastics, swordsmanship, and roller-skating. The main feature was that a scantily clad 'lady parachutist' leapt out from van Tassel's balloon, and performed gymnastics hanging from a trapeze bar suspended below her parachute, all the way down to earth. Park van Tassel had a daughter named Jenny who did parachute jumps from balloons, but the two young ladies accompanying him in Australia were the sisters Valerie and Gladys

Freitas, both performing under the name of van Tassel. They appear to have been quite skilful performers, never coming to grief during a series of performances in 1890 and 1891. The 'lady parachutist' stunt was considered quite outrageous by the Australian clergy, particularly when performed on a Sunday, installing lecherous thoughts into the minds of the impressionable youngsters.

In 1892, Park van Tassel went on to India, where he was joined by his daughter Jenny. At the time, the subcontinent was full of wealthy nabobs, many of whom had a fondness for the performances of female parachutists. But when performing in front of the Nawab of Dhaka in March 1892, poor Jenny crashed into a tree. She was severely injured and died a couple of days later. For her, there was no coming back from the dead.

Park van Tassel himself kept performing for many years. In September 1930, the seventy-eight-year-old daredevil was featured in the *New York Times*, the very same newspaper that had erroneously reported his demise forty-one years earlier. Captain van Tassel, as he now styled himself, freely told the journalist about the ups and downs of his adventurous life: in Siam he had crash-landed into a large mulberry tree, and in India he had nearly been lynched by fanatics who feared he would bring malevolent devils of the air with him in his balloon. His experiences covered more than a century, van Tassel boasted, and he had jumped from balloons in almost every country in the world. The following month, Park van Tassel died from heart disease in Oakland, California, and his death was reported, this time correctly, in the *New York Times*.

Succi, The Fasting Man

Giovanni Succi was born in the coastal town of Cesenatico, Italy, in 1853. His early career was uneventful, and he became a bank clerk in Rome, but in the 1880s, he travelled as a commercial agent in Madagascar and East Africa, and claimed to have discovered an elixir that enabled him to fast for extended periods of time, without any ill effect. To prove that his elixir worked, he made himself available to the medical profession in Italy and France. Experiments began in Paris, where Succi fasted for fourteen days and nights. In August 1886, he completed a thirty-day fast in Milan, and in December the same year, he won a bet for 15,000 francs by repeating the same feat in Paris. In 1888, he was awarded a diploma by the Medico-Physical Academy of Florence after successfully completing another thirty-day fast. 'Fasting Artists' were considered quite a novelty in the 1880s and 1890s, and Succi could make a comfortable living travelling around in Europe to show off his fasting prowess. A short, black-haired man with typical Italian looks, he was agile and muscular, and an excellent fencer.

In March 1890, Giovanni Succi came to the Westminster Aquarium, where he wanted to complete a forty-day fast. There was immediate interest from the Londoners, who took a keen interest in fasting artists, as well as from the medical profession, who saw a golden opportunity to study the physiology of fasting first-hand. According to Dr George N. Robins, Succi's personal medical attendant, the Italian was five feet five inches in height and slightly built. He seemed quietly confident that the fast would be a success, and ate heartily the days before it was to be commenced. After beginning to fast, Succi took neither solid nor liquid nourishment; he drank only water, and regularly sipped small quantities of his elixir. He smoked one or two pipes each day, and occasionally a cigar or cigarette. After ten days of fasting, Succi had lost more than sixteen pounds in weight, but he seemed none the worse for his abstinence from nourishment. He sometimes suffered from biliousness, which he treated using warm water as an emetic. On the fortieth day of fasting, Succi remained in good health: his pulse was regular and fairly firm, and his heart sounds, though feeble, were distinct. He had lost more than thirty-four pounds in weight, in excess of 26.5 per cent of his original body mass!

After the forty-day fast at the Royal Aquarium, Giovanni Succi became the most famous fasting artist in the world. He was paid £3,000 for his ordeal, and had no shortage of other offers. Later in 1890, he completed a forty-five-day fast in New York. In 1892, he was back at the Royal Aquarium for an intended fifty-two-day fast, but he felt very ill on the forty-fourth day, and had to take nourishment. For several years to come, he travelled around in Europe, performing various fasting stunts, sometimes combined with gymnastic performances. When he came to Vienna, disaster struck: during a fifty-day fast, it was discovered that he had nourishment smuggled in to him. This exposure did not end his career, however: in Verona, he was bricked up inside a small prison without windows, and in Florence, he was imprisoned in a cell without food. He took up spiritualism, and bragged that he was host to the Spirit of the Lion, which enabled him to live without taking nourishment; in expansive moods, he claimed to be the second incarnation of Jesus Christ. In December 1896, when Succi was performing at a music-hall in Paris, he went stark raving mad and broke everything in his room. When two police constables appeared on the scene, the frenzied Italian threw empty champagne bottles at them, until he was eventually secured and tightly bound. He 'yelled out Italian songs all the way to the station, to the great delight of a crowd of several hundred people who followed behind'. After being taken to the depot infirmary, his reason was restored within a week, and he was set at large to continue his career. There were quite a few other fasting artists at large at the time, and after Succi had left Britain, two competitors tried to usurp his fame, namely Giuseppe Sacco-Homann

Succi the Fasting Man at the Aquarium, from the *IPN*, 26 April 1890.

End of Succi's fast, from the *IPN*, 3 May 1890.

The two fasting usurpers Ricardo Sacco and Giuseppe Sacco-Homann, from signed postcards sold at their performances.

and Ricardo Sacco, who both flourished into Edwardian times, and had picture postcards printed to celebrate their exploits.

As for the original performer, Giovanni Succi, he fell on evil times in the 1900s, since fasting artists had gone out of fashion. In Vienna, he was paid only £20 for a thirty-day fast. According to a newspaper article from 1908, Succi was working as a male nurse at the asylum in Nanterre outside Paris, commenting, 'Fasting does not feed the faster!' Another newspaper report said that in 1918, Succi had died destitute in Florence; after fasting had completely gone out of fashion during the Great War, the once-famous artist could no longer support himself. He was said to have been seventy years old at the time of his death, but the real Succi was just sixty-five at the time. It also attracts suspicion that, according to Oettermann & Spiegel's *Lexikon der Zauberkünstler*, Succi was still alive in 1924.

Fasting performers have always been regarded with suspicion, and there have been several instances of the drinking water being mixed with nutrients, and cloths saturated with broth. But a writer in the *British Medical Journal*, who reported on Succi's forty-day fast in 1890, declared himself certain that there had been no deception; after all, the man had lost more than 26.5 per cent of his body weight. After having eaten heartily for a week after his fast, he had regained more than fourteen of the thirty-four pounds he had lost. Extreme fasting of this kind can lead to serious electrolyte disorders, and Succi was fortunate to survive his foolhardy exploits; his 'madness' in 1897 may well have been related to some dangerous fluctuation in his serum levels of sodium and/or potassium. As a recent scholarly article has pointed out, his 1888 fast in Florence was also rigorously controlled with regard to experimental physiology, and unlikely to have involved any cheating. Later, during an even longer fast in Vienna, Succi is recorded to have been exposed as a cheat, and this of course undermines the confidence in the authenticity of his other exploits, although the careful monitoring of his Florence and London fasts in 1888 and 1890 was quite impressive. Succi's 'elixir' may well have contained some primitive appetite suppressant, although I would put it beyond the witch-doctors of East Africa to make any important breakthrough in this field. A jocular London paper recommended that Succi's elixir should be mixed with the drinking water of the paupers and workhouse inmates, in order to reduce the bills for food to maintain the poor; with this rather Swiftian modest proposal, the tale of the Italian fasting performer shall end.

Lion Wagers

A small file of cuttings from the *IPN* and other newspapers, with the heading 'Lion Wagers', provides some curious information about a *fin-de-siècle* craze that has not yet found its historian: the performance of various foolhardy stunts inside cages full of lions.

In January 1890, the champion long-distance runner George Littlewood received a challenge from some of his friends: that he would not dare to enter the lion's cage at Wombwell's Menagerie. In front of an enormous crowd, the runner accomplished this feat with commendable intrepidity. Although he got separated from Orenzo the lion-tamer, and although the massive beasts were jumping around in a dangerous manner, Littlewood made it out of the cage unharmed, and the first recorded Lion Wager was won.

In August 1894, a Paris barber made a bet that he would dare to shave the lion tamer of the Juliano menagerie in a barber's chair situated inside the lions' cage itself. The lions looked on with interest throughout the procedure, which lasted twenty minutes. Once or twice, they came up to see what the barber was doing, but the lathered tamer shooed them away. When the same stunt was repeated by another barber, in Vichy, he narrowly escaped being bitten by a lion named d'Artagnan. In June 1895, when a travelling menagerie visited Tullins in France, the local barber made a bet that he would shave one of his customers inside the lion cage. Again, he won the Lion Wager: held in check by their tamer, the lions observed these bizarre proceedings with the greatest indifference. In St Louis, the animal trainer Pauline Devere married the cowboy Harry Bishop inside the lion cage at Wombwell's Circus, with six lions and lionesses acting as best men and bridesmaids. This was the first recorded Lion Wedding, considered as quite a curiosity at the time, and featured in many newspapers including the *IPN*.

In September 1895, the Lyons railway porter Léon Eyssete made a bet that he would dare to have his photograph taken inside the lion cage

Shaved in a lion's den, from the *IPN*, 8 June 1895.

Married inside a lion's cage, from the *IPN*, 15 June 1895.

when Castanet & Pezon's menagerie visited that city. Having read about the various barbers plying their trade in the same surroundings without any ill-effect, the foolish young Frenchman had become convinced that lions were placid and friendly animals, who would welcome his visit to

Léon Eyssete loses his Lion Wager, from the *IPN*, 21 September 1895.

their quarters. Eschewing the conventions of having a lion tamer handy at the time of the Wager, and making sure the beasts were well fed beforehand, the foolhardy young railwayman entered the lion cage just when the animals were to be fed. Before the photograph could be taken, a large lion named Romulus leapt at him and literally tore his head off. Léon Eyssete lost his Lion Wager.

The sad outcome of the Lyons Lion Wager did not prevent three jolly Frenchmen from having a bet of their own when the Salvator menagerie visited Bourg in November the same year: this time, they would play a game of cards inside the lion cage. To begin with, this Wager proceeded in good order: the three gentlemen sat down, set up their gaming-table, and began to play. But then a lion walked up to M. Chaveau, one of the card-players, and sniffed at his clothes. Wanting to display his courage, the Frenchman pushed the animal's head away. The lion immediately pounced, knocking him off his chair, and grabbing hold of his jacket. The other two card-players fled yelling, but the intrepid lion-tamer seized hold of the lion's tongue, and twisted it until the animal released its hold with a howl of pain. M. Chaveau was unharmed, although his clothes were torn to pieces, and the Lion Wager lost.

In January 1898, a Bolton publican won a Lion Wager of £25 through entering a cage containing three lions. A year later, a cyclist won a Wager by pedalling his machine inside a lion's cage. In March 1902, two Brighton daredevils played a game of ping-pong inside a large cage full of lions, with several thousand spectators in attendance. Again the Lion Wager was won, although squeamish people criticised the Brighton

A narrow escape for the card-playing Frenchmen, from the *IPN*, 30 November 1895.

A bicyclist inside a lion's cage, from the *IPN*, 7 January 1899.

A DANGEROUS GAME.—Ping-Pong Match in a Lion's Cage.

Ping-pong inside a lion's cage; from the *IPN*, 15 March 1902.

THE LIONS SPRANG UPON THE GIRLS.

The French tightrope dancers come to grief, and the lions attack, from the *IPN*, 11 May 1907.

A PLUCKY BARMAID WINS A WAGER

The lion looks on in amazement as the barmaid wins her plucky wager, from the *IPN*, 1 February 1908.

authorities for allowing such a dangerous exhibition to take place. At about the same time, two Welsh lasses from Merthyr Tydfil won a Wager for £20 through dancing the can-can inside a lion cage. When two French girls tried to emulate them by performing a tightrope routine just above a lion cage, the rope broke and they fell right on top of the lions. Although severely mauled, they both survived, but the Lion Wager was lost.

The final recorded Lion Wager occurred in 1908, when intrepid young barmaid Carrie Baker danced a hornpipe inside a lion cage in Liverpool. The ultimate notice in the 'Lion Wagers' dossier is that in 1910, Bostock's menagerie advertised a 'jungle wedding', with three lions acting the part of groomsmen and the same number of lionesses as bridesmaids.

Lively Goings-On at a Trance Show, 1896

'Professor' Mark Moores was a phrenologist and mesmerist who kept the Phrenological Museum in Morecambe. His son Harry Moores, born in 1868, also became a mesmerist and hypnotist. Already as a teenager he started performing in the provinces, through hypnotising volunteers from the audience, to considerable acclaim. He used the stage names 'Professor Leon Vint', 'Dr Dexter Vint', and 'Oubas the Mysterious' interchangeably. In December 1891, when he was performing in Wolverhampton, the Town Clerk prosecuted him before the local magistrates, alleging that his hypnotism was a complete fraud, and that the 'volunteers' were in fact men in his employ. And indeed, a witness had been struck by the fact that the same 'volunteers' appeared on stage at several different performances, and that they were laughing and joking together as if they knew each other. Although Mark Moores the phrenologist, and the Baptist minister

Lively goings-on at Professor Vint's trance show, from the *IPN*, 10 October 1896.

of Bury, acted as character witnesses, and although several people who had been hypnotised by young Moores swore that they were not in his employ, he was found guilty of unlawfully using pretended hypnotism and mesmerism to deceive and impose upon Her Majesty's subjects. He was fined a total of £5 5s, and had to pay in excess of £19 costs, or face three months in prison.

After this hard blow to his budding career, Leon Vint, as he henceforth would be calling himself, toured the provinces for several years to come. It would take until October 1896 for him to make the news, again unfortunately for all the wrong reasons. At this time, he was performing in Chester, with an act involving his assistant being put in a trance on a Monday, to be woken up on Saturday night. The assistant, dressed only in a nightshirt, was sleeping in a coffin. The problem was that Leon Vint had promised that the local medical men, and any other interested parties, should be allowed to witness the trance, to satisfy themselves that no fraud was involved. A number of local roughs took him up on this offer, bringing a bottle of whisky and a pack of cards to amuse themselves in the room with the coffin. After they had stuck pins into the sleeping man, and burnt his nose with a cigar, he was miraculously 'cured' from his trance: he leapt out of the coffin, and struck out at his tormentors, challenging the shortest of them to a fight. One of the tallest and stoutest of the rowdy visitors instead accepted the challenge, but then 'Professor' Vint came dashing into the room, threatening him with a revolver! If a police constable had not arrived to calm things down, some nasty scenes might have ensued, but once he saw the constable, the 'corpse' jumped back into the coffin and resumed his 'trance'.

These undignified scenes in Chester were discussed in many newspapers, the *IPN* adding a hilarious illustration of the night-shirted man and the coffin. The foolhardy 'Professor' managed to explain that the revolver he had been waving around was only a cigar-cutter in the shape of a revolver! A *Cheshire Observer* journalist had been knocked on the head by a ruffian in Vint's employ at some stage of the uproar, and the 'Professor' was taken to court again, this time being fined £12 and costs. In spite of the Chester fiasco, he continued as a showman, although trance shows were strictly avoided: instead, he employed a twenty-strong female choir and a pianoforte player in his grand 'Globe Choir and Scenorama' that toured the provincial music halls and mechanics' institutes. As the choir performed, Leon Vint exhibited a series of moving and panoramic pictures, and 'Madame Vint' showed her clairvoyant talents in a séance. Vint's Globe Choir and Scenorama was particularly popular in Wales, where he struck a chord with the labouring men in the valleys. In 1912, he rented the Nuneaton Theatre and reopened it as Vint's Electric Theatre, but according to the *Stage Year Book* for 1919, he was back in London by that time. The popularity of the cinema meant that such unambitious theatrical performances became a thing of the past, too old-fashioned even for the most backward Welsh valleys, and 'Professor' Leon Vint, who had once become notorious for the lively goings-on at his trance show, died in obscurity in 1943.

Death of the Champion Diver, 1897

Thomas 'Tommy' Burns was born in Liverpool in 1867. He learnt to swim at an early age, and excelled at many sporting activities, like diving, running and boxing. He became the captain of the Sefton Swimming Club, and worked as an attendant at the local baths, advancing to become a swimming teacher. In his early twenties, Tommy became a professional daredevil who specialised in diving from tall bridges. In 1890, he dived from the middle arch of Runcorn Bridge, plunging eighty-five feet into the Mersey; the dive went perfectly, and after swimming ashore, he received an ovation from a thousand-strong crowd. In June 1890, Tommy challenged the American athlete Carlisle Graham to a wager; they both dived from the Runcorn railway bridge, and Tommy was first ashore. They then went for a ten-mile run, and although the American led for much of the distance, Tommy overtook him and won easily.

Tommy Burns had clearly found his calling in life. He dived off the Forth Bridge, the Tay Bridge, Jamaica Bridge in Glasgow, London Bridge, and the O'Connell Bridge in Dublin. After Tommy had taken a dive from New Brighton Pier in Cheshire, he was attacked by a young shark, five feet in length, and bitten hard in the arm; assisted by some boatmen, who handed him a large knife, he managed to dispatch the shark and bring it ashore in triumph. The police and railway authorities took a dim view of people who risked life and limb diving from tall bridges, and Tommy was often in danger of being arrested for trespass on the railway. He went to elaborate lengths to outwit these spoil-sports, through disguising himself as a farmer, a miner, or an old woman, when he was approaching the railway. In August 1890, Tommy was arrested after diving off the O'Connell Bridge into the Liffey, but the police treated him well, and gave him several tots of brandy. In November 1891, he was arrested for trespass on the railway when he tried to sneak onto the Earlstown railway bridge disguised as a collier, and fined twenty shillings and costs.

In August 1892, Tommy Burns gave diving exhibitions at the Southport Centenary Exhibition; in November the same year, he took a dive from a tramcar in Liverpool; in December, he was 'nabbed' by the police after attempting to dive from the Liverpool Pier-head. In March 1893, 'Professor' Tommy Burns made the headlines as the new star of the Westminster Aquarium, diving from a high trapeze into a tank of water on the stage. In August the same year, when he was to dive seventy feet from a platform into a tank of water at the Sheffield Botanical Gardens, a piece of timber broke as he was being hoisted up to the platform, and he fell heavily to the ground and was taken to hospital in an unconscious state. Tommy had married by this time, and his wife was in the audience. But after making a full recovery, the indestructible Tommy was soon up to his old ways again. In September 1894, he was to make an attempt to dive into the Ship Canal from the Trafford Bridge. Since the police were up in arms against the railway trespasser, he disguised himself as a fishwife and travelled to the bridge in a fishmonger's cart. The police were wise to this trick, and the 'Professor' was arrested and frog-marched to the local police station by six sturdy constables. But the indefatigable diver was back at the Royal Aquarium in March 1895, where he dived from the roof into a tank only six feet deep.

In September 1895, Tommy Burns wanted to dive from the Tay Bridge, but the police and railway officials were aware of the Champion Diver's activities, and he again suffered the ignominy of being arrested. A year later, he again made the news with further foolhardy exploits: he made a wager that he would go from a public house in Tabard Street, Borough, to London Bridge, leap into the Thames, and then run to Great Yarmouth, where he would dive off the Britannia Pier into the sea, all within twenty-four hours. He made it all the way to London Bridge, where he plunged into the Thames like a champion, but an enormous crowd had congregated to see him, and he was arrested by the police and brought before the Lord Mayor, to enter into his own recognisances to keep the peace for six months.

In late 1896, Tommy Burns leapt from the Forth Bridge early in the morning of 21 December; he made it all the way, and did not seem at all put out by his experience. In January 1897, he made use of a novel stratagem to get a jump off the Tay Bridge: he booked a railway ticket into Dundee, where he had many admirers, and climbed from the carriage window up onto the roof while the train was in motion across the bridge! He then leapt from the carriage roof into the River Tay like a champion, but the boats that had been kept in readiness to save him from the ice-cold water had taken a wrong turning, and the diver had to swim for his life. He had been at least five minutes in the water when he was eventually picked up by the Tay Bridge steam launch, and carried down below to be placed next to the stove, which was burning brightly. Once he was brought ashore, the daredevil diver had perked up, and he was very proud of his latest stunt which had broken every record in the annals of foolhardiness.

In July 1897, Tommy Burns was getting ready for a swimming and diving display in Rhyl: he was to dive from a specially erected platform 100 feet above the water, at the Pier-head, in front of three thousand spectators. He arrived early, looking unwell and the worse for drink,

TOMMY BURNS, THE CELEBRATED HIGH DIVER,
MAKES HIS LAST DIVE FROM RHYL PIER.

The final dive of Tommy Burns, from the *IPN*, 17 July 1897.

having journeyed from Edinburgh to Liverpool non-stop the evening before, without food or sleep. He took a room at a hotel and slept a few hours, before having three large glasses of gin and seltzer to perk himself up. Sensible people were objecting that a high wind was blowing, and that the sea was very rough, but the daredevil ignored them. When leaping off the platform, Tommy fell over on his back, and landed very heavily in the rough sea. He was still able to swim, but seemed dazed and disoriented. Although boats were launched to bring him ashore, he was dead when they reached him, and his lifeless body was brought up to the pier by means of ropes. The Champion Diver, who had cheated death by a narrow margin several times before, had finally run out of luck.

Paul Tetzel, the Champion Butcher, 1898

The earliest butchery competition considered newsworthy by the national press was held at the Standard Theatre in Gateshead in April 1898. The London champion butcher Edward Harper had been challenged by the Gateshead butcher Matthew Ramsey, known as the winner of a local beef-dressing competition the previous year. Each man had to skin and dress two large, fat bullocks, watched by a referee and a time-keeper. A special train had been run from London, full of cattle dealers, drovers and butchers, who were keen to have a few pints of strong Northern bitter and to have a bet on the London champion Edward Harper.

The four bullocks were duly slaughtered, and the two butchers went to work, cheered on by a large and uproarious audience. Edward Harper was a fine figure of a man, twenty-five years old and very strong and sturdy; Matthew Ramsey was smaller and also incapacitated by blood poisoning in one hand. The London butcher was by far the superior performer: he finished his two bullocks in twenty-one minutes and ten seconds, whereas the Gateshead man took twenty-six minutes and seven seconds. There was much cheering as the result was announced, and the jolly London butchers went for another extended pub crawl, before boarding another special train that was to return them to the Metropolis.

In June 1898, Edward Harper was challenged by the champion butcher of America, Paul Tetzel, a native of Chicago. Another butchery competition was arranged at the Wood Green Athletic Grounds, for £200 a side. The stipulations were the same as those for the Gateshead match, and thousands of pounds were bet on the result. The attendance exceeded all precedents, and several men were doing a good trade selling silk handkerchief trophies of the event. The Old Butchers' Band of the Metropolitan Cattle Market was in attendance, playing marrow-bones and cleavers to great acclaim. When the four fat bullocks were slaughtered, there was a roar of anticipation as the two rival butchers went to work.

Edward Harper looked like a proper butcher, large and stout, and with a red, perspiring face. In contrast, Paul Tetzel was a thin, dapper-looking

The Wood Green butchery competition, from the *IPN*, 25 June 1898.

cove, whose waist-belt would not have reached round half of his opponent's well-nourished bulk. But still, Tetzel had the head off his first bullock well before his opponent, and he proceeded to skin both beasts with extreme rapidity. In the end, Tetzel had his two carcases ready for the market in eighteen minutes and thirty-two seconds, whereas Harper took just over twenty minutes. Paul Tetzel was the new undisputed champion butcher of the world.

The working men's newspapers of the time reported on the Wood Green butchery competition with extreme enthusiasm. 'International Beef-Dressing Competition for £200 a Side and the Championship!' exclaimed the *IPN*. At least 4,000 people had watched this bloodbath, which had 'aroused a tremendous amount of excitement throughout the butchery trade in England'. Trade newspapers like the *Butcher's Advocate* were also enthusiastic about the Wood Green encounter, and the prospect of future butchery competitions. But squeamish middle-class people objected to such a sanguinary display being enacted in front of a large paying audience. When there was a question in Parliament whether it was really appropriate for butchery to be performed in a place of public amusement, the Home Secretary, Sir Matthew White Ridley, gave a rather vague answer. Although the Wood Green track had given an assurance that butchery contests would not be allowed there in the future, the butchery trade might well find alternate venues for their 'beef-dressing competitions'.

Paul Tetzel liked his novel fame among the London butchers. Showing no urgency to return to his native land, he settled down at a butcher's shop in Greenwich. The 1901 Census finds him and his family in a three-storey Victorian terraced house at No. 59 Endwell Road: his wife Amelia, son George and daughter Caroline. He had been born in Germany in 1867, but his parents had brought him to New York in 1881. Paul Tetzel called himself the Champion Butcher of the World, and was always ready to defend his title. In 1901, he was challenged by J. Marsh, the Champion Sheep-dresser of Manchester, to a contest at the Salford Football Club for a stake of £50 a side, that he could not dress a bullock in less time than his local rival would dress a sheep. Again, several thousand spectators were present, many of them butchers from Manchester or the Midlands. Councillor Hornby, of Manchester, acted as judge, and Mr Mills, of Birkenhead, as time-keeper. Once more, Paul Tetzel was the winner, taking just three minutes and 16 seconds to get his bullock ready for the market, whereas Marsh took more than half a minute longer to dress his sheep.

In 1903, Paul Tetzel outclassed all local competitors at a butchery contest in Glasgow. A few years later, the Champion Butcher performed at Gilbert's Circus in Sherwood Street, Nottingham, to general acclaim. The 1910 US Census finds Paul Tetzel at No. 19 Manhattan Ward, New York, with his wife and three children. According to an internet source, Tetzel remained active much longer than that, showing off his skills at fairs and markets on both sides of the Atlantic. His year of death is not known, but since his son George was listed in the 1940 US Census, with four children alive, the Champion Butcher may well have living descendants today.

Strange Performers at the Royal Aquarium, 1898

The *IPN* took a vigorous interest in London's popular entertainments, whether it was the exhibition of human freaks, strange stage performers, or trained animals on show. In 1898, Mr Josiah Ritchie had recruited some decidedly strange performers at the Royal Aquarium, where an *IPN* journalist paid them a visit.

Firstly, there was Madame Christensen, said to be a native of Sweden, who would fast for thirty days. Her portrait shows a sturdy dame looking far from half-starved. Mme Christensen would be under observation throughout her fast, and there was light-hearted newspaper speculation that some German-speaking joker would try to tempt her by speaking about the delicious *Frankfurterwurst* and *Rothkraut* she was missing out on. There were regular bulletins to the press once the fast had begun, and the first fifteen days were completed in good order. But after eighteen days of fasting, Mme Christensen's medical attendants recommended that she should 'throw in the towel' and start taking nourishment again. This was an anticlimactic ending to this much-publicised fast, but Mme Christensen kept performing. As shown by the fame of Signor Succi, there was a strong interest in various fasting artists in the 1890s, and Mme Christensen was still at the Royal Aquarium in 1902, when she was said to have completed a thirty-five-day fast. Her later activities have remained unrecorded; in Edwardian times, fasting artists went out of fashion just as quickly as they had become popular a decade earlier.

The trio of rotund performers featured in the *IPN* illustration were the Australian Giant Family: the siblings Clara, Anna and Tom Snell. They were natives of Gippsland, and started their show business careers at the Melbourne Waxworks Museum in 1886. Their father William Snell was of normal size, as was his wife Elizabeth, but three of his five children were extremely tall and heavy: Clara was over six feet tall and weighed 40 stone, and Anna and Tom both weighed around 26 stone. In 1888, the Australian Giant Family went on a world tour, visiting London and various European cities before going on to the United States, where they shared the stage with Buffalo Bill and Sitting Bull. Tom then retired from show business at the age of just twenty-one, lost much weight, and became the storekeeper at Nar Nar Goon in Gippsland. The two girls went on another world tour, earning enough money to be able to buy the Robin Hood hotel near Drouin. They were both eventually married, Anna to a certain Mr Small. Clara, who remained very heavy throughout her life, died in 1914 at the age of just forty-one; Anna died in 1930 aged fifty-four, and Tom lived on until 1949. They were all buried in the Bunyip Cemetery.

Mlle Paula, the Queen of the Reptiles, had been active at the Royal Aquarium since June 1890. A native of Bavaria, she had married Captain

A VISIT TO THE ROYAL AQUARIUM.
ASTUTE MANAGER RITCHIE PROVIDES PLENTY OF NOVELTIES FOR HIS PATRONS.

Strange performers at the Aquarium, from the *IPN*, 1 October 1898.

Swann, himself a prominent snake-charmer until he had the misfortune of losing his eyesight. A tall and handsome blonde with luxuriant hair, Mlle Paula had long specialised in handling large snakes and alligators. Dressed in a tight-fitting green outfit, she wrestled a fully grown boa constrictor and two Indian pythons. Two Mississippi alligators were then introduced, and although the reptiles objected to being handled, Mlle Paula lifted them up like if they had been lap-dogs. A particularly large and ferocious alligator was then introduced, but when it dashed at Mlle Paula, she threw a cloth over its head and demonstrated its gaping jaws. When interviewed by a *Pall Mall Gazette* journalist, Mlle Paula could show the scars from some nasty bites to her hands and arms, but her courage and knowledge of the habits of the animals made sure that she never suffered any severe injury; she kept performing, with complete success, at least until 1899.

Terrible Parachute Fatality, 1902

As we have seen from the life and adventures of Zazel, Zaeo and Leona Dare, female daredevils were popular in late Victorian times. Although the misogynists objected that being fired from cannon, swinging in a trapeze, or jumping from a balloon with a parachute put too formidable a strain on the frail female physique, various lady performers flourished at the time, and it was considered novel and curious to see them in action. One of these female daredevils was Miss Maude Brookes, the Lady Parachutist. She used to ascend to a height of several thousand feet in a gas balloon operated by her manager Lieutenant George Philip Lempriere, and then leap from a trapeze with a primitive parachute. By 1902, she had made several dozen of these perilous descents, landing alive and well each time.

Maude Brookes had a younger sister named Edith, who also wanted to become a daredevil. There were no academies for Lady Parachutists at this time, and the only opportunity for her to learn her trade was by literally taking the plunge. The twenty-three-year-old Edith Brookes made her debut at a gala held at the Wednesday football ground in Sheffield on 19 May 1902: the balloon ascended to a height of several thousand feet, and young Edith jumped with her parachute, alighting safely near Neepsend Station, on the Great Central Railway, about a mile and a half from the football ground. In contrast, Lieutenant Lempriere crash-landed his balloon on the roof of a house, but fortunately, as it was thought at the time, the contraption could be repaired for a second parachute jump on the following day.

On 20 May, Lieutenant Lempriere's balloon was in readiness at twenty minutes to eight in the morning. Lady Parachutists were quite a novelty in Sheffield in those days, and in spite of the early hour, thousands of spectators had congregated inside and outside the football ground, anticipating another successful performance. Amidst hearty cheers, the balloon soared aloft, with Lieutenant Lempriere at the controls and young Edith Brookes sitting on her trapeze, which was suspended from the balloon. But at a height of just 700 feet, Edith Brookes began tugging at the ropes to her parachute. She then suddenly dropped from the balloon, but the parachute did not open. To the horror of the spectators, the large, ungainly canvas just flapped around and dropped like a wet rag. As she fell with tremendous speed, Edith Brookes could be seen desperately pulling at the ropes of the parachute, before she landed with a heavy thud in Hillsborough Park, just a few hundred yards from the football ground.

Lieutenant Lempriere and the organisers of the gala rushed to the spot where Edith Brookes had fallen. She was said to have been still alive when found, but she soon succumbed to her terrible injuries. The tragedy caused much consternation throughout Sheffield, and the gala in the football field was at once abandoned. At the coroner's inquest on Edith Brookes, various theories as to the cause of the accident were discussed. The misogynist speculation that she had fainted and fallen off the balloon does not appear likely, since the spectators had seen her pulling at the ropes for the parachute as she fell. The reason she had jumped at a height of just 700 feet was never made clear. There was a suggestion that the man who had prepared the parachute had done so in a cack-handed manner, and at the inquest he admitted twisting the cords to prevent them from being blown against the Lady Parachutist during the descent. He said that the twist would have come out once the weight of the parachutist had rested on the ropes.

There was sensation when Maude Brookes, the original Lady Parachutist, gave evidence. Her real name was Mrs Frank Edward Morgan, but she had maintained her maiden name for her parachuting career. When Lieutenant Lempriere had contracted her for the Sheffield show, the careless young officer had not thought of checking Maude's availability, and she had in fact been booked in for another show in Carmarthen, with a different aviator. Maude Brookes knew that young Edith had been begging hard to be given a trial as a Lady Parachutist, and she thought it would not do her any harm to make her debut in Sheffield, in spite of her total lack of experience as a parachutist. After all, Lieutenant Lempriere had only signed a contract that he would procure a Lady Parachutist for two ascents and descents; he had not specified who it would be. And indeed, Edith had been advertised as the celebrated Maude Brookes on the placards and handbills for the Sheffield gala, and some early newspaper reports of the tragedy had named Maude Brookes as the victim.

The grieving father of Edith Brookes had written a letter to the coroner, asking that such foolhardy performances should be prohibited by law. The coroner's jury seconded this motion, but when a question was eventually asked in Parliament, the Home Secretary said that the present state of

Poor Edith Brookes falls from the balloon, from the *IPN*, 31 May 1902.

TERRIBLE PARACHUTE FATALITY AT SHEFFIELD.
UNFORTUNATE EDITH BROOKES DASHED TO THE GROUND FROM A HEIGHT OF 700 FEET.

the law did not allow Lady Parachutists being banned from the sky. Among the newspapers, some agreed that demand created supply, and if the public would pay good money to see these female daredevils risking their lives, nothing could prevent it. Other newspapers pointed out that since dangerous professions already abounded, their number should not be increased unnecessarily. People who tempted the public to attend such foolhardy performances had a great responsibility on their shoulders, and they should not be allowed to make any money in this way. The daredevil career of young Edith Brookes had ended after just her second parachute jump; a planned performance in London the same week had to be cancelled. As for Maude Brookes, whose decision to perform in front of the Carmarthen Taffies instead of the Sheffield Steelmen had such tragic consequences, she did not enter a nunnery to mourn her dead sister: some press cuttings from 1905 show that she was still performing as a Lady Parachutist at that time.

8

Strange People

The Cat Woman of Rottingdean

Robert Dennis Chantrell was a distinguished architect, a pupil of Sir John Soane, and the designer of many churches in Yorkshire and elsewhere. In 1846, he retired aged just fifty-three and settled in London. In addition to his wife, the mother of his eight children, he kept a mistress, Miss Mary Elizabeth Dear, an aspiring artist he had met at the Society of Arts. After the death of his wife in 1863, Chantrell settled down with his mistress at Ivy Cottage, a large detached property facing the high street of the seaside village of Rottingdean, not far from Brighton. Since Miss Dear was not always of sound mind, Chantrell appointed himself her guardian. Her habits were very odd: she fancied herself as a painter, and wanted to keep large numbers of animals for use as models. She was particularly fond of cats, keeping not less than a hundred of these animals, of all shapes and sizes.

But although he was formally her guardian, the aging Robert Dennis Chantrell was entirely incapable of controlling his demented, cat-hoarding paramour. She had several times made forays into the yards and gardens of her neighbours in Rottingdean to extend her collection of cats. In February 1866, after a certain Mr Moody had lost three favourite cats, Miss Dear was suspected of having stolen them. After the police and magistrate had been called in, a search warrant was executed. When searched, Ivy Cottage and its outhouses were found to contain 150 living cats, and fifty dead ones; there were also fifteen dogs, and a tame fox. The whole place was in a very filthy state, and the stench was awful. Six dead cats were putrefying in Miss Dear's bedroom. Chantrell was sternly ordered by the magistrate to clean up this nuisance.

In May 1867, the Rottingdean surgeon Mr J. Noakes, inspector of nuisances to the Newhaven board of guardians, was ordered to inspect Robert Dennis Chantrell's house, due to the very noxious smell

'Extraordinary Collection of Cats', from the *IPN*, 1 June 1867.

emanating from these premises. In the garden, fifty cats were running about, and in the kitchen, a similar number of these animals were making themselves comfortable in front of the fire. In a yard nearby, Mr Noakes saw upwards of twenty cats, a fox, a goat, and many turkeys, geese, and fowls of every description. He estimated the total number of cats on the premises to more than 100, some of them very dirty. Since the excrements of all these cats had not been removed for many months, the smell was 'offensive in the extreme and most injurious to health'. When summoned before the Lewes petty sessions, Robert Dennis Chantrell said that all the animals belonged to his ward Miss Dear, who fancied herself as an animal painter. She was a great friend of the feline tribe, making regular trips to purchase more of these animals. The bench of magistrates ordered Chantrell to abate the nuisance in three days, or the animals would have to be removed.

The old architect was at his wits' end. He was quite a feeble man, and to add to his worries, Miss Dear had recently been arrested for debt. Even seven maids with an equal number of mops would have faced a stern challenge to clean up this Rottingdean Augia's stable; the dotard Robert Dennis Chantrell and his elderly, long-suffering domestics were entirely unable to remove the accumulated filth of several years of neglect. Due to the vile smell emanating from Ivy Cottage, Chantrell was extremely unpopular locally: people booed and hooted him, and once he was slapped in the face with a wet fish, since his filthy house stunk down all of Rottingdean. After he had unwisely put up a sign in one of his front windows, saying that a Londoner could never find peace among such uneducated country bumpkins, the locals made a sport of breaking his windows at night.

When Ivy Cottage was again inspected by Mr Noakes, things had not improved in the slightest. The healthy animals were taken away, the sick or starving ones put down, and Robert Dennis Chantrell presented with a hefty bill for all the cleaning work. With the help of a solicitor, Chantrell managed to pay his debts, and bail Miss Dear out of prison. What she said when she saw the spotlessly clean Ivy Cottage, and the nine cats that had been allowed to remain, is unfortunately not known. Chantrell had escaped to Belgium to avoid the wrath of the Cat Woman.

There was eventually a reconciliation between the seventy-five-year-old former architect and the thirty-six-year-old cat hoarder. After she had claimed she was pregnant, Robert Dennis Chantrell offered to marry her. The old architect's children from his previous marriage of course did their best to dissuade him from marrying such a lunatic, but there is no fool like an old fool: this mismatched couple wed at the Old Church, St Pancras, and later had the daughter Marion Felicia, presumed to have been fathered by Chantrell. As could be expected, the marriage between these two oddballs was not a particularly happy one. The Cat Woman began collecting animals again, and appeared to lose her wits altogether. Her fierce and angry temper, and the smell and filth of the animals, forced old Chantrell to escape to lodgings in Croydon, where he expired in January 1872. His entry in the Oxford DNB mentions nothing about his sad declining years.

Later in 1872, the Cat Woman of Rottingdean was again prosecuted, this time for cruelty to animals. She had left eighteen dogs and fourteen cats to starve after going away and not leaving the domestics with enough money to feed them. The dogs had eaten the fowls, and some of the cats, for want of proper nourishment. In court, the Cat Woman objected that her husband's sons from his previous marriage were contesting his will, leaving her to struggle for money. She was fined £5, with costs in excess of £15, and harshly warned that if she kept hoarding animals, and did not look after them properly, she would be sent to prison. The angry locals booed her all the way to the railway station. After the *IPN* had published a feature on this case, a friend of the Cat Woman threatened legal action, claiming that the animals had been far more healthy-looking

'Starving Cats and Dogs at Rottingdean' from the *IPN*, 17 August 1872.

The Cat Woman is hooted by the mob, from the *IPN*, 17 August 1872.

than the half-starved wretches depicted by the *IPN*'s artists. George Purkess replied that the illustration was based on drawings provided by a local artist, although it might of course be that this individual had been mistaken, and that Mrs Chantrell was more sinned against than sinning.

It turned out that the will of Robert Dennis Chantrell had been 'doctored' by his wife, with the help of a dodgy solicitor. In May 1874, the Court of Probate awarded the old architect's worldly possessions to the children from his first marriage. Later the same year, the Cat Woman was twice more prosecuted for cruelty to animals. The enraged locals broke down her front door to allow the constables to enter. Although the Cat Woman flew at them with a poker, yelling like a lunatic, she was unable to prevent the constables from removing the emaciated cats and dogs, which all had to be put down. She was sentenced to two months in prison, and heavily fined. Ivy Cottage was later repossessed and sold at auction. The Cat Woman may well have ended her days in an asylum. On a brighter note, her daughter Marion Felicia, whose childhood must have been unconventional to say the least, later married and went to Australia, where she became an artist and musician.

Animal hoarding by various deranged people is a phenomenon regularly reported in the newspapers. A confused, elderly person is found in a squalid, dilapidated house or flat, surrounded by rubbish, waste, and miserable, half-starved animals. The psychopathology of this maladaptive, destructive behaviour is poorly understood, although it is believed there is a link to obsessive-compulsive disorders. Three-quarters of animal hoarders are women, often living in squalor, equally incapable of recognising the neglect to themselves or the cruelty to the animals. In fact, just like the Cat Woman, they claim to be great friends of animals, and 'rescue' poor cats and dogs from the cruel outside world. A recent review on animal hoarding has claimed that this phenomenon was first described in 1981, but there were in fact several instances of this unsavoury phenomenon from Victorian times, the Cat Woman of Rottingdean probably the most extreme of them. As I have demonstrated in my book *Queen Victoria's Stalker*, certain types of aberrant human behaviour, whether stalking of celebrities or hoarding animals, have existed for several hundred years, although they have gone under different names.

Suicide from the Clifton Suspension Bridge

The Clifton Suspension Bridge, an architectural wonder designed by Isambard Kingdom Brunel, was opened in 1864. The tall and impressive bridge, 245 feet over the high-water level of the River Avon, become one of the landmarks of Bristol, and it has kept that status to the present day.

The *IPN* normally did not care much for bridges or architecture, but the Clifton Suspension Bridge made it onto its first page on 11 September 1869, when a young pastry-cook named Joel Cousins had committed suicide by leaping off the bridge. He had paid his toll at the gate and proceeded to the middle of the bridge, where he took off his hat, coat and waistcoat, and leapt over the side. For a while, he held on to the rail of the bridge with both hands, but then he let go, and there was a loud thud

Clifton Suspension Bridge.

... *One for your collection. From Madeline S. Scott.*

Above: Clifton Suspension Bridge, from a postcard stamped and posted in 1903.

Right: Joel Cousins falls to his death, from the *IPN*, 11 September 1869.

SUICIDE FROM THE BRIDGE AT CLIFTON

as he landed in the mud below. Cousins was only nineteen years old, and was presumed to have led a fast life and spent his money recklessly.

Joel Cousins was not the first man to commit suicide by jumping off the Clifton Suspension Bridge, however. His sole predecessor, the wealthy Portishead factory owner George Green, had taken his leap in May 1866, vaulting over the side of the bridge and landing in the muddy bank of the Avon with a dull thud. In September 1870, an old coachman named George Bates leapt to his death from the bridge, and the following month, the young labouring man William Henry Felling followed suit. In 1871, a young woman named Amelia Stone committed suicide by throwing herself off the bridge.

SUICIDE FROM CLIFTON SUSPENSION BRIDGE ON THE 9TH INST.

The *IPN* failed to feature the suicide of George Green, the first ever off the Clifton Suspension Bridge, but the *Penny Illustrated Paper* of 19 May 1866 did not miss out on this opportunity, although its drawing was certainly no masterpiece.

SUICIDE FROM THE CLIFTON SUSPENSION BRIDGE

Mr James Vinson falls to his death, from the *IPN*, 17 August 1872.

In August 1872, a well-dressed gentleman was observed to behave oddly in the Clifton area. When a police constable demanded his name and address, the gentleman introduced himself as Mr James Vinson, of No. 35 Langton Street, Cathay. Mr Vinson proceeded to purchase a ticket to cross the Suspension Bridge, which he made use of at ten in the evening. Soon after he had disappeared in the dusk, there was a sound like the report of a pistol, caused by his body hitting the muddy bank of the Avon. There was insanity in Mr Vinson's family, and his friends had for some time been fearful that he was losing his mind. In an illustrated account of Mr Vinson's sad fate, the *IPN* wrongly stated that he was the fourth person to commit suicide off the Clifton Suspension Bridge; he was in fact the sixth, and by no means the last, as we will see.

Some light relief from this constant suicidal gloom was provided by the twenty-two-year-old barmaid Sarah Ann Henley, who leapt from Clifton Suspension Bridge in May 1885 after a tiff with her boyfriend. But it was a very blustery day, and the wind caught her voluminous skirts, slowing her descent very markedly. Still, she landed feet first on the soft bank of the Avon with such force that it took three workmen to dig her out of the mud. Amazingly, she had not suffered any broken bones, and the workmen took her to a railway tavern nearby for a much-needed glass of brandy. A doctor at the tavern recommended that she should be sent to the infirmary, and a cab was hailed. The driver refused to transport poor Sarah, however, since her clothes were so very dirty, with the remarkable words, 'I don't care! Let her die!'

Thus the workmen had to carry Sarah all the way to the Bristol Infirmary on a stretcher, a journey taking more than an hour. She remained in hospital for more than a week, being treated for severe shock and unspecified 'internal injuries'; these latter were not formidable enough to prevent her from making a complete recovery from her foolhardy adventure. Due to all the newspaper publicity, she received several offers of marriage, but she turned them all down. The cruel cab driver defended his actions in a letter to the *Bristol Times & Mirror*, stating that he had only just had his cab cleaned, and did not want to get the seats dirty. He called for a fund to be set up to assist cabbies in these circumstances and pointed out that the corporation should have had an ambulance available for incidents like this. As for Sarah Ann Henley herself, she refrained from further rash acts, married the labouring man Edward Lane in 1900, and lived to be eighty-four years old. The Bristol poet William E. Heasell serenaded her in laborious verse:

> Once in Victoria's golden age
> When crinolines were all the rage
> A dame in fashionable attire
> Would change her life for one up higher

> So up to Clifton Bridge she went
> And made a parachute descent
> But though, 'twas not the lady's wish
> A boatman hooked her like a fish
> And thus a slave to fashion's laws
> Was snatched from out of Death's hungry jaws ...

In August 1896, the *IPN* reported the suicide of the old tailor Thomas Smale off Clifton Suspension Bridge, adding that he was the thirty-third person to suffer this fate. The following month, there was further drama when a bankrupt Birmingham grocer named Charles Albert Browne threw two of his children, twelve-year-old Ruby and three-year-old Elsie, headlong off the Clifton Suspension Bridge. Amazingly, both girls survived this attempt to murder them, and Ruby was able to testify against her father in court. Browne was found guilty but insane and was committed to Broadmoor. Amazingly, he was released as early as 1899, apparently without making any further attempts to decimate his family.

The Clifton Suspension Bridge has remained one of the most notorious 'suicide bridges' in the world; the total death toll is said to exceed 400. According to a scholarly article, 127 people leapt or fell off the bridge between 1974 and 1993; the mortality among them was greater than 95 per cent. It was noted that the presence of the suspension bridge affected the local pattern of suicide very dramatically, and that local residents were twice as likely to commit suicide by jumping as inhabitants of the remainder of England and Wales. In December 1998, two tall wire barriers were erected on the Clifton Suspension Bridge, and these halved the suicide rate from 8.2 to 4.0 per year, providing evidence in favour of the preventive role of 'suicide barriers' on tall bridges. Since many acts of suicide are impulsive in nature, restricting access to commonly used methods can reduce both method-specific and overall suicide rates.

The Strange Case of Boulton and Park, 1871

Ernest Boulton was a young London bank clerk with very unusual interests. From an early age, he had been obsessed with wearing female clothes. He was very effeminate and had once managed to trick his own grandmother into believing that he was the new parlour-maid. Ernest took to the mid-Victorian homosexual underworld like a fish took to water. Together with his best friend, the law student Frederick William Park, he joined a theatrical company, both of them playing feminine parts. Ernest was quite a talented actor, with a fine soprano voice; he received many bouquets after the performances, some from his own set, others from people who did not realize that he was really a man.

Off the stage, Ernest and his friend dressed alternately in male and female attire. When dressed up as women, calling themselves 'Stella' and 'Fanny', their use of make-up, and their choice of flashy and risqué outfits, often led to them being mistaken for prostitutes. It seems to have been of rare occurrence that any person suspected that they were men; in fact, they were sometimes suspected of being women in disguise when wearing male attire! By 1868, when he was twenty years old, Ernest had acquired a permanent boyfriend, none less than Lord Arthur Clinton MP, the son of the Duke of Newcastle. A strange-looking cove with a balding head, a weak chin, and bushy whiskers, Lord Arthur became infatuated with the good-looking young Ernest. They even appeared on stage together, in the roles of Sir Edward Ardent and Mrs Chillington in the play *A Morning Call*.

When Ernest felt monogamous, he wrote love letters to Lord Arthur, wore the expensive wedding ring he had been given, and ordered calling cards in the name of 'Lady Stella Clinton'. But when they felt up to some serious hanky-panky, gay young 'Stella' and 'Fanny' went cruising at the Burlington Arcade and other haunts for homosexuals and transvestites, where they never had any difficulty in picking up fun-loving friends. They also liked flirting with heterosexual men, teasing them and keeping them at arm's length. A certain Mr Cox very much fancied the pretty 'Stella', whom he kissed at a jolly champagne luncheon. When he learnt, quite by chance, the truth about his new lady friend, his jaw must have dropped. When he next met 'Stella' and 'Fanny', dressed in their usual finery, he angrily cried out, 'You damned set of infernal scoundrels, you ought to be kicked out of this place!'

Carefree young 'Stella' and 'Fanny' were wholly undeterred by this regrettable episode, however. In female attire, they attended the Oxford and Cambridge Boat Race, the old Surrey Theatre in Blackfriars Road, and the Alhambra Theatre in Leicester Square. 'I am consoling myself in

Boulton and Park partying in London, from the *IPN*, 28 May 1870.

your absence by getting screwed,' Ernest wrote to Lord Arthur in 1869; his Lordship's reaction to this outspoken missive is unfortunately not known. Two of Ernest's other boyfriends were Louis Hurt, a clerk in the Post Office, and John Fiske, US Consul at Leith. Since his consular duties kept him in Scotland most of the time, the amorous American had to be content with sending his beloved 'Stella' long and passionate letters, which the latter kept.

In early 1870, the Metropolitan Police wanted to teach those infesting the Burlington Arcade a hard lesson. They had had their eyes on the fun-loving 'Stella' and 'Fanny' for quite some time. After these two had attended a ball at Haxell's Strand Hotel in full female attire, they were arrested and taken to the Bow Street police station. Without any court order, a police surgeon pulled up their elegant long dresses and examined their anuses to find evidence of 'pedication'. Still in female dress, they appeared at the magistrate's court the next day, to be charged with conspiring and inciting people to commit an unnatural offence. Ernest wore a cherry-coloured silk evening gown trimmed with white lace, bracelets on bare arms, a wig, and a plaited chignon. This lugubrious scene was just what the *IPN* thrived on. The 'Capture of Men dressed as

Boulton and Park are arrested, from the *IPN*, 7 May 1870.

Boulton and Park are taken to prison, from the *IPN*, 14 May 1870.

'Cor Blimey, look at these!' A jolly policeman makes an inventory of Boulton's wardrobe. From the *IPN*, 14 May 1870.

Women' could be milked for weeks, with drawings of the two miscreants being arrested, their cavorting with Lord Arthur and other admirers, the ignominious ending to Mr Cox's romance, and a grinning police constable making an inventory of Ernest's considerable wardrobe of dresses, wigs and elegant hats.

For stern Victorian moralists, the Boulton and Park scandal represented everything that was wrong with modern Britain: its loose morals, depraved young men, and the easy-going levity of the throng. It was thought perverted and obscene that a hearty London man of the town would be at risk of picking up what he presumed to be a 'fast girl' at Burlington Arcade, only to find out that 'she' was really a man. Long before they were tried, Boulton and Park were marked men. Ernest's indiscreet letters from his various admirers led to these individuals being added to the charge-sheet. Lord Arthur Clinton died the month after, allegedly from scarlet fever, but more probably from suicide, although there was persistent gossip that he had in fact faked his death and gone abroad under an assumed name.

The police tried to cajole Hurt and Fiske to denounce Ernest, but these two showed unexpected bottle and 'stood by their man' with admirable constancy. When the case finally went to trial, in May 1871, the evidence for the prosecution seemed very feeble indeed. This time, the two main accused appeared in male attire; on the insistence of their solicitor, Ernest had grown a moustache and Park whiskers. In court, they appeared like a pair of silly and immoral young men, who had hob-nobbed with various 'consenting adults' within their own set, and certainly not incited any person to commit an unnatural offence. It was thought wholly unfair that they had been submitted to an anal examination by the police without permission from a higher authority. As a result, they were acquitted

Boulton and Park in court, from the *IPN*, 14 May 1870.

amidst cheers from members of their own set. In spite of his 'butch' moustachioed appearance, Ernest fainted when he heard the verdict, like the heroine of a Victorian novel.

The homophobic 'hearties' ground their teeth when they heard that these two transvestite buggers had been let off scot-free, without even a reprimand. What was Britain coming to when such catamites were allowed to prance round the streets, perverting public morals? When Ernest resumed his theatrical career, rotten vegetables came his way more often than bouquets. In Aldershot, he was nearly lynched by some young officers, but managed to make his escape after the gas had been turned down. Clearly, there was nothing else to do but to change his name and flee the country.

In 1874, two novel artists appeared on the New York stage, the brothers Ernest and Gerard Byne, female impersonators. They had very considerable success, particularly the talented Ernest with his excellent voice. Their photographs sold very well, and newspaper reviews of their performances were excellent. Together with some male and female musicians, they formed a theatrical troupe of their own. In 1877, 'The Wonderful Bynes' came to Britain, touring the country and appearing in London, Wolverhampton, Gloucester, Hereford and other parts. But when they came to the Stuart Hall in Cardiff in April 1879, a very disagreeable letter appeared in the *Western Mail*. 'An Indignant Nonconformist' had seen a naughty poster for 'The Wonderful Bynes', with a picture of a gaudily attired female displaying a large amount of stocking. He wanted it to be confirmed that the Bynes did not, as had been rumoured, include either of that notorious pair, Boulton and Park.

Clearly, the immense prejudice against Boulton and Park was still out there. The Bynes took refuge on the Channel Islands for some months, hoping the homophobic nonconformist's letter would be speedily forgotten, as it deserved to be. But in January 1881, the columnist H. Chance Newton ('Carados' of the *Referee* newspaper) boldly stated that the once so notorious Ernest Boulton was still going in for female impersonations, now under the name Ernest Byne. After this cowardly disclosure, 'The Wonderful Bynes' disappeared for good. Frederick William Park, who was not the same person as 'Gerard Byne', went to New York, where he hoped to act under the name 'Fred Fenton', but his career failed and he died from syphilis in 1881, aged just thirty-four. At the time of the 1881 Census, 'Ernest Byne' was lodging at No. 21 Euston Street, St Pancras; he described himself as an actor, and gave his age as twenty-seven (he was at least thirty-three at the time). In 1882, Gerard Byne and Ernest Boulton resurfaced as the acting duo Gerard and Ernest Blair. The 'Brothers Blair' toured Britain performing various comedy routines, Gerard in male attire, Ernest in female dress. They had good success, and reviewers pointed out that Ernest was very funny, without being vulgar in the slightest degree. As the years went by, Ernest became a middle-aged drag queen, and success evaded him; when he died from a brain tumour in 1903, aged fifty-four, there was just enough money to pay for the funeral.

Wikipedia has a short and wayward entry on the Boulton and Park case, which concludes that it demonstrates the relative freedom of the Victorian homosexual sub-culture. This is not exactly the impression of a more astute observer, however, since without committing any crime, Boulton and Park were twice hounded out of the country by the hatred and prejudice against them. And what about Lord Arthur Clinton, who might have had to pay a much higher price for his indiscretions? The homophobic attitude to Boulton and Park, and what they represented, is well illustrated by the following deplorable limerick:

> There was an old person of Sark
> Who buggered a pig in the dark;
> The swine in surprise
> Murmured: 'God blast your eyes
> Do you take me for Boulton or Park?'

Mynheer van Klaes, the King of Smokers, 1872

In May 1872, the *IPN* could announce that one of the most eccentric characters in Holland had expired: Mynheer van Klaes, the celebrated King of Smokers. This gentleman had made a considerable fortune in the Indian linen trade, and settled down to spend his old age in a comfortable mansion he had erected for himself in Rotterdam. A handsome apartment in this house contained his Tobacco Museum, containing specimens of tobacco from all parts of the world; cigars, cigarettes and cigarillos of every description; and an enormous collection of pipes. There were pipes of every country and of every period, from those used by ancient barbarians to smoke hemp, to the splendid meerschaum and amber pipes, ornamented with carved figures and bands of gold, like those seen in the finest stores of Paris. The museum was open to visitors, to each of whom, after he had aired his knowledge on the subject of pipe-collecting, Mynheer van Klaes gave a pouch filled with tobacco and cigars, and a catalogue of the museum in a velvet cover.

A rotund, bald-headed figure, Mynheer van Klaes was seldom seen without his large Dutch pipe, at which he was puffing incessantly. Since his consumption of schnapps, genever and Dordrecht beer was also very considerable, many thought that van Klaes was not destined for a long and healthy life. But the sturdy Dutchman defied them all, living well into his eighties in his Rotterdam house, surrounded by a thick

The Singular History of Mynheer van Klaes, from the *IPN*, 18 May 1872.

cloud of tobacco smoke. Every day, Mynheer van Klaes smoked 150 grams of tobacco, and he died at the ripe old age of ninety-eight years; consequently, if we assume that he began to smoke when he was eighteen years old, he consumed in the course of his life 4,383 kilograms. If this quantity of tobacco could be laid down in a continuous black line, it would extend twenty French leagues.

When Mynheer van Klaes felt death approaching, he summoned a notary and dictated his will. After he had bequeathed the greater part of his fortune to relatives, friends, and charities, he added:

> I wish every smoker in the kingdom to be invited to my funeral in every way possible, by letter, circular, and advertisement. Every smoker who takes advantage of the invitation shall receive as a present ten pounds of tobacco, and two pipes on which shall be engraved my name, my crest, and the date of my death. The poor of the neighbourhood who accompany my bier shall receive every year on the anniversary of my death ten pounds of tobacco and a cask of good beer. I make the condition that all those who assist at my funeral, if they wish to partake of the benefits of my will, must smoke without interruption during the entire ceremony. My body shall be placed in a coffin lined throughout with the wood of my old Havana cigar-boxes. At the foot of the coffin shall be placed a box of the French tobacco called 'caporal' and a package of our old Dutch tobacco. At my side place my favourite pipe and a box of matches ... for one never knows what may happen. When the bier rests in the vault, all the persons in the funeral procession are requested to cast upon it the ashes of their pipes as they pass it on their departure from the grounds.

If we are to believe a waggish writer in the *Daily Telegraph*, this bizarre funeral ceremony was carried out just as planned, and when the words 'Ashes to ashes, dust to dust' were intoned, all the mourners emptied their pipes over the coffin. Since there was not much interesting news in May 1872, the curious story of van Klaes spread like wildfire: many provincial newspapers in Britain abstracted it, often with some facetious comments of their own. The *IPN* was the only paper to publish the portrait of this prodigious smoker. The story spread further to American, Australian and New Zealand papers, and got taller as it went along. Even the sombre *Lancet* quoted the case of van Klaes as a remarkable instance of tolerance of the human system of the excessive use of tobacco: the singular Dutchman had survived the fumes of more than four tons of this noxious weed! But when a monthly magazine for the tobacco trade, Cope's *Tobacco Plant*, made some inquiries in August 1872, they found that the story of the King of Smokers was pure fiction. An offer of a £100 reward to 'any person or persons who shall accord such information as shall lead to the identification of Mynheer van Klaes, the Smoking King of Rotterdam, and establish the correctness of the history propounded by the *Daily Telegraph*' was never claimed. But Cope's *Tobacco Plant* was not a widely read periodical, and as a result, the rotund figure of the King of Smokers has never gone up in smoke. In fact, the spectre of Mynheer van Klaes is still alive and well, puffing away merrily in various ill-researched modern books and articles about the history of tobacco smoking. Although there is today a curious Pipe Museum at the Prinzengracht in Amsterdam, its custodians have no knowledge of their alleged predecessor van Klaes, and they express incredulity as to his very existence.

Tragic Effects of Practical Joking, 1875

In Victorian times, fun-loving gentlemen involved in practical joking had to be aware that women and children were delicate creatures, with very sensitive nervous systems. Under no circumstances should they sneak up on women or children when wearing some kind of theatrical costume, since people dressed as devils or monsters could trigger the most dreadful hysterical attacks. In spite of these precautions on the part of the pranksters in disguise, there were some distressing incidents in late 1875, seized upon with glee by the *IPN*.

Mr Stackhouse, a fun-loving gentleman residing near Middleton, went to a rather jolly Christmas party in 1875, where he ate and drank well. His friends persuaded him to play the part of a clown in a pantomime, which he did to everyone's amusement. After the show, the inebriated Mr Stackhouse had to be helped home by his mischievous friends, who thought it very funny that he was still wearing the extravagant clown's outfit. But when Mr Stackhouse staggered into his bedroom, his wife thought a stranger had entered the house. She gave a series of piercing screams, which were followed by three hysterical fits. By the time the 1 January issue of the *IPN* went to press, she had still not recovered,

Mrs Stackhouse suffers a fit when she sees the drunken clown, and the dragon frightens the children out of their wits. In addition, for no extra charge, we have a madman up a steeple, a railwayman falling to his death, and an old man seeing a ghost and confessing to a murder committed thirty years earlier. Happy New Year to all, from the *IPN* editorial office, dated 1 January 1876!

and her life was despaired of. Mr Stackhouse was inconsolable, and his friends very much regretted their imprudent joking.

On 27 December 1875, only a few days after the mishap to poor Mrs Stackhouse, some other jolly young people were holding a Christmas party at Tatchet House in Derbyshire, the home of a wealthy gentleman named Johnson. When a mischievous and inebriated young man named Mr Brounger had dressed up in an elaborate dragon costume, he thought it would be very funny to burst into the room of some of his friends, to give them a fright. Unfortunately, he went into the nursery by mistake. Thinking it must be a real dragon, the children stampeded out of the room, screaming hysterically, and the nursemaid herself suffered a protracted fit. The *IPN* summed the situation up very succinctly: 'Two of the children were so frightened that for some time their lives were despaired of; and, indeed, it is very questionable if they ever recover from the terrible effect of the sudden fright. The maid-servant is seriously unwell in consequence. This incident, it is to be hoped, will act as a warning to hilarious young gentlemen who are fond of practical jokes.'

Laura Julia Addiscott, the Female Wackford Squeers, 1879

In 1877, the twenty-two-year-old Miss Laura Julia Addiscott went canvassing in Deptford and its surroundings, advertising her Home for Friendless Girls at No. 104 Deptford High Street. A demure, good-looking young lady, she described herself as a trained nurse and cook. She was born in Devonport and came from a respectable West Country family: her father James Lucas Addiscott was a customs officer, and she had four brothers and two sisters alive. Miss Addiscott had always been very religious, and she believed that God wanted her to help the destitute orphans of London's eastern suburbs. Many people were impressed with her obvious candour, and donated money to support the Home. A clergyman and a doctor volunteered their services, and a number of Friendless Girls were recruited from workhouses and children's homes. This would have been good if Miss Addiscott had restricted her reading to the Bible and various cookery and nursing manuals, but unfortunately for the Friendless Girls who entered her clutches, she was also a close student of *Nicholas Nickleby*, by one Mr Dickens.

Miss Addiscott advertised for Friendless Girls in the newspapers, and many people who had unwanted girls to spare, and money to support them, decided to deposit them in the Home. Soon, there were more than twenty inmates on the premises. Since Miss Addiscott was convinced that girls older than twelve were too old to go to school, and that those below that age should concentrate on studying the Good Book, she did not need to exert herself as an educator. Instead, she sent troops of girls out to collect money to support the Home, and ordered others to clean the house. Miss Addiscott's invalid mother also lived on the premises, but did no work at all. There was also a cook and a general servant, who took turns in supervising the Friendless Girls.

Miss Addiscott and some of her Friendless Girls, from the *IPN*, 16 August 1879.

In her first semi-annual report, Miss Addiscott stated that: 'The results and general good conduct of the inmates has encouraged us still to persevere in the effort to provide a shelter for the orphan and friendless – that they might find a home for a time and a glorious life through the Lord Jesus for eternity being our great aim.' And indeed, the local clergy and workhouse authorities appear to have regarded the Home for Friendless Girls a wholesome influence for good in Deptford and its surroundings. But although the girls were on their best behaviour when the workhouse guardians came to visit, trouble was brewing at the Home. Miss Addiscott was a stern disciplinarian, who always carried a large whip, which she made liberal use of to chastise her pupils. The hapless inmates were fed a starvation diet of bread, milk and rice; meat was only served on some Sundays, and on Christmas Day. A Friendless Girl who had the temerity to ask for a second helping received the full 'Oliver Twist' treatment from the furious Miss Addiscott. Another girl, who had gone begging for food instead of money, had a boot thrown into her face. Ellen Smith, a Friendless Girl whose sister was one of several children who had died at the Home, was scalded with hot coffee as a punishment for overturning a cup, and then chased downstairs by the virago Miss Addiscott, who belaboured her head and shoulders with a poker all the way down. A rolling-pin and a clothes-line were also made use of at times when no more suitable weapon was handy, to discipline the Friendless Girls.

If Miss Addiscott had established her Home in some desolate part of the country, she may well have got away with her scam for much longer, but the Deptford workhouse guardians found it strange that although her takings were relatively modest, the Home seemed to be prospering, and they decided to investigate. An unannounced inspection in early 1879 revealed that the girls were looking very thin and unwell. As soon as they were taken away from the Home, they told all about the cruel treatment and starvation diet. It was strongly suspected that several girls had died as a result of the wholesale neglect, and Miss Addiscott was arrested. On trial for the manslaughter of Kate Smith, a miserable, Smike-like waif who had died of tuberculosis at the Home, she was acquitted due to lack of evidence. But the workhouse guardians went on to prosecute the Female Wackford Squeers for assault and neglect of children, and a number of Friendless Girls provided some very damning evidence against her. Her barrister Mr Grain tried his best to cross-examine them: had they never been beaten by their own parents, and had they always had enough to eat when living at home? The often sordid motives of their families in disposing of them at the Home were exposed, and it looked like Miss Addiscott might well get off scot-free. But the workhouse guardians had made sure that the Friendless Girls had been examined by a competent doctor when they were removed from the Home, and he described them as being very emaciated, dirty and suffering from the itch, and their hair had to be cropped short since they were swarming with vermin. Miss Addiscott was exposed as a liar and a cheat: her nursing education was non-existent, her cookery skills unimpressive, and her religion just unctous bigotry. She was soundly hissed when taken out of court to begin an eighteen-month prison sentence.

There was much writing in the newspapers about the Deptford Girl's Home Scandal. A sneering editorial in the *Morning Post* commented that: 'The severe sentence passed upon Laura Julia Addiscott will, we hope, act as a wholesome warning to that increasing class of pseudo-philanthropists who, not being already provided for and having no taste for work, make a lazy and undignified living out of the pickings of charitable institutions.' The *Bury and Norwich Post* agreed that the case was a loathsome one, due to the terrible and brutal neglect: 'The wretched children placed under her care wandered about the streets in search of subscriptions, to return at night to stripes, squalor, and starvation.' Other newspapers, the *IPN* included, made some Dickensian puns about the weird goings-on at the Deptford 'Do-the-Girls Hall' and wondered what reflections the Female Wackford Squeers would make about 'wheels within wheels, a prison within a prison'. Laura Julia Addiscott is recorded to have left prison alive in 1881, changed her name to Louisa Addiscott, and moved in with her parents and siblings in lodgings at Wentworth Road, Mile End. She died under her assumed name in January 1882, from advanced tuberculosis according to her death certificate. As for the former Friend for Homeless Girls at No. 104 Deptford High Street, it has been changed into commercial premises and is now home to the Sea Food Centre.

Daring Robbery at Maria Marten's Cottage, 1883

The Red Barn at Polstead, where William Corder murdered Maria Marten in 1828, achieved considerable notoriety, since this was one of the first 'media murders'. Many people who had read about the romantic

MARIA MARTIN'S COTTAGE - SERIOUS ASSAULT

Maria Marten's cottage, from the *IPN*, 25 August 1883.

story of the pretty mole-catcher's daughter and her dalliance with the scoundrel Corder came to see Polstead, and the obscure Suffolk village became a tourist venue of some repute. The Red Barn and the Martens' cottage excited particular interest. The barn was stripped for souvenirs, and even the planks removed from the walls, broken up and sold as toothpicks. The Red Barn was planned to be demolished after the trial, but it was left standing and eventually burnt down in 1842. Even Maria Marten's gravestone, in St Mary's Churchyard, Polstead, was eventually chipped away to nothing by souvenir hunters.

Although she was just twenty-six years old when she was murdered in the Red Barn, Maria Marten had given birth to three illegitimate children, all with different fathers. Two of them died young, but Thomas Henry Marten, whose father Philip Matthews, a well-respected gentleman with relatives in Polstead, provided a regular allowance for the upkeep of his child, lived on for many years. At the time of the 1881 Census, Thomas Henry Marten, who now called himself Henry Martin, lived in Maria Marten's cottage in Polstead. At the age of fifty-six, he still worked as an agricultural labourer, and his sixty-one-year-old wife Isabella looked after the cottage. Through the kindness of the Revd T. A. Cooke, the impoverished labourer held the cottage at the nominal rent of a shilling a year. The cottage was in good order, and its garden well stocked with fruit trees.

On the early morning of 17 August 1883, Henry Martin left Maria Marten's cottage for a long day's work in the fields, leaving his wife behind. She locked the front door, but since she was busy with the laundry, she left the back door open and unlocked. At ten in the morning, while she was washing away in the backhouse, a man stepped in through the back door and seized hold of her with a hearty goodwill. 'Goodness gracious, what are you going to do?' the startled woman exclaimed. 'I will show you shortly what I am going to do!' the intruder growled, as he pulled her clothes over her head and wrestled her to the backhouse floor. With an oath, he ordered her to tell him where the money was kept, but this question she could not answer, since there was no money in the house. He then left her to ransack the house, but when Mrs Martin heard the noise and clatter as the thief rummaged through the house, she became quite desperate and began shouting 'Help! Murder!' The intruder returned with some large blankets and counterpanes, which he made use of to wrap her up tightly in their folds, threatening that he would murder her if she did not keep quiet. Baffled that the impoverished household seemed to possess nothing of any value, he stole Mrs Martin's wedding ring and ran off into the forest.

It took poor Mrs Martin two full hours to escape from the blankets and counterpanes that the ruffian had wrapped her up in. At just after twelve o'clock, the distraught old woman ran from the house into the road outside to give the alarm. Police Constable Noller was soon at the scene, but since the miscreant had got two hours' head start, the police were unable to find him, particularly since Mrs Martin had failed to see his face clearly during her ordeal. Mrs Martin had always been held in high esteem by her neighbours, as a quiet respectable woman, and there was much local sympathy for the old woman who had been so shamefully treated. The story of the Daring Robbery at Maria Marten's Cottage even made it into the national press, due to the notoriety of the place from the famous murder committed more than half a century earlier. Maria Marten's cottage still stands today, in Marten's Lane, Polstead.

The Lichfield Yeomanry Outrages, 1884

The Queen's Own Royal Staffordshire Yeomanry was one of several volunteer regiments raised in 1794 to repel foreign invasion. As we know, Napoleon never carried out a full-scale invasion of Britain, but the Staffordshire Yeomanry remained for many decades to come: a volunteer cavalry regiment run to archaic and feudal standards by the local nobility and gentry.

In June 1884, the Staffordshire Yeomanry went to Lichfield for its summer meeting, led by their Colonel, the wealthy magnate William

Bromley-Davenport, MP. He was sixty-three years old and had never seen active military service in his life, but still he was popular and respected, and known as the 'Father of the Regiment' for his long service. The Marquis of Anglesey was the Lieutenant-Colonel of the Staffordshire Yeomanry, and the Marquis of Stafford, Sir C. M. Wolseley, and other members of the aristocracy and gentry served as officers. The problem was that these officers had little authority over the men, and that some of them were irresponsible youngsters of a giddy and frolicsome disposition.

There was instant dislike between the Lichfield townsmen and the Staffordshire Yeomanry. The soldiers were rude and insulting, and the local police had no authority over them. Discipline was non-existent, and the troops were up to all kinds of mischief in town. When a party of officers from the Staffordshire Yeomanry attended a performance of Gilbert & Sullivan's *Queen Ida* by Mr D'Oyly Carte's theatrical ensemble, they behaved very obnoxiously, shouting and yahooing, and 'improving' the play with various coarse jokes. When the theatrical manager objected to this outrage, two of the officers frog-marched him to an upstairs room and locked him in. The officers then charged the stage, putting 'Queen Ida' and her fellow thespians to headlong flight.

In the meantime, troops of soldiers from the Staffordshire Yeomanry made their presence felt in Lichfield, drinking and carousing. Several public houses had extended their opening hours to accommodate the soldiery, and the foolishness of this soon became apparent. Fights broke out, and one soldier leapt onto a cart, pulled the driver's hat down over his eyes, and shoved him off the box. A soldier then cut one of the horses loose, and rode off on it. Another soldier, who had been knocked down by one of the enraged locals, was arrested by a party of police constables, but

The yeomanry officers assault Dr Johnson's statue in Lichfield, and other incidents from the riots, from the *IPN*, 28 June 1884.

Dr Johnson's statue in Lichfield, a postcard stamped and posted in 1907; the blacking had clearly been cleaned off the lexicographer's face by this time.

the other troopers charged the police and liberated their comrade in arms. Several constables were knocked down, and had their trousers pulled off. The young officers who had just put an end to the performance of *Queen Ida* had an even better idea, however: would it not be capital fun to deface the statue of Lichfield's most famous son, Dr Samuel Johnson?

The statue of the great lexicographer at Market Square in Lichfield had been erected in 1838, on a tall plinth with railings to protect it from vandals. But the young officers got hold of a tall ladder and a large bottle of 'Nubian Black', which they made use of to blacken Dr Johnson's face. Major Graves had alerted Colonel Bromley-Davenport to his officers and soldiers running riot in town, and the elderly officer came up to plead with the soldiers to return to their makeshift barracks. They did not obey him, however, and the major shortly after saw the hapless colonel lurch off towards Yeomanry House; on his way there, he dropped dead in the street.

There was consternation among both the military and civilian inhabitants of Lichfield at Colonel Bromley-Davenport's unexpected demise. At first, it was thought that one of the enraged locals had murdered him, but Major Graves had seen no other person nearby, and the colonel had been unwell with heart disease for some time. At the inquest, a verdict of death from natural causes was returned. The verdict of the press on the Lichfield Yeomanry Outrages was a more severe one, however. In spite of acrid soap and bristly brushes being applied to Dr Johnson's face, the application of 'Nubian Black' was still obvious. One of the police constables had himself had his face daubed with blacking, and several others had been assaulted and debagged. Windows had been broken, and innocent townsmen beaten up. What kind of soldiers were these coarse yeomanry brutes, and what about the officers who had actually led the assault on Dr Johnson? They ought to be drummed out of the regiment! Other newspaper editors called for the entire regiment to be disbanded, and claimed that the Marquess of Anglesey, who had taken command after the untimely death of his superior officer, had deliberately misled the journalists about the extent of the rioting.

But in the end, the officers and men of the Staffordshire Yeomanry appear to have got off more or less scot-free. This lenience did not have the desired effect: when the regiment met in Lichfield in June 1885, there were again fights with the police. Windows were broken, and Dr Johnson's face daubed with blacking a second time! But just as the great lexicographer's face was eventually cleaned up by the locals, the equally black stain on the reputation of the Staffordshire Yeomanry was removed by the regiment's valiant wartime conduct. The Staffordshire Yeomanry did well in both World Wars, equipped with horses in the first and tanks in the second. The regiment was amalgamated with another yeomanry unit in 1992, and no longer exists. In contrast, Dr Johnson's statue still stands in Lichfield, proving that in the end, the pen is mightier than the sword.

Dick Schick, the Female Errand-Boy, 1886

In January 1886, a cheeky-looking young lad who gave his name as Dick Schick was employed as an errand-boy by Messrs Goodman & Davis, the Oxford Street tailors. Dick said that he was fifteen years old, and that since his mother's work as a furrier could not support the family, he decided to get a job himself. Dick seemed an honest and upright young lad, and although he had a fondness for drinking and smoking at various pubs, his partying habits did not differ much from those of other young London errand-boys. But worryingly, various garments started disappearing from the tailor's shop. Another boy was dismissed on suspicion, but the thefts continued. One day, Mr Davis saw that the dapper-looking Dick Schick was wearing a pair of trousers and a waistcoat made from his own stolen material! He collared Dick and took him to the Tottenham Court Road police station, but for reasons undisclosed, he decided against pressing charges.

After being fired by Goodman & Davis in June 1886, Dick quickly secured another job as an errand-boy, this time for the respectable glover Frederick Noble Jones, of Burlington Arcade. His mother, Mrs Lois Eunice Schick, gave him a good character. When gloves and other garments started disappearing, Dick became a suspect. This time, the cunning Dick wrote an anonymous note blaming another boy, but after this individual had been dismissed, the thieving continued. One day in October, Mr Jones got the idea to compare the anonymous letter with some of Dick's handwriting; they were an excellent match. The police raided the Schick lodgings and found some of the missing garments, along with forty pawn tickets for other items of clothing. This was not the only noteworthy discovery of the day, however; when examined by a doctor, 'Dick' turned out to be not just a Schick, but a 'chick'. The twenty-year-old Miss Lois Schick had successfully masqueraded as a fifteen-year-old London errand-boy for nearly a year.

The impecunious clerk William Schick, said to have been of German extraction, had used to lodge at No. 78 Elmore Street, Islington, with his wife Lois Eunice; here, they hatched seven little Schicks, five of whom survived infancy. The 1881 census has William working as an 'advertising clerk', whereas his wife and his eldest daughter Lois, born in March 1866 and later to become 'Dick', were both 'machinists'. After the death of William Schick in March 1882, the family became near-destitute. Mrs Schick worked as a furrier for a while, and her teenage daughters Lois and Mary also tried to find work, albeit with little success.

There was a good deal of writing about the Female Errand-Boy in the London newspapers, although they did not quite get her name right, calling her Schwick or Schwich instead of Schick. Motivated by a mixture of sensationalism and vague proto-feminist sentiments, the rabble-rousing editor W. T. Stead tried to put a spin on the 'Dick Schick' case in his *Pall Mall Gazette*: was it not a shame that young women were so discriminated against with regard to finding employment, and had young Lois Schick not been forced by poverty to don male attire? Some other newspapers followed suit, calling young Lois a brave lass who had just wanted to

Lois Schick, the Boy Moore and other players in the case, from the *IPN*, 30 October 1886.

get a job and support her family. In an interview, Mrs Schick praised her daughter for helping to save her younger siblings from starvation. There was even a Schick Relief Fund, organised by the solicitor Bernard Abrahams; in its first week, it collected £10.

The *IPN* found the 'Dick Schick' case quite hilarious, and published portraits of its leading characters, including the heroine herself. Also featured was 'The Boy Moore', a young Soho sword-maker who had liked to drink and smoke with 'Dick', allegedly without suspicion that his friend was actually a woman. 'Dick' had once given him a (stolen) handkerchief, saying, 'Here is a present for you; we must "lush" together when we go out!'

When Lois Schick was charged with theft at the Marlborough-street police court on 13 October 1886, she seemed quite undeterred by having to wear her male attire in court, looking as cheeky as ever. The momentum was clearly against her, however: in relentless testimony, her career of dishonesty was exposed. In particular, it was considered 'not cricket' that this artful young woman had twice successfully 'framed' other errand-boys for the thefts, causing them to be dismissed from their jobs. The credibility of Mrs Schick was seriously harmed after it had been exposed that she had clearly acted as her daughter's accomplice, through providing her with a false reference and hiding the stolen goods. An uncharitable clergyman wrote a letter to the *Lloyd's Weekly Newspaper* to point out that the Schick family had been supported by the parish for some time, that Lois' younger sister Mary had found employment without resorting to cross-dressing, and that Lois had actually posed as 'a nephew' for four years or more. At the Middlesex Sessions, Lois Schick was later sentenced to eight months in prison with hard labour, for stealing articles to the value of £75.

The almost incredible tale of 'Dick Schick', a jolly, cross-dressing working-class girl amusing herself in Victorian London's shady underworld, and 'nicking' some new trousers when she felt like it, seems rather like the theme for a ribald and explicit modern novel; still, the facts are well verified through independent newspaper accounts, and supported by census and demographic records. We know, from the case of Boulton and Park, that London had an established upper-class male homosexual and transvestite underworld. It is very likely there were also regular haunts for young women wearing men's clothes. Lois Schick's motives for cross-dressing were clearly not merely to facilitate her criminal career, since she had been wearing male attire for three years before starting her career as a dishonest errand-boy.

But what happened to Lois Schick after she had been released from prison? She completely disappeared. Although it is still possible to follow the humble careers of the other Schicks in various demographic records, like for example her mother who expired in late 1905, Lois herself is nowhere to be found in the genealogical records. Did she emigrate to the United States, or perhaps start a new life as 'Dick Brown' in some London suburb? The Ancestry genealogical database provides two possible sightings of 'Dick': a thirty-year-old Miss Lois Schick departed from London for Thursday Island in August 1899, on the ship *Zaida*, and a sixty-nine-year-old Lois Schick, described as white and widowed, was lodging at No. 47 Harrison Street, Sussex, New Jersey, at the time of the 1940 US Census. We can only speculate whether either of these sightings concerns the erstwhile 'Dick', and whether her life, which began as a hilarious picaresque novel, ended up in oblivion, tragi-comedy, or premature death as a recluse.

Mystery at Mr Cooke's School of Anatomy

Born in Buffalo, New York, in 1841, Thomas Cooke was the only son of Mr John Hawley Cooke, a Shrewsbury gentleman, and his wife Jane, the daughter of the Hon. Richard Hawley. His globetrotting parents took him to Paris as an infant, and he was later privately educated there, before becoming a medical student. Thomas Cooke graduated in 1862 and set out to become an anatomist. He made excellent progress as a medical scientist, but the Siege of Paris put an end to his prospects in late 1870. After moving to London, he managed to become Demonstrator of Anatomy and Physiology, and Assistant Surgeon, at Westminster Hospital. One of the high points in his rather sad life came the year after, when he made a favourable marriage to Aglae, the daughter of the Comte de Hamel de Manin.

Thomas Cooke was proud of the superior anatomical education he had received in Paris, and hopeful of a brilliant career in London's medical world. His colleagues at the Westminster Hospital agreed that Thomas Cooke was a skilful anatomist and useful teacher. Unfortunately for him, they also agreed that he was a clumsy, dangerous surgeon, incapable of adapting to the Listerian principles of antisepsis. When vacancies occurred at the hospital, he was not promoted to full surgeon, and he was eventually relieved of all clinical duties. For obvious reasons, he was also unable to set himself up in private practice.

In 1875, the chagrined Mr Cooke decided to open his own anatomy school. Controversially, he did so in his own home, No. 31 New Bridge Street, Blackfriars. Not unsurprisingly, the neighbours were soon up in arms against this malodorous enterprise in private medical education. In January 1877, they had Mr Cooke prosecuted at the Guildhall Police Court. When the police had raided the premises, they had found a putrid human body, and the equally seasoned cadavers of a rabbit and a large baboon. The magistrate Sir Thomas Gabriel declared Mr Cooke's School of Anatomy a

Mr Cooke's portrait, from the *Graphic*,
18 February 1899.

THE LATE MR. THOMAS COOKE

nuisance and ordered it to be closed down forthwith. Mr Cooke complied,
although he lamented that it would cost him £500. Some ribald writing
in the London newspapers prompted the anatomist to complain, in the
Medical Times & Gazette, how harshly he had been treated at the police
court, and how severely he had been libelled in the press.

But Mr Cooke was a very stubborn man. Oblivious to the argument
that private medical schools were a thing of the past, more suited to
Dickens' Bob Sawyer than to modern medical education, or the equally
potent argument that London's great teaching hospitals already had
perfectly good anatomy departments, he was hell-bent on setting up his
School of Anatomy at a more suitable location. The persistent anatomist
purchased a plot in an old graveyard at the corner of Handel Street and
Henrietta Mews, Bloomsbury, which was large enough for the anatomy
school not to stink down the neighbourhood, or so at least he presumed.
The new school was ready in 1878. It was entered from a small gate
in Henrietta Mews, a notice over the door having the sign 'Anatomy,
Physiology, and Surgery'. Mr Cooke's new School of Anatomy had a large
dissecting-room, a laboratory, and an anatomical tank full of corrosive
sublimate [mercury chloride], in which not less than seventeen cadavers
could be stored. There were no close neighbours, since the anatomy
school was surrounded by the old graveyard, with the tombstones
remaining. This had once been the joint burial ground of St George's
Church, Bloomsbury Way, and St George the Martyr, Queen Square, but
burials had ceased in 1855.

But once more, the neighbours in Handel Street were soon up in
arms against the anatomy school. Not only did they feel that such an
establishment should not exist outside an established hospital, they also

alleged that insanitary smells emanated from the dissecting-room. But this time, Mr Cooke fared better when summoned before the sanitary authorities of St Pancras in July 1880. He pointed out that his school was 106 feet away from the nearest building, and 350 feet away from the house of the main complainant. He managed to persuade the authorities that his anatomy school was a modern, sanitary enterprise, and that its position could not be better. A deputation of the local inhabitants tried to force their way into the courtroom, quite possibly to lynch the anatomist, but they were ordered to retire by two sturdy police constables. Mr Cooke had won the day, although he continued to be very unpopular locally. Rotten vegetables were thrown at his coach, and the windows of the anatomy school were surreptitiously broken.

The 1881 Census finds Mr Cooke and his family at No. 16 Woburn Place, not far from his anatomy school. He was thirty-nine years old at the time, and his wife Aglae thirty-seven. They had five children, of whom the eldest son Granville was at Charterhouse, his private school. The young daughters Florence and Evelyn were at home, as were their brothers Francis and Reginald. Four medical students lodged in the large house, and the Cookes employed four servants. Mr Cooke was an enthusiastic teacher, and by some stratagem or other, he was also able to ensure that his school's supply of cadavers exceeded those of the London teaching hospitals. As a result, many a backward medical student took classes to brush up his anatomy there before the exams, and London's only private anatomy school flourished. The dissecting room was never short of pupils, and in spite of his failed hospital career, and lack of private practice, Mr Cooke made a comfortable living as an anatomy teacher, with more than a hundred pupils a year.

One of Mr Cooke's early pupils was John Bland-Sutton, later to become a distinguished surgeon. In his memoirs *The Story of a Surgeon*, Sir John Bland-Sutton, as he had become, had nothing but good to say about Mr Cooke. The anatomy school was large and well attended, and the supply of cadavers excellent. 'Cooke was an admirable teacher and had a system of his own, teaching over the freshly dissected body; and the course was so arranged that the whole of the body was quickly reviewed in three months. With a good class there was a brisk round of questions and answers for an hour, often enlightened with sallies of wit and repartee, brilliant and delightful.' Mr Cooke wrote a series of cram-books, popularly known as 'Cooke's Tablets', which he printed himself at the anatomy school. Since Bland-Sutton was an excellent anatomist, Mr Cooke offered him a salaried post as his demonstrator at the anatomy school, but due to the establishment's dubious reputation, he turned it down. Instead, Mr Cooke employed an impecunious young doctor named Edward Knight as his assistant, and this individual would remain associated with the school for many years.

Mr Cooke remained fearful that the locals would be up to mischief, and try to vandalise his anatomy school. He had a cottage erected adjacent to it, to house a night watchman, and also a shed for the storage of his printing press and his stockpile of anatomy books. In early 1886, a suspicious fire was started at the premises, and a number of Mr Cooke's valuable anatomical specimens were destroyed. Mr Cooke blamed the night watchman for being in cahoots with the locals, conspiring to burn his school down. He evicted the watchman and instead rented the cottage to a man named Henry Walker, sewerman to St Pancras Parish. Mr Cooke equipped his new tenant with a pistol, for use against potential vandals and arsonists. Henry Walker had strong political interests: in spite of his humble background and employment, he was a stout-hearted Conservative, and a great enemy of Irish Home Rule. A soap box orator, the 'English Orangeman', as he was called, kept haranguing the people of Bloomsbury, although crowds of Irish labouring men made threats to lynch him.

In early October 1887, Henry Walker came to the Hunter Street police station, to report that someone had tried to murder him! Late the previous evening, he had come home from a political meeting, noticing a cab parked nearby. When he and his son sat down in the front parlour, they saw a shadowy figure outside and heard two shots, and a report like if something had struck the window. The two Walkers ran upstairs and hid in their beds. The morning after, a neighbour found a pellet embedded in the window frame, and another on the ground nearby. The evening of the shooting, Walker had spoken at an open-air political meeting,

The watchman Henry Walker is under fire, from the *IPN*, 8 October 1887.

ALLEGED MOONLIGHTING OUTRAGE IN ST PANCRAS

trouncing his Irish opponent severely, and as a result, some Fenian roughs had threatened his life. The police questioned whether some political enemy had tried to murder Walker, or if the night watchman had been mistaken for the unpopular Mr Cooke? Walker was congratulated by the President of the local Conservative Association for his narrow escape. A journalist alleged that in spite of making use of phrases like 'dastardly attempt' and 'cowardly Moonlighters', Walker had shuddered visibly when reminded of the awful danger he was in, although he had been given police protection. But a *Pall Mall Gazette* journalist suspected that the alleged assassination attempt was nothing but a hoax: Walker had in fact not been seconded by a single person at the political meeting, and the only threats had been uttered by himself. He might well have made use of the pistol provided by Mr Cooke to fake the alleged attack. Why had Mrs Walker not heard the shots, why had Walker not raised the alarm until the next morning, and why had he not returned fire at the suspected assassin?

After the events of 1886 and 1887, Mr Cooke went on to enjoy a period of relative calm at his School of Anatomy. The students kept coming, and business remained brisk. But in the late 1890s, the establishment started to decline, since Mr Cooke was not getting any younger: his teaching had always been old-fashioned, and he was unable to keep up with modern medical science. Mr Cooke died from a burst aortic aneurysm in 1899, not while demonstrating at his school, as his biographers have alleged, but at his house in No. 40 Brunswick Square. He was succeeded by his second son Dr Francis Gerard Cooke, who had previously assisted him at the school, along with the stalwart Edward Knight, but in spite of their efforts, the decline of the school continued. Young Cooke left in 1904, to take up a position in India, but the persistent Knight remained at the premises. In spite of its outdated premises and equipment, the improved anatomy teaching at the London medical schools, the Great War, and various other calamities, the Cooke School of Anatomy struggled on until 1920. It has been presumed, by a competent medical historian, that the old anatomy school was closed and demolished in or around 1920. But some very queer goings-on in 1925 indicate otherwise.

Thomas Cooke's oldest son, Granville Hawley Egerton Cooke, born in 1872, received a superior education at Charterhouse, and at Bonn University. When he married Mabel Violet Wright in 1896, he was still living in his father's house at No. 40 Brunswick Square. The scapegrace Granville Cooke tried his hand as a poet, an inventor, and an authority on bicycles and motor cars, but without any success. In 1897, he thought of a disastrous scheme to 'get rich quick'. He opened a bogus private employment agency, offering to find people work for a fee of 3s 6d. More than 1,000 letters were sent to his alleged 'office', a poste restante box in Old Street, many of them enclosing money, and Granville prospered briefly as a result. But two men he had promised employment charged him with obtaining money on false pretences, and in March 1898, he was prosecuted at the Clerkenwell police court. There was no doubt that the 'London and Provincial Employment Agency' was a bluff, and that Granville Cooke had swindled hundreds of people out of their paltry 3s 6d. The only defence his barrister could think of was that his client was the son of a respectable medical practitioner, and that he had recently been ill, so that he could not open the letters in the Old Street office. In May 1898, Granville was sentenced to twelve months' hard labour at the Old Bailey, the Common Serjeant adding that since offences of this kind were getting far too common, his punishment was very well deserved. Granville had a previous conviction for obtaining 5s 6d on false pretences in July 1896.

Granville Cooke's life of pointless and cowardly crimes continued. Emerging from jail in late 1899, he was employed as a traveller by a Huddersfield bicycle shop owner named Hubert Brooks. Granville went around on his bicycle to deliver spares and accessories to dealers and customers. But various bicycle parts kept disappearing from Mr Brooks' shop, and Granville was soon suspected. He was found to have stockpiled twenty-one bicycle air tubes, seventeen brakes, nine bells, thirteen bags and various other property, to the value of £50 in all. The stolen property was recovered, and at the Liverpool Assizes, Granville was sentenced to three years' penal servitude. While in prison, he savagely attacked a warder who had annoyed him, and was soundly whipped as a punishment.

After being released from Maidstone Gaol in July 1904, Granville Cooke was soon again in court, this time seeking divorce from his wife Mabel. Much dirty laundry was hung out to dry, revealing the gramophone salesman Granville Cooke's dalliance with his young typist Mary Hawthorne, and Mabel's adulterous affairs with two men named George Mason and the Hon. Charles Gordon Duff. Mabel's barrister made sure that Granville Cooke's life of dishonesty was mercilessly revealed, but at the end of the divorce trial, Granville was granted a decree nisi, and custody of the couple's young son Cyril Athelston Cooke: the judge clearly thought his wife as bad as Granville.

In 1910, Granville Cooke made a rare appearance in court as plaintiff: he had fallen foul of a gang of racecourse blackguards led by a billiards instructor named Arthur Smythe, and been cheated out of £120. These individuals had thought of an elaborate scheme to make drunken 'plungers' believe that the results of various horse-races had been fixed, and that a vast syndicate was controlling their outcome. Granville made a surprisingly good impression in court, saying that after being heartily ashamed of his past exploits, he had changed his name to Egerton Hawley, in order not to embarrass his respectable family any more. Under this name, he had earned an honest living for three years, as a civil engineer taking out patents in connection with the motor trade. In the end, Smythe was convicted of fraud, and sentenced to four months in prison.

After lying low during the Great War, Granville Cooke resurfaced in 1920, with a poem entitled 'Cry Not Farewell', honouring the war dead. His career reached an unexpected high when he received a letter of acceptance from Queen Alexandra. It then plumbed an all-time low when he was convicted for converting to his own use money obtained for St Dunstan's Blind Institute from the sale of copies of this poem, and sentenced to eighteen months in prison. After emerging from prison, he married a much younger woman named Bertha Scott, but she left him in 1925 on account of his dissolute life. A sturdy, barrel-chested cove, Granville smoked like a chimney and drank like the proverbial fish. He gambled hard and frequently lost, and tried various cowardly scams selling patents and inventions, at times narrowly escaping prosecution.

In early 1925, after his wife had left him, the now fifty-three-year-old Granville Cooke moved into the cottage at Mr Cooke's School of Anatomy. This was the very same cottage that had been at the centre of the alleged 'moonlighting' scandal back in 1887. With him was his young friend Selwyn Foster, the scapegrace son of a recently deceased Yorkshire wool merchant. A harum-scarum, scatter-brained young man, he had given Granville control of his affairs, something that this experienced fraudster used to extort money from the wealthy Foster family. Although lacking any medical education, Granville Cooke took possession of the School of Anatomy. His brother Francis was in India, and although Edward Knight was still alive, he had left the school and was in very indifferent health. Granville used the school laboratory for his chemical experiments, and built up a stockpile of poisons; enough, he declared, to kill all Londoners. He was delighted to find a headless corpse in the anatomical tank, and proudly demonstrated it to his lady friends. Granville Cooke and Selwyn Foster led a riotous life at the School of Anatomy. Granville rummaged around in the laboratory, and tried his best to write some poems, but young Foster slept all day and was awake all night. Every evening, the two friends went out partying, often bringing some young floozies with them to the School of Anatomy in the wee hours.

The little cottage inhabited by Granville Cooke and Selwyn Foster had not seen a lick of paint for decades, and Granville made use of some of his friend's money to restore it. The two workmen he employed, Harold Skinner and Samuel Pearson, found the cottage in a most dilapidated state. There was a kitchen, a sitting-room and two bedrooms, one of them occupied by the stuporous Selwyn Foster. Granville Cooke could not decide whether he wanted to occupy the cottage himself, or let it to some card-sharpers for a good figure. His mother, the erstwhile Countess Aglae, came to visit Granville more than once. She told the workmen about the School of Anatomy's former glory, and her late husband's troubles with the locals. Once, Mr Cooke had 300 students there at one time. Remarkably, she added that Mr Cooke had a tunnel constructed from his house in Brunswick Square to the anatomy school, so that he and the students who lodged with him could travel to the school in safety, without being pelted by the angry locals; this tunnel had since been boarded up. The bonhomous Granville Cooke showed the two slack-jawed workmen the dissecting-room, the headless corpse, and his stockpile of poisons.

On 1 April 1925, when the two workmen came to the cottage at Mr Cooke's School of Anatomy, they found the lifeless bodies of Granville Cooke and Selwyn Foster. Two of the oven taps were on, and the room was full of gas. 'Two Men Dead! Mystery of School of Anatomy!' said *The Times*, 'Discoveries at House of Death!' exclaimed the *Daily Mirror*, and 'London's Mystery House!' was the headline of the *IPN*. Thirty detectives were working hard to solve this mysterious case. Was this a suicide pact, murder-suicide, or a case of double murder? They searched the mystery house throughout the night, taking up the floors and removing piles of documents. A strong force of police constables was needed to keep out the crowd of sightseers, who had come to admire London's House of Mystery.

Granville Cooke's disastrous career was soon exposed in the newspapers, including that he had recently been frequenting some very dubious boxing clubs to find 'the Great White Hope', and that he associated with a gang of forgers. Had he poisoned his friend and then gassed himself? Selwyn Foster had recently served a term of five months' imprisonment for false pretences, something that was said to have broken his respectable mother's heart. Still, this disreputable pair had led a jolly life at the School of Anatomy, and Granville Cooke had clearly been making plans for the future. At the coroner's inquest on the two men, an impressive number of journalists were in attendance, hoping for some juicy titbits about the drama at London's Mystery House. Mrs Bertha Cooke, becomingly dressed in a black sealskin coat [said the *Daily Mirror*; the seals would hardly have agreed], said that her husband had always been very careless with the gas, since he was often drunk, and his sense of smell quite defective. She had recently received some long and rambling letters from him, but they had contained nothing to suggest that he was planning to destroy himself.

Mrs Emily Foster, mother of young Selwyn, said that her son had always been foolish and easily led, and his mental condition had been far from good. He had obtained funds by selling reversionary interests in his father's estate, something she had very much disapproved of. The post-mortem examination indicated that both men had died from carbon monoxide poisoning. There were some dirty and greasy glasses on the table, but they contained nothing poisonous. Selwyn Foster had some caked amorphous powder around his mouth, but again this was no

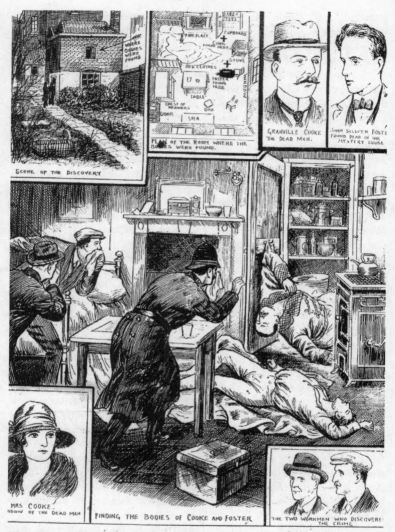

LONDON'S MYSTERY HOUSE.— MEN'S BODIES IN ROOM.

Mr Cooke's School of Anatomy, and other sketches concerning London's Mystery House, from the *IPN*, 9 April 1925.

poison. The inquest was adjourned, and speculation was rife about the goings-on in London's Mystery House. The two workmen Harold Skinner and Samuel Pearson sold an exclusive interview to the *Daily Chronicle* about their singular meeting with Granville Cooke and his mother just a few days before his death. The death certificates for Granville Cooke and John Selwyn Foster, signed by Mr Walter Schröder, the Coroner for London, give the cause of death as carbon monoxide poisoning, leaving it open how the escape of gas had come about.

Mr Cooke's School of Anatomy was pulled down soon after the tragedy. But for an illustration in that valuable newspaper the *IPN*, we would not even have known what it looked like. The Wellcome Collection has some photographs of two odd-looking coves rummaging around on the premises, and posing with a cadaver and a skeleton, said to be dating from the 1920s. They are definitely genuine, but the men are not Granville Cooke and Selwyn Foster, perhaps rather Edward Knight and his assistant. Today, the site of the old anatomy school is part of St George's Gardens. Henrietta Mews still exists, just off Handel Street on the western boundary of the gardens. There is still a door in the boundary wall, one that once might have had the sign 'Anatomy, Physiology, and Surgery'. Interestingly, there are also some buildings remaining, including an old cottage, but its proportions and the location of its chimneys do not match those of London's Mystery House, as judged from the sketch in the *IPN*. These buildings can be seen already on the 1871 Ordnance Survey map of North Bloomsbury, whereas Mr Cooke's anatomy school and its adjoining cottage were not constructed until seven years later.

I am reliably informed that the former site of Mr Cooke's School of Anatomy is not haunted. To a close student of the works of Elliott O'Donnell, the Great Ghost-Hunter, this sounds well-nigh incredible. Surely there must be a phantom coach, pelted by some spectral guttersnipes, a ghostly Irishman firing off his pistol at the Cottage of Death, and a weird dissecting-room scene enacted by headless corpses, with the anatomist emerging from a hidden tunnel like a jack-in-the box? And surely, the site must also be haunted by a sturdy, inebriated ghost, surrounded by a cloud of nebulous gas, making a theatrical gesture and declaiming:

> Cry not farewell, O anguish-stricken heart,
> When cruel death tears loving ones apart,
> Be not disconsolate, though hope has fled,
> And all worth cherishing on earth is dead ...

The Sleeping Frenchman of Soho, 1887

In March 1887, a Frenchman named M. Chauffat came to stay at the Hotel Français at No. 36 Greek Street, Soho. A native of Annecy, Haute Savoie, Chauffat was a commercial traveller, employed by a French wine merchant, and he had been to London before. Albeit a middle-aged man,

M. Chauffat was keen to go partying in the Metropolis. Along with two other hotel guests, he went to a club in Rathbone Place, and then to the Hotel de Paris in Leicester Square. The others had had enough, but the 'party animal' Chauffat went on to a house (or perhaps rather brothel) in Tottenham Court Road, riding in a cab along with two 'ladies' who had invited him there. Inside the house, the drunken Frenchman was robbed of £32 and a gold watch, and then unceremoniously kicked out of the premises.

Several people saw the dazed Chauffat bumbling around in Tottenham Court Road, including the cabman who had driven him there. But when the Frenchman appealed to him for help, the cab driver just grimaced and drove away in his vehicle. Clearly, he had been in cahoots with the two deceitful 'ladies' who had decoyed Chauffat to the house of ill-repute. Since Chauffat could not speak a word of English, and since he did not know where to find the Hotel Français, he was in immediate danger of further misadventures. Fortunately, a kind lady rescued him and took him back to the hotel in a cab. Too drunk (and perhaps also ashamed) to explain what had happened, Chauffat just lurched up to his bedroom.

But strangely, this strange Frenchman did not get out of bed again. At first, M. Bougeret the hotel-keeper thought that he was just 'sleeping it off', but after a few days, Dr Jean Keser from the French Hospital was called in. Dr Keser found his patient in a state of deep lethargy, and it was impossible to rouse him by shouts, pinches, or shining a strong light into his eyes. Chauffat had lost one of his arms in active service in the Franco-Prussian war, but otherwise his physical health seemed quite good. He did not appear drunk or drugged. The inner pocket of his coat contained a card stating that he was under treatment at the famous Salpetrière hospital in Paris for a dangerous form of catalepsy. If he was found in a state of nervous collapse or profound sleep, he should immediately be returned to that hospital, under the care of Dr Jean-Marie Charcot.

The problem was who would pay for the transportation of this lethargic patient back to the Paris hospital. The Tottenham Court Road robbers had done a thorough job, leaving the Sleeping Frenchman of Soho entirely penniless. Dr Keser worried about his fees, and M. Bougeret was fearful that his soporific countryman might not be able to pay his hotel bill. Dr Keser spread the word about his singular patient in London's medical world, and on 30 March, Sir William MacCormac, Dr Beevor and Mr Brudenell Carter went with him to the Hotel Français, where M. Chauffat was fast asleep in the top-floor front room. The doctors found the lifeless figure in the bed very interesting, and tried various experiments to try to stimulate his nervous system. They found it curious that if the Frenchman's arm was raised, it remained in an upright position until pushed down again. When his large bushy moustache was pulled, he grimaced with pain. M. Chauffat was unable to move his extremities voluntarily, or to take any nourishment. The doctors pronounced his case one of the most extraordinary ever seen in Britain.

There was not a lot of interesting news in March and April 1887, and the Sleeping Frenchman of Soho soon became a newspaper celebrity. The *Standard* and other newspapers published daily reports about his condition. On 1 April, another party of medical men went to see Chauffat, and his case was discussed in a leading article in the *Lancet*. After a week in bed, the Frenchman was getting seriously hungry, and he drank *bouillon* and brandy with avidity, even being able to masticate some bread. A frolicsome young doctor suggested that the itching-powder should be applied, or that some noxious substance should be mixed with the patient's soup, but Dr Keser did not allow such indignities to his famous patient. When '*Ouvrez les yeux!*' was shouted into the Frenchman's ear, his eyelids twitched. Dr Charcot had not answered the letter appealing for help, and both Dr Keser and M. Bougeret were becoming increasingly fearful that their bills would not be paid. Moreover, inquiries had revealed that Chauffat had no wealthy *tante d'heritance* to pay his medical bills; his parents were both dead, and his four sisters in a feeble state of health themselves. On 7 April, Dr Keser made an appeal in the *Morning Post*, asking the generous Londoners for contributions to the Chauffat Relief Fund, intended to pay the penniless Frenchman's bills in London, and to assist his repatriation to his native land.

On 9 April, when the Sleeping Frenchman of Soho was featured in the *IPN*, he was still in a state of deep lethargy, although now capable of moving his extremities, and of taking nourishment. When the musician M. Boichet, of the Hippodrome, played the 'Marseillaise' on the oboe to cheer up his soporific countryman, M. Chauffat professed not to recognise the tune, 'and seemed anything but pleased with the performance'. But on 16 April, the Sleeping Frenchman of Soho was finally out of bed after his nineteen-day slumber: he finished his morning toilet, wrote some letters, and read about himself in the French newspapers with great interest.

The hotel at No. 36 Greek Street, a portrait of M. Chauffat, and the doctors examining the Sleeping Frenchman of Soho, from the *IPN*, 9 April 1887.

'The Soho Sleeper wakes up!' announced the *Lloyd's Weekly Newspaper* of 17 April. The Chauffat Relief Fund had enjoyed considerable success, and after all his London bills had been paid, there was still enough money to convey the patient to Paris, where Dr Charcot made sure he was taken into hospital. Eschewing patient confidentiality, this distinguished neuro-psychiatrist wrote a newspaper bulletin of his own, pooh-poohing the London doctors' great interest in the Sleeping Frenchman of Soho. M. Chauffat was just a hysterical patient whose illness assumed the form of 'attacks of sleep' rather than convulsive attacks. Such cases were by no means rare in France, he pontificated: there was, at the present time, a woman at the Salpetrière Hospital who had been asleep for months.

In August 1887, M. Bougeret the hotel-keeper in Greek Street wrote to the newspapers that the Sleeping Frenchman of Soho was still under Dr Charcot in a Paris hospital. In November 1888, M. Chauffat was back in London, where he suffered another attack of catalepsy. But although his attending physician Dr Speed wrote to the *Lancet* and the London newspapers, nobody was much interested in last year's celebrity. The Sleeping Frenchman woke up after a few weeks, probably dismayed at the lack of publicity. Nothing is known about M. Chauffat's later vicissitudes, but it is curious that the old hotel at No. 36 Greek Street, where this marathon sleeper once held court, looks virtually unchanged since 1887, although the ground floor is now an oriental restaurant. If I had been able to afford it, I would have purchased the freehold of this historic house, to live in the upper floors. In spite of the busy nightlife of those parts, it would surely have been easy to enjoy a refreshing night's sleep in the chamber vacated by the Sleeping Frenchman of Soho. The ground floor should of course be a *French* restaurant, named 'The Snoring Frog', where I would have a reserved table to enjoy a meal of *escargots*, *grenouilles* and *hômards*.

Miss Vint and Her Reincarnated Cats, 1892

Early October 1892 was a disappointing time from an *IPN* point of view: there had not been a murder for several weeks, nor any other sanguinary outrages, and the rich and famous had been behaving themselves with decorum. The only thing for the *IPN* to do was to bolster up the newspaper through publishing what today would have been termed a 'human interest' story, about the eccentric London spinster Miss Vint and her extraordinary cats.

The elderly Miss Vint, who lived in a little cottage at Eden Gardens, Walworth, and was known for her belief in the transmigration of souls, freely demonstrated her eight cats to the journalists. They were all sturdy, contented-looking animals, well looked after by Miss Vint and her domestics.

Miss Vint had always been very fond of her Devonshire grandmother. This ancient lady was very odd-looking, with a large wart on her nose, and eyes of different shades of grey. She was very nervous, and since the grating of a lucifer-match sent her into hysterics, she adhered to the old-fashioned flint-and-steel way of making light.

One day, Miss Vint was distraught to hear that this strange old lady had expired, at a very advanced age. The very same day, she found a tiny kitten on her doorstep, and brought it inside. Examining the animal, she was astonished to see that it had a wart on its nose, and that its eyes were different shades of grey. When Miss Vint struck a match, it gave a squeal of terror ...

Having added her reincarnated grandmother to the household, Miss Vint kept looking for other family members in feline form. Her sister Minnie had been the beauty of the family, with large blue eyes, and a fondness for pink dresses. After she had died, Miss Vint found a pretty blue-eyed white kitten for sale at a street stall, with a frilly pink ribbon around its neck. 'Sister Minnie' was still alive in 1892, and Miss Vint introduced her to the journalists: a handsome, large white cat, which was very fond of her mistress.

Not long after, Miss Vint's eldest brother Micah, a very obese character, died after being hit on the head by a brick dropped from a building site. The day after, Miss Vint saw some street ragamuffins throwing stones at a very fat cat! She belaboured them with her umbrella and rescued the cat. 'Brother Micah' was also formally introduced to the journalists: a very

Miss Vint and her Reincarnated Cats, from the *IPN*, 8 October 1892.

stout, whiskerless cat, who disapproved of locomotion and liked to drink large saucers of cream.

The black sheep of the Vint family had been her brother Job, who had lived a dissolute life before going abroad as a sailor; his last letter to his sister had been sent from Persia. After it had been rumoured that Job had been lost at sea, Miss Vint found a half-drowned Persian cat in her water-cistern. She saved the cat and took care of it, but 'Brother Job' showed her little gratitude, being a most disreputable cat, with a fondness for philandering. The only person he was fond of was the cat's meat man, and he ignored the comfortable bed Miss Vint had provided for him, preferring to sleep in the dustbin.

Disbelievers in reincarnation, the journalists thought Miss Vint as mad as a hatter, albeit harmless and kind. Sinisterly, they wrote that if she had possessed a fortune, her grasping relatives would surely have had her committed into an asylum, to get their hands on her money. But fortunately for her, Miss Vint had an income of just a little more than a hundred pounds per annum, and she could remain in her little Walworth cottage, living contentedly with her feline family.

The story of Miss Vint and her Reincarnated Cats originated in the *Daily Telegraph* before spreading to various other London and provincial papers, the *IPN* included. When I did some research to find out Miss Vint's first name, and to verify the story, it turned out that no such lady resided in Walworth at the time of the 1881 and 1891 censuses; nor was there any record suggesting that a Job or Micah Vint ever existed. But surely, the *honest* London journalists could not have *invented* the story – *or could they?*

The Strange Tale of Professor Beaurigard, 1894

In late 1894, a strange newspaper story swept the globe. It was said to emanate from Dalziel's correspondent in Buenos Aires, and concerned Professor Beaurigard, of the Ecole de Medicin in that city. Beaurigard was a distinguished medical scientist, who specialised in pathology and bacteriology. As a leading proponent of the bacterial origin of disease, he was in advance of the great Koch of Germany.

Professor Beaurigard was a polished linguist and a great entertainer, who was famous for his dinner parties, to which never more than three guests were invited. The problem was that it was of frequent occurrence that these guests died within twenty-four hours of the party! The doctors attributed the deaths to cholera or yellow fever, and no trace of poison was ever found in the bodies of the victims. After fifteen dinner guests had been dispatched in this manner, the police arrested Professor Beaurigard and charged him with murder. The case against him was of the flimsiest character, and was in danger of breaking down altogether, when the prosecution called a last-minute witness. This individual merely pointed his finger at the accused man. The plan was for the mystery witness to make a full revelation of the facts the following day, but Beaurigard was found dead in his cell the following morning, killed by a drop of deadly poison hidden in a diminutive gold capsule inside a hollow tooth.

The public prosecutor made a statement that the last-minute witness had been the former butler of Professor Beaurigard, whose tasks in the household included supervising his dinner parties. The butler had noticed that after the coffee, the professor brought a block of ice from his laboratory and had it crushed into small pieces, for the guests to have

The sinister Professor Beaurigard supervises his lethal dinner party, from the *IPN*, 6 October 1894.

iced crème de menthe. Himself, he always had a second cognac instead. One day, the butler had collected the ice left over, and when it had melted, it had an unpleasant smell. It turned out to be a living mass of cholera bacilli. The demented Professor Beaurigard had been experimenting on his dinner guests, intending to prove that the cholera bacilli would withstand freezing without losing their pathogenic power!

'Disgusting!' I hear the readers exclaim. But is this extraordinary tale of that modern Borgia, Professor Beaurigard, really true? It was reproduced in many American newspapers, and in nine British ones, although the *Western Mail* called it 'A Sensational Story' and the *Dundee Courier* an 'Extraordinary Story from America'. As for the *IPN*, it depicted the Mephistophelian Professor Beaurigard on the front page, supervising his experiment on the dinner guests with a sinister smirk. Several Australian and New Zealand newspapers also reproduced the story, the Perth *Western Mail* stating that it had been reported in full in the *New York Herald*. It attracts suspicion that neither the *New York Times* nor the London *Times* mentioned Professor Beaurigard, however, and it must be remembered that the newspaper press of the 1890s sometimes invented extraordinary stories said to have happened in some faraway part of the globe. These canards would sometimes travel the world, being regurgitated in newspapers in many countries.

So, was Professor Beaurigard an invention? Poisoning by cholera bacilli was a popular topic in contemporary popular fiction: the hero in Grant Allen's *The Devil's Die* poisons a man using cholera germs, and several of the novels of William Le Queux features villains making nefarious use of noxious bacteria. That cholera bacilli are capable of withstanding freezing was a novel and disagreeable fact back in the 1890s, one that might have inspired some unscrupulous American journalist to invent a newspaper story from faraway Argentina. Apart from some online newspaper repositories, the internet has nothing whatsoever to say about Professor Beaurigard and his criminal activities; one would have thought that such a scientific pioneer, and prolific mass poisoner, would have been remembered by some Argentinian historian of crime or science. The crucial test comes from the Web of Science and its online repository of cited references. A search for references to Robert Koch's old papers shows that not less than 783 writers have cited them. One would have thought that the works of Professor Beaurigard, stated to have been in advance of the great German bacteriologist, would also have been honoured by later writers, but not a single person has made reference to them. Thus the murderous Professor Beaurigard would appear to be an invention. And a successful newspaper hoax at the time, which was never seen through. It is amazing that the strange tale of the Professor's misdeeds was so widely and uncritically regurgitated in the worldwide press; clearly, a good story was considered to be better than a true one at the time.

9

Misdeeds of the Rich and Famous

A Dismal Tale from the Peerage, 1867

Lodge Evans Morres, an Irish barrister, made himself useful to the government of the day; he was rewarded with a barony in 1800, and a viscountcy in 1816. He changed his name, assuming the title of Viscount Frankfort de Montmorency, incurring the anger of the ancient French Montmorencys, who did not like an Irish newcomer perching on their distinguished heraldic tree. The first Viscount had several daughters, and also the son, Lodge Reymond, who succeeded him in 1822. The second Viscount Frankfort de Montmorency was an officer in the 10th Hussars for a short while before settling down to an idle life in London. In 1835, he married Miss Georgiana Frederica Henchy, daughter of Peter FitzGibbon Henchy QC, and they soon had a son and a daughter.

It would take until 1842 for Lord Frankfort de Montmorency to make the news, for all the wrong reasons. He was living apart from his wife at this time, at No. 17 Southwick Crescent [today Hyde Park Crescent; the house no longer stands], Paddington. He had befriended the young actress Alice Lowe, and installed her in his house at as his permanent mistress. She was not the only young woman invited to this Hyde Park seraglio by the lecherous nobleman, who liked to change his lady friends at regular intervals. After two months with the Viscount, young Alice moved out, taking with her a quantity of valuable jewellery that she claimed he had given to her. Since Lord Frankfort was furious with her, he made the disastrous decision to prosecute her for theft. There was much astonishment that a thirty-six-year-old Viscount should make a fool of himself by taking a nineteen-year-old actress to court, but Lord Frankfort brought his case to the Old Bailey. Here, he was subjected to a searching cross-examination by the opposing barrister, and reminded that he was himself his only witness. Young Alice Lowe made a very good impression in court, and made use of her acting talents to personify an injured and persecuted heroine, with complete success. Without leaving the box, the jury returned a verdict of Not Guilty, and Alice Lowe was loudly cheered as she triumphantly came out of court.

The prosecution of Alice Lowe was widely reported in the newspapers, and Lord Frankfort de Montmorency was a ruined man. In society, exception was taken to his immoral conduct: not only was it far from conventional for a middle-aged nobleman to take a girl of just nineteen as his mistress, but it was definitely 'not cricket' to prosecute her to reclaim articles that may well have been given to her for 'services rendered'. Lord Frankfort was hounded out of his clubs, and his wife obtained a divorce on account of his adultery with Alice Lowe and many other young women, with a yearly allowance of £800. In 1852, Lord Frankfort was again involved in a painful judicial scandal. It turned out that some person had printed poison-pen letters about the immoral conduct of Lord Henry Lennox and others, and distributed them widely in society under the name of 'Mr Macbeath'. It was suspected that Lord Frankfort was the man responsible for these scurrilous missives, and his maidservant was arrested one evening as she was taking a basketful of anonymous letters out to be posted. His lordship had set up a small printing-press in his kitchen, and expert evidence proved that this contraption had been used to print the poison-pen letters. For this cowardly crime, Lord Frankfort was sentenced to twelve months in prison, which he served in the Middlesex House of Corrections, Coldbath Fields. With the payment of a fee of 5s per week, his lordship was exempted from oakum picking and the treadmill, but all the other indignities of prison life were there for him to share.

After suffering the ignominy of being imprisoned, Lord Frankfort de Montmorency disappeared into obscurity; had he remained a member of any clubs, he would have been hounded out of them. What he was doing in 1867 is not known, except that if he had learned his lessons from the two disastrous legal actions in which he had been involved, he is likely to have taken good care not to seduce young actresses, or to print poison-pen letters in his kitchen. But instead, Lady Frankfort de Montmorency made the news in 1867, again for all the wrong reasons, earning the distinction of being depicted in the *IPN*. That year, she was residing at No. 123 Marina in Hastings, a nice Georgian seaside residence that is still standing today. Her sister Elizabeth Ann Hentley lived with her, and they had a maid-of-all-works named Sarah Rebecca Morey. Both Lady Frankfort and her sister were very deaf, and her ladyship also had a strong sense of household economy. When the servant Morey asked for a candle, she refused to give her one, since one a day was enough for the kitchen. When the servant took a piece of candle from a bedroom candlestick, without permission, Lady Frankfort jumped up and took the poker out of the fire, exclaiming, 'I will knock your — brains out with this poker!' Sarah

Rebecca Morey tried to escape, but her ladyship seized her by the hair and dragged her violently across the room. The poor servant was then frog-marched downstairs and locked out of the house, and she had to go to a nearby public house for shelter. When she brought an action against Lady Frankfort for assault, before the Hastings magistrates, her ladyship had not made an appearance, in spite of being summoned. The mistreated servant gave a clear account of how she had been assaulted, and although Elizabeth Ann Hentley, the deaf sister, objected in sign language, the outcome was that her ladyship was fined £2 and 15s costs, or in default one month's imprisonment. Not wishing to join her estranged husband in the ranks of the jail-birds, Lady Frankfort duly paid her fine.

The action against Lady Frankfort was widely reported in the newspapers, as a sign that law and justice applied both to titled ladies and to their household servants; it was considered encouraging that her ladyship had ended up on the losing side, and that the mistreated maid-of-all-works had been compensated for her injuries. Lord and Lady Frankfort de Montmorency never did anything newsworthy again. She died in Brighton in April 1885, and he lived on until 1889; in spite of their high rank, neither of them was honoured by a newspaper obituary of any description. The peerage to which they had added so little lustre became extinct in 1917.

Lady Frankfort de Montmorency attacks the servant Sarah Rebecca Morey, from the *IPN*, 9 November 1867.

The Strange Story of the Countess of Derwentwater

In 1715, James Radcliffe, the 3rd Earl of Derwentwater, was executed for his participation in the Jacobite rebellion. The Hanoverian government cast covetous eyes on the rebel Earl's vast estates in south-west Northumberland, but Lord Derwentwater had settled them on his infant son John, and the legality of this move was upheld in 1719. The martyred Earl's family had wisely made themselves scarce, bringing young John with them to the Netherlands, where Jacobites were much safer than in England. But in 1731, there must have been a great shout of 'Hup! Hup! Huzza!' in the London government buildings, when it was announced that John Radcliffe had died a minor. The Derwentwater estates were entrusted to (some would say usurped by) Greenwich Hospital, and in 1865, it was announced that they had been transferred to the Commissioners of the Admiralty.

But in August 1866, the newspapers in Northumberland could report an extraordinary development: Countess Amelia Matilda, the rightful heiress to the Derwentwater estates, had taken up residence in Blaydon-on-Tyne. She explained that young John Radcliffe had staged an accident and faked his death in 1731, in order to escape the Hanoverian agents plotting to murder him. He had married well and lived for many years. His second son James had married a Princess Sobiesky, and Countess Amelia was his only living child. The Countess had some private means, she alleged, and she also had custody of a considerable stockpile of furniture, paintings and other valuable objects belonging to her distinguished family. A distinguished-looking, middle-aged lady who sometimes liked to dress in military uniform, the Countess became quite popular locally. She gave generously to charity, insinuated herself with various dignitaries, and promised the needy that after she had taken over the Derwentwater estates, poverty would become a distant memory, and the paupers would dine from her table in style.

The Northumberland authorities kept the rabble-rousing pseudo-noblewoman under observation, but since she seemed entirely sane and respectable, they did not fear that she would stage an uprising or rebellion. But they were proven wrong when Countess Amelia went to war on 29 September 1868. Dressed in an Austrian uniform, complete with a sword, she led two of her stoutest followers, and a cart containing her belongings, to her ancestral home, ruined Dilston Castle. Since the castle was uninhabited, she could raise a canopy in one of the roofless rooms, and fill it with her possessions. When her occupation of the castle became known, Amelia's followers brought her food and other supplies, to be rewarded with generous promises of future prosperity, once the Derwentwater lands had been restored to their rightful owner. These credulous supporters believed her every word, and imagined feudal pleasures to come once she had established her rights. One of Amelia's adherents praised her in a poem:

Oh, could the human hand obtain
   Then all it could bestow,
Again would Countess Amelia reign
   Where her sires did long ago.
Then justice, mercy and gratitude,
   Go hand in hand,
And give to the heart its latitude
   And Countess Amelia her land.

But the agent of the Admiralty Commissioners, a certain Charles Grey, was not amused by this impromptu uprising. He raided the castle with a troop of sturdy men, put Amelia's followers to flight, and removed her furniture. When the gallant noblewoman drew her sword in a threatening manner, they disarmed her, put her in a chair, and unceremoniously carried her out of the castle grounds.

THE COUNTESS OF DERWENTWATER EJECTED FROM DILSTON CASTLE

Above: The Countess of Derwentwater keeps Grey and his henchmen at bay with her sword, from the *IPN*, 10 October 1868.

Right: Dilston Castle, from a postcard stamped and posted in 1907.

Dilston Castle.   Near Corbridge.

233

The chagrined Countess erected her tent just outside the castle, over a flooded ditch, but in spite of these insalubrious living conditions, she still upheld her claim. Some of her followers warned her about the damp, but since Countess Amelia was determined to stay where she was, they built her a small hut instead. The proprietor of the *Newcastle Chronicle*, Mr Joseph Cowen Jr, known as 'The Blaydon Brick', openly supported her claim, and some other newspapers also found it cruel that a middle-aged woman was forcibly evicted from what she claimed to be the castle of her forebears. One of Amelia's supporters composed an amusing poem in the local dialect:

Then the Blaydin Bricks torn'doot, and Cowins' mang the swarm
This swore be Trooth an' Honor's cawse She shuddint suffor harm,
Oh maw canny, bonny lass, but aw like ye for yor neym;
For nowt but mordor teuk the heed frey Dorrintwettor – sheym!
Oh! bliss the Coontis is she eeves in the funny leukin' tent,
She'll get hor reets sum time, aw hope, an' bliss the boonty sent
For she's the reetful hair aw naw, an' bellangs the greet istates,
An'ef she gets them bless her soul! there'll soon be open gates,
Egh, the hungory she'll feed fat, an' the feebil she'll meyk strang,
An'a' the orfin bairns neerby'll raise a jolly sang,
Singin' 'Life an' Happiness tiv ivvory soul on Tyne
An' glory to Armeeley's cause – for Justis is divine!'

But the Hexham Highway Board declared the hut of the Countess an obstruction, fined her 10*s*, and dismantled it. In a book entitled *Jottings of Original Matter from the Diary of Amelia Countess of Derwentwater*, sold and published by Joseph Cowen, the noblewoman was most indignant about this state of affairs. Parts of this book are in French and Latin, severely testing the linguistic abilities of Amelia's Northumberland followers. It was illustrated with various amateur drawings, some of them executed by Countess Amelia's own hand, and with a surprisingly youthful-looking photograph said to depict this illustrious lady.

Protected by her small band of followers, Countess Amelia lay low for a year. But on 19 November 1869, she marched to the agent Grey's office at the head of her supporters, and told him that he had no right to demand rent from her tenants. An angry scuffle broke out, and the sword of the Countess was broken in two. She claimed that Grey had seized hold of her and ordered two of his henchmen to throw her downstairs; he denied this, and instead claimed that the angry noblewoman had rapped him over the knuckles with her stick. The next move was that Henry Brown, a former bailiff who had become Amelia's leading supporter, led a mob of her followers to a farm on the Derwentwater estates, and rustled twenty-two sheep, eleven cows and two horses. All these animals were

THE COUNTESS of DERWENTWATER ASSERTING HER CLAIM

The Countess again confronts Grey and his men, from the *IPN*, 27 November 1869.

sold by auction, along with various tools and implements stolen from the farm, to help boost Countess Amelia's fighting funds. But the police arrested Brown and ten of Amelia's other supporters, and the cattle-rustler was rewarded with nine months' imprisonment with hard labour.

The imprisonment of Henry Brown was a major blow to the Countess, who had actually borrowed money to support her claim. Her creditors clamoured for the return of their funds, and forced her to sell her heirlooms at auctions. But although Amelia had claimed that these treasures, some famous Old Master paintings among them, were worth at least £200,000, the auction buyers did not agree, casting doubt on the authenticity of the grubby old paintings. A 1520 painting by Albrecht Dürer went for £2 15s, two splendid battle scenes by Rubens fetched £2 10s together, and *St Jerome in the Desert* by Leonardo da Vinci fetched 7s 6d. This dismal auction finally broke the spirit of the haughty Countess, and she was imprisoned in Newcastle Gaol as bankrupt. Once released, she broke with Brown and many of her other supporters, and died destitute in 1880, still maintaining her claim.

Who was this remarkable claimant, Countess Amelia of Derwentwater? Well, competent historians have asserted that John Radcliffe really died without issue in 1731, making it unlikely that this Northumberland woman of mystery was a legitimate descendant of his. Nor is there any record of a Princess Sobiesky marrying a man named Radcliffe, or for that matter any mystery Englishman. Countess Amelia did possess some genuine pieces of furniture belonging to the Radcliffes, as well as some bona fide documents, and it is of course possible that she was the descendant of some person connected with the Radcliffes, perhaps by an unsanctified liaison. Mr Cadwallader J. Bates, author of the *History of Northumberland*, proposed that Amelia was a lady's maid from Dover who had moved to Germany, where she came across an old novel in which the son of Lord Derwentwater settled in that country after a mock funeral. This version would have been easier to believe if Bates had provided the title of this novel, and the name of its author. Nor did he explain how a Dover lady's maid could have learnt Latin, French and German, languages in which Amelia was proficient. The pseudo-noblewoman's knowledge of history was excellent, and her grasp of the annals of the Derwentwater peers well-nigh encyclopaedic. In the annals of claimants of great estates, she stands between John Nichols Thom, the Kentish fanatic, whose swordplay antics she emulated, and that man of mystery, the Tichborne Claimant.

A Bonaparte on Trial for Murder, 1870

Pierre-Napoléon Bonaparte was born in 1815, the son of the Great Napoleon's brother Lucien. A wild youth who laughed in the face of various authority figures, he freely roamed the vast family estate outside Rome, consorting with shepherds, vagabonds and bandits. In 1831, after spending six months in prison for assault, he went to the United States to visit his uncle Joseph, formerly King of Spain, who lived in Bordenstown, New Jersey. Since Pierre did not like the Americans very much, he proceeded to Colombia, where he was given a commission in the army of General Santander. After falling ill, he returned to Italy, continuing his riotous life in the same manner as before. One day, a bandit named Saltamachione tried to hold up Pierre and one of his brothers, but the two Bonapartes wounded and captured the bandit, before frog-marching him to the nearest police station. But since the bandit claimed that the Bonapartes had beaten him up without provocation, a police troop was sent to arrest them. Thinking it was the bandit's gang coming to exact revenge, Pierre lashed out with his large hunting-knife and killed a young lieutenant. He was tried and sentenced to death, but was reprieved by the Pope after spending nine months in jail, on condition that he never set foot in the Papal States again.

Pierre Bonaparte's irregular life continued after this narrow escape. In addition to his long-term mistress Rose Hesnard, he slept with other young women at every opportunity. On a hunting expedition to Albania, he killed two brigands who had tried to ambush his party. After the 1848 revolution, Pierre went to Paris to try his hand as a politician, claiming that in spite of his name, he was really quite a radical. He got elected as deputy for Corsica and took part in various political shenanigans during these turbulent times. After the successful 1851 *coup d'état* by his cousin Louis Napoléon, Pierre made a complete volte-face with regard to his political opinions, and supported the new regime. He was rewarded with the title of Prince. After the death of Rose Hesnard in 1852, the thirty-seven-year-old Prince Pierre secretly married the nineteen-year-old Nina Ruffin, the daughter of a foundry worker. As a result of this *mésalliance*, and his various other shortcomings, Napoleon III took a firm dislike to Prince Pierre, and snubbed him at court. The disgruntled Pierre moved back to Corsica, where he amused himself by hunting and womanising, leaving a trail of illegitimate little princes and princesses all over the island.

In 1870, Prince Pierre returned to Paris, hoping to get back into his cousin's favour. He quarrelled with a writer named Paschal Grousset, who challenged the Prince to a duel. Although Prince Pierre was a short, stocky man, and by now fifty-five years old, he was as tough as ever, and a crack shot. M. Grousset seems to have had second thoughts about facing such a dangerous character, since he sent two roughs to seek out the Prince, allegedly to set the terms for the duel. One of them, a brutal character named Victor Noir, famous for the enormous size of his private parts, tried to strike Prince Pierre, who seized up a large revolver and shot him dead, on the spot. There was widespread outrage in Paris, where 100,000 people attended Noir's funeral. The republicans insisted that Prince Pierre should be tried for murder. The man who had accompanied Noir testified that after an angry quarrel, the Prince had slapped Noir's face, and then shot him. Prince Pierre testified that after Noir had struck him a glancing

Prince Pierre Bonaparte shoots M. Noir, from the *IPN*, 22 January 1870.

blow on the cheek with a heavy cane, he had acted in self-defence. It was proven that both roughs had been carrying loaded revolvers. As a result, the Prince was acquitted, although Napoleon III had now definitely had enough of him, and he was a ruined man.

His mistress Nina Ruffin insisted that Prince Pierre ought to marry her properly, since they had now been living together for nearly twenty years, and had two children. After Pierre had reluctantly agreed, Princess Nina promptly left him and decamped to London, taking her children with her. She opened a high-class dress shop, with her name and title proudly displayed over the door. Prince Pierre replaced this deceitful woman with yet another mistress, a young serving girl. He died in 1881, from complications from diabetes, and is buried in the Cimetière des Gonards in Versailles. The tomb of his victim Victor Noir, at the Père Lachaise cemetery in Paris, is much more famous than of the violent, trigger-happy Prince. It has a life-size bronze statue of Noir, which a recent guide book claims to be admired by ladies of all ages, due to the large protuberance in the trousers.

The Gooch Scandal, 1878

In 1872, Sir Edward Gooch, 7th Baronet, died at the age of just thirty. He belonged to a wealthy and distinguished family, who had their seat at stately Benacre Hall near Lowestoft in Suffolk. He was succeeded by his younger brother Sir Francis Gooch, who inherited the house, land and £25,000. One would have expected a spirited young man to make good use of these considerable advantages, but Sir Francis was a gloomy, introspective character who did not care for revelry and high life. He spent much time at Benacre Hall, but occasionally went travelling on the continent. Later in 1872, he met Annie Louisa Sutherland, and they married after a brief acquaintance. Tragedy struck in late 1873, when the couple's only son Francis died, at the age of just four months.

For several years, Sir Francis and Lady Gooch cohabited quietly together, but as the years went by, she became increasingly obsessed with having a child. Not only did she deplore being barren, but there was also a need to provide a son and heir to the estate, which would otherwise be usurped by Sir Francis' younger brother Alfred, with whom the Baronet was on bad terms. In 1878, Lady Gooch lost whatever remained of her common sense, and her behaviour became increasingly unbalanced; she kept telling her ailing husband that she was pregnant, but although she wore padded clothing, he did not believe her.

Lady Gooch tried to persuade the family doctor that she was indeed with child, but again without success; the desperate lady then tried to swear him into a conspiracy: he was to put her up in a home for pregnant

Ribald sketches of the Gooch charade, and a sketch of Lady Gooch in court, from the *IPN*, 30 November 1878.

ladies, and procure a baby that she would then pass off as her own! But the doctor put enough value on his Hippocratic oath to refrain from such undignified shenanigans. He instead recommended that the Gooches should adopt a child, but she objected that in that case, they would not have a son and heir, and the detested Alfred would take over Benacre Hall after her husband had expired. After the doctor had threatened her that if she tried to embroil him in her plans any further, he would tell her husband, the demented Lady Gooch decided to act alone. She knew of a crooked infants' home in Great Coram Street, and after paying a fee, she was able to leave with a two-week-old little boy. She hired a 'nurse' who called herself Mrs Annie Walker and arranged to take a suite at the Grosvenor Hotel; the following day, Annie Walker emerged from this suite, to announce that Lady Gooch had given birth, and that there was now an heir to Benacre Hall.

But although he was not the shrewdest of men, Sir Francis Gooch was not taken in by his wife's conspiracy to deceive him, and he refused to accept the child as his own. He thought she deserved punishment for her foolish conduct, and although wiser people objected that he would sully the family name unnecessarily, he took out a summons against her and Annie Walker for conspiring to palm off on him a strange child, with intent to defraud and deceive. The result of this sensational summons was that the doings of Lady Gooch became headline material in every newspaper in the country, and that the family name was dragged through the mud. There was amazement at the extraordinary conduct of Lady Gooch, and astonishment that it was, in the year 1878, possible to purchase a recently born baby in such a brazen manner. Poor Lady Gooch appeared to be very ill and feeble, and she once fainted in court; the wretched woman felt her public disgrace keenly, and lamented that her private affairs were discussed in the newspapers. Miss Elizabeth Garrod, the housekeeper at Benacre Hall, testified against her. In the end, the jury could not find a true bill against Lady Gooch, and she was acquitted, but the damage had been done; if Sir Francis Gooch had intended to teach his wife a hard lesson for her foolishness, he had certainly succeeded. But the 'collateral damage' to the family name, which had been tarred black throughout the country, must have been a severe blow to the padded Baronet.

Not at all unreasonably, after having been so shamefully treated, Lady Gooch made haste to divorce her husband. The 'Gooch Matrimonial Case' hit the news in March 1879, but poor Lady Gooch would not have long to celebrate being free from the cad Sir Francis: she expired at Norwood in October 1879. A newspaper commented that, 'The unfortunate event in which Lady Gooch was the principal actor a few months ago will be fresh in the memory of our readers.' Sir Francis took a permanent mistress after her death, and moved her into Benacre Hall. When Sir Francis Gooch died in 1881, his brother Alfred inherited the estate. Sir Francis had written a will granting his mistress Mrs Shippey all his personal property, and also a valuable racehorse; although Sir Alfred contested the will, he lost the case after protracted legal wrangling. In 1893, there was again trouble at Benacre Hall, when Sir Alfred divorced his wife; much mud was flung in court about the extra-marital peccadilloes of both husband and wife. Both Sir Francis and Sir Alfred Gooch certainly had a very loose definition of gentlemanly behaviour.

Since the 1890s, the Gooches have behaved themselves more decorously, and kept away from the law-courts: the present-day holder of the title is Sir Arthur Brian Sherlock Heywood Gooch, a retired brigadier-general and an aide-de camp to the Queen. The Gooch Scandal is well-nigh forgotten today, and if it had not been for two engravings in the *IPN*, we would not even have known what the principal actors in the Gooch drama had looked like. The indiscretions of the tragic Lady Gooch lie hidden in the yellowed pages of old newspapers, as do the cruel actions

Lady Gooch faints in court, and portraits of Miss Garrod and the forbidding-looking Annie Walker, from the *IPN*, 14 December 1878.

of her overbearing husband; as for Sir Alfred, his major claim to fame today is that he donated land for the construction of the Birmingham Dogs' Home.

The Fearneaux Frauds, 1882

The reader will recall the sensational 1870 case of the two male transvestites Ernest Boulton and Frederick Park, alias Stella and Fanny, and their gay life in London's homosexual underworld. Ernest Boulton had befriended Lord Arthur Pelham Clinton, a former naval officer and MP, who was the third son of the Duke of Newcastle. A strange-looking cove with a bald head, a small moustache and long side-whiskers, he was besotted with the pretty young 'Stella', and they even appeared on stage together. After the scandal had broken, and Boulton and Park were to stand trial for conspiring and inciting people to commit an unnatural offence, Lord Arthur was called to testify, since 'Stella' had kept all his love letters, which were read by the police. Lord Arthur was said to have died from scarlet fever in June 1870, after having received his subpoena for the trial. A Press Association telegram told that he had been staying at a cottage in Muddeford, near Christchurch in Hampshire, under the name Captain Edward Gray, when he had fallen ill with a fever and revealed his true identity. His solicitor Mr W. H. Roberts wrote to the *Morning Post* about the premature death of his unfortunate client, enclosing a letter said to have been written by Lord Arthur on his death-bed, in which he explained his involvement in the case as a simple frolic among light-hearted theatrical characters.

Lord Arthur Clinton's brief obituary was published in many newspapers, detailing his undistinguished naval service, his brief parliamentary career, and his bankruptcy in 1868, and quoting the *Morning Post* letter with regard to the recent disastrous turn in Lord Arthur's career. He was buried on 23 June 1870, the ceremony being a very plain one, with the Duke of Newcastle, Lord Thomas Clinton, the solicitor and the family doctor as the only mourners. There were early rumours that Lord Arthur had faked his death and escaped abroad, however. There had been three coffins at the funeral, one of them made of lead, and several newspapers voiced their suspicions that the inner one of them had contained nothing more than a sack of sawdust. In October 1872, the *New York Mercury* could report that Lord Arthur Clinton had been sighted more than once at the New York theatres, and clearly identified.

There had also been sightings of the unfortunate nobleman closer to home, however. In late 1871, a mysterious woman lodged in Birmingham; she gave her name as Mary Jane Fearneaux, and sometimes smoked cigarettes and wore male clothing. She confided to some people that

Mary Jane Fearneaux in prison dress and in disguise, from the IPN, March 4 1882.

she was really Lord Arthur Clinton, who had donned female attire after faking his death to escape facing the music in the Boulton and Park scandal. To make people believe he was dead, he had been chloroformed and put in the coffin, but rescued at the last minute. Many people believed her, including a clergyman, and these supporters lent her money in advance for some substantial legacies that were said to be coming Lord Arthur's way. In November 1871, Mary Jane Fearneaux was exposed as a swindler, however, and committed to stand trial at the Birmingham Police Court; in the end, she was sentenced to twelve months in prison.

As the years went by, there were sightings of the mystery man Lord Arthur Clinton all over the world. In 1875, he is said to have attended the funeral of his sister Lady Susan Vane-Tempest at Long Newton; in 1878, he was recorded among those present at a congregation of Irish Freemasons; in 1879, he was stated by an Antipodean newspaper to have spent many years in Australia, preparing to make a comeback in London society; in 1881, the *Bath Herald* could report that Lord Arthur's coffin had been empty, and that the fugitive nobleman he had recently been seen in London. But in the meantime, the Midlands adventuress Mary Jane Fearneaux had returned to her wicked old ways. Spreading her net wider this time, she had succeeded in persuading many foolish and credulous people in Birmingham and its surroundings that she was really Lord Arthur Clinton in disguise. In February 1882, she and her suspected accomplice James Gething were charged with receiving £5,000 from two of her most ardent followers, under false pretences. There was much writing in the newspapers about this strange sequel to the Boulton and Park case, and amazement that for upwards of ten years, a woman had been able to impersonate an English nobleman with complete success, taking in many people and persuading them to part with large sums of money. In the end, she was sentenced to seven years in prison, whereas Gething was acquitted. In 1894, Mary Jane Fearneaux made a comeback in Leeds, cheating various people out of money and valuables in a series of property frauds, and in 1896, she is recorded still to have been in prison. She may well be the 'Mary Jane Furneaux' who died in Coventry in

Vignettes on the Fearneaux case,
from the *IPN*, 13 May 1882.

1901. What happened to the real Lord Arthur Clinton in the end is unclear, but there is reason to believe that he may well have faked his death and fled abroad back in 1870, to seek out a perilous colonial existence instead of cavorting with dubious young men in London's theatrical demi-monde.

The Garmoyle Breach of Promise Case, 1884

Emily May Finney was born in 1862, the daughter of a London coal merchant. After her father's business had failed in 1881, she became an actress under the name May Fortescue, enjoying immediate success as a member of the D'Oyly Carte Opera Company. Good-looking and vivacious, she became a great favourite with the male clientele of the Savoy Theatre, and cabinet card photographs of her sold like hot cakes. She acted in Gilbert and Sullivan's operas, and became a friend of W. S. Gilbert himself.

In 1882, May Fortescue met the twenty-one-year-old Arthur William Cairns, known by the courtesy title of Viscount Garmoyle, since he was the eldest surviving son of the Earl Cairns, a distinguished lawyer and politician who was Lord Chancellor in Benjamin Disraeli's government. Lord Garmoyle was an awkward-looking fellow: tall, thin and narrow-shouldered. Educated at Eton and Cambridge, he was intent on a military career, but found it difficult to pass the relevant examinations to enter Sandhurst. It did not help that he was something of an idler, and a great friend of the London theatrical world. A regular at the Savoy Theatre, Lord Garmoyle was much taken by the pretty May Fortescue. What she thought of this unmanly-looking swain we can only guess at, but it was of course in his favour that he was the heir to an Earldom.

In July 1883, Lord Garmoyle proposed marriage to May Fortescue, and she accepted him. Lord Cairns was of course not happy that his

Lord Garmoyle and Miss Fortescue, from the *IPN*, 22 November 1884.

son was going to marry an actress, but at least she was a pretty and good-mannered one. Since the dour Lord Cairns had a great antipathy for the stage, May Fortescue agreed to leave the theatre, for good. Lady Cairns wrote the actress a friendly letter, and she later visited Lord and Lady Cairns at their country house in Scotland. Everything seemed to work in favour of May Fortescue going from chorus to coronet, and marrying into the aristocracy, except that Lord Garmoyle was a foolish, vacillating young man who was beginning to fear that he would be ridiculed in society for marrying beneath him. Since his military training did not progress satisfactorily, Lord Cairns suggested that the marriage should be delayed, and this drawback appears to have unsettled the feeble young nobleman further. In January 1884, Lord Garmoyle broke off the engagement and went to travel abroad.

May Fortescue, who had been so basely deserted, consulted her friend W. S. Gilbert, and he agreed to supply her with a team of solicitors to take Lord Garmoyle to court for breach of promise. The Garmoyle Breach of Promise Case became one of the legal sensations of 1884. There was much public sympathy for May Fortescue, and an equal amount of odium for the hapless Lord Garmoyle. The case plodded on throughout 1884, and the legal bills for both sides grew steadily. The outcome of the case was a clear victory for May Fortescue: she was awarded £10,000, by far the heaviest damages ever awarded for breach of promise. Lord Garmoyle was harshly criticised in the press, and called a weak-minded simpleton, a booby and a cad; his heartless conduct in jilting his paramour admitted no possible excuse, it was pontificated.

May Fortescue made use of her £10,000 fortune to set up her own company of actors. She enjoyed a long and fruitful career on the stage, often performing in her friend W. S. Gilbert's plays, both in Britain and in the United States. After her dismal experience with Lord Garmoyle, she stayed away from wicked men throughout her career, and never married.

She died in 1950, aged eighty-eight. As for Lord Garmoyle, he had a narrow escape a few years later while travelling in India, having to shoot off his great toe with a revolver because a cobra had attached itself to it. He became the second Earl Cairns when his father died in 1885. After being jilted by an American heiress, he married a clergyman's daughter in 1887, but died from pneumonia in 1890 aged just twenty-eight. A London wag wrote a poem alluding to the single newsworthy action of his late Lordship:

> Cairns has left this world of care,
> Cairns has climbed the golden stair,
> Will he pay 'ten thousand' there
> For jilting of an angel fair?

The Earldom of Cairns is still extant, and the later holders of the title have handled their matrimonial affairs in a more conventional manner that the erstwhile Lord Garmoyle.

The Dunlo Sensation, 1890

Isabel Maude Bilton was born in 1868, the daughter of an artillery sergeant. At an early age, Belle Bilton, as she was called, took to the stage along with her younger sister Florence. Since the Sisters Bilton were both very pretty and had good singing voices, they soon made quite a success on the London tiles, and counted many male admirers. In 1888, Belle Bilton fell in love with the American Alden Weston, a glib-tongued confidence trickster who frequented the theatres, and she became his mistress and carried his child. But soon disaster followed: not only did Alden Weston already have a wife, but he was also prosecuted for swindling various people under the names of 'Lord Fairfax' and 'Baron de Loanda'. Although Belle borrowed money to pay for his defence, he was found guilty and sentenced to eighteen months in prison.

When the prison gates closed upon Alden Weston, Belle Bilton's situation in life was not a pleasant one: she was out of employment, heavily pregnant, and without any support in the world. But fortunately for her, the young Jewish businessman Isidor Wertheimer took pity on her and supplied her with a comfortable Maidenhead cottage and a doctor and nurse to make sure her child was born without any unforeseen complications. When she had given birth and could travel, he took her to Trouville for a holiday, and then he made arrangements for both Belle and Florence Bilton to live in his house in St John's Wood. But although Isidor Wertheimer's intentions appear to have been fully honourable, and he was genuinely anxious to marry her, his parents took exception to his involvement with a disreputable London actress, and they shipped him off to America on business to avoid any further mischief.

Belle Bilton went back to the stage to continue her music-hall career as well as she could. At the Corinthian Club, she met William Frederick Le Poer Trench, son and heir of Earl of Clancarty, who held the courtesy title of Viscount Dunlo. An awkward, feeble-minded youth, he had been incapable of passing the entrance tests to Sandhurst, but he remained a close student of the London stage and bars, and the various race-courses near the Metropolis. He fell in love with Belle and asked her to marry him, and was accepted after due consideration. Knowing that his father was a snob, and a stern disciplinarian, Lord Dunlo was very fearful of parental censure after he had married Belle, and here he was not far wrong. Lord Clancarty was much upset to find that his son and heir had married a music-hall actress: he refused to accept Belle as his daughter-in-law, and sent Lord Dunlo to Australia with a tutor, to make sure he was out of harm's way.

The creature Alden Weston was out of prison by this time, and soon up to mischief again: he found out that Belle Bilton had been pursued by Isidor Wertheimer, who had returned to London after his exile in America, and decided to forge some cheques with Wertheimer's name on them. When arrested, Weston made a frantic appeal to Belle, but she had had enough of him by this time, and he was sentenced to seven years of penal servitude. Lord Clancarty consulted his solicitors and had private detectives follow Belle around the clock. When he had evidence that she was seeing Wertheimer behind the back of her husband in faraway Australia, he demanded that Lord Dunlo should petition for divorce. The solicitors sent Dunlo a bundle of papers to sign, and the weak-willed young man, who was used to doing what his father told him, duly signed them.

The leading lights from the Dunlo divorce case, from the *IPN*, 2 August 1890.

Lord Dunlo returned to London in the summer of 1890, just in time for the hearing of his petition for divorce, citing his wife's adultery with Isidor Wertheimer, in front of Sir James Hannen, president of the Divorce Court, and a special jury. Lord Clancarty had employed the eloquent Sir Charles Russell, and a strong team of supporting legal counsel, to conduct the case, but Wertheimer had made sure that both he himself and Belle Bilton were also well represented. It was not contested that Wertheimer and Belle had gone to Paris and Trouville together, or that she had lived in his house at St John's Wood. Lady Dunlo was very much the senior of her husband in worldly experience, as Sir Charles Russell expressed it, and in possession of considerable personal attractions. Surely, Wertheimer must have had impure motives when consorting with her while her husband was in Australia. Lord Dunlo was put into the box, where he said what his father had told him to say about the petition for divorce, but he was exposed as the cad he was by a hostile cross-examination: at the very same time he had petitioned for divorce, he had written her some pathetic love letters. Belle's letters to him were read aloud, and she made no secret of Wertheimer showing her attention. Lord Clancarty's private detectives gave evidence at length, but these professional peeping Toms had not really seen much that was indecent: Wertheimer had more than once taken Belle out in his coach, and they had once been observed standing together at a window. Wertheimer had once put his hand round her waist, and she had once been observed smoking a cigarette and drinking champagne with him. Lord Clancarty made an unsympathetic impression in court, whereas both Wertheimer and Belle performed very well. Isidor Wertheimer could not be shaken when he asserted his platonic attachment to the celebrated music hall singer, and Belle told the tale of Alden Weston's crookery, and Wertheimer's admiration for herself, with complete candour. The verdict was that Lord Dunlo's petition for divorce was dismissed, with costs.

There was much writing in the newspapers about this sensational lawsuit, and a good deal of sympathy for Belle Bilton, who had been so very shamefully treated. There was a similar amount of newspaper ire for the dismal Lord Clancarty: had the House of Lords had a 'Booby of the

The end of the Dunlo divorce case, from the *IPN*, 9 August 1890.

Year' competition for 1890, he would have been a strong bet for achieving that dubious honour. Much odium was also reserved for the slow-witted Lord Dunlo, and had Belle Bilton been a heroine in a Victorian novel, she would surely have jilted her cad of a husband. But she was aware of his feeble and weak-willed nature, and reasoned that once he was removed from his father's influence, his character would improve. This plan worked a treat, and the couple settled down to a happy uxorious life.

The gloomy old Lord Clancarty never forgave his son for his *mésalliance*, nor did he ever acknowledge his daughter-in-law. When he died of paralysis soon after, having suffered badly from gout for many months, Lord Dunlo inherited the title and became the 5th Earl of Clancarty. He and Belle had five children alive, and lived quietly at the family estate in County Galway for many years. Having moved from chorus to coronet, Isabel Countess of Clancarty was a popular society figure. When she died prematurely from cancer in 1906, her grieving husband never remarried. The title is still extant, and the 9th and current Earl has been able to hold on to his seat in the House of Lords.

Spiritualism and Animal Hoarding in Thomas Carlyle's House, 1892

Thomas Carlyle, the celebrated historian and literary lion of Victorian times, lived at No. 5 (today No. 24) Cheyne Row, Chelsea. His fine town house dating from 1708 still remains today, in one of London's best preserved early Georgian streets. But the *IPN* provides details of some distinctively weird goings-on in Thomas Carlyle's house a few years after his death in 1881.

In 1850, the twenty-four-year-old Elizabeth Ann Caulfield married the army surgeon James William Cottell. He served in India for some considerable period of time, but was back in England in 1858. James William Cottell died unexpectedly in 1860, leaving his not inconsiderable savings to his wife and children under an indenture of settlement. Mrs Cottell tried to get her hands on the money directly, but was repulsed in the Court of Chancery. The trustees of the marriage settlement proved not to be ungenerous, however, and she could educate her four sons in good schools, and live in some style at No. 26 Cheyne Row, Chelsea. Two of the sons grew up to become army surgeons just like their father; the third became a midshipman. But in the 1880s, when her children had all fled the nest and gone abroad, Mrs Cottell's behaviour became increasingly odd. She developed a strong interest in spiritualism, and an equally powerful fondness for cats and dogs.

In 1887, six years after her famous neighbour Thomas Carlyle had died, Elizabeth Ann Cottell bought the lease of his house and moved into No. 24

Above: Mongrels and tabbies in Thomas Carlyle's old house, from the *IPN*, 17 December 1892.

Right: Thomas Carlyle in 1860, from *The Homes and Haunts of Thomas Carlyle*.

Cheyne Row. The move into 'Carlyle House', as she called her new town house, seems to have unhinged her mind permanently. A great friend of stray cats, she provided free meals for these animals. Cats from all over Chelsea congregated in Cheyne Row to enjoy these feline banquets, amidst much caterwauling. Inside Carlyle House, Mrs Cottell kept a dozen dogs, which she kept well fed on bins full of tripe and cat's meat that was delivered daily.

The two-legged inhabitants of Carlyle House were of an equally queer standard. The New York sisters Leah, Margaret and Kate Fox had become quite notorious in America as spiritualist mediums. In 1888, the sisters quarrelled, and Margaret confessed that their 'spirit rappings' had been a fraud all along, to devastating effect for their future careers. Kate had married a London barrister named Jencken, who had died in 1881 leaving her with two sons. In some way or other, her path had crossed that of the animal-hoarding weirdo Elizabeth Ann Cottell, and in 1888, Kate Fox Jencken moved into Carlyle House, where she held several seances, to the perfect satisfaction of her hostess. It is not mentioned if Thomas Carlyle's spirit made itself known. When there was newspaper publicity about the spiritualists in Thomas Carlyle's house, Mrs Cottell wrote back saying that she was the sole proprietor of the premises, having bought the lease, and that Mrs Jencken and her children merely were her visitors. Kate Fox Jencken was a hard drinker, and it appears as if Mrs Cottell also took to drink during the transatlantic spiritualist's stay at Carlyle House.

In 1889, Mrs Cottell got fed up with Kate Fox Jencken and her children, and they were evicted from Carlyle House, probably because they had objected to the twenty dogs sharing the house with them. The once celebrated spiritualist ended her days in miserable circumstances, dying in 1892 and being buried in a pauper's grave. Mrs Cottell had been one of her last supporters, and some letters from her are quoted in Sir Arthur Conan Doyle's *History of Spiritualism*. The 1891 Census finds Elizabeth Ann Cottell living at No. 24 Cheyne Row, with the boarder William Littler, who described himself as an artist, two female servants and a young errand-boy.

In August 1892, the other residents of Cheyne Row had finally had enough of the twenty dogs kept at No. 24, and they summoned Mrs Cottell under the Public Health Act. The barrister prosecuting for the Chelsea Vestry said that the magistrate probably knew of the Chelsea Sage's fondness for cats and dogs, but Carlyle would certainly have objected if he had known that his old-world retreat had been converted into a menagerie. Mrs Cottell was fined £10 and strictly warned that further action would be taken if the nuisance continued. Just a few days later, there was 'Another Scene at Carlyle's Old House', as the newspapers recorded it: the servant Emma Stanton, who had complained after being pushed downstairs by a large dog, had been locked out of Carlyle House by the angry Mrs Cottell, who had told her through the letter box that she was fired. The magistrate ordered that Emma's clothes should be returned to her, and that Mrs Cottell should pay 23s costs.

In December 1892, the Chelsea Vestry again summoned Elizabeth Ann Cottell before the Westminster Police Court. Mr Grant, one of the sanitary inspectors of Chelsea, had found eleven dogs and six cats in the dining room of Carlyle House. But when the door was opened, as the *Daily News* expressed it, 'In rushed mongrels and tabbies from up stairs and down stairs with a velocity that nearly made the Sanitary Inspector's head turn. He manfully tried to continue the census, but the animals refused to stand still. They ran in and out – barking, howling, yelping, mewing and miaulling – in such inextricable confusion that the enumeration broke down ...' Although the animals seemed to be in good cheer, healthy and well fed, the house was very dirty, and the stench far from pleasant. This time, Mrs Cottell was fined £11 23s and a further fine of £2 per day the nuisance continued. There was widespread newspaper publicity about the neglect and animal hoarding going on in Carlyle's house. The *IPN* thought the case most hilarious, and published a drawing of the mongrels and tabbies of No. 24 Cheyne Row.

Further prosecutions followed, in April and June 1893, and bailiffs entered Carlyle House to remove Mrs Cottell's furniture in lieu of the fines she had refused to pay. During the June hearing, Mrs Cottell lay down on the floor and pretended to go to sleep. The magistrate said that since she had kept his court busy for nearly a twelvemonth, and refused to pay the fines ordered by the court, she was clearly not in her right mind. The RSPCA accused Mrs Cottell of starving her remaining four dogs and three cats, but the old lady provided evidence that the cat's meat man provided plentiful amounts

Carlyle's house, a drawing from *The Homes and Haunts of Thomas Carlyle*.

Cats and dogs in Carlyle's house, a drawing from *The Homes and Haunts of Thomas Carlyle*.

of food for them. In September 1893, an admirer of Thomas Carlyle made a pilgrimage to the old house in Cheyne Row, the sad results of which he described in a letter to the *Daily Chronicle*. Mrs Cottell was away at the time, but she had left a caretaker to look after the house. This was not a task that this individual had taken particularly seriously, however, since the house was very dirty, the windows broken, and the rooms almost devoid of furniture. In 1893, Thomas Carlyle was still a household name, and many Londoners found it distasteful that his old house would meet with such a dismal fate.

In November 1893, although still in possession of a handsome annuity, Elizabeth Ann Cottell is recorded to have been in a Brighton workhouse. She died of delirium tremens in Richmond in July 1894. The old Chelsea chronicler Reginald Blunt described the decay of Carlyle's house, and the dog-hoarding Mrs Cottell's appearances in the police courts, adding the spicy remark that, 'A climax was reached when the lady herself succumbed, and a servant who continued in occupation introduced inhabitants far more objectionable than Persian cats and Maltese spaniels.' But in late 1894, the house was cleaned and repaired, and its undesirable inhabitant evicted. The author of an article on Carlyle's house in the *Woman's Signal* magazine could report that although No. 24 Cheyne Row had now been cleansed of Mrs Cottell and her animals, there were still many stray cats nearby, perhaps vainly waiting for one of the feline banquets that Mrs Cottell had used to arrange for them. As demonstrated in the story of the demented 'Cat Woman of Rottingdean', animal hoarding is not a modern phenomenon. Several instances of this unsavoury phenomenon are on record from Victorian times, in the *IPN* and other newspapers.

Mr George Lumsden, an admirer of Thomas Carlyle, was very much pained by the indignities his hero's old house had had to suffer.

He gathered together a group of kindred spirits, and pondered how to save the house. Lumsden and his friends found out that Mrs Cottell was in dire straits, and that her seven-year lease of the house was about to expire. They managed to raise £1,750, by public subscription, to purchase the house. After the house had been cleared up, and much of the Carlyles' original furniture repurchased, No. 24 Cheyne Row was opened to the public in 1895. Although Carlyle's ponderous prose was going out of fashion already in late Victorian times, there were still enough admirers of his weighty tomes to keep the turnstiles ticking over at a steady rate. Run by the National Trust since 1936, Carlyle's House is still open today, and admirers of his work, or of old London architecture, should take care not to miss it. Having visited it more than once, I am assured that it is not haunted by a horde of ghostly cats and dogs.

Above left: A postcard of Carlyle's house, stamped and posted in 1906.

Above right: A postcard stamped and posted in 1909, showing Carlyle's statue in the Chelsea Embankment Garden.

The Strange Case of Lord William Nevill, 1898

Lord William Beauchamp Nevill was born in 1860, the fourth son of the Marquess of Abergavenny. He was sent to Eton and then became an officer in the Royal West Kent Regiment. He was aide-de-camp to the Duke of Marlborough when he was Viceroy of India. Lord William then went into business, joining the firm of the Marques de Santurce, a wealthy foreign nobleman. In 1889, he married Luisa Maria Carmen de Murrieta, the eldest daughter of the Marques; they had quite a society wedding, attended by the Prince and Princess of Wales, and many other royal and noble characters. For a while, Lord William lived contentedly in London, but soon the South American business speculations of the Marques began to go seriously wrong, and Lord William had to rely on his own resources. He was not the shrewdest of men, nor the most energetic, and we all know who it is that finds work for idle hands to do ...

In 1897, Lord William Nevill was mixed up with a very queer set of London crooks and moneylenders. He had set up an office as an insurance agent, with indifferent success, and soon found it difficult to make a living. The only good news for him was that he had befriended a foolish young man named Herbert Clay, who had inherited considerable wealth. Clay could easily be persuaded to sign a roll of paper alleged by Lord William to concern his sister's divorce proceedings, but the cunning nobleman had 'doctored' this document by cutting out two squares in the paper, so that Clay was really signing two promissory notes for more than £11,000, payable to the moneylender Sam Lewis, of Cork Street. After a while, Clay's financial advisors found out about the forgery, and Lord William Nevill was arrested in February 1898 and ordered to stand trial at the Old Bailey, for fraud and forgery. A drawing of him in the dock shows a rum-looking cove with a receding hairline and a prominent nose. The case against him was rock solid, and he was found guilty and sentenced to not less than five years of penal servitude. Lord William hung his head in shame when Mr Justice Lawrence spoke of his noble family being dishonoured, and sorrow, suffering and shame brought to those near and dear to him; his crime had been great, and his punishment must be severe, this far from bonhomous judge proclaimed.

An 1899 feature in *The Times* on celebrated prisoners lists Lord William Nevill as a prisoner in Parkhurst Prison, Isle of Wight, and he was still there at the time of the 1901 Census. In November 1901, Lord William was released from prison, after three years and eight months 'inside'. One would have expected to see the disgraced nobleman 'leave well alone' and try to become a useful member of society, but in 1903, he published his prison memoirs *Penal Servitude*, anonymously under the alias 'W.B.N.' He complained at length of the injustice of his sentence and the severity of the Old Bailey judge; since the man Clay had been so

Lord William Nevill being sentenced to five years of penal servitude, from the *IPN*, 26 February 1898.

very rich and thoughtless, he had never missed the £11,000 he had been swindled out of, so Lord William's crime had in reality been one without a victim! Lord William gave a realistic account of his experiences in prison, with its many indignities. Being something of a gourmet, he found the prison grub very unpalatable, with its poorly baked bread, rotten potatoes and rubber-like meat. He became very thin, but the unfeeling prison authorities kept working him hard as an agricultural labourer. The book of prison memoirs sold poorly and is today relatively scarce.

Again, one would have expected someone who spent 309 pages of a book whingeing about the horrors of prison life to 'go straight' after being released, but Lord William must have suffered from some mental quirk that made him incapable of making an honest living. In 1907, it was 'porridge' again for Lord William: he was sentenced to twelve months' imprisonment for stealing £350 worth of jewels by means of trickery, in what was called the 'Black Diamonds' case. A drawing of him in the dock demonstrates that in spite of having lost much hair, he had grown a large handle-bar moustache. This time, he was released from Wormwood Scrubs in February 1908.

In 1919, Lord William Nevill received positive mention in *The Times* for having set up a club for foreign servicemen two years earlier. The same newspaper mentioned him once or twice in its society column in the coming decades, indicating that Lord William may well have landed on his feet after his second stint in prison, and been able to rejoin London society in a more humble capacity. In April 1931, he received some cheering news, when the prima donna Dame Nellie Melba left him a legacy of £1,000 in her will. In April 1934, there was renewed odium when Charles Francis Field, formerly butler to Lord William Nevill, took him to court for publishing

Lord William Nevill in the dock again, from the *Penny Illustrated Paper*, 20 April 1907.

a defamatory libel, namely that the butler and his wife were crooks and blackmailers. Lord William was bound over in the sum of £100 to keep the peace for two years, and ordered to pay ten guineas in costs. This was the final newsworthy action of this all-rounder in crime, however: he died in May 1937, aged seventy-eight, from bronchopneumonia, cerebral softening and generalised arteriosclerosis according to his death certificate. Several newspapers published his obituary, since he was after all the uncle of the present Marquess of Abergavenny. Lady William Nevill, who had loyally stood by her husband through thick and thin, lived on to see another war, before expiring in 1951 at the age of eighty-seven.

The Poulett Claimant, 1899

In the summer of 1849, when some jolly young English officers in Dublin sat drinking and gambling in their mess-room, one of them thought of an amusing bet. If another of their number, Lieutenant William Poulett, agreed to marry the first woman he saw after walking out of the barracks, he would win £500; otherwise he would forfeit the same amount of money. Drunken young William Poulett, the nephew of the Earl of the same name, thought this a capital idea. And he did not 'chicken out' of his bet: when he met Miss Eliza Newman, the daughter of a humble Dublin pilot, he politely asked her hand in marriage. After they had wed a week later, Poulett cashed in £500 from his friends.

The caddish young Poulett installed Eliza in his quarters, without telling anybody that she was actually his wife. When the Colonel came to call on her, in the belief that Poulett was illicitly keeping a mistress in his quarters, she indignantly showed him the marriage certificate. Lieutenant Poulett received a severe reprimand for his foolish conduct, and became the laughing-stock of the regiment. In a furious temper, he returned to his quarters, beat up his wife mercilessly, and kicked her out of the barracks, promising more ill-usage should she ever return. Poor Mrs Poulett went to join her mother in Portsmouth, where six months later she gave birth to her infant son William. With the help of a small allowance from her cad of a husband, she was able to send her son to the French and English College at Merton, but there was no money for him to attend any higher education. Instead, young William wanted to become an actor. He played the leading role in 'Sweeney Todd' at the Garrick for a salary of 25s per week. This enabled him to marry the young ballet dancer Lydia Shippey, and set up a humble family home in London. But not long after, disaster struck: William accidentally stumbled down an open trapdoor, breaking the fall with his jaw. He became disfigured for life, and could only play comical parts, where his chinless appearance would actually be an advantage. In the end, he became a circus clown.

In the meantime, Lieutenant William Poulett had been hounded out of his regiment as a result of his scandalous marriage. He joined the 22nd Foot instead and went to India, serving in the Mutiny. His relatives back in England started dying off at an alarming rate, however, and after old Earl Poulett had expired in 1861, Captain William Poulett inherited the title. Overjoyed, he retired from the military, settled down at stately Hinton House near Crewkerne, and built up a stable of expensive racehorses. The year 1871 was a good one for Earl Poulett: firstly, his horse 'The Lamb' won the Grand National, and secondly, his estranged wife died, allowing him to marry again. The caddish nobleman wanted to make this a hat-trick of breakthroughs in his career. He invited his 'son' the circus clown to his club, and offered him a handsome yearly allowance if he went to India or some equally far-away place. If the Earl had used some degree of tact or astuteness, he might well have been able to 'export' poor William abroad, but instead he acted in his usual snobbish manner, declaring that William was a bastard in more ways than one: he was definitely the son of the man who had 'kept' his mother prior to her marriage. After William had refused to go abroad, the Earl cut him off without a penny.

Fortunately for William, he received financial help from the dowager Duchess of Cleveland, who was on bad terms with Earl Poulett. She provided William with some money, and he assumed the family's courtesy title of Viscount Hinton. The Duchess also helped him to set up 'Lord Hinton's Burlesque and Comedy Company', a travelling circus. They toured for a few months, visiting Crewkerne to annoy the Earl, before the money ran out. The kind Duchess again helped William to get on his feet, setting him up as a clown and female impersonator at St James's Theatre. In the early 1880s, after developing some kind of speech impediment, William had to retire from the theatre. Instead, he fell in with a gang of criminals, who wanted to use the weak and foolish Viscount as a front to their fraudulent company. In 1886, they were all arrested, and William was sentenced to twelve months in prison, with hard labour. His poor wife screamed and fainted in court, since she was fearful her ailing husband would die in prison. After his release in 1887, the Viscount was in desperate straits. He took to tramping London with a street organ, with a placard saying: 'I am Viscount Hinton, eldest son of Earl Poulett. I have adopted this as a means of earning a living, my father having refused to assist me through no fault of my own.'

The Viscount turned organ-grinder became one of the curiosities of London: people of all classes came to see him, and to put a penny into the collecting-box of the thin, careworn-looking man grinding away at his instrument.

In January 1899, Earl Poulett expired at the age of seventy-two. Although his habit of purchasing expensive but slow racehorses, and

Some ribald images from the varied career of the organ-grinding Viscount, from *IPN*, 4 February 1899.

betting large sums of money on these animals, had seriously depleted the family coffers, there was still stately Hinton House and a wealth of other real estate that the Earl had not had the time to squander. The organ-grinding Viscount lost no time to consult a solicitor and claim the Earldom; his rival was the old Earl's son in his third marriage. For a few heady months, the Viscount was a major newspaper celebrity. Since an organ-grinder aspiring to become an Earl was certainly *Illustrated Police news*, there were some lengthy features about him in this newspaper, illustrated with ribald original drawings. The Viscount seemed quite optimistic that he would finally to be able to cast off the yoke of poverty, and to claim the title and family estates. He sold his street organ to Madame Tussaud's for £60, before sitting for his likeness, modelled by Mr John Tussaud and dressed in a suit of his own shabby clothes.

But the organ-grinding Viscount was up against wealthy and powerful enemies. The old Earl had never made it a secret that he preferred the son from his third marriage, and detested the organ-grinding clown his first wife had tried to foist upon him. Since the Committee of Privileges of the House of Lords was not a body that believed in hasty action, the Poulett peerage hearing did not begin until July 1903. The Viscount could present his mother's marriage certificate and his own birth certificate, proving that she had been married to Lieutenant Poulett at the time he himself had been born. At this time, it was standard to presume that a child born in wedlock was not a bastard. But after due deliberation, the Committee rejected the Viscount's claim, since he had been born just six months after the marriage. The proper reason was probably that the organ-grinding Viscount was such a very unattractive specimen of humanity, whereas the younger claimant was a handsome young gentleman. The heartbroken 'Viscount', who was now just Mr William Turnour, went back to Madame Tussaud's to reclaim his organ, before setting out to tramp the endless streets of London once again. He died at the infirmary of Holborn Union Workhouse in 1909, from hypertrophy and fatty degeneration of the heart according to his death certificate.

Young Earl Poulett married an actress and became a popular society figure. He died of influenza while serving as an army captain in the Great War. He was succeeded by his young son, who also married an actress, although she later deserted him. When the last Earl Poulett died childless in 1973, all his titles became extinct. Hinton House has been sold and is today subdivided into flats. Are they perhaps haunted by a slow, shuffling gait of a broken old man, and the ghostly sound of an old-fashioned street organ?

The old Earl, the junior claimant, and some other images from the Poulett family, from *IPN*, 18 February 1899.

10

Crime and Mystery

The Great Speke Mystery, 1868

In early 1868, the Revd Benjamin Speke had been the rector of Dowlish Wake, a quiet Somerset village, for eleven years. Since the wealthy Speke family was very powerful locally, his promotion to rector of a good parish, at quite a young age, may well have been the result of nepotism. He was the brother of the adventurous explorer Captain John Hanning Speke, who had discovered the sources of the Nile, and died in a mysterious hunting accident in 1864. Himself, Benjamin Speke had never done anything interesting or newsworthy in his life. A confirmed bachelor, he looked after the spiritual welfare of his flock of just four hundred souls, and busied himself with the restoration of the church. He was quite popular among his parishioners, thanks to his kindness and generosity, and his heartfelt and traditional theological views. But this obscure West Country parson's humdrum life was just about to change.

On 8 January 1868, the Revd Benjamin Speke wanted to attend the marriage of an old friend in London. He was driven to Chard station, where he bought a return ticket to Waterloo. The train was a few minutes late, arriving at about 4.45 in the afternoon. Speke hailed a cab and went to his brother-in-law's house in Eccleston Square. Arriving there five minutes later, he told a footman that he was going to Warwick Street to buy a new hat, and then to Westminster on business. Later the same day, he would be dining with a friend at seven, although he insisted that he would be back to the house in time to change. Several witnesses attested that Benjamin Speke made it to the Warwick Street hatters, where he chose a top hat and ordered it to be delivered to his brother-in-law's house, not later than 6.45 since it would be required the same evening. But after leaving the hatters, the Revd Benjamin Speke disappeared into thin air.

PORTRAIT OF THE REV. MR. SPEKE AND VIEW OF HIS SISTER'S HOUSE.

The Revd Benjamin Speke, from the *IPN*, 22 February 1868.

Worried that Speke might have been murdered or kidnapped, his brother-in-law Mr Murdoch immediately contacted the police. It was initially hoped that it would be easy to track down a dog-collared Somerset clergyman in the busy London streets, but the only result of the hue and cry was that a workman reported to the police station, carrying a top hat. He had found it in Birdcage Walk at 7.30 the same evening Speke had disappeared, and originally planned to keep it for himself. But then he read about the missing clergyman in the newspapers, and saw that its lining was marked with 'Speke'. The police regarded the finding of the hat as a clear indication that Speke had not disappeared from his own free will. The clergyman's friends agreed: what reason could there be for this wealthy gentleman of high moral character and unchallenged integrity to 'go underground' and abscond from his previous life?

The lost country parson became headline news in all the London papers. Numerous amateur detectives brought forward the most extraordinary theories for how Speke might have been done away with. Had some criminal gang burgled the Eccleston Square house, murdered Speke, and hidden his dismembered remains underneath the floorboards? Or had the unfortunate clergyman been decoyed into a cab by a gang of foreign criminals, to be knocked out cold by a boxing glove fitted to a powerful spring, shot by a hidden air-gun, or rendered unconscious by chloroform pumped into the vehicle? Speculation was also rife as to whether these gangsters had murdered Speke and stolen the money in his wallet, or whether he actually might be held for ransom to extort a fortune from his wealthy family. There was even lewd speculation that Speke might be on his way, in a drugged or fettered condition, to some vile brothel in Tunis or Tangiers, cities where the most horrible and unnatural vices were current. Another set of obvious suspects, at least for the xenophobic London journalists, were closer to home. Had the dastardly Fenians perhaps mistaken Speke for the Home Secretary Mr Gathorne Hardy, and kidnapped the clergyman by mistake? Unamused, the police objected that Mr Hardy was twenty years older than Speke, and not in the habit of wearing clerical attire.

There was much scare-mongering about the Great Speke Mystery in the London newspapers. Many other people, clergymen prominent among them, claimed to have had disturbing experiences with foreign-looking ruffians trying to waylay or abduct them. Mr White, Chaplain of the Savoy, claimed that they had tried to decoy him into a cab, saying that he was wanted to give evidence by the Chief Magistrate at Bow Street. *The Sunday Times* claimed that several other well-to-do Londoners had recently disappeared. Surely, there must be a well-organised gang of assassins at work in the Metropolis, with an ample supply of decoy hansom cabs equipped with air-guns and chloroform-pumps. Having plundered their victims, these villains dismembered their bodies and left the remains in the countryside, to be devoured by foxes and badgers. Another horror-story involved the discovery of a chopping-block in a London slum dwelling. It could be opened by a spring mechanism, and underneath was an opening to a main sewer: was this where Speke and the dastardly gang's other victims had been dismembered and unceremoniously dumped? *The Times* exposed this particular story as a newspaper canard, however.

Originally, Benjamin Speke's friends had posted a reward of just £3 for the recovery of the missing clergyman, but as the moral panic about the Great Speke Mystery kept growing, so did the reward. Even an offer of £500 did not produce the desired result, however, and no trace of Speke was found; nor was any worthwhile clue. *The Spectator* wrote that, 'Twenty or thirty thousand minds have been at work upon the case, including the whole body of Police, the entire Bar, and the whole body of Clubmen.' By late February, the journalists entertained little hope that Speke would ever be seen again. Surely, no self-respecting kidnapper would 'sit on' his victim for more than a month and a half, before sending a demand for money to the wealthy Spekes, enclosing a blood-stained dog-collar. They concluded that the unfortunate clergyman had been the victims of one of London's well-organised criminal gangs.

On 24 February 1868, Police Sergeant Soady, of the Cornwall Constabulary, saw a rum-looking cove trudge down the main street in Padstow. He was dressed like a cattle-drover, but seemed to have seen better days. Sergeant Soady thought he looked rather like a swindler named Ayre, who was wanted by the Hull police for stealing a large sum of money from his employers. When the tramp was arrested and searched, a large sum of money in banknotes was found in his pockets and wallet. Proud to have captured the Hull miscreant, the Cornwall coppers communicated with the Chief Constable and the Superintendent of Police. But when these gentlemen had interviewed the suspect, they found nothing to suggest that he was the Hull swindler. Instead, the senior policemen looked through their files of other fugitives and missing people, and found the description of the Revd Benjamin Speke; the Padstow mystery man fitted it perfectly.

When challenged with being the missing clergyman, the man became very agitated, before admitting that he was really the Revd Benjamin Speke. He said that he had believed that all his friends and relatives were against him, and decided to 'disappear'. Leaving his tall hat in Birdcage Walk as a decoy, he left London in disguise and tramped around the West Country for many weeks, visiting various churches and monuments. He bought the newspapers every day, to read about himself. His original plan had been to start life afresh in the United States, he said, but he could not explain why, in that case, he had dallied so long in England.

Taken back to London, the Revd Benjamin Speke was examined by a team of competent physicians, who diagnosed 'a depressing form of hypochondriasis' which had been aggravated by certain quack medicines imbibed by the patient. Some waggish journalists disputed this diagnosis, however. The *Western Morning News* thought that Speke's excessive biblical study had led to religious monomania. A *Times* correspondent had heard rumours that Speke had a morbid dread of marriage, and presumed that he had absconded to avoid an unwanted marriage arranged by his family. *The Spectator* wrote that, 'We never heard of Mr Speke in his life until Mr Murdoch published his first letter, and shall be delighted never to hear of him again, – considering that he ought in common decency to have been murdered in a cab by foreigners.'

The London Correspondent of the *New York Times* hade definitely had enough of the Revd Benjamin Speke:

> You will have heard all about Mr Speke by telegraph. He has had an immense success – been the talk of the town for nearly a month, and had as many leaders written about him as if he had conquered a world. No doubt you read some of the elaborate and ingenious theories which were put forward to account for his disappearance. I believe, however, that I may claim the credit of having sent to you, in a letter written nearly three weeks ago, the explanation which turned out to be the true one. I declared my conviction (founded on experience among 'bolters') that he had run away to escape marriage. That is now asserted to be the fact. Speke's friends are trying to make out that he is a little touched in the head, but there is no reason to believe that he has ever been anything else than a fool. He has now been playing a cruel and wicked part, and his friends in paying £500 for his recovery have given exactly £499 19s 113/4 more than he is worth. He pretends to have some peculiar religious ideas, and to be aiming for America – attracted thither, I suppose, by Mr Hepworth Dixon's indecent and imbecile books. Enough of him! He will now sink into sudden and general contempt.

And indeed, the Revd Benjamin Speke returned to his flock in Dowlish Wake, and well-deserved obscurity. In 1869, he became engaged to marry his first cousin Miss Fuller, the daughter of a Wiltshire squire. There was light-hearted newspaper speculation whether he would be absconding again, but this time he made it all the way to the altar. The couple went on to be fruitful and replenish the earth, having not less than eight children. But tragedy struck in 1881: Mrs Speke died on 23 February, and her heartbroken husband drowned himself the following day, leaving his numerous brood of children orphans. The Revd Benjamin Speke's obituary in *The Times* mostly deals with his escapade back in 1868, although it states that in spite of his rash actions, he was descended from a respectable old Somerset family.

A Thieves' Supper

Ned Wright, a young London hooligan, was quite incorrigible at school, and imprisoned for theft not long after. He became a prize-fighter, and later a sailor, but his nautical career did not last long: he was severely flogged and imprisoned for some unspecified misdemeanour. Ned married a young woman named Maria Beard, but he remained a drunkard and treated her cruelly. Although Ned still occasionally fought in the ring, his main source of income came from burglary.

One day, Ned attended a street prayer-meeting, an experience that made this London street rough think about religion, probably for the first time. He brought Maria to another meeting, where they both became converted Christians. But although Ned now had religion, he could not find a job. Nobody wanted to employ a former thief and drunkard. When Ned had spent thirteen weeks searching for work, he and his wife prayed for food, and Lo! they found a penny loaf in the cupboard. This was clearly Divine intervention, and Ned decided to spend the remainder of his life in the service of the Lord. In spite of being quite uneducated, he began preaching in the streets, and no amount of derision could distract this singular lay preacher from his mission. There were already churches and cathedrals for the wealthy, Ned reasoned, but what God wanted him to do was to convert London's thieves and vagabonds to the Christian faith.

Despairing of persuading the London thieves to attend his sermons, Ned invented the 'Thieves' Supper'. At these extraordinary religious meetings, convicted thieves were invited to a supper of strong pea soup and loaves of bread. In January 1870, the first recorded Thieves' Supper was held at Ned Wright's Gospel Hall in the New Cut, Lambeth. Not less than 220 thieves sat at table, eagerly awaiting the soup and bread. As Ned was overseeing proceedings, he received a fair bit of 'chaff' from his dinner guests, which he put a stop to by saying, 'You're going to have a clinking clump of bread each, and if you make your jaws ache now, they'll be no use when you get the tommy (bread).' When Ned gave the sign, the bread and soup was devoured with the rapidity of extreme hunger.

When the thieves had cleared the table, the sturdy, muscular Ned Wright began his sermon. For nearly an hour, he kept his audience spellbound with his adventurous religious parallels, using anecdotes from his own career. When he had been a pugilist, a boxing promoter had offered him £1,000 to throw a fight, but Ned smote the Philistine and threw him out of the house. Another time, Ned had rescued a boy from drowning in the Thames; were the thieves in the audience not as helpless as the drowning lad, and as dependent on him for their salvation? He told them how the loaf had miraculously appeared in his cupboard, and how his first-born son had been taken from him to test his faith. After some rousing hymns had been sung, the slack-jawed thieves trudged away into the night, their bellies full of soup and bread, and their minds equally saturated with Ned's odd religious ideas.

Ned Wright was the man of the day. Many journalists praised him for his practical Christianity, and he found sponsors for further Thieves' Suppers at the Gospel Hall. Female thieves and juvenile delinquents got suppers of their own, so that they would not have to consort with the more hardened wretches. Although the thieves were keen to get their hands on some more promising food, Ned strictly adhered to his 'bread and soup' formula, with which he was able to nourish large congregations at very little cost. Ned was also praised for his philanthropy. Through one of his sponsors, he purchased thirty costermongers' barrows, and tried to recruit as many thieves to pull them. Each thief would be given a shilling each to begin business for himself: 'many a thriving salesman has risen from so small a capital to independence'. Another of his schemes, outlined in a remarkable advertisement, was even more adventurous:

HONEST EMPLOYMENT FOR THIEVES
Sir – Permit me to solicit your helping hand to temporarily rescue poor thieves from their miserable position, hundreds of whom are at this moment ready to work at carrying advertisement boards in the streets, also delivering circulars &c &c at a small return.
Apply to Edward Wright. Boards and men always in readiness.

But as Ned Wright became something of a London celebrity, there was a media backlash against 'the converted burglar' and his bizarre activities. Was it not counterproductive to nourish the criminal classes, so that they emerged from the Gospel Hall sturdy and well fed, and ready for burglary and murder? 'Supper for thieves indeed! The only proper meal is what our forefathers would have given them – Old English whipping-cheer!' exclaimed *Punch*. The mainstream clergy found Ned's liberal use of Cockney rhyming slang in his sermons more than a little unsettling. And surely, they reasoned, his religious oratory was quite blasphemous. Once, he claimed that after his conversion, the bruiser Mike Madden had tried to break his jaw for refusing to fight him in the ring, but Mike's

Ned Wright's Supper for Female Thieves, from the *IPN*, 5 February 1870.

A Thieves' Supper, from the *IPN*, 13 December 1884.

clenched fist had been averted by the hand of Providence. Through the same means, Ned had been saved from a large stone that an evil-minded person had directed against his head during one of his sermons. In another sermon, Ned described how a kind ship's corporal had once comforted him with some water after he had received two dozen lashes. Foaming at the mouth, the evangelist continued, 'Yes, he pitied me, and gave me to drink; but when He was dying on the Cross and cried out, "I thirst!", what did they give Him? Vinegar and gall on a sponge! And yet He forgave His enemies and saved the world!'

Ned Wright remained active throughout the 1870s and 1880s, holding many Thieves' Suppers in London and the provinces. In 1873, he published his autobiography, *The Story of My Life*. In 1876, work was begun on his new Mission Hall, in George Street, Clerkenwell. His marriage to Maria was a happy and long-lasting one, and although their eldest son Edward had died prematurely in 1884, they had five daughters and a son who all grew to adulthood. In 1886, Ned Wright advertised a Free Tea for Rogues, Thieves, and Vagabonds, at the Lillie Road Mission Hall, West Brompton. Not less than 150 thieves enjoyed a hearty meal, and were afterwards treated to the exhortations of Ned Wright. In the 1890s, Ned gradually sunk into obscurity, although he kept touring the country to preach to all who would listen to him. The 1901 Census finds Ned and Maria Wright living in a comfortable semi-detached house at No. 10 Greenhill Park, Willesden. All their children had fled the nest, but a female amanuensis and a young general servant completed the household. In July 1908, the newspapers could announce that Ned Wright had died in Tintagel while on a mission to Cornwall, just as he was looking forward to going home to Harlesden to celebrate his birthday. The more positive of his ideas had been absorbed by charities controlled by the mainstream clergy; they held the last recorded Thieves' Supper at the St Giles' Christian Mission in December 1891.

The Great Twiss Mystery

The *London Gazette* of April 1872 contained the following cryptic announcement, published under the authority of the Lord Chamberlain: 'The presentation of Lady Twiss at the Drawing-room attended by her in 1869 is cancelled.' For mere mortals, it is hardly possible to cancel a previous introduction to some unsavoury character, but royalty has a different code of conduct; clearly, Queen Victoria had not been at all amused by the conduct of this mysterious Lady Twiss. Indeed, the main accuser of the errant lady boldly claimed that it had been his duty 'to expose such an outrageous scandal on society, and such an unprecedented insult to Her Majesty'. So had Lady Twiss stolen Queen Victoria's underwear, or spied on her in her dressing-room, like that enterprising persecutor of royalty, Edward 'The Boy' Jones? Or was her ladyship one of the deranged individuals who had fired off an old flintlock pistol in the general direction of the Queen's carriage? No, the misdeeds of Lady Twiss were more subtle and mysterious than those of the royal stalker and would-be assassins. The Great Twiss Mystery of 1872, in which the young and beautiful wife of a distinguished advocate was accused of having led a secret life as a prostitute, has awaited its solution for nearly a century and a half.

Travers Twiss was born in 1809, the eldest son of a capitalist clergyman. After a distinguished Oxford career, he was elected Fellow of University College and published a series of weighty treatises, mainly about international law, an area where he was fast becoming an authority. In 1855, he was appointed Regius Professor of Civil Law in Oxford, a post that he would hold for many years. Travers Twiss became an advocate at Doctor's Commons, an archaic institution specialising in a variety of civil law cases. Considered a man of superior integrity and high moral qualities, he also acquired a number of well-paid legal appointments within the Church of England, becoming Vicar General of the Archbishop of Canterbury, and Chancellor of the Diocese of London. Travers Twiss made use of the income from his flourishing legal practice to purchase a fashionable town house at No. 19 Park Lane. On 29 August 1862, the fifty-three-year-old Travers Twiss married, at the British Legation in Dresden, a young lady who gave her name as Pharailde Rosalie Van Lynseele, her place of birth as Courtrai, and her age as just twenty-two. In a letter to a friend, Travers Twiss described how he had 'narrowly escaped finding no clergyman, since the Revd Mr Dale, a self-supporting clergyman, only returned by the same train which brought me'. And indeed, the marriage certificate is signed by 'Henry Dale, British Chaplain at Dresden', and looks fully legitimate.

Travers Twiss proudly brought his young wife back to London and installed her at No. 19 Park Lane. The contrast between the two could not have been greater: he was thick-set, bewhiskered and elderly-looking, but she was quite beautiful, with long dark hair and refined features. Mrs Pharailde Twiss took to life in London society like a duck to water: she spoke good English with a charming French accent, and seemed the perfect gentlewoman. If anything, there was surprise among the romantics that such an attractive young lady would have married a much older man, but the realists pointed out the very healthy state of her husband's coffers, and his fine Park Lane residence. Since Travers Twiss was fond of showing off his young 'trophy wife' in society, she attended many lavish parties, and had her own box at the Opera. She met Dr Tait, the Archbishop of Canterbury, and Dr Jackson, the Bishop of London. In 1867, Twiss was made the Queen's Advocate, and later the same year, he was knighted. Sir Travers Twiss was now at the height of his powers, and there was speculation that he might one day proceed to the Woolsack, or to high government office. In 1869, when Sir Travers and Lady Twiss attended a Drawing-Room at Buckingham Palace, she made her curtsy to the Queen.

Sir Travers Twiss, Lady Twiss and Alexander Chaffers, from the *IPN*, 23 March 1872. This is the only known likeness of Lady Twiss.

Old houses in Park Lane, a postcard stamped and posted in 1904. There is reason to believe that the Twiss house at No. 19 is one of the houses furthest to the right on this case; it has since been demolished, and the Hilton Hotel stands on the site.

Sir Travers Twiss had one implacable enemy, the small-time solicitor Alexander Chaffers. Poor as a church mouse, Chaffers must have envied the prominent advocate's wealth and prominent position in society. He approached Sir Travers Twiss after his marriage, claiming that his wife owed him money for some legal services. Chaffers sent a bill for £150, but the canny Sir Travers reduced the amount to £50 and made Chaffers sign an affidavit that his claim had been settled in full. This rebuff appears to have unhinged the mind of the already paranoid solicitor, and inspired a deadly hatred against Sir Travers and his wife. Alexander Chaffers kept writing them ambiguous and threatening letters, hinting that he possessed dangerous information about Lady Twiss and her early life, and that he would be collecting further evidence about her immoral past. Suspecting that he was dealing with a blackmailer, Sir Travers ignored him, something that angered the demented Chaffers further.

On 4 April 1871, Alexander Chaffers went to the Bow Street Police Court, where he made a statutory declaration in front of one of the magistrates. He swore that Lady Twiss had resided in London for several years prior to 1862, as a prostitute under the name Madame Marie Gelas. Chaffers had first met her in April 1859: he had picked her up in Regent Street, accompanied her to her lodgings in Upper Berkeley Street, remained with her a couple of hours and given her a sovereign. He afterwards visited her on regular intervals, constantly passing the whole night with her. In the summer of 1859, he had frequently seen Marie Gelas at Cremorne Gardens and at the Holborn Casino, sometimes alone, sometimes in company with another foreign prostitute. In August 1859, Marie had told Chaffers that she had met Travers Twiss, and that he had agreed to keep her as his mistress, allowing her £5 a week. In March 1862, he sent her to Dresden, having purchased her hand in marriage for four promissory notes for £500 each. This cunning plan had worked a treat: they had married in August, he had brought her back to London, and she had been fully accepted in society.

The malicious Chaffers distributed copies of this unpleasant document to various legal and clerical luminaries, including the Archbishop of Canterbury, the Lord Mayor, and the Queen's Proctor. The Lord Chamberlain, who had also received a copy, spoke with Sir Travers and Lady Twiss, and declared himself convinced that the accusations were entirely baseless. He recommended that Twiss should take Chaffers to court for libel, but Sir Travers, who knew what his opponent was capable of, hesitated for some time, until Archbishop Tait told him that he could delay no longer. In February 1872, Chaffers was summoned before the Southwark Police Court, before Mr Ralph Benson the magistrate, for maliciously publishing defamatory and wicked libels upon Sir Travers and Lady Twiss, with intent to extort money.

The prosecution of Alexander Chaffers was conducted by the barrister Harry Poland: when opening his case, he asserted that the Twisses had nothing to hide, and that they invited the fullest inquiry. As for Chaffers, he was merely a vulgar and dastardly blackmailer. When Lady Twiss was called as a witness, there was breathless interest in court. She declared herself to be the orphan daughter of Major General Count Raoul Van Lynseele, a Polish officer who had resided in Belgium. When the Count went to Java, he left his daughter behind in Brussels, to be looked after by her guardian, Count Felix Jastrzebski, in his house in the Boulevard de Waterloo. Between 1859 and 1861, she had been living with her governess Madame Marie Gelas at South Street in London, in order to study English, in which language she was not then proficient. When she fell dangerously ill, she decided to execute a will, making use of the solicitor Alexander Chaffers, who came recommended by Madame Gelas, to draw it up. She then went to Courtrai for a while, to study German, before going on to Dresden where she met and married Travers Twiss.

In Harry Poland's examination, Lady Twiss confidently denied all Chaffers' allegations, declaring that she and Madame Gelas had been two different people. The possible past misdeeds of her former governess thus had nothing to do with herself. The only time she had seen Chaffers before her marriage was when he drew up her will, and all his vile allegations were entirely false. At the beginning of his cross-examination in court, the venomous Chaffers sneered at Lady Twiss and promised that he would have a lot of questions for her. And he was as bad as his word. In a highly scurrilous and indecent cross-examination, he suggested that the background she had just given was an invention: she had been born in Courtrai of humble parentage, before becoming the notorious London prostitute Madame Gelas. Her parents and brother had accompanied her to London. Chaffers had more than once taken her to the Argyll Rooms, and to the Holborn Casino, where the tipsy young Madame Gelas had danced with her hair hanging down her back, and so misconducted herself that the master of ceremonies had reprimanded her. In September 1860, Chaffers and Madame Gelas had gone for a romantic journey to Courtrai, where they had lived together at No. 15 Grand Place. Madame Gelas had been arrested for debt, and seen the inside of a sponging-house, and she had once received treatment for venereal disease from a certain Dr Straube. Lady Twiss stalwartly denied all his scandalous allegations, and declared that there had never been the smallest familiarity between the defendant and herself. She had known Dr Straube as the doctor of Madame Gelas, but she had never been treated by him. As for Sir Travers Twiss, Chaffers pointed out that he had previously kept the notorious courtesan Agnes Willoughby as his mistress, before 'buying her off' with £8,000 and all the furniture she had stolen from his house in Park Lane.

After Lady Twiss had been tormented for two full hours, it was time for the witnesses for the defence to be called. Felix Jastrzebski exclaimed that he would have sacrificed his life for Lady Twiss: he had come all the way from Brussels to defend her honour, which was as dear to him as his own! He corroborated all the details Lady Twiss had given concerning her schooling and early life: he had known her governess Madame Gelas, and they were two different people. Louisa Harrison, formerly lady's maid to Pharailde Van Lynseele, had also known Madame Gelas, who did not in the slightest resemble Pharailde, being short, with a dark complexion, and several years older. Chaffers had once approached Louisa Harrison, promising her £150 if she swore that Sir Travers had been intimate with Pharailde before their marriage, but the stalwart former lady's maid would not be a party to such perjury. Four other witnesses then swore that Madame Gelas and Pharailde Van Lynseele were two different people, and that they did not resemble each other in the slightest: among them the Brussels artist M. Guillaume who had painted Pharailde's portrait, and her former music master M. Des Marès.

Since the defence witnesses had made an excellent impression in court, things were not looking good for the creature Chaffers. The plan was for Harry Poland to sum up his case, before Chaffers called his own witnesses. The police court was full to capacity on 13 March, when the case was expected to conclude, and both the spectators and the journalists expected that Lady Twiss would triumph, and her cowardly assailant be committed for trial. But when Harry Poland appeared in court, it was with a very glum face. Lady Twiss had resolved not to reappear in court, and she had left London! The prosecution against Alexander Chaffers was withdrawn, and he was a free man. But before the gloating Chaffers could leave the dock, the irate Mr Benson addressed him in ringing tones, saying that in the history of criminal proceedings, there had never been one that ended with such utterly demoralising results. For his abominable cross-examination of Lady Twiss, Chaffers would become an object of contempt to all honest and right-thinking men.

After Lady Twiss had fled London, Sir Travers resigned all his offices and sought refuge with her in Lausanne. The disastrous outcome of the Twiss Libel Case was headline news, in papers all over the British Empire. Alexander Chaffers published *The Twiss Libel Case*, a short pamphlet in which he reproduced what he alleged was the true birth certificate of Lady Twiss: she had been born on 5 October 1834, daughter of the carpenter Pierre Denis Van Lynseele and his wife Barbe Thérèse Vanderschoore, and christened Pharailde Rosalie the following day. The certificate states that since the father and one of the witnesses could not write, only the first witness signed his name along that of the civil registration officer. This document alone proved that Lady Twiss had committed perjury on no less than six points. In addition, she had been twenty-eight years old when she married Sir Travers in 1862, and not twenty-two as she had alleged. Chaffers also possessed an affidavit from the jeweller Denis Faure, who had many times visited the prostitute Marie Gelas, whose real name was Pharailde Van Lynseele, at the time she resided at Brompton. The testimony of the buffoon 'Count Jastrzebski', a title likely to have been conferred by himself, had been of a very perjurious nature, as had that of Messieurs Guillaume and Des Marès. Interestingly, Chaffers writes that the flight of Lady Twiss had been brought about by the few questions that he had put to the latter gentleman. The wicked Lady Twiss had then perceived that Chaffers was better acquainted than she expected, as to her recent life in Brussels while her husband had been absent. And indeed, *The Times* trial transcript shows that Chaffers pressed M. Des Marès hard with regard to another Brussels resident with the same name, who lived in a certain house at Rue de la Paille. The *soi-disant* music master denied that he was identical to the man in question, but refused to state their relationship, although he admitted previously living in the Rue de la Paille house himself. Reading between the lines, the 'certain house' was of course a brothel, and its resident the brothel-keeper.

Sir Travers Twiss would have been in danger of disappearing into obscurity altogether, had he not found a useful friend and kindred spirit in the international arena. When King Leopold II of Belgium employed him to provide legal justification for the creation of his Congo Free State, it took all of Sir Travers' capacity for legal wrangling to manipulate the law into allowing the Belgian tyrant's exploitation of his Congo empire, one of the most disgraceful episodes in the annals of colonialism. Feeble health and indifferent finances darkened the old advocate's declining years; he died in his terraced Fulham house in 1897, aged eighty-eight. There is reason to believe that Lady Twiss ended her days in an asylum in Brussels. As for Alexander Chaffers, he developed a mania for legal actions against various prominent people, and the Vexatious Actions Act of 1896 was designed to impede his litigation mania. Having had the satisfaction of surviving his great enemy Sir Travers Twiss, he died in St Pancras Workhouse in April 1899.

The earliest chronicler of the Great Twiss Mystery was the old crime writer Horace Wyndham, who quoted a passage from a book of memoirs of Sir Harry Poland, in which the former barrister of Lady Twiss recapitulated this very painful case, of the most terrible character. The next person to investigate the mystery was John Sparrow, the celebrated Oxford academic. He took an interest in 'Count Jastrzebski', who had turned up in London for the trial, and it turned out that Felix Jastrzebski [1805–1874] had served as an officer in the Polish Uprising in 1830. The year after, he had settled down in Brussels and become a manufacturer of pianos, with considerable success. Felix Jastrzebski came from a well-known Polish family, although he had no claim to the title of Count. He had a cousin named Jean-Pierre, born in 1805 and a former military surgeon. 'Major-General Van Lynseele' was an invention: no such person had ever served in the Polish, Dutch or Belgian armies. John Sparrow thought it possible that Lady Twiss was the daughter of Pierre Denis, and born in Courtrai in 1834 just like Chaffers had alleged, but he could not understand why the respectable Felix Jastrzebski would become the guardian of the daughter of a humble carpenter. He also speculated that she might have been the illegitimate daughter of either Jastrzebski himself, or his cousin Jean-Pierre. Although aided by two Polish antiquaries resident in France and Belgium, John Sparrow was no closer to solving the Great Twiss Mystery after two years of research, and he eventually gave up his efforts.

My immediate reflection, after pondering the Great Twiss Mystery, was that modern genealogical resources could be made use of to solve it. Although the elusive Lady Twiss had been good at dodging the authorities, she surely could not have dodged them all? We remember that she testified in court that in 1861, she lived at No. 11 South Street [today South Terrace, just off Thurloe Square], as Mlle Pharailde Rosalie Van Lynseele, together with her governess Madame Marie Gelas. Alexander Chaffers and his witness Denis Faure alleged that at the same time, Pharailde had lived at No. 11 South Street as the prostitute Madame

Gelas, with her parents and brother. To decide who was right, here is an extract from the 1861 Census:

11 South Street, Kensington
Marie Pharaelde Gelas, Head, aged 26, born Belgium.
Therese Vangemeude [?], Servant, aged 55, born France.
Pierre Denis, Boarder, aged 54, born France.

This extract firmly merges Pharailde and Madame Gelas into one person, and it lists as the other inhabitants of No. 11 South Street two people of the same age, and near-identical names, as the couple alleged by Chaffers to be Pharailde's parents. It is not known if Pharailde married, at some stage of her adventurous career, a Frenchman named Gelas, or whether 'Madame Gelas' was simply her nom de plume as a London prostitute, as alleged by Denis Faure.

To psychoanalyse the main dramatis personae of the Great Twiss Mystery would have been a challenge even for Sigmund Freud. As for the heroine herself, her sense of morality seems to have been seriously defective. If we accept that she had grown up in Belgium, before settling down in London as Madame Gelas the reasonably successful, fun-loving prostitute, she must have been delighted when Travers Twiss first agreed to 'keep' her permanently, and then arranged to marry her abroad. There are indications that Lady Twiss was residing abroad from time to time: at the time of the 1871 Census, she was not at No. 19 Park Lane, although her lady's maid was on the premises. Was Chaffers perhaps right that she was staying in Brussels, at the brothel in Rue de la Paille run by the mysterious M. Des Marès? As for Alexander Chaffers, he was clearly quite insane already at the time of the Twiss Libel Case, a victim of litigant paranoia. Still, Chaffers was no fool, and he realised that his enemy Sir Travers Twiss was ripe for blackmail, since Chaffers knew the dark secrets of his wife. When merely ignoring the blackmailer, Sir Travers greatly underestimated the determination and venomousness of this litigant Herostratos, however: the demented Chaffers was perfectly capable of laying waste to his own life and career, merely in order to obtain the satisfaction of ruining his old enemy. Sir Travers Twiss himself is the hardest case to crack for the Freudian analyst. Although presenting an ultra-respective façade to the world, and being trusted by some of the highest authorities of the Church of England, he seems to have had a particular liking for harum-scarum young ladies of dubious virtue. We only have the word of Alexander Chaffers for the Agnes Willoughby episode, but it seems fully credible. Then to get involved with another young prostitute is bad enough, but to hatch a plot to marry her, set up a bogus defence in court to prevent being found out, and arrange for 'witnesses' to perjure themselves wholesale, is quite without precedent. It is ironic that the slimy old Sir Travers ended up prostituting *himself*, by perverting the course of international law in favour of his sole remaining friend and ally, the tyrant Leopold of Belgium.

The Penge Mystery, 1877

In 1875, the twenty-four-year-old auctioneer's clerk Louis Staunton married the eleven-years-older Harriet Richardson. Mrs Richardson, the bride's mother, knew that her daughter was quite feeble-minded, and suspected that Louis was marrying her to get his hands on the £3,000 she had inherited. Since Harriet herself was very keen to get married, she resented her mother's meddling. Although Mrs Richardson applied to the Court of Chancery to have Harriet placed under control as a person of weak intellect, she was unsuccessful to prevent the wedding from taking place as planned.

Louis and Harriet Staunton went to live at No. 8 Loughborough Park Road, Brixton. His brother Patrick lived across the road at No. 9, with his wife Elizabeth. In March 1876, Harriet Staunton gave birth to a son, christened Tommy. But by that time, Louis was already on intimate terms with Patrick's young sister-in-law Alice Rhodes. Harriet was plain and feeble-minded, whereas Alice was young and pretty, and very much in love with the moustachioed, bushy-whiskered Louis. It was probably around this time that the Staunton brothers, two cruel and calculating scoundrels, made plans to dispose of Harriet and little Tommy. Since Harriet was quite half-witted, given to violent temper tantrums, and addicted to the bottle, Louis could no longer stand her. Later in 1876, Patrick and his wife moved to a lonely cottage near Cudham in Kent. Louis decided that Harriet and her child should live with them. Himself, he rented a farmhouse nearby, living there with Alice as Mr and Mrs Staunton.

Harriet did not like Patrick Staunton, and he returned her dislike in full. He struck her more than once, and made sure she was systematically starved. Mrs Richardson suspected foul play, but Louis and Patrick fobbed her off when she demanded to see her daughter. When she went to London and entered the cottage where the Stauntons kept Harriet, Patrick forcibly threw her out. In early April 1877, Louis Staunton took the ailing little Tommy to Guy's Hospital. The wretched child died not long after, from long-standing starvation. Nobody seems to have suspected unnatural death, and Louis went to Guy's under an assumed name to collect the tiny corpse. He drove a hard bargain at the funeral parlour, and Tommy ended up having to share a coffin with another pathetic little London waif. Later the same month, the brothers Louis and Patrick Staunton, aided and abetted by Elizabeth Staunton and Alice Rhodes, considered themselves close to success. Since they thought Harriet could not live much longer, they removed the feeble, emaciated invalid to No. 34 Forbes [today Mosslea] Road, Penge, where she died the very next day. A careless local doctor, who had only seen the patient in a dying condition, was persuaded to sign a death certificate that Harriet had died of 'apoplexy'.

Would the scoundrelly Stauntons get away with it? They very nearly did. By mere chance, it happened that Harriet's brother-in-law was in a shop in Forbes Road, when a stranger came in to register the death of a lady from Cudham in Kent, at No. 34. The brother-in-law knew that Harriet had been kept in Cudham, and that Mrs Richardson was very keen to trace her current whereabouts. He went to see the doctor, and to identify the deceased as his thirty-six-year-old sister-in-law Harriet Staunton. The police were notified, the death certificate withdrawn, and the hastily arranged funeral postponed. An inquest was held, and since a panel of medical experts had assigned Harriet's death to starvation, the Stauntons and Alice Rhodes were committed to stand trial at the Old Bailey for her murder, before Sir Henry Hawkins, who was known for his severity.

HARRIET STAUNTON THE BRIDAL DAY — HARRIET STAUNTON THE LAST HOURS

THE LATE MRS HARRIET STAUNTON

Above: Harriet Staunton at her wedding and at her miserable death, and portraits of the four Penge miscreants, from the *IPN*, 6 October 1877.

Left: A cabinet card portrait of Harriet Staunton.

Clara Brown, the former housemaid of Patrick Staunton, provided some very damning testimony about how he had beaten and mistreated poor Harriet. Mrs Richardson described how Louis had married her daughter for money, and then kept her captive in Cudham. The medical evidence was of a disgusting nature. Harriet had been systematically starved, and her weak, emaciated body was dirty and swarming with vermin. Due to the long-standing louse infestation, her skin was thickened to a remarkable degree. The counsel for the prisoners faced an uphill task. Mr Edward Clarke, representing Patrick Staunton, tried to attack the medical evidence, aided by two doctors who testified that Harriet might have died from meningeal tuberculosis. It is true that the autopsy revealed that she had a small tubercular lesion at the apex of the right lung. The doctors speculated that 'some small patches of rough millet-seed like deposit in the meshes of the pia mater' might be a sign of meningeal tuberculosis, but Sir Henry Hawkins pooh-poohed their evidence, remarking that they had themselves not seen the body. In a marathon summing-up, lasting more than ten hours, he effectively closed every loop-hole for the four prisoners; in particular, he reminded the jury that all four were equally culpable.

Due to Sir Henry's oratory, the time was close to 10 p.m. when the jury finally retired. They sat for ninety minutes before returning a verdict of guilty. Alice Rhodes fainted dead away, and the other three prisoners

The autopsy of Harriet Staunton, and a drawing of the murder house, from the *IPN*, 2 June 1877.

The Stauntons in the dock receiving sentence.

sat trembling like leaves as Sir Henry Hawkins, who looked even more sinister than usual in the dark, candle-lit court-room, sentenced all four to death for 'a crime so black and hideous that I believe in all the records of crime it would be difficult to find its parallel'.

Although there was little sympathy for the Staunton brothers, many people thought Sir Henry Hawkins had gone too far when he sentenced the two women to death. As the medical debate about Harriet's cause of death continued in the *Lancet*, some correspondents still upheld the possibility of meningeal tuberculosis. This led to the Home Secretary reopening the case and respiting the executions. In the end, the three Stauntons were sentenced to life imprisonment, and Alice Rhodes, against whom the evidence had been feeble to say the least, was acquitted. Alice got a job as a barmaid after her narrow escape. One day, she pulled a pint for Sir Henry Hawkins, who remarked that surely, he had seen her somewhere before.

'You have, my Lord. I am Alice Rhodes, and your Lordship once sentenced me to death.'
'Good heavens! I hope you are now doing well for yourself?'
'I am, quite well – no thanks to your Lordship!'

Patrick Staunton died in prison in 1881, and Elizabeth was released three years later. She married an art dealer and led a respectable life until her death, well into her seventies. As for the selfish, cruel Louis Staunton, he became a changed man in prison. A model prisoner and a devout Roman Catholic, he admitted his guilt, and said he deserved his punishment. In 1898, he was released from Dartmoor Prison, having served twenty-two years behind bars. It is pleasing to recount, in a tale as dark and disturbing as this one, that he was met by his loyal Alice, who had been waiting for him all those years. They were married in Brighton, and had offspring. Alice died just before the Great War, but Louis remarried. He was by then a successful estate agent and auctioneer. He died in 1934, aged eighty-three.

Although the Staunton house in Loughborough Park Road has been 'developed' since it was pictured in local historian Dorothy Cox's 1989 book *Brotherly Love; or, the Cudham Quartet*, quite a few of the other houses associated with the Penge Mystery remain. No. 6 Colby Road, Gipsy Hill, where Louis and Harriet lived before she was taken to Cudham, still remains, and Dorothy Cox reproduced recent photographs of both the Cudham farmhouses. Forbes Road was renamed Mosslea Road after the murder, but the houses were not renumbered. A woman growing up there in the 1950s remembers the lurid tales told about No. 34, not far from where her family lived. When it was featured by Dorothy Cox in 1989, No. 34 Mosslea Road was in a rather shabby condition, but when I saw it in 2012, the murder house was looking quite well cared for.

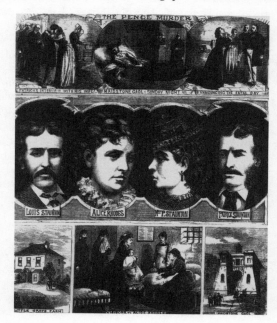

Vignettes from the Penge Murder, from the *IPN*, 20 October 1877.

The Harley Street Mystery, 1880

In 1880, the large terraced Georgian town house at No. 139 Harley Street was owned by sixty-eight-year-old Mr Jacob Quixano Henriques, a wealthy Jewish banker and merchant, who had lived there for more than twenty years. At times, when Mr Henriques was travelling abroad, the large house was inhabited only by a caretaker and his wife. Once he was back in London, Mr Henriques had to employ a butler and a full staff of servants. This system did not work particularly well, since the servants hired at such short notice were often of an inferior quality.

In early June 1880, Mr Henriques had been back in residence at No. 139 for around eighteen months. His wife Elizabeth and three adult daughters also lived on the premises. His butler John Spendlove was doing a good job running the household, and supervising the other six servants. One day, Spendlove told his master that he had become aware of a very noxious smell emanating from the cellars. At first, the drains were blamed, and a plumber was called in, but all the closets and drains were found to be in good working order. In order to find the source of the smell, the butler and the plumber decided to clear the largest cellar room, which extended underneath the pavement. In a corner was a large cistern on four wooden legs; underneath it was a wooden barrel and a quantity of other lumber. When the two men dragged the barrel out, it seemed unexpectedly heavy. The butler peered inside and exclaimed, 'There's somebody in here!'

A party of police constables, led by Chief Inspector Lucas, came to No. 139 to investigate the unexpected finding of a dead body in the cellar of Mr Henriques. When they unceremoniously turned the barrel upside down, a badly decomposed, partially mummified human body hit the floor. It was removed to the infirmary at Marylebone workhouse for a proper medical examination by the pathologist Professor Pepper, and two police surgeons. The medical specialists found that the Harley Street cadaver was that of a woman, very short (just four feet seven inches tall), aged between forty and fifty years, and with dark brown hair. Her front teeth looked very peculiar: short and with blunt ends, like if they had been cut or filed. The cause of death was that she had been stabbed in the chest. It was estimated that she had been in the barrel for between eighteen and thirty-six months.

At the coroner's inquest on the unknown Harley Street murder victim, the police were roundly criticised for their clumsiness: valuable clues must have been destroyed when the body had been expelled from the barrel. The police had searched London and the Home Counties for former servants in Mr Henriques' household, for the last five years; these domestics had all been tracked down, in a healthy and living condition. They all denied any knowledge of the body in the barrel, or any

Spendlove the butler finding the body, the front of the murder house, and the jury visiting the cellar, among other images of the Harley Street Mystery, from the *IPN*, 19 June 1880.

The cellar entrance, and other images relating to the Harley Street Mystery, from the *IPN*, 26 June 1880.

acquaintance with a very short woman with dark brown hair and strange-looking teeth. The former butler Henry Smith, who had been sacked for drunkenness by Mr Henriques back in 1878, was now a soldier in the 3rd Surrey Regiment. He testified that during his tenure in the household, the gate leading to the area steps had regularly been left unlocked on purpose, to allow the servants to come and go after hours, as it pleased them, or to smuggle various visitors into the house. The police had been curious why some bricks from the cellar floor had been removed, but Henry Smith freely explained that he had been in the habit of burying stale bread down there, so that Mr Henriques would not complain of his wastefulness!

Neither Mr Henriques himself nor Spendlove the butler had anything important or interesting to say at the coroner's inquest, except that the latter admitted that his eagerness to track down the source of the noxious smell had been prompted by the fact that his own bedroom was situated below stairs. Goodley, the plumber who had helped to find the body, provided some light relief when he said that he had not sensed any bad smell in the cellar, since 'plumbers do not notice them so much as other people'. The verdict of the coroner's inquest on the unknown woman was that she had been wilfully murdered by some person unknown. The police did not ever find a suspect, and the Harley Street Mystery remains unsolved today. It was by no means the only unsolved London murder at the time: indeed, the *IPN* published a gloomy list of various unavenged outrages in the Metropolis.

Dr Frederick William Spurgin had been the Divisional Police Surgeon in charge of the Harley Street Mystery. He had left his papers to his son Dr Percy B. Spurgin, who gave a lecture on the case before the Medico-Legal Society in April 1931, quoting at length from his father's memorandum. According to old Dr Spurgin, Mr Henriques had experienced the unpleasant smell from the basement, but he otherwise had no knowledge of the case. The two male servants in his household, the butler Spendlove and the footman Tinapp, both had a good character, and had been in the service of Mr Henriques for more than a year and a half. A caretaker named Woodroffe, and his wife and son, had been looking after the house when Mr Henriques was away, for a period of six years; he denied having any idea where the body was coming from, although he had seen the barrel in the cellar as early at the autumn of 1878. According to old Dr Spurgin, the body had been inside the barrel for at least two years. It was much decomposed, and in part dried and mummified, and the face was quite unrecognisable. The woman had been between forty and forty-five years old when she was murdered, old Dr Spurgin speculated; she had been very short, and lacked several molars in the upper jaw. Her clothes had been of a very inferior quality, inducing old Dr Spurgin to speculate that she had come from the lower classes of society.

There was much interest in the Harley Street Mystery among the members of the Medico-Legal Society. None less than Sir Bernard Spilsbury speculated that this might have been a case of an abortion gone wrong, but young Dr Spurgin retorted that the house had not been used by any medical man at the time. There was also a discussion whether this was a case of accident, suicide or murder, and the latter theory was adhered to, with the added speculation that the victim may well have been stabbed through her clothes. It may be suspected that the dishonest butler Henry Smith, or one of the other servants employed at the time, had smuggled a prostitute into the house through the unlocked gate to the area steps, and later murdered her and hid the body in the barrel. It is true that the victim was an extremely short woman aged between forty and fifty, with very peculiar-looking teeth, but the Victorians were far from fastidious with regard to the prostitutes they went to bed with. Samples of hair and textile were secured from the Harley Street murder victim, and casts were made of both jaws; all these objects are today at the Scotland Yard's Crime Museum.

Mr Jacob Quixano Henriques was not afraid of ghosts, nor was he worried about the reputation that often stuck to murder houses in those days. He stayed at No. 139 Harley Street for many years to come, living there until his death in late 1898, at the age of eighty-seven. At some stage, a bay window was added to the ground and lower ground floors. In later years, No. 139 Harley Street has been turned into medical and dental consulting rooms, as have so many other houses along this famous avenue of private medical enterprise. Apart from the prominent bay window, the murder house looks very much like it had done in 1880.

The Mystery of Lieutenant Roper, 1881

Lieutenant Percy Lyon Ormsby Roper was a twenty-two-year-old officer of good family, stationed at Brompton Barracks in Chatham. A handsome, martial-looking young man with a dark moustache, he belonged to the Royal Engineers and had just finished a two-year course at the School of Military Engineering. On the evening of 11 February 1881, Percy Roper seemed to be in a good mood, since he was to report at the War Office in London the following day before going on extended leave to visit his relations in Germany. After Lieutenant Roper had gone down to mess, his friend Lieutenant Stewart Davidson sent him a note inviting him to an evening gathering, and Roper wrote back that he wanted to write a letter after dinner, but would be glad to come a little later.

Percy Roper had his rooms in House No. 9, next to the central archway at Brompton Barracks. Five other young officers lived on the premises, and they had a staff of four servants looking after their needs. Lieutenant Roper sat down in his sitting-room and wrote some letters, but ended one of them abruptly: 'Dear Mrs Adams, I finally go up to the A.A.G. on Monday, and as probably that will take all day …' Another officer, Lieutenant Vidal, kept some dogs at the house, and they suddenly started barking furiously. Mrs Gerside, wife of one of the servants, went to quieten them. There was a sentry in front of the house, and he heard a cracking noise, followed by the barking of the dogs. He stood for a

LIEUT ROPER.
THE VICTIM OF THE CHATHAM MURDER

A portrait of Percy Roper, from the *IPN*, 26 February 1881.

while pondering what had happened, and heard a low groaning noise emanating from the house, but could not tell from which part. Another sentry heard a sound like the breaking of china coming from the house, but did not think twice about it.

When Mrs Gerside returned after comforting the frightened dogs, she saw the figure of a man in an officer's uniform on the stairs. She told another servant, William Gallagher, that one of the young gentlemen was larking about, and he went to have a look at what was happening, along with his wife. Gallagher saw that the man was lying down on the upper flight of stairs, with his face to the railings. When the servant turned him over, he gave a groan, and Gallagher saw that it was his master, Lieutenant Percy Roper. Blood was pouring from a wound in his side. Leaving Roper with his wife, Gallagher rushed outdoors to get help. At the foot of the staircase, he met the assistant commandant, Lieutenant Colonel Duff, who was just returning from the mess, and gasped out, 'Oh, sir, my master! Somebody had stabbed him!' Colonel Duff examined the recumbent Lieutenant Roper, and tersely said, 'He is not stabbed. He is shot. Somebody has shot him or he has shot himself.' The servants carried the unconscious young officer into his sitting-room and put him on the sofa there. Mrs Gallagher went for Dr Blood, the resident doctor at Brompton Barracks, but he was away at the time, so she instead fetched a certain Dr Henry Weekes, who came with her to the barracks. The doctor could do nothing for Percy Roper, however, since the bullet had passed between the fifth and sixth ribs and caused severe internal injuries. The patient expired shortly after ten in the evening.

On the top stair was discovered a six-chambered revolver with five loaded chambers; the cartridge in the sixth chamber had just been exploded. Scattered about the landing were six other cartridges, a poker from Lieutenant Roper's fireplace, his watch and purse, and a bundle of clothes from his drawers. The candles in his room were still burning, and the unfinished letter was lying on the blotting pad. The revolver belonged to Lieutenant Henry Kendall Stothert, who lived next door to Lieutenant Roper. Stothert said that he had gone straight from the mess to the card-room, where he had remained until after the discovery of the crime. The very same morning, the servant James Gerside had cleaned and oiled this revolver, which hung in its holster next to Stothert's bed. Since Stothert had no ammunition in his possession that fitted this revolver, which was not army issue, and which he had won as a prize, he presumed that some person must have brought the cartridges along and loaded it.

The coroner's inquest on Lieutenant Percy Roper was opened on 14 February. The servants described how they had found the dying lieutenant on the stairs. The kitchen-maid Margaret Cruft had left the mess at a quarter to nine. When passing House No. 9, she heard a sound like the crack of a stick, and afterwards two or three moans. There was a sound like a scuffle on the stairs, and three dogs came running out of the house like if they had been frightened. Amelia Privett, the wife of Colonel Duff's groom, had been in one of the basement kitchens of House No. 9, and heard sounds of a scuffle on the stairs, followed by a knock and the sound of some person falling down. Dr Weekes described the wound, and gave his opinion that it was not self-inflicted. The deceased could not have fired the revolver with his right hand, and it was highly improbable that he had done so with the left. Dr Blood, who had assisted with the post-mortem examination, agreed that this was not a case of suicide. The reason the sound of the shot had been muffled was that the weapon had been pressed hard into the victim's waistcoat. The gunsmith E. Palmer, of Rochester, testified that he had sold a box of cartridges similar to those found near the body. The person who had bought them had been a military looking man between thirty and thirty-five, possibly an officer. After having been shown a photograph of Lieutenant Roper, he declared that he was not the purchaser.

Superintendent Coppinger, of the Kent County Constabulary, received help from Chief Inspector Sherlock and a team of Scotland Yard detectives in unravelling the mystery of Lieutenant Roper. There was no particular reason for Roper to have committed suicide, and the medical evidence spoke in favour of murder. There was early newspaper speculation that Roper had been killed by the Fenians, and some Irish labouring men fitting tanks in the attic space were investigated, but without anything incriminating being found. Then there was the possibility of some enemy of Lieutenant Roper murdering him, but all the other five officers who lived in No. 9 House were supposed to have been away from the house at the time of the murder, and most of them had solid alibis. The servants

Three vignettes from the mystery of Lieutenant Roper, from the *IPN*, 26 February 1881.

were elderly and had a good character, and no reason could be discerned for any of them to shoot Percy Roper. The police rather favoured the hypothesis of a burglar sneaking up to the house and entering it, thinking that all the young officers were away. But when searching Stothert's room, the burglar alerts Lieutenant Roper, who grabs the poker and goes out to investigate, but only to be gunned down with the revolver the burglar had just stolen from Stothert's room. But none of the sentries had seen any sign of an intruder entering or leaving the house, there was no technical evidence of a forced entry, and nothing seemed to have been stolen.

On 28 February, the coroner's inquest on Percy Roper returned a verdict of murder against some person or persons unknown. The police were quite baffled by the mystery, and without a single worthwhile clue to the identity of the murderer. But on 22 March, a man who gave his name as Alfred William Johnson gave himself up for the murder in Leamington Spa. He had met Lieutenant Roper on the staircase near his quarters, and shot him with a brother officer's pistol, he said. He had not committed the murder for robbery, and now he could not keep his secret any longer. This sounded promising, the police thought, and 'Johnson' was promptly sent to Chatham, where inquiries were made about his background and character. A short and insignificant-looking man, just five feet four inches tall, and of very slight build, he looked nothing like a cool, calculating murderer. It turned out that his real name was Arthur Jardine, and that he had been hitting the bottle hard in recent times. He had left his mother's house in Walton Street, Oxford, to get a job as a travelling draper in Leamington Spa. After a few days in police custody, he said that his confession was wholly untrue, and that he had never been in Chatham. The police found nothing to suggest that he had been anywhere near Chatham at the time of the murder, and he was released with admonitions for wasting police time.

The next newsworthy development in the Roper case came in November 1881, when Percy Lefroy Mapleton, who had murdered Mr Gold in a Brighton railway carriage, confessed to the murder of Lieutenant Roper while he was awaiting execution. Lefroy said that when he had been strolling in Pall Mall one evening, he had heard two gentlemen speaking slightingly of the actress Miss Violet Cameron, for whom Lefroy expressed a deep devotion. He confronted one of the gentlemen, and demanded his card: it turned out to be none other than Percy Roper! Lefroy decided that the young officer had to die for his imprudent remark about Violet Cameron, and one evening he entered Brompton Barracks in disguise, wearing false whiskers, gunned down Lieutenant Roper and successfully made his escape. Members of Lefroy's family testified that he had been in a state of high excitement at the time of the murder, and that in prison, he had confessed to his sister that he had committed the murder. But the police believed that Lefroy was just making a story up to get the execution delayed. His story about walking into Brompton Barracks wearing false whiskers is too good to be believed, and much of the confession did not add up: he said he had bought a gun in the Strand, whereas the murder weapon had really belonged to Lieutenant Stothert. Lefroy withdrew the confession after knowing that he was not believed.

In January 1885, there were some very interesting developments in the Roper mystery. News had reached England that a young officer in the Royal Engineers, Lieutenant Stothert, who was stationed in India, had committed suicide through shooting himself with a revolver while suffering from mental depression. It was said that the revolver used in the suicide was the same weapon with which Lieutenant Roper had been murdered at Chatham nearly four years ago. It was commented that, 'The case has given rise to some very strange speculations in Chatham, where both officers were well known.' Two weeks later, there was another newspaper account, which deserves being quoted in full:

Some sensation has been caused in military circles in Dover by a report just arrived there from India, that an officer, who was formerly stationed at Chatham, has blown his brains out, after having written a letter confessing that he shot Lieutenant Roper, who was found lying dead in the barrack-yard, Chatham garrison. The tragedy is said to have followed a dispute about a love affair.

As late as October 1892, a man named William Dalton, alias Coulter, alias Park, confessed that he had murdered Percy Roper. He had been serving as a private soldier in the Royal Engineers at the time, and been stationed at Chatham. One day, he had sneaked into the officers' quarters and shot Lieutenant Roper down, without any particular motive for the deed. Dalton was taken into police custody, and his background investigated: it turned out that he was indeed a sapper at the time, but stationed in Malta, far away from Chatham. Moreover, at the time of the murder, he was serving a sentence of eighteen months' imprisonment for a military offence. Dalton then denied all knowledge of the murder, and said that his confession had been due to the influence of drink.

For an analysis of the mystery of Lieutenant Percy Roper, the initial question is whether he was really murdered. Can suicide and accidental death be ruled out? Yes, according to the medical evidence, and considering that Roper had for some reason felt threatened, and armed himself with a poker. There had been Irish labouring men at work at the barracks during daytime, but they were no longer there in the evening, and the police were able to rule out any Fenian involvement. Thirdly, there is the burglar hypothesis, favoured by the police at the time. But what kind of suicidal burglar would break into a house inside a large military barracks, guarded by armed sentries, and inhabited by young and alert officers with access to loaded firearms? The idea of an outside avenger, like Lefroy, meets with the same objections. Three sentries were posted near the house, and it was a clear moonlit evening, but none of them saw any suspicious person either enter or leave the premises. There were no signs that an intruder had forced any window or door, and if a burglar or avenger would come strolling in through the main door, he would be at risk of being challenged by the servants.

An avenue of thought that does not seem to have been considered at the time is that one of the servants in the house committed the murder. After all, they had the opportunity to roam the house at will, and perhaps do some pilfering from the empty rooms of the young officers; one of them might have nourished a grudge against young Roper, and looked forward to settling the score with him. After the murder, it would have been easy for the murderer to take refuge in the basement. At least five servants were in House No. 9 at the time of the murder: the married couples William and Winnie Gallagher and James and Mary Gerside, and also the woman Amelia Privett. Since the police file on the Roper case is not kept at the National Archives, we can only speculate what interest the detectives took in ascertaining exactly who was inside the house at the time of the murder. The reason the police did not take more interest in the servants is probably that they were elderly former soldiers and their wives, and viewed as harmless and loyal old retainers without any homicidal intent.

In my view, the most promising solution to the Roper mystery is that he was murdered by an enemy among his fellow officers, who hid inside House No. 9 before and after the murder. Percy Roper was said to have been very popular, without an enemy in the world, but this should really be 'without a known enemy in the world'. There may well have been a Judas at Brompton Barracks: a determined rival of Lieutenant Roper, full of hatred against the young officer, who had determined that he must die. The prime candidate for being this avenger is of course Lieutenant Stothert, said in 1885 to have committed suicide after writing a letter confessing to the murder, which was due to rivalry following a love affair. It turns out that Henry Kendall Stothert was born in Bath in late 1860, the son of the prosperous civil engineer John Lum Stothert. He had three younger brothers and a younger sister. He joined the army as a young man, and in July 1880, he was promoted from gentleman cadet to lieutenant. The 1881 Census finds him a lieutenant on the active list of the Royal Engineers, stationed at the School of Military Engineering, Brompton Barracks, Chatham. He is not listed in the 1891, 1901 or 1911 Censuses, indicating that the report that he committed suicide in India in early 1885 is likely to be correct.

But if we accept Henry Kendall Stothert as the main suspect, there are a number of immediate difficulties. According to the contemporary newspapers, he was purported to have had an alibi, having gone from the mess to the card-room, where he was presumably seen by many people. And even if we presume that he was able to leave the card-room, sneak into the murder house, load his pistol and shoot Lieutenant Roper, this leaves unexplained why he was not spotted by the sentries entering the house, and how he managed to escape after the murder. Furthermore, although the report of Stothert's suicide in 1885 is likely to be reliable, the Victorian newspapers of the 1880s were not unknown to falsify a 'solution' to historical murders by reporting idle gossip as fact. Maybe the solution to the mystery of Lieutenant Roper is hidden in the yellowing pages of some obscure Anglo-Indian newspaper reporting on his suicide; perhaps it lies concealed in a bundle of inquest papers in some Indian archive; most probably, the truth will never be known.

The Mystery of Urban Napoleon Stanger, 1881

Urban Napoleon Stanger was a German baker, born in 1846 and said to have been a native of Kreuznach. He went to London as a young man, and in August 1869, when he was twenty-three years old, he married the twenty-one-year-old Elizabeth Gallon. On their marriage certificate, Urban Napoleon's father is given as John Stanger, gardener, and the bride's father as the farmer Christian Gallon. The two Stangers lived at No. 21 Curtain Road, Shoreditch, at the time. The marriage witnesses were Felix Stumm and Ann Elizabeth Cooper.

Urban Napoleon Stanger later settled down in a baker's shop at No. 136 Lever Street, in the parish of St Luke's, Whitechapel. This was a densely populated East End neighbourhood, full of immigrants, many of them Jews, Eastern Europeans, and Germans. Stanger was an honest, industrious tradesman, and his baker's shop did well from the start: he was able to save money, and live comfortably in the maisonette flat on the two floors above the shop. Elizabeth Stanger was a tall, sturdy dame, and the baker himself quite short and insignificant-looking; there was gossip in the neighbourhood that she was the person in charge of the household, ordering the meek little baker about at will. But still, the two Stangers seemed to be getting on quite well. Elizabeth served behind the shop counter as her husband was beavering away in his bakery in the cellar, assisted by the journeyman baker Christian Zentler and by a young boy. There was also a servant girl in the household. Urban Napoleon had an old friend, the German master baker Franz Felix Stumm, who had got into debt and did not have a baker's shop of his own. He is very likely to have been the 'Felix Stumm' who was a witness at Stanger's wedding back in 1869. Stumm was often helping out in the busy little shop at No. 136 Lever Street, and he soon became more than familiar with Elizabeth Stanger. These two were a far from romantic pair, Stumm being quite villainous-looking, with an ugly face, a hooked nose and a short, bushy beard, and Elizabeth looking quite coarse and bloated, but nevertheless the neighbourhood gossips were whispering that Mrs Stanger was becoming very friendly with her husband's assistant. Although Urban Napoleon's main interest in life seems to have been the accumulation of money in his bank account, he may well have been aware of what was going on in his household.

Franz Felix Stumm and Elizabeth Stanger, sketches made in court, from the *IPN*, 14 October 1882.

At shortly before midnight on 12 November 1881, the journeyman baker Christian Zentler saw four men standing outside the baker's shop at No. 136 Lever Street: Urban Napoleon Stanger, Franz Felix Stumm, and two Englishmen named Long and Cramer. They seemed to be talking together on amicable terms. Zentler then saw Stanger enter the shop, while the other three men walked away. The following day, when Zentler came to work at No. 136 Lever Street at 8 a.m., Urban Napoleon Stanger was nowhere to be seen. Elizabeth showed no particular interest in his whereabouts, but she was adamant that Zentler should go to Stumm's lodgings at once and make sure that he made his way to No. 136 Lever Street without any delay. And indeed, the sturdy, bushy-bearded Stumm soon made himself comfortable on the premises. There was a Mrs Stumm, but she seems to have been a most accommodating woman, who did not at all object to her husband looking after the baker's shop at No. 136, and consorting with Mrs Stanger. Indeed, after her mother had made a fuss about Stumm's shenanigans with Mrs Stanger, Mrs Stumm moved into No. 136 herself. Week followed week, and Urban Napoleon Stanger did not make an appearance. The vanished baker had no close friends or relations, but when a few business colleagues asked about his whereabouts, Stumm and Mrs Stanger said that he was recuperating from an illness in the countryside, or that he had gone abroad. After a few months, the name 'U. N. Stanger' was erased from the shop front, to be replaced by 'F. F. Stumm'!

For several months to come, Franz Felix Stumm and Elizabeth Stanger had success usurping the business of Urban Napoleon Stanger. Although the change of name on the shop front had caused gossip, and although there were lurid stories that Stanger had been murdered and turned into meat pies sold on the premises, the two conspirators were fortunate that no person took much interest in Stanger's whereabouts. There was one exception, however: the flour factor Georg Giesel, who had several times called at No. 136 Lever Street to collect money for flour supplied to Stanger. The first time, Stumm had told him that Stanger was recuperating in the countryside, having broken a blood vessel; the second time, that the vanished baker was probably to be found back in Kreuznach, having fled London due to his outstanding debts. But since Giesel knew that Stanger's finances were in a very solid condition, he suspected that Stumm had in some way managed to do away with him. In April 1882, Giesel approached a private detective, and newspaper advertisements and handbills with the following text were circulated:

Fifty pounds reward. Mysteriously disappeared, since the early part of November last, from his residence No. 136 Lever Street, City Road, Urban Napoleon Stanger, master baker, native of Kreuznach, Germany. Any person who will give information leading to his discovery will receive the above reward. Wendel Scherer, Private Inquiry Agent, 28 Chepstow Place, Bayswater.

This advertisement put the cat among the pigeons, and the gossip concerning the vanished baker in Lever Street and its neighbourhood reached new heights. Had Urban Napoleon Stanger been made into German sausages, for sale in the Shop of Horrors, or had he been roasted in his own oven? After Mrs Stanger had been booed and hooted in the street, she moved into new lodgings in Kingsland, along with Mrs Stumm. Franz Felix Stumm remained in residence, however: the obstinate German crook would not admit defeat and leave the baker's shop. His enemy Georg Giesel kept making inquiries about Stanger's disappearance, however. He found out that Stumm had opened an account in the London & County Bank, the same establishment where Stanger had hoarded his savings of not less that £414. Through forging cheques, Stumm had been able to lay his hands on much of this money. As one of the executors of Stanger's will, Giesel saw a solicitor and took legal action against Stumm, for uttering a forged cheque with intent to defraud.

THE MYSTERIOUS DISAPPEARANCE OF MR. STANGER FROM ST. LUKE'S: SKETCHES OF PERSONS INTERESTED IN THE CASE.—(See "Law and Crime.")

FROM THIS SHOP A BAKER DISAPPEARED AND HAS NOT SINCE BEEN HEARD OF.

Above left: Sketches concerning the St Luke's Mystery, from the *Penny Illustrated Paper*, 14 October 1882.

Above right: The former baker's shop at No. 136 Lever Street, from *Harmsworth's Magazine*, Christmas 1898.

It took until October 1882 before Franz Felix Stumm appeared before the Worship Street magistrates, charged with forging and uttering a cheque for the payment of £76 15s, with intent to defraud, and conspiring with Elizabeth Stanger to defraud Georg Giesel of the same sum. *Lloyd's Weekly Newspaper* described the defendant in unflattering terms: 'Stumm is said to be a man of about 34 years of age, but he looks older. He is a big stout man of thoroughly German appearance.' Two illustrations of his sinister countenance, in the *IPN* and the *Penny Illustrated Paper*, bore out this impression in the full. Giesel and his legal representatives had prepared themselves well, and there was a steady flow of incriminating evidence against the sturdy, unwholesome-looking Stumm. He had been telling untruths about the activities of Urban Napoleon Stanger, namely that he had either been taken ill, was convalescing in a country resort, or had returned to his native Germany to escape his creditors. Christian Zentler told his story about being the last man to see Stanger alive, and Georg Giesel told how Stumm had been trying to empty Stanger's bank account by uttering forged cheques; a number of German witnesses described how they had visited Kreuznach, and seen Stanger's brothers and sisters there, but without finding any trace of the vanished baker. The outcome of the magisterial inquisition was that Franz Felix Stumm was taken into custody, and committed to stand trial for forgery at the Old Bailey. Mrs Stanger, who was expecting a child, was given bail of £50 to appear in court, but Stumm was refused bail, since it was feared that he would abscond to Germany.

The trial of Franz Felix Stumm, for deception and forgery, began on 20 November 1882, before Mr Justice Hawkins, a judge noted for his severity. The evidence against Stumm appeared rock solid: the forged cheques were declared by an expert not to have been signed by Stanger, Giesel told all about the takeover of No. 136 Lever Street and the attempt to empty Stanger's bank account, and a number of German witnesses testified that Stanger had not been seen anywhere near his home town of Kreuznach. The main defence witness was Elizabeth Stanger, who swore that her husband had not disappeared on 12 November, as suggested by Zentler's evidence, but that that after a domestic quarrel on the evening of 19 November, he had declared that he would leave her, for good. After having discovered, on the following morning, that Stanger had carried out his threat, she had called her friend Franz Felix Stumm to look after the shop. It was in fact she herself who had signed her husband's name on the cheques, since she was in the habit of signing various documents for him. In a hostile cross-examination, she contradicted herself on many points, and when she left the court with a stout female companion, said by some to have been Mrs Stumm, she was loudly hooted and hissed. Montagu Williams, who defended Stumm, had a hopeless task due to the weight of evidence against his client; he did not mention the case in his memoirs, but according to the old crime writer Guy Logan, he believed that Mrs Stanger had murdered her husband on the night of 12 November, and that Stumm had merely helped her to dispose of the body. After a hostile summing-up from Mr Justice Hawkins, the jury brought in a verdict of 'Guilty' against Stumm. White with fury, the sturdy German gripped the rails of the dock, and screamed that his legal counsel had bungled the case shamefully: he was the victim of a conspiracy on the part of Stanger's relatives in Germany, and there was 'no justice in vile England for a foreigner'! Mr Justice Hawkins took no notice of his outburst, but calmly sentenced him to ten years of penal servitude. Not long after the trial, on 6 October, Mrs Stanger gave birth to a daughter named Elizabeth; on her birth certificate, the name of the father is omitted! Save for a medical miracle, it cannot have been poor Urban Napoleon, who had been missing for eleven months. Mrs Stanger's disgraceful performance in court was not forgotten: in March 1883, she was found guilty of perjury, and sentenced to twelve months in prison, with hard labour. Little Elizabeth was probably taken into a workhouse or children's home during her mother's period of incarceration.

According to Guy Logan, who took a great interest in the Stanger Mystery, Elizabeth Stanger got out of prison in 1884, and joined the tolerant Mrs Stumm in Germany. Hopefully she stopped at the workhouse to pick up little Elizabeth, who was after all her only child. Franz Felix Stumm proved to be an intractable and violent convict, who had to serve his full ten years before he could join his two 'wives' back in the *Vaterland*. Guy Logan had heard that he died in Frankfurt as early as 1896: a short and evil life, if this is true, for this unprepossessing German miscreant. A portrait model of Stumm was exhibited at Madame Tussaud's for a few years in the 1880s, but no likeness of it seems to have been preserved. As for Urban Napoleon Stanger himself, the story of his wife and the creature Stumm, that he had gone to Germany and left everything behind, is a ridiculous one, since Stanger was a careful and prudent man who would surely have made sure he brought plenty of money if he cut himself adrift from home. It would appear that he was murdered in the late evening of 12 November, either by his wife alone or by her and her lover Stumm. The 'Sweeney Todd' theory that Stanger's remains were made into pies is not without its merits, but then Stumm was a baker, with access to a capacious oven, in which human remains could be reduced to cinders. It seems very likely that Stanger's body was roasted in his own oven, and that Stumm then successfully managed to dispose of the charred remains. As for the shop at No. 136 Lever Street, it still stood in 1898, to be depicted in a feature on London murder houses, but it has been long gone, a victim of either wartime bombings or post-war 'development'.

The Ardlamont Mystery, 1893

Alfred John Monson was born at Bedale, Yorkshire, in May 1860, the son of the Revd Thomas John Monson and his wife the Hon. Caroline Isabella Monckton, a daughter of Viscount Galway. He would later claim to have been educated at Rugby and Oxford, but there is nothing to suggest that he possessed an Oxford degree. The 1881 Census lists him as a 'Tutor Schoolteacher' living with the Mercer family in Winchester, and educating their five children. In October 1881, we find him in South Africa, where he married Agnes Maude Day, the daughter of a Yorkshire landowner. Monson made his living as a gentleman tutor, and as a dealer in horses. In 1886, he took over the lease of Chesney Court, a large country house near Ledbury, but just after he had insured this mansion against fire, it burnt down. In the late 1880s, Monson got involved with various shady London moneylenders. In 1890, he was arrested in Harrogate for obtaining £200 by fraud from a usurer named Brown, and charged at the Clerkenwell Police Court, although not prosecuted any further, probably because his family bailed him out.

In 1889, Alfred John Monson had got acquainted with Major Dudley Hambrough, who employed him as a tutor for his son Cecil, who was intended for the army. Cecil was to live with Monson and his wife while receiving education. Monson proceeded to take another stately home, Risely Hall in Yorkshire, but his income from Major Hambrough was not enough to pay his considerable debts, and in August 1892, he was declared a bankrupt. This did not prevent him from taking another grand country residence, Ardlamont House near Tignabruaich in Scotland. Although

Features from the Ardlamont Mystery, from the *IPN*, 9 September 1893.

an undischarged bankrupt with very considerable debts, the grandiose Monson spoke of buying the entire Ardlamont Estate for £80,000, and a nice steam yacht as well; the trusting Scots believed his every word, and thought him the perfect gentleman. Major Hambrough changed his mind and wanted Cecil to return home, but Cecil was a rather foolish, trusting young man, who had become entirely dominated by Monson. He refused to leave his sinister tutor, in spite of his father's entreaties, and Monson lost no time before making plans to exploit this state of affairs. He insured Cecil's life for £20,000, with Mrs Monson as the beneficiary, and the thoughtless lad willingly signed all the paperwork, without suspecting that anything sinister was afoot.

Cecil Hambrough, who was fond of outdoor pursuits, looked forward to enjoying the shooting and fishing at Ardlamont. There was a mishap when Cecil and Monson went out in a boat to lay some nets, however: the boat sank and Monson swam ashore. He seemed very worried that Cecil, who could not swim at all, would perish, but the accident-prone young man managed to wade ashore unscathed. By this time, the party at Ardlamont House had been joined a man who was introduced by Monson as Edward Scott, an engineer who would help with Monson's yacht. On 10 August 1893, Monson, Hambrough and Scott went out for some

(THE ABOVE ILLUSTRATIONS ARE FROM SKETCHES BY OUR SPECIAL ARTISTS.)

Monson and Scott, from the *IPN*, 23 December 1893.

shooting. Monson and Hambrough had guns, and the former managed to shoot a rabbit. When Scott wanted to act as retriever, Monson told him that they would collect the game on their way back. Monson and Hambrough then parted and walked their different ways. All of a sudden, there was the report of a gun, and Monson came back saying that there had been another misadventure: young Cecil's gun had accidentally gone off, killing him. His body was taken back to Ardlamont House, where a friendly local doctor signed a death certificate with 'accidental death'. The following day, the man Scott absconded, leaving no forwarding address. Cecil was quickly buried in the family vault, and Monson offered his condolences to the grieving Major Hambrough and his wife. But it soon became clear to the police that the 'Ardlamont Shooting Tragedy' had many mysterious aspects, and Monson was arrested and charged with murder, while the hue and cry was up for the fugitive Scott.

When Alfred John Monson stood trial for murder at the High Court in Edinburgh, there was much evidence in favour of his guilt. He was a man of the lowest repute, a swindler, and an undischarged bankrupt who had been living much above his means. The incident with the boat that sank under Monson and Hambrough turned out to be caused by a plug in the bottom having been removed beforehand, and this was strongly suspected to have been the first attempt on Cecil Hamburgh's life. The body had been exhumed and examined by reliable forensic experts: their verdict was that Hambrough had been murdered, by some person shooting him at a range of nine feet. He had been shot by a twelve-bore gun, one similar to that carried by Monson. There was no blood in the ditch where Cecil was supposed to have fallen, and the ground did not appear disturbed or trampled on in any way. Major Hambrough was called as a witness, and he testified that after he had been summoned to Ardlamont after the death of his son, Monson had told him that Cecil had been the only person carrying a gun at the time of the shooting. Then there was the matter of the still missing 'Mr Scott', who turned out to

Monson on trial, from the *IPN*, 30 December 1893.

be a London bookmaker named Edward Sweeney; the gravest suspicions were entertained concerning this mysterious individual, and his role in the boat incident and the shooting of Cecil Hambrough. But still, Alfred John Monson appeared calm and confident in court, and he was well defended by the eloquent Comrie Thomson. A number of witnesses testified that Monson and Hambrough had always been on very good terms, and that young Cecil had been very clumsy and careless with guns, and once shot a dog by accident. The jury was out for seventy-three minutes before returning a verdict of 'Not Proven' and Monson was a free man.

Was Alfred John Monson guilty of murder? I rather think he was. Monson was a thoroughly amoral individual, and very short of money: to him, Cecil Hambrough was worth just an income of £300 a year when he was alive, but a cool £20,000 once he was dead. The forensic evidence indicates that young Hambrough was murdered, and the incident with the sabotaged boat indicates that Monson had attempted to take his life before, and disguise the murder as an accident. It may be argued that as a white collar criminal, Monson lacked the killer instinct. But in the 1886 Chesney Court conflagration, Monson had intended to incinerate a stable full of horses, all heavily insured, although the animals were eventually saved from the flames. Now a man capable of roasting his horses alive for the insurance money would surely be capable of pulling the trigger of a shotgun to obtain £20,000. And if we presume that for some reason, Monson was squeamish about committing murder, the role of the man Edward Sweeney merits investigation. He was not a close friend of Monson, just an acquaintance, and surely, inviting an unreliable witness along when planning to murder some person is not a good idea. And why did Monson lie about Sweeney's name and background? Was Sweeney the man hired to shoot Hambrough with Monson's gun, and then to make himself scarce in order to obscure the case?

If Alfred John Monson had been found guilty of murder, he would surely have been hanged, since the crime of which he had stood accused was a premeditated and dastardly one. One would have expected an individual who had just been saved from the hangman's noose, by a very narrow margin, to have changed his wicked ways and made sure that he never saw the interior of a courtroom again. But all Monson knew was how to be a crook, and a brazen scoundrel at that. Using the name Wyvill to disguise his Ardlamont notoriety, he became a moneylender's tout, specialising in introducing foolhardy young men from wealthy families to these usurers. He took Madame Tussaud's to court to force them to remove his effigy from a position just outside the Chamber of Horrors. In 1893, he published a pamphlet about the Ardlamont Mystery, arguing his innocence and criticising the Scottish legal system, to which he appended what was purported to be the man Scott's diary. The outcome of this was that Edward Sweeney, formerly Scott, who was no longer a wanted man, spoke to the press, saying that he had never kept a diary in his life. In 1894, Sweeney sold his story to the *Pall Mall Gazette*, but the erstwhile Ardlamont fugitive expressed himself vaguely and cautiously, refusing to admit any guilt or to accuse Monson; he attributed his flight to moral cowardice. In 1895, Monson was back in Edinburgh, to take part in a show with a mesmerist who would put him in a trance and ask him if he had committed the Ardlamont Murder; the result was a firm denial. In 1898, Monson petitioned to divorce his wife of seventeen years, the mother of his six children, citing her purported adultery with Cecil Hambrough at the Hotel Metropole in London; he did not go through with the legal action, but the wife understandably left him, for good. Later the same year, Monson was convicted for an insurance swindle, together with the moneylender Victor Honor, and they were each sentenced to five years in prison.

The 1901 Census finds Alfred John Monson a convict at Parkhurst Prison, Isle of Wight. It was reported in the newspapers that after being released from prison, he was allowed to emigrate to South Africa. And indeed, a letter from Monson to Viscount Galway, dated 12 September 1902 and sent from Reitfontein, Burghersdorp, Cape Colony, tells us that he had been in South Africa for a few months, and was studying agriculture. He had met two Englishmen who had imported a Cleveland stallion worth £220, and rented a farm with thirty-seven mares, and hoped that Lord Galway would support him in purchasing a partnership in this venture. Since he had changed his name, the response was to be sent via Monson's mother, but there is no record that Lord Galway, who must have known what kind of man he was dealing with, ever took any notice of Monson's begging letter. Monson's wife and daughters remained in Britain, and the 1911 Census lists them as living in Brighton under the name of Wyvill. Mrs Monson died in 1942, and two of the daughters lived well into the late 1970s, but none of them left any hint what further mischief Alfred John Monson, perhaps alias Wyvill, had been up to in South Africa.

Indeed, after being snubbed by Lord Galway in 1902, Alfred John Monson disappears from view, for good. He was just forty-two years old when he emigrated, so he had accomplished much wickedness in his short and evil career, and nothing even resembling good. Evelyn Waugh and Graham Greene, both fond of chronicling the misadventures of various colonial outcasts in faraway lands, would have been worthwhile biographers of Alfred John Monson, but the pages would have been blank, the book without contents, unless some South African genealogist could perform a miracle of research to ferret out the ultimate fate of the elusive 'Mr Wyvill'. How did this monster fare in South Africa, an unforgiving country that abounded with murderous brigands, noxious animals and dangerous epidemics? There was no 'Not Proven' in South

Africa: one must either swim or sink, and I rather suspect that Monson did not have what it takes to stay afloat. He had deserted his family, lacked any religious belief with which to console him, and possessed no useful education or skills to help him make a living in a hostile environment; all he knew was how to be a crook and cheat people out of money. Did Alfred John Monson end his miserable life in some primitive South African hospital, trembling with fever and with no hope of succour; and was he, *in extremis*, given a newspaper from back home, only to read an advertisement inserted every year for many a decade: 'In loving memory of our dear son, Windsor Dudley Cecil Hambrough, found shot dead in a wood near Ardlamont, Argyllshire, August 10th, 1893, in his 21st year. "Vengeance is Mine, I will repay, saith the Lord."'

The Greenwich Bomb Outrage, 1894

On the afternoon of 15 February 1894, a foreign-looking young man was seen briskly walking up the zigzag path to Greenwich Observatory. When he was within fifty yards of the observatory, there was a tremendous explosion. Some schoolboys heard the blast and saw a plume of smoke rise through the trees. When they ran to the scene, they met with a horrible sight: the foreign-looking man was covered in blood, his left hand was entirely blown off, and his abdomen was severely lacerated. Unaware of his the extent of his injuries, he asked the boys to fetch him a cab. They instead called some park-keepers. 'Take me home!' the wounded man demanded, but instead a doctor was called and the man was taken to the nearby Royal Naval Hospital, where he expired shortly afterwards, his intestines protruding from his abdominal wound.

The man was identified as Martial Bourdin, a French tailor who was active in the anarchist movement. These radical left-wingers considered the national state unnatural and harmful, and instead promoted the idea of a stateless society, or anarchy. They were anti-royalists by nature, and found it perfectly reasonable to use force and terrorism to promote their aims. There was, at this time, a considerable presence of foreign anarchists in London, congregating in the Autonomic Club, in Windmill Street. In France and other continental countries, the anarchists were firing off their bombs with abandon, sometimes to assassinate public figures, at other times in random terrorist outrages. Severely persecuted in many countries, the anarchists had found a safe haven in England. Some politicians found it more than a little precarious to import this dangerous foreign riff-raff; how long would it take, they queried, before these fanatical terrorists would start blowing things up in their adopted country?

The newspapers were full of the Greenwich Bomb Outrage, and there was much speculation what business Martial Bourdin had at Greenwich

Observatory, carrying a powerful bomb. The immediate suggestion was of course that the dastardly anarchist had wanted to blow up the observatory, and this was also the conclusion of Colonel Vivian Magendie, the government's explosives expert, at the coroner's inquest on Bourdin. The anarchists themselves retorted that it was against their principles to target scientific institutions that were dedicated to the advancement of humanity, but the journalists did not believe them. There was also a suggestion that Bourdin had been carrying the bomb along, intending to pass it on to some other anarchist, for export to France, where it would be used against some obnoxious government figure. But surely, it would be a very dangerous practice to carry powerful explosive devices about as if they had been cauliflowers, and surely, the French anarchists had access to their own bomb factories.

In his 1897 pamphlet *The Greenwich Mystery*, a certain David Nicoll claimed that acting as a government agent, Bourdin's brother-in-law H. B. Samuels had provided him with the material to make a bomb. There was further speculation that Samuels and Bourdin were perhaps not the best of friends, and that the crooked Samuels had considered the Frenchman 'expendable' and deliberately equipped him with a defective bomb. The aim of this plot would of course have been to discredit the

Martial Bourdin is blown up, from the *IPN*, 24 February 1894.

foreign anarchists, and give the impression that they were planning further bomb outrages in London. The pamphlet writer Nicoll believed that thirty Russian agents were active in London, spying on the radicals and plotting to turn the British government against them.

None less than Joseph Conrad was inspired by the various conspiracy theories around the Greenwich Bomb Outrage when he wrote his novel *The Secret Agent*. The dismal anti-hero Stevie, whose body is scattered all over Greenwich Park, after the bomb he had been persuaded into carrying had detonated prematurely, was of course based on the unfortunate Bourdin. The sinister villain Verloc was the agent provocateur Samuels, as seen through Conrad's fertile imagination.

The Nicholls-Popejoy Affair, 1897

In October 1896, the sixteen-year-old Emily Jane Popejoy left the family home at Laurel Cottage, Jenkins Hill, Bagshot, to go into service in the household of Mrs Camilla Nicholls, a wealthy and fashionable Kensington lady living in the large terraced house at No. 14 Pitt Street. Her wages were to be 6s per month, and her board and lodgings. She was to share the domestic duties with another young maidservant, and an elderly cook, and also take Mrs Nicholls' invalid daughter for a daily airing in a large perambulator, in Kensington Gardens. Jane Popejoy was a sturdy, healthy girl, who had never been seriously ill in her life. She occasionally wrote home in the year to come, once complaining that she was worked very hard, and did not get enough to eat, although she took this back in her next letter.

On Christmas Eve 1897, Jane Popejoy was brought back to Bagshot, in a dreadful state. She had a black eye, her nose was broken, and her arms and legs were covered with cuts and bruises. She was severely emaciated, weighing just 65 lbs, and seemed generally unwell. Her family recognised her only from her voice. Dr Osburn, an experienced Bagshot practitioner, was called in to see her on Boxing Day. It was clear to him that Jane Popejoy was gravely ill with emaciation and broncho-pneumonia. Since he considered the case to be a suspicious one, he contacted the police and arranged for the dying girl's depositions to be taken. When asked about the origin of her extensive bruising, she said that her mistress had beaten her with a stick. Jane Popejoy died on 28 December, and Dr Osburn made sure that Mr G. F. Roumiou, the local coroner, was communicated with.

The coroner's inquest on Jane Popejoy went on throughout January and February 1898. Camilla Nicholls identified herself as a widow, aged forty-two years and living at No. 14 Pitt Street. She testified that Jane Popejoy had been a most unpromising servant: dirty, clumsy and sometimes smelling of strong drink. She had been very fond of running after men, and Mrs Nicholls had once seen her behaving improperly in Kensington Gardens, in broad daylight. The reason she had not been sent home to Bagshot sooner had been that she had complained that her father had beaten her, and her mother kept her without food. Jane Popejoy had led a comfortable life at No. 14 Pitt Street, Mrs Nicholls asserted: she had eaten bacon, bread and butter, and roast meat, vegetables and pudding for her dinner. She had been prone to falling over, and this might have accounted for some of her injuries.

Dr Osburn and his colleague Dr Creasy described the findings from the post-mortem examination of Jane Popejoy. The body had been extremely emaciated, and contained no fat at all. The large bowel was in an extraordinarily contracted condition, indicative of very little food being ingested for some considerable period of time. The extensive bruising to the body was consistent with repeated blows, and the nasal cartilage was separated from the bone. Death had been caused by pneumonia of both lungs, and there was a tuberculous cavity to one of them. The girl was *virgo intacta*, so the tales told by Mrs Nicholls about her immoral tendencies must have been exaggerated.

Mr William Thomas Rayne testified that Jane Popejoy had once been a servant at his house when he lived at Bagshot: she had been a strong, healthy-looking girl who had carried out her duties cheerfully. Jessie McNeil, a former servant to Mrs Nicholls, described how she had run away from the household after being beaten with a stick. Elizabeth Janaway, another servant at No. 14 Pitt Street, described the bad food served in the household, and told how Jane Popejoy had been scolded after writing to her parents, and forced to write another letter at Mrs Nicholls' dictation. The servant Edith Garrett also spoke of the poor diet in the household, adding that due to the lack of food, Jane Popejoy had used to pick up bread crusts in the street. She had heard Jane scream when Mrs Nicholls beat her with a walking stick; the invalid also screamed at regular intervals, presumably after being the recipient of some parental chastisement, but in a thin voice like a child. A small white terrier also had the misfortune to live in the house of horrors at No. 14 Pitt Street, and Mrs Nicholls kept a dog whip to discipline it, although she sometimes used this whip on the servants as well.

A number of neighbours had seen Mrs Nicholls beat and mistreat her servants, although none of them had taken any action to prevent these outrages. Elizabeth Croxford, of No. 12 Pitt Street, had seen Jane Popejoy become very thin, and heard the sound of heavy blows being administered next doors, with Mrs Nicholls screaming unflattering zoological epithets like 'Cow!', 'Sow!' and 'Filthy beast!' George Henry Taylor, page boy at No. 16 Pitt Street, had seen Mrs Nicholls beat Jane Popejoy, and the local postman and several other people living nearby had made similar observations. The jury was out for twenty minutes before returning a verdict of 'Manslaughter by starvation and ill treatment on the part of Mrs Nicholls'. After examinations before the magistrates at Chertsey and Bow Street, where Mrs Nicholls was hooted by an excited mob, and pelted with bread crusts, she was committed to stand trial for manslaughter at the Old Bailey. There was considerable media interest in the Nicholls-Popejoy affair: the conservative newspapers expressed themselves with caution, and pointed out that servants were sometimes deserving of some chastisement, but the liberal press, particularly the cheap Sunday newspapers, were wholly anti-Nicholls. The populist *Weekly Dispatch* predicted a lengthy period of incarceration for the unpopular Mrs Nicholls, and promised to arrange a subscription for the erection of a memorial cross to the blameless Jane Popejoy in Bagshot Cemetery.

The trial of Camilla Nicholls for manslaughter began at the Central Criminal Court on 28 April, before Mr Justice Phillimore. Having realised, from the amount of hostile evidence against her at the coroner's inquest, that she needed a first-rate barrister to defend her, this Kensington harridan had employed the celebrated Edward Marshall Hall. The evidence provided in court was much the same as that in the coroner's inquest, except that the servant girl Edith Garrett went to much greater lengths describing the mistreatment she and Jane Popejoy had been exposed to in the house of horrors at No. 14 Pitt Street. She had still been frightened of her former mistress when giving evidence at the inquest, she explained, but now she no longer felt fearful, and could speak the truth. She detailed how Jane Popejoy had been beaten and degraded, adding some spicy details, like that once, Camilla Nicholls had been advancing on Jane, brandishing a red hot poker, but the brave Edith Garrett had stood up in front of her. Marshall Hall bullied the doctors at length about the correct cause of death: for some reason, he felt convinced that Jane Popejoy had died from diabetes, but the doctors did not agree. He then presented a 'tame doctor' for the defence, Dr Humphrey Davy Rolleston, who pointed out that diabetes might well have been the real cause of death; moreover, patients with diabetes bled very easily, which could explain the multitude of bruises on poor Jane's body. He had to admit, however, that the doctors who had actually performed the post mortem would be better judges than him when it came to the true cause of death.

Having harried the medical witnesses, the filibustering Edward Marshall Hall introduced his 'plan B'. The Countess of Harrowby testified that she had for many years supported Mrs Nicholls, since she admired her selfless devotion to 'this hapless being' as she referred to the invalid. Another London do-gooder, Mr Beverley Edward Saurin, said that he had known Mrs Nicholls for twenty years, and that he had approached Lady Harrowby for a charitable fund to be set up for her. Mr Saurin had seen nothing wrong with Jane Popejoy when he had visited No. 14 Pitt

Street, he said. Then there was sensation when an elderly woman wearing an old-fashioned coal-scuttle bonnet shuffled up to the witness-box. She introduced herself as Catherine Harrington, eighty-four years old and cook at No. 14 Pitt Street. She then said that Mrs Nicholls was in fact her illegitimate daughter. They had lived together for many years, with the old woman acting as housekeeper for her daughter. The husband of Mrs Nicholls had left her fifteen years ago, and she had had to take care of 'that child' as the invalid was referred to, ever since. Catherine Harrington stoutly denied that she had ever seen Jane Popejoy being mistreated in any way: she had been a very dirty girl and an unsatisfactory servant. This predicament she had shared with Edith Garrett, who had been very untruthful and quarrelsome in the household.

Edward Marshall Hall addressed the jury at length, trying to persuade them that Jane Popejoy had suffered from diabetes, and that it was by no means proven that she had been starved through the wicked negligence of the prisoner. He called Edith Garrett, who had changed her testimony a good deal from the coroner's inquest, a coward, a liar and a sneak: she had been fed the same diet as Jane Popejoy, and yet appeared in the witness box the picture of health and impudence. He then did his best to create some sympathy for the accused: she was a woman born under a cloud, deserted by her husband, left with an invalid child, without money, but happily not without friends. There was applause in court celebrating the eloquent exhortations of 'the great defender'. Mr Charles Mathews, for the prosecution, drily pointed out that there was in fact no evidence that Mrs Nicholls had ever been deserted by her husband, and that at the coroner's inquest, she had been passing for a widow. As testified by the doctors who had performed the post mortem, the emaciation of Jane Popejoy had been caused by the prolonged withholding of sufficient food. Three former servants at No. 14 Pitt Street had described the mistreatment dealt out to themselves and Jane Popejoy on the premises, and the constant starvation. After a brief summing-up from Mr Justice Phillimore, the jury withdrew for just twenty minutes, before returning a verdict of 'Guilty'. Mrs Nicholls fell back in a state of collapse. With the stern words, 'The law, madam, will be more humane towards you, than you were to that poor girl!' Mr Justice Phillimore sentenced her to penal servitude for seven years. There was a cheer in court then the sentence was announced, and a huge mob waited outside, to hoot the detested Mrs Nicholls as she was taken off to Wormwood Scrubs.

There was joy in the liberal and populist newspapers that the termagant Mrs Nicholls had been taught a hard lesson, and that the honour of poor Jane Popejoy had been upheld. The *IPN* published a large drawing of the ghost of Jane Popejoy appearing to haunt Mrs Nicholls in her prison cell. In May 1898, a *Weekly Dispatch* journalist could present a masterpiece of late Victorian investigative journalism: the background

THE SENTENCE

THE VISION OF JANE POPEJOY

The ghost of Jane Popejoy comes to haunt the imprisoned Mrs Nicholls, from the *IPN*, 14 May 1898.

of the much-despised Camilla Nicholls was nothing but a tissue of lies! To start with, her real name was Harriet Harrington, and she was the illegitimate daughter of a poor Aldershot washerwoman. Harriet helped her mother with the washing for a while, but hard graft and honest toil was not to her liking. Being reasonably good-looking, she went to London at the age of sixteen and tried to set herself up as an actress, but with modest success only. In January 1865, at the age of nineteen, she married James Charles Nicholls, who made a living as a scenic artist. They lived together for quite a while, and had their invalid daughter Camilla Gustava in late 1876, but Harriet tired of her husband and left him in 1877, never to return. She set herself up as a begging-letter writer in Brighton, apparently with some degree of success, since she soon had a plentiful supply of money. Her husband thought she might be living in sin with some gentleman of means, and he may well have been right. Mrs Nicholls kept moving up in the world, and in the 1880s, she changed her name to Camilla and set herself up as a wealthy Kensington lady, always elegantly dressed and wearing expensive furs, and with a quantity of fine jewellery. She lived in a series of large and well-appointed houses, and had a number of servants, often recruited from the destitute young children of the neighbourhood, and miserably treated for as long as they would stay with her.

So, what happened to that wicked woman Camilla alias Harriet Nicholls, after her conviction? She was incarcerated at Wormwood Scrubs, and proved a difficult prisoner. She was fond of writing letters to various authorities petitioning for her release, but since her crime had been a dastardly one, she had little success. She persistently complained of feeling unwell, and at first it was thought she was shamming, but in September 1898 she was examined by a certain Dr Smalley, and found to be suffering from an abdominal tumour. An operation was called for to remove this tumour, but the obnoxious Mrs Nicholls at first refused to give consent for surgical treatment, if she was not allowed to make a statement on oath about her case. She eventually changed her mind, and the operation was scheduled for December; since it would cost £125 to have a specialist come to Wormwood Scrubs, and just £30 to perform the operation at Westminster Hospital, she was removed there under conditional license. The operation was successfully performed on 21 December, and Mrs Nicholls was back at Wormwood Scrubs in early January 1899. The 1901 Census finds her a convict at Aylesbury Prison; it is interesting that her true age is now given as fifty-one, implying that she had aged nine years since 1898! She was released into the care of the Royal Discharged Prisoners Aid Society on 21 August 1901, having served three years and 246 days of her original sentence. According to a letter dated 16 December 1901, Mrs Nicholls had behaved herself since being released, and she was no longer required to report to the police. According to her death certificate, 'Camilla Harriet Nicholls', annuitant, died at No. 17 Ranelagh Gardens on 29 June 1907, from heart failure secondary to long standing valvular disease; there was no cheating the Grim Reaper, and her age at death was correctly stated as fifty-seven years. She left a total of £997 and change to her daughter Camilla Gustava, a person of unsound mind, but the poor 'invalid' herself expired in early 1910, aged just thirty-three.

Since Mr Justice Phillimore had pointed out that a key point of the Nicholls-Popejoy case was that the enfeebled servant had been unable to escape the control of her mistress, who was mistreating her and denying her food, this implied that a master who withheld food from a servant who was unable to withdraw from his employ was liable to be prosecuted for manslaughter or even murder. The Nicholls-Popejoy case was quoted in several books on household management, to shed light on the law relating to master and servant. The erstwhile house of horrors at No. 14 Pitt Street still stands, looking quite unchanged since the goings-on back in 1897, but otherwise no memorial is left of the harridan 'Camilla Harriet Nicholls', rather befittingly considering her miserable career of cruelty. In contrast, Laurel Cottage, where Jane Popejoy grew up, still stands, although it has been subdivided into two tiny cottages: Nos 165 and 167 London Road, Bagshot. The *Weekly Dispatch* was as good as its word, and an ornate marble cross to the memory of Jane Popejoy was erected in Bagshot Cemetery. Repaired after being wantonly vandalised by some mindless thug, it still stands today, under a large cypress near the Chapel Lane entrance to the cemetery.

The Presumed Murder of a Fortune-Teller, 1899

In early January 1899, the Dutchman Willem de Swart, owner of a lodging-house at No. 8 Whitfield Street, near Tottenham Court Road, was dismayed to find that without consulting him, his wife had let two first-floor rooms to a German couple named Fritz and Augusta Briesenick. His qualms were not eased when he found that the two Germans seemed like very queer characters. Fritz was a tall and good-looking youth, who said he was twenty-five years old although he looked even younger. He introduced himself as an unemployed baker, but was well dressed and smoked expensive cigars. His 'wife' said she was thirty-six years old; although flashily dressed, she looked much older. But when Mrs Briesenick pulled out a large purse filled with gold sovereigns, to pay the rent in advance, the money-loving landlord immediately realised that these strange Germans were good tenants.

In the coming months, Willem de Swart kept a close eye on his weird lodgers. In spite of the vast difference in age, they seemed to be on good terms with each other, and never quarrelled. Fritz was a very idle fellow, who never showed any inclination to do any work. He seemed to be entirely dependent on his wife for money, even the amount of twopence to buy stamps. Augusta was very coy about her line of business, until one day, de Swart saw an advertisement in a German newspaper published in London, where Mrs Briesenick claimed to be a distinguished fortune-teller, with access to life's hidden mysteries. When challenged, Fritz freely admitted that his wife worked as a masseuse and fortune-teller; she had several wealthy clients, one of them a famous German actress. Willem de Swart did not approve of fortune-telling going on in his respectable house, but the regular payment of the rent made sure he did not press this point any further.

In March, Mrs Briesenick seemed intent to change her career. She put another advertisement into the newspaper, seeking a post as house-keeper. Fritz kept lounging about, smoking his expensive cigars, but the idle young German did not look as jaunty and carefree as before. In the late evening of 2 March, Willem de Swart was returning home after having enjoyed a few pints at the local pub. Looking up at the first-floor window of his house, he saw Fritz standing there, puffing at a cigar. He shouted, 'Hullo! Good evening, countryman! A nice night, eh?' but the lodger looked quite unlike his usual jovial self, merely replying, 'Yes, but I am going off to sleep. Good-night!'

This was the last Willem de Swart ever saw of the mysterious Fritz Briesenick. The next day, he received a postcard saying that the Briesenicks had gone away, but that they would return soon. But there was the matter of a very unpleasant smell emanating from Mrs Briesenick's room. When de Swart broke open the door, he could see a half-naked corpse lying on the bed. When the police arrived, the hysterical de Swart was running about gabbling inarticulately. Screaming 'Mein Gott!', he opened the bedroom door, before running away. Two doctors next arrived; they

The discovery of the body in the bedroom at No. 8 Whitfield Street [the house no longer stands], from the *IPN*, 18 March 1899.

MYSTERIOUS TRAGEDY IN THE WEST END.
A FORTUNE-TELLER FOUND DEAD IN BED WITH MARKS OF ILL-USAGE.

believed death had been the result of suffocation, and that the blackening of the dead woman's face had been caused by blows. Willem de Swart, his wife, and another lodger named Ghood all identified the deceased as Frau Augusta Briesenick. At the first session of the coroner's inquest, it was suspected that Fritz Briesenick had murdered his wife, before escaping.

Giving evidence at the second session of the inquest, the servant Minnie Gransow testified that she had also seen the body of the deceased, and that she was certain it was *not* Augusta Briesenick. The corpse in the bedroom had been that of a tall, stout woman; Frau Briesenick had been short and thin. Moreover, Augusta Briesenick's hair had looked very strange indeed: in the front, she wore a false fringe of greyish brown, in the middle her hair was bright red, and at the back, it was dyed jet black. The hair of the corpse had exhibited no such peculiarities. Accordingly, the coroner had the body exhumed, to be inspected by a number of people who had known Augusta Briesenick. The de Swarts and Ghood changed their minds: they were now fully satisfied that the deceased was not the Augusta Briesenick they had known. Instead, the police found evidence to suggest that the corpse in the bedroom was the Swiss housemaid Sophie Richard, who had 'got into the family way' and consulted the sinister Frau Briesenick, whose bag of tricks apparently included abortionism. Changing their minds, the doctors thought there might have been some mishap during the abortion, although they still favoured that death had been the result of suffocation. Later, to confound things further, it was claimed that the corpse's intestines had contained traces of a certain chemical used as an abortifacient.

As the witnesses and doctors were dithering, the London detectives found evidence that the Briesenicks had absconded back to the *Vaterland*, presumably to Berlin. And sure enough, the Berlin detectives saw two queer-looking individuals disembarking a train: a flashily dressed, middle-aged woman and a tall, indolent cove smoking a cigar. They were both arrested, and taken to the main police station. Since the German detectives had ways of making people talk, the young cigar-smoker was soon singing like a bird. His real name was Fritz Metz, and he had been apprentice to the wealthy Berlin baker and confectioner Adolf Briesenick. After the baker's femme fatale of a wife had seduced him, they had stolen Briesenick's money, and set off to London to start a new career as international criminals. The wicked Frau Briesenick had performed abortions, swindled people by telling their fortunes, and robbed a famous German actress who had employed her as a masseuse.

When Fritz Metz and Augusta Briesenick were tried in November 1899, the craven Metz turned Kaiser's evidence against his former partner in crime. He was duly acquitted, whereas Augusta Briesenick would have been severely dealt with, had she not 'become insane and unable to plead', as *Lloyd's Weekly Newspaper* expressed it. She was duly detained in a lunatic asylum. It is a pity these extraordinary scenes were but rudimentarily summarised in the newspapers of the time: we will never know whether the straitjacketed Augusta Briesenick screamed 'Burn in hell, you *Schweinhund*' at the coward Metz, or whether the latter, emerging from the court unscathed, took a welcome puff at his cigar before exclaiming, 'Well, that was a *damned* close thing!' Did this strange character continue his life of crime, was he killed in the Great War, or did he live to fight another day, after Hitler had made Germany a country fit for scoundrels to live in?

The Case of Kitty Byron, 1902

In 1902, life was not looking good for Mr Reginald Baker. Although a solicitor of respectable background, and just forty-four years old, severe alcoholism had reduced him to a wreck of a man. A stocky, barrel-chested fellow with an enormous handle-bar moustache, Reggie Baker kept swigging hard from his whisky-bottle almost around the clock, to stave off the DTs. He tried gambling at the stock exchange, with disastrous results; to pay back his debts, he had to sell the London flat he had shared with his wife Mabel. Quoting her husband's repeated adultery, cruelty, and constant abusive language, and his giving her a venereal disease, Mabel petitioned for divorce. Reggie moved into cheap lodgings with his latest mistress, the unemployed milliner Emma 'Kitty' Byron, and continued his idle, worthless life. He was kind to Kitty when he was sober, but unfortunately for her, he was almost always drunk. He constantly ill-treated her, and threatened to murder her more than once.

One day in November 1902, Kitty was distraught to hear from her landlady Madame Adrienne Liard that Reggie had referred to her as a prostitute, whom he would soon be leaving behind. Understandably, the landlady herself had little sympathy for Reggie, asking Kitty, 'Why do you live with a brute like that for?' The pathetic Kitty, who had hoped that Reggie would marry her, replied that she loved him, and that after being seduced and living in sin, she would never obtain a good character again. Influenced by some forthright advice from Madame Liard, Kitty packed her few belongings and planned to move away from her caddish boyfriend. But since his insults still rankled, she went out and bought a formidable knife, drank several glasses of brandy on an empty stomach, and invited Reggie to meet her at a post office nearby. After they started quarrelling, she pulled the knife out of her muff and stabbed him hard four times. His aorta severed, Reggie dropped dead, on the spot. Making no attempt to escape, the hysterical Kitty pleaded with the people who had seized her that she must be allowed to kiss her dear Reggie one last time.

Kitty Byron stabs
Reggie Baker,
from the *IPN*,
22 November 1902.

The murder of Reggie Baker took place on the pavement opposite the Lombard Street post office. It was witnessed by several people, and Kitty did not deny stabbing Reggie to death. Nor was it possible for her to deny premeditation, since the sharp knife had been purchased in advance, and carried in her muff ready for action. But one feature of the murder of Reggie Baker was quite singular: no person had any sympathy for the victim himself. Reggie had been a drunk, a scrounger, an adulterer and a cad. His former colleagues at the Stock Exchange drank a toast to celebrate his death, and clubbed together to make sure Kitty got a good barrister. Their choice was Mr Henry Dickens, the son of Charles. Like other men who came into contact with the pathetic Kitty Byron, Dickens pitied her intensely; was she not a wronged, working-class young woman, who had been driven to desperation by her cruel middle-class seducer? Kitty was young and quite good-looking, with a child-like and artless mien that would be of great benefit to her throughout her adventures.

The *IPN* and other popular newspapers all published Kitty's portrait, and tried their best to put a spin on her pathetic story. Was it really right to prosecute a wronged woman like Kitty for murder, and should women really suffer capital punishment? There were petitions from thousands of working people all over Britain that Kitty should be spared the gallows, since she had been driven to despair by the cruel Reggie. When tried at the Old Bailey later in 1902, Kitty was ably defended by Henry Dickens. She was fortunate that the old-fashioned 'hanging judge' like Sir Henry Hawkins had become near-extinct by this time; although the humane Mr Justice Darling did sentence her to death, he also supported the jury's recommendation of mercy. Accordingly, the Home Secretary commuted

Two vignettes of Kitty Byron in court, from the *IPN*, 27 December 1902.

Kitty's sentence to life imprisonment in December 1902. This verdict did not take into account that there had clearly been premeditation, nor that Reggie had been stabbed hard not less than four times. A damning psychiatrist's report, which stated that Kitty had attempted suicide twice in her teens, that she regularly consumed alcohol, and that she had been sexually promiscuous since an early age, not only with older males but also with members of her own sex, was also disregarded.

During Kitty Byron's years in prison, Henry Dickens and her other friends did not forget her. There were several petitions for her early release, signed by many London stockbrokers and professional men, but they went unheeded since it was practice that people jailed for life should serve at least seven years. But in October 1908, Adeline Duchess of Bedford took an interest in Kitty, petitioning the government that she should be released to Duxhurst Farm, a refuge for alcoholic women run by Lady Henry Somerset, the sister of the Duchess. The logic behind this move is not immediately discernible: even if Kitty may well have enjoyed a few too many back in 1902, she surely cannot have had access to strong drink during her six years behind bars. And the activities of Lady Henry Somerset, involving proto-psychotherapeutic methods supervised by nurses or laypeople, were far from uncontroversial. Still, the pro-Kitty *Daily Mail* expressed relief that their heroine would obtain a refuge at:

> A quiet half-way house between prison and freedom at Lady Henry Somerset's beautifully situated industrial colony at Duxhurst, near Reigate. Here for a year, although she will be under a certain supervision, she will be permitted to wander through gardens and secluded walks, and have the companionship of other women.

Kitty Byron, who had been a model prisoner throughout her six years in jail, was soon up to mischief at Duxhurst Farm. Nevertheless, in

December 1909, she volunteered to stay at the home for another year. But a nurse named Annie Mapplebeck, who had been Kitty's therapist, complained that throughout her stay at the alcoholic's home, her charge had shown some very sinister tendencies. Kitty had fallen violently in love with Nurse Mapplebeck, and she became very jealous when the nurse spent time with other inmates; plates and glasses were thrown, and bloodcurdling curses screamed. Kitty had threatened to murder Nurse Mapplebeck more than once, and these threats were far from empty; once, Kitty had been caught secreting a sharp pen-knife, and another time, she had tried to set fire to the farm. The same day the long-suffering nurse reported Kitty to Lady Henry, this sinister young woman had procured a bottle of poison, which she tried to persuade Nurse Mapplebeck to drink.

Lady Henry Somerset was in a quandary, and she referred the matter to the Prison Commission. To send Kitty back to prison, or to have her incarcerated in a lunatic asylum, would enrage the many friends of the murderess, and cause adverse newspaper publicity. It would also reflect badly on the faddist methods employed at Duxhurst Farm. After a bitter society scandal when she had divorced her husband on grounds of his homosexuality, Lady Henry was wary of publicity. There was a tame doctor at Duxhurst Farm, and he was willing to have Kitty committed to a private asylum, but the signatures of two doctors were needed for such transactions, and Kitty was quite lucid most of the time. To keep this sinister woman at Duxhurst Farm was equally impossible: what if she burnt the place down, or dosed the soup with poison and killed off all the other inmates? In the end, Lady Henry and the Prison Commission decided to have Kitty released into the care of her unmarried elder sister Agnes. At the time of the 1911 Census, Kitty Byron was living in Coventry, and there is reason to believe that she died in early 1954, aged seventy-five; if she ever killed anyone else, she must have gotten away with it.

The Disappearance of a Lady Doctor, 1903

The sensation of the summer of 1903 was the mysterious disappearance of the twenty-nine-year-old doctor Miss Sophia Frances Hickman. She had been a brilliant medical student, achieving several prizes, before starting work at the Royal Free Hospital in a junior locum position. Miss Hickman had appeared her normal cheerful self on 15 August 1903, seeing patients and doing her work on the wards, before going out for her luncheon. She never returned.

At first, the police took the matter of Miss Hickman's disappearance lightly, but her father, the wealthy merchant Edwin Francis Hickman, soon stirred them into action. Sophia had always been a very good girl, he said; shy, industrious and reliable. Never, even as a teenager, had she shown any disposition to chase boys, so the police could discard the hypothesis that she might have gone off with some man. Sophia had still been living with her parents, sisters and invalid brother at Courtfield Gardens, SW. She was a strong, healthy woman, fond of walking, swimming and other wholesome outdoor pursuits. The police questioned Miss Hickman's hospital colleagues, who agreed with her father that she had been very steady and industrious, and never showed any tendency to consort with wicked men. She was well-liked at the hospital, and popular among the local poor for her kindness and charity.

There was widespread newspaper publicity about the lost lady doctor. The lurid theories about this mysterious disappearance varied widely: had Miss Hickman been kidnapped for ransom, murdered for her purse and jewels by some local rough, or was she kept as a sex slave in some concealed brothel? The white slavery scaremongers of course suspected that a drugged Miss Hickman was kept captive in a large wooden box on board ship, addressed to 'Sheik Abdul, The Harem, Araby.' Edwin Francis Hickman had a dotty theory of his own: he suspected that his daughter had been kidnapped by some sinister Roman Catholic priests, who held her captive in a convent and tried to convert her into becoming a nun.

The rabble-rousing editor W. T. Stead made much of the case of the missing lady doctor: was it not a shame that a decent, law-abiding English woman could not be safe on the streets of the Metropolis! He circulated various conspiracy theories about the disappearance of Miss Hickman, many of them involving lustful foreign villains. Since Stead was interested in spiritualism, he got hold of a psychic detective and a seance was held, in which the medium had a vision of the missing lady doctor lying on a bed in a small attic room. Since this useful medium could describe the house and surroundings, a detective who was present called in his colleagues. The house was identified, the door broken open and the attic room stormed by plain-clothes police. The bed was found to contain

Miss Sophia Hickman, the Missing Lady Doctor, from the *Tatler*, 2 September 1903.

nothing more interesting than a cantankerous old woman, who was most irate at being woken up in the middle of the night!

A writer in the *Lancet* came up with a slightly better suggestion. Might Miss Hickman not be suffering from 'automatic wandering', a fashionable diagnosis at the time? These automatic wanderers were presumed to suddenly lose their memory and scour the countryside in a half-dazed condition, entirely unaware of their own identity. The police took this notion quite seriously, and added it to posters offering a £200 reward from the Royal Free Hospital to the person who recovered the lost lady doctor. A wealthy Scot, who for some reason was convinced that Miss Hickman was automatic wandering in the Highlands, issued a £100 reward of his own. As a result, any haughty Englishwoman who resembled Miss Hickman, and who declined to identify herself when challenged by the kilted locals, was in danger of being frog-marched to the nearest police station.

By October 1903, doom and gloom pervaded the newspaper coverage of the search for the lost lady doctor: she was either murdered, held captive in a drugged condition, or kept as a white slave in the harem of some Arabic magnate. But on 18 October, two young boys discovered the dead body of Sophia Frances Hickman, in a densely wooded area of Richmond Park. 'Orrible Murder!' exclaimed the newspaper headlines, since her purse was missing, the head completely severed from the body, and a hospital knife found nearby.

But the competent forensic experts who examined the body found that it was in a condition to suggest that it had been in Richmond Park ever since Miss Hickman had disappeared. The reason the head and neck were very badly damaged was that rodents and other animals had fed from the corpse. The autopsy showed no suspicious injuries, and Miss Hickman

The finding of Miss Hickman's body, from the *IPN*, 24 October 1903.

Scenes from the inquest on Miss Hickman, from the *IPN*, 31 October 1903.

was *virgo intacta*. Nearby, the doctors found a syringe and needle, and a bottle of morphine; traces of this drug was found in the corpse's intestinal tract, and a pharmacist, who had sold a quantity of morphine to Miss Hickman some days before she disappeared, could identify the bottle. Thus it was concluded that the missing lady doctor had committed suicide. The reason for absence of the purse was probably that some tramp had stolen it from the dead body. It is curious that in a 1927 newspaper feature, none less that ex-Superintendent Percy Savage declared himself unimpressed with the evidence in favour of suicide, pointing out the advanced decomposition of the body, that one of Miss Hickman's hospital colleagues thought it absurd that she would destroy herself, and that if she had left the hospital by her own free will, she would surely have been wearing her overcoat. Superintendent Savage speculated that she might have been lured away from the hospital by some person with murder in mind, but after twenty-four years had gone by, his grasp of the case was not the strongest, and a recent academic article on the case agrees with the contemporary press that Miss Hickman committed suicide.

The evening newspaper journalists were very disappointed at this anticlimactic ending to the mystery of the missing lady doctor. Instead of imaging murderous robbers or foreign villains, they were struggling to grasp why this secure, successful young woman had taken her own life, without confiding in any person. The misogynist brigade, whose mouths had not yet been obturated by Madame Curie and other successful female doctors and medical scientists, of course made the most of the situation, suggesting that Miss Hickman's death was yet another example that the female intellect was incapable of coping with the demand of a higher education. Medicine, in particular, was far too demanding for them, and unless the doors of every medical school was barred against these female interlopers, the streets of London would be cluttered with the corpses of lady doctors who had destroyed themselves as a result of not coping with the demands of their profession.

It is good to see that neither the *Lancet* nor the *British Medical Journal* was taken in by this misogynist claptrap. These journals pointed out that Miss Hickman had coped very well with the demands of her profession; far from being a stressed, underachieving doctor, she had been quite a popular and successful one. Women had been allowed to study medicine for quite some time, and many of these lady doctors had done the medical profession considerable credit. Nor was it unheard-of that male medical practitioners destroyed themselves. None of these journals dared to speculate why Miss Hickman had committed suicide, however, and the motives will be buried forever in her inner mind. If there was a man, or perhaps a woman, involved in the case, they never came forward. The lady doctor who had remained a very good girl, to use her father's parlance, well into her womanhood, had confided in no one; we cannot fathom what dark, solitary thoughts must have tormented her mind when she took the morphine and lay down to her final rest in Richmond Park.

An Exciting Episode from the Life of Mr Kenneth Grahame, 1903

On 24 November, 1903, a well-dressed man came into the lobby of the Bank of England, presented a card with the name 'Mr G. F. Robinson' and demanded to see the Governor, Sir Augustus Prevost. He was politely told that Sir Augustus was busy, but that the Secretary of the Bank of England, Mr Kenneth Grahame, was available. Robinson agreed to see him instead. A short man with a slight moustache, Robinson was elegantly dressed and looked the perfect City gentleman; nobody could guess that not only was he a Socialist Anarchist, but a stark raving lunatic as well. When ushered into Mr Grahame's office, Robinson promptly and wordlessly handed him a roll of paper, tied up at one end with black tape, and at the other with white tape. Robinson knew that if Grahame took the white end, he was one of the Good Bankers, a loyal servant of his country; if he took the black end, he was one of the Bad Bankers, who hoarded the money of the poor in his bottomless vaults. 'Mr G. F. Robinson' was that kind of lunatic.

Kenneth Grahame took the black end and unfolded three pages of foolscap, all with the only words 'All are concerned!' Understanding that his silent and sinister visitor was clearly not quite sane, Grahame told him he did not have the time to read his documents. Robinson's response was to draw a heavy Colt revolver and fire at him from nearly point-blank range. Amazed that he was still alive, Kenneth Grahame shouted for Tolmie, the head waiter. Screaming 'I did it for the good of everybody!' Robinson kept firing his revolver more and less at random: splinters flew from the office furniture as the heavy-calibre bullets struck home, and plaster showered from the perforated ceiling. When Tolmie showed his face in the door, the lunatic fired several shots at him, and pursued him out into the corridor. The shaken Mr Grahame and his fellow bankers took to their heels, leaving Robinson in possession of one wing of the Bank of England. The brave Tolmie, who crept after the lunatic, could see him stalking through the empty offices, holding his smoking revolver high, and exclaiming 'Where are you, cowards!'

A frightened bank messenger came rushing out of the Bank of England and called Detective Inspector Bacon and his colleague Detective Constable Digby, of the City Police. In the public lobby, the two policemen were met by Mr Grahame, who told them there was an armed man at large in the Bank. Behind him, some bank messengers were holding a door shut, to prevent the lunatic's egress. When the two detectives opened this door a little, they could see Robinson standing a few yards down the corridor; he aimed his heavy revolver at them and shouted 'Come on, you cowards!'

The two policemen swiftly slammed the door shut and directed the messengers to keep holding it. Bravely, they themselves tried another entrance to the corridor, in the hope of surprising the lunatic, but they found he had retreated into the Bank Library and bolted the door from

The lunatic Robinson on the rampage, from the *IPN*, 5 December 1903.

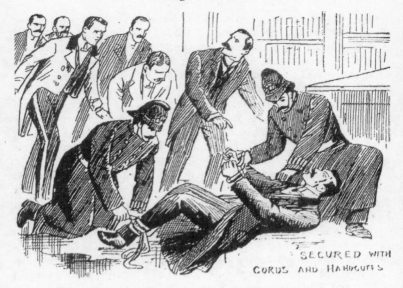

SECURED WITH
CORDS AND HANDCUFFS

Robinson is subdued, from the *IPN*, 5 December 1903.

the inside. They tried to reason with him, asking why on earth he had gone on a rampage inside the Bank, and eventually he drew the bolts, as if to invite them to come in. When the policemen bravely entered the room, Robinson sat down in an armchair, aimed his revolver at them, and exclaimed 'If you come a step further I fire!'

The two unarmed officers had to withdraw, leaving the lunatic in possession of the Bank Library. Inspector Bacon had got an idea, however. Lord Revelstoke, the Director of the Bank of England, had come to the scene, and the Inspector asked for permission to make use of the Bank's powerful fire hose to pacify the lunatic. After his Lordship had given his consent, the Bank's firemen got the contraption ready for use. The library door was burst open, and Robinson caught the first jet of water straight in the chest. As he was swept off his feet, both police and porters attacked him. Jumping to his feet, the lunatic threw his revolver at them, but he missed and the weapon went through the glass front of a bookcase. Undeterred, Robinson swung a heavy chair at Inspector Bacon, but the agile officer dodged underneath it and the chair smashed to pieces against a table.

Constable Digby, who had retrieved Robinson's heavy revolver, struck him on the head with the butt of this weapon, but the crushing impact against the lunatic's rock-hard skull did little to pacify him. Screaming 'All money is wrongly distributed!' he desperately struggled against the police and porters, as the hose played all over them, until Inspector Bacon dealt him another heavy blow with a chair, knocking him out cold. Robinson was promptly tied to a stretcher and removed to Bow Infirmary, where his bruised and lacerated head was dressed. The only policeman to be injured was Constable Digby, whose hand had been bitten by the lunatic during the melée. The library was very much destroyed, and entirely flooded with water.

It turned out that George Frederick Robinson, to give the lunatic his full name, had run away from home when just sixteen years old, vainly hoping to get rich in the Klondyke gold rush. After being bitten by an infuriated sled dog, he nearly lost his arm after walking eighty miles to get the wound treated, and contracting septicaemia. He later joined the army and served in the Canadian Yeomanry during the Boer War, not without distinction. While in Africa, he caught malaria, and this was believed to have affected his brain, since when he returned to his respectable family in England he behaved very oddly, saying it was the fault of the banks that so many people were poor. The Bank of England ought to open its vaults and hand out their contents to the needy, he exclaimed to his astonished father. On trial, Robinson seemed quite mad, asking the judge whether he could have his revolver back when it was shown in court. He was certified insane and committed to Broadmoor. Perhaps he is today haunting the old asylum, frightening the other inmates by groaning and waving his heavy revolver about, and exclaiming, 'I was right about those damned bankers all along! I *told* you they could not be trusted!'

Mr Kenneth Grahame, who had had such a narrow escape, became a changed man as a result. Fed up with the modern world and its unpredictable, trigger-happy Socialist Anarchists, he lost interest in banking and began writing stories for children, quaint and bucolic tales featuring talking animals living quietly in the countryside. Five years after the shooting incident, he retired from the Bank of England at the age of just forty-nine, four months before the publication of *The Wind in the Willows*.

11

Victorian Weirdness

The death of Queen Victoria in January 1901 put the *IPN* into deep mourning: there were illustrated features about her eventful reign, and drawings of her funeral cortege. The newspaper continued its career into the reign of jolly King Edward; its finances were in a healthy state and its circulation very considerable, in spite of the persistent competition from that miserable rag, the *Illustrated Police Budget*. The outbreak of the Second Boer War provoked an orgy of jingoistic flag-waving in the pages of the *IPN*. The Boers were depicted as sub-human brutes, with coarse features and large bushy beards; they were fond of strip-searching English ladies, and making use of various cowardly and unsporting military ruses. The *IPN* headlines about the Boer War include gems such as 'Another Dastardly Instance of Boer Trickery', 'Mafeking as Plucky and Buoyant as Ever' and 'Her Majesty Graciously Receives the Wounded Boy Bugler'.

Some naughty Boers amusing themselves, from the *IPN*, 8 July 1899.

After the Boer War had been won, the *IPN* returned to normal, featuring sensational recent crimes, boxers and racehorses, actresses and music hall performers, and a variety of serialised novels, some of them with 'fierce' titles like Douglas Stewart's *The Wild Tribes of London* and *The Fiend of the Bomb, or the Anarchist's Doom*. One of the most prolific contributors to the *IPN* in this period was the journalist Guy Logan, who would later become a distinguished crime historian. He provided many articles on historical crimes, a number of serialised novels about the South African war, Jack the Ripper and other sensational topics, and sentimental Christmas poems in the manner of George R. Sims. In January 1903, the *IPN* was further expanded to sixteen pages, the additional space being filled with sporting news, fiction, and advertisements. Not a few articles and illustrations from this period have an unpleasant racist odour: in the Southern states of the United States, dastardly Negro criminals attack and outrage white women, only to be lynched by the Ku Klux Klan, whose activities were approvingly described. That dismal downmarket rival of the *IPN*, the *Illustrated Police Budget*, finally gave up the ghost in 1912, having struggled for years in London's competitive newspaper world, but the *IPN* itself continued to prosper. In February 1914, the newspaper's golden jubilee was briefly and frugally celebrated: a replica of an 1864 cover was reproduced, and readers were invited to collect and submit a series of coupons, to take part in a raffle to win a clock.

Guy Logan's poem 'The Centre Figure', from the *IPN*, 27 December 1902.

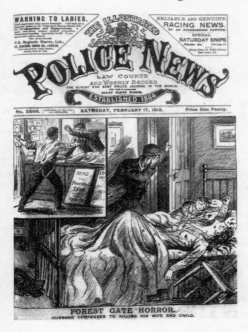

The first page of the *IPN*, 17 February 1912, featuring a double murder in Forest Gate.

When the Great War broke out, the *IPN* was ready for another orgy in flag-waving ultra-patriotism. It has to be admitted that the dastardly Huns excelled in brutal and sanguinary outrages, however, and the *IPN* artists did not need to exaggerate when describing the wholesale murder of civilians, the burning of churches and cathedrals, the bombardment of Lowestoft and the shooting of Nurse Cavell. With a large proportion of the younger male population of Britain in uniform abroad, the potential readership of the *IPN* had been severely decimated by the war, and the newspaper soon hit evil times. Filled with depressing and repetitive war news, only spiced up by the occasional murder on the home front, its circulation steadily decreased, and in April 1916, it went back down to twelve pages. A year later, the price for an issue of the *IPN* was increased to three halfpennies, after it had remained a penny newspaper for fifty-three years.

In March 1918, the struggling *IPN* went down to eight pages, and the newspaper must have been literally saved by the bell when the Great War finally ended. The racism and xenophobia continued in the post-war period: German white slavers infested London, illegal aliens ought to be deported, and American negroes were up to mischief again, although kept in check by the upstanding members of the Ku Klux Klan. Ghosts and hermits, human and animal freaks, weirdoes and strange performers

Sketches from the murder of Olive Young by the demented playboy Ronald True, from the *IPN*, 16 March 1922.

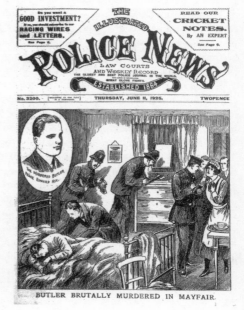

The first page of the *IPN*, 11 June 1925, featuring the murder of the Mayfair butler Francis Rix by the pantry boy Arthur Henry Bishop.

were shunned from this time onwards: the post-war *IPN* concentrated on criminals at home and abroad, sportsmen and music-hall performers. In May 1920, the price of an issue of the *IPN* rose to twopence. The newspaper was something of an archaic oddity in London's competitive publishing world by this time: in the age of photography, it relied on its draughtsmen just like it had done in the 1860s; nor had its standards of journalism been significantly improved since that time. Still, the *IPN* managed to struggle on throughout the 1920s and early 1930s, and it continued to describe the celebrated murders of the day with gusto, like those committed by Ronald True and Henry Jacoby, the 'Wimbledon Matricide' of 1934, and the unsolved 'Soho Slayings' of Marie Jeanet Cotton and Leah Hinds. As I have demonstrated in my trilogy about the *Murder Houses of London*, the quality of the *IPN*'s illustrations remained quite high: in spite of its obvious decline, and the invasion of its pages by bruisers and footballers, it still prided itself on its accurate portraits of criminals, and its reliable drawings of houses where celebrated murders had taken place. Although it was no longer customary among London newspapers to publish the addresses of the scenes of celebrated crimes, the *IPN* remained the murder house detective's greatest friend.

In June 1934, the *IPN* went back to twelve pages, featuring more film news and sporting pursuits. Guy Logan's old features from before the Great War were reused, with the original illustrations, as were some of his serialised novels. By this time, the newspaper was nearly entirely devoid of Forteana, apart from the solitary marauding eagle snatching away a child or two. In early 1937, the *IPN* was back up to sixteen pages, but the pernicious adulteration of its contents continued, with football pools and boxing matches sharing the limelight with the criminals. In March 1937, the *IPN* published its first ever photograph: a study of the Boat Race that appeared on the first page. Photos of muscle-bound bruisers and pretty chorus girls continued to appear in the issues to come. In September, the title strapline changed from 'Law Courts and Weekly Record', which had been there since the inauguration in 1864, to 'Sporting Weekly Record'. This did not augur well for the newspaper's future, and indeed, the woeful day of 3 March 1938 saw the publication of the *ultimus* of the once famous *IPN*, the title of which was henceforth permanently changed to *The Sporting Record*. Having degenerated into a worthless newspaper for pointless old men hanging around in bookmakers' shops, it nevertheless survived the Second World War, Clement Attlee, Harold Wilson, and various other calamities. As the *Greyhound and Sporting Record*, it finally perished in the first spring of the Thatcherian renaissance, the last issue ever being published on 2 August 1980.

During its Purkessian heyday, the *IPN* was very much a child of its times: a product of the demand from a large working-class audience who wanted an easy-to-read weekly newspaper that was mainly about

The first page of the *IPN*,
14 May 1931, featuring a
Croydon matricide.

The first page of the *IPN*,
12 March 1936, featuring a
Tooting family tragedy.

criminals, and the supply of such a newspaper from the vigorous London publishing industry. Its decline in the post-Purkess period, which accelerated after the outbreak of the Great War, meant that in the end, the IPN survived itself. It was far from a novel enterprise in the 1860s, old-fashioned by the 1890s, outdated in the 1910s, and positively archaic in the 1930s. But although the times were changing fast, and the young readership turned their backs to the *IPN*, there were still enough old-fashioned, traditionalist countrymen, who would not contemplate changing their favourite reading material, for the newspaper to keep going until 1938. The concept of a present-day *IPN* would of course be entirely preposterous, at a time when even the very concept of traditional printed newspapers is under threat from the internet. The big London daily newspapers have tried to counter this spectral menace through making part of their contents available online, either by subscription of for free; the smaller country papers, who lack this option, are going out of business as a result. As old-fashioned *Daily Express* readers are dying off at a steady rate, and new generations brought up with the internet gain maturity, there are those who predict that in ten or twenty years' time, all printed newspapers will be as extinct as the *IPN*, joining carbon-paper, slide-rules, typewriters, box cameras and old-fashioned printed books like this one in a ghostly 'museum of technology past' sent into oblivion by the computer age.

But in spite of the onslaught of the internet, a considerable number of London and provincial tabloid newspapers are alive and well at the time of the publication of this book. Do they have any similarities with the long-lost *IPN*? One likeness is obvious, namely that that the fascination with recent sensational murders is still with us: the *Sun* and the *Daily Mirror* both chronicled the activities of Mark Dixie, who murdered Sally Anne Bowman; Mark Bridger, who murdered April Jones; Stuart Hazell, who murdered Tia Sharp; the spree killers Derrick Bird and Raoul Moat; and the sinister serial killers Joanna Dennehy and Levi Bellfield. Criminals convicted for historical murders, whether in prison or out of it, become public hate figures, like Ian Huntley, Maxine Carr, the Yorkshire Ripper Peter Sutcliffe, and the juvenile monsters Jon Venables and Robert Thompson, to say nothing of the detested paedophile brigade, counting members like Gary Glitter, Rolf Harris and Max Clifford, and recruiting new ones all the time. The old-fashioned drawings of the *IPN* have been replaced with cold hard photographs, and the sentimentalism of olden times, depicting the murderer's old mother weeping, or imagining the convict's last dream before execution, has been replaced with cold hard vilification: in present-day tabloid journalism, the murderer or the paedophile does not possess a single honest bone in his body, and can accomplish nothing good or positive. A second recurring theme is the puerile approach to politics: politicians are either good or evil, depending on which party the tabloid supports: either upstanding patriots on a crusade to save the country after decades of misrule, or penny-pinching killjoys and Ebenezer Scrooges intent on ruining the honest working family's Christmas holiday. The xenophobia of the old *IPN* is also still with us, albeit in a somewhat different guise: it is easier to pity the downtrodden East End vagabonds lampooned by the *IPN* than the foreign scroungers of the present time, and more natural to feel sympathy for the black Americans harried by the Ku Klux Klan than the bushy-bearded 'Hate Preachers' kept in check by the anti-terrorist authorities. The medical advertisements in today's tabloids are touting magnetic bracelets, a time-honoured quack 'cure' for arthritis and various other ills, instead of nostrums to increase male sexual potency, and make the hair regrow on balding pates. The reactionary tabloid cartoon strips strike another archaic note, the dreadful 'Andy Capp' in particular.

***

The journalism of the *IPN* was fully competent during the Purkess era, although the newspaper often regurgitated material from other large newspapers. Its reporting of recent high-profile London murders was excellent, often outclassing the mainstream papers. Even in the 1920s, when the *IPN* was otherwise a shadow of its former vigorous self, it could still enjoy a good murder. The second strength of the *IPN* was its extensive coverage of strange and macabre news from all over the world, achieved through the sifting of much British and foreign newspaper hardcopy. From time to time, the newspaper repeated obvious canards, like the invented tale of Miss Vint and her Reincarnated Cats, the bogus American yarn of the murderous Professor Beaurigard, the story of the non-existent chain-smoker Mynheer van Klaes, and the various 'buried alive' newspaper fantasies imported from France and Austria. Although the politics of the *IPN* were radical at the time of the Purkess takeover in 1865, they never played much of a role in influencing the newspaper's contents, and were gradually diluted by traditionalism, patriotism and xenophobia in the years to come.

The major reason that the *IPN* is still remembered today is the quality of its illustrations, which was good already in 1864, and outstanding throughout the Purkess era, to my mind superior to those in the *Illustrated London News* and the *Penny Illustrated Paper*. Many illustrations were fully realistic, depicting the Dog-faced Men, Krao, the conjoined twins, the White Gorilla and various performers like Zaeo, Teddy Wick and Leona Dare as they really were. Similarly, without the *IPN*, we would not have known what some of the protagonists in sensational Victorian dramas and mysteries had looked like: Dick Schick, Lady Twiss, Lieutenant Roper, the Revd Benjamin Speke and the Poulett Claimant. These realistic illustrations are a valuable contribution to the social history of the period. Then we have another group of illustrations, namely those that are fanciful or exaggerated: ghosts appear and disappear, somnambulists fall from the roofs, eagles the size of aeroplanes swoop down in search of little children to abduct, and sub-human criminal types enjoy a thieves' supper. These fanciful images are often quite hilarious to the modern reader.

When lecturing to the Cardiff medical students, I sometimes used to provide some light relief during the break, making use of the computer-assisted projector to introduce them to the strange world of the *IPN*. The students laughed uproariously when they saw the child-snatching eagles, the White Gorilla, the Ratting Monkey of Manchester and Dick Schick the Female Errand Boy, although some felt sorry for the pseudo-gorilla that had been so shamefully treated. And indeed, the Victorian exploitation of the human and animal freaks revealed by the *IPN* sometimes makes for dismal reading: the exhibition of the ailing Dog-faced Man, the profiting from making little Krao out as a human monkey, and putting the Scottish Giant on show when he was in fact a dying man. In spite of its praiseworthy canophilia during the Purkess period, and a firm anti-vivisection stance, the *IPN* had little sympathy for the animal kingdom as a whole. Both the human spectators and the dogs involved seemed to have liked a bit of ratting, but I can see nothing to suggest that the rats themselves ever showed any enthusiasm for this gory 'sport'. An elephant hit by a railway train, or polar bears kept in captivity, are not as prepossessing today as they were for a Victorian reader of the *IPN*; nor is there anything particularly uplifting about the use of caged lions for ludicrous and foolhardy Lion Wagers. The *IPN* was the true mirror of its times, without squeamishness or political correctness.

Throughout the Purkess era, and well into Edwardian times, the *IPN* had a strong fascination for the spectral world, and over the years, the newspaper published many illustrated ghost stories, a good few of which are retold in this book. The most extraordinary of them concerns the Haunted Murder House near Chard, where both the murder and the subsequent haunting were well verified in the local papers. Being something of an aficionado of haunted murder houses, I very much regret that it has proven impossible, due to the sheer amount of humble working man's cottages in those parts, to determine if this West Country house of horrors is still standing today. The tales of the Manchester Ghost, and the Mystery of Sarah Duckett, are also genuinely spooky, and both remain unexplained. In contrast, the Hackney Ghost and the Fairwater Mystery are both much ado about nothing in my opinion, and this predicament they share with that much-hyped doyen of Metropolitan spectres, the Ghost of Berkeley Square. The Jumping Ghost of Peckham, the Plumstead Ghost and the Fighting Ghost of Tondu are all amusing instances of suburban ghost imitators being up to mischief. Undeterred by the dismal fate of the Hammersmith Ghost, which was shot dead by a ghost hunter in 1804, these frolicsome youngsters acted the part of Spring-Heeled Jack with enthusiasm, sometimes frightening men, women and children, and giving rise to veritable ghost hysterias.

Some of the 'human interest' stories told by the *IPN* are uplifting tales, none more so than the biography of Ned Wright, who was inspired by God to shun prize-fighting and burglary, and who became the founder of the thieves' supper and a much-respected evangelist as a result. Teddy Wick, the Fastest Barber in the West, and Paul Tetzel, the Champion Butcher, also appear to have led quite jolly, independent lives. As a direct result of the Bank of England Shooting Outrage, Kenneth Grahame turned his back on the uninspiring world of banking, and became a famous author instead. As for the not inconsiderable daredevil element in the pages of this book, some of them, like Park van Tassel, Zazel and Leona Dare, survived against the odds, and were able to tell the stories of their extraordinary careers in old age and security; others, like Vincent de Groof, Tommy Burns, Edith Brookes and various luckless Lion Wager enthusiasts, perished miserably in their prime. It would have been interesting to track down the later career of that Soho marathon sleeper M. Chauffat, but his first name was never published in the newspapers, and there were too many Chauffats in France at the time, awake or asleep, for the true identity of the Soho Sleeper to be successfully established. To be sure, it would also have been most intriguing to learn about the later career of that cross-dressing young woman of mystery Miss Lois Schick, also known as 'Dick', but she has also been able to dodge the present-day internet genealogists with impunity.

Other of the *IPN* stories are cruel and disturbing tales. Nothing good can be said about the demented animal hoarders Mary Elizabeth Dear and Elizabeth Ann Cottell. Lady Gooch must have suffered from some strange mental quirk when she thought she could foist the child she had purchased in Great Coram Street onto her husband as the Heir to Benacre Hall. Nor is the tale of Laura Julia Addiscott, the Female Wackford Squeers, a particularly pleasant one: how could a religious young woman from a respectable middle-class family establish a 'Dothegirls Hall' house of horrors worthy of a Marquise de Sade? Had the tale of the *ci-devant* Countess of Derwentwater been a work of fiction, its author would have been taken to task for his lack of realism when describing the foolhardy adventures of the sword-toting pseudo-noblewoman; had the pathetic story of the Poulett Claimant been an invention, its author would have been lambasted for laying on the sob-stuff too thick, in an attempt to rival Smike and Little Nell, when outlining the misadventures of the organ-grinding former circus clown who tried to claim an Earldom.

Through setting out the relevant hypothesis, and testing it using online genealogical tools, I can claim to have solved the Great Twiss Mystery of

1872: Lady Twiss had really led a double life as a prostitute before her marriage, and her husband is likely to have known all about it. With regard to the Roper Mystery, I feel convinced that the Lieutenant was wilfully murdered, and there is now a prime suspect, his colleague Lieutenant Henry Kendall Stothert. I also believe that Alfred John Monson was responsible for the Ardlamont Tragedy, and that either he himself, or the henchman Sweeney alias Scott, gunned down young Cecil Hambrough. I strongly suspect that Urban Napoleon Stanger was murdered, either by his wife Elizabeth or by his rival Franz Felix Stumm, and that his remains were roasted in the oven in the bakery at No. 136 Lever Street. Nor is there any doubt that the scoundrelly Stauntons caused the death of Harriet Richardson through wilful neglect, although the role played by tuberculosis may well obscure the point whether their crime was really that of murder. The Harley Street Mystery is the most baffling of them all, since the identity of the murder victim is not known. I do not think she was a servant at No. 139 Harley Street, nor the victim of an abortion gone wrong; rather a foreign prostitute who was murdered by one of the locum servants, put inside that sinister barrel in the basement, and missed by no one after she had disappeared. The hair and textile samples held by the Crime Museum were a poignant reminder of this celebrated London mystery when I saw them at the Museum of London in December 2015.

Many protagonists from the 'Mysteries' department also came to sticky ends. Sir Travers and Lady Twiss were both ruined, for good, by their implacable enemy Anthony Chaffers; a case study of pathological hatred, brought on by paranoia, from this legal Herostratos. The Revd Benjamin Speke and Sophia Hickman both ended their days as suicides. The singularly unattractive Alfred John Monson got off scot-free after the Ardlamont Tragedy, but he may well have received a both long-awaited and well-deserved come-uppance later in life, through the *nemesis divina*. There can be no sympathy for the inhumanly cruel Stauntons, for the unprepossessing German crook Franz Felix Stumm, or for that terrible virago Camilla Nicholls. Many of the stories in this book are real-life Victorian *contes cruels*, worthy of the pen of Poe or Maupassant, and alternately tragic, horrific, pathetic and hilarious; reflected in the contemporary *IPN* illustrations, they simultaneously fascinate and repel.

Sources

1 The History of The Illustrated Police News

De Vries, L., *'Orrible Murder* (London: Macdonald, 1974), West, J., *Studies in Scarlet* (Chester-le-Street: Casdec, 1994) and Jones, S., *The Illustrated Police News* (Nottingham: Wicked Publications, 2002) published various extracts from the *IPN*, whereas Stratmann, L., *Cruel Deeds and Dreadful Calamities* (London: British Library, 2011) provided a full history of this newspaper, with high-quality illustrations. Magazine and newspaper sources include *London Review* 28 May 1864, 579, *Punch* 22 July 1865, *Macmillan's Magazine* 43 [1880–1881], 397 and *Pall Mall Gazette* 23 November 1886. See also Bondeson, J., (*Fortean Times* 247 [2009], 44–9 and 274 [2011], 50–3), the internet paper 'Predators and Prey' by A. O'Day, and various entries in john-adcock.blogspot.com about Victorian and Edwardian newspaper history.

2 Medical Freaks

Somnambulists in Peril:
IPN 1 June 1867, 19 February 1870, 9 July 1878, 8 August 1885, 18 August 1888, 17 April 1897.

Andrian the Dog-faced Man:
IPN 7 February 1874; Bondeson, J., *Freaks* (Stroud: Tempus, 2006), 21–66.

Conjoined Twins:
IPN 31 January 1874, 27 November 1880, 17 September 1892; Quigley, C., *Conjoined Twins* (Jefferson NC: McFarland, 2003), Bondeson, J., *Freaks* (Stroud: Tempus, 2006), 237–58.

Buried Alive:
IPN 11 April 1874, 4 October 1874, 28 June 1884, 26 January 1889, 25 May 1895, 14 December 1901, 7 May 1904; Bondeson, J., *Buried Alive* (New York: Norton, 2001) and *Fortean Times* 146 [2001], 34–9 and 247 [2009], 44–9.

The Scottish Giant:
IPN 8 June 1878; *Era* 17 and 24 March 1878, *Funny Folks* 6 April 1878, *The Times* 24 April 1878, *Lancaster Gazette* 29 May 1878, *Otago Witness* 3 August 1878, 20 and 27 September 1879; *Lancet* i [1878], 297, *British Medical Journal* i [1878], 441, Bondeson, J., *Freaks* (Stroud: Tempus, 2006), 112–36.

Marian, the Giant Amazon Queen:
IPN 29 July 1882; *Lloyd's Weekly Newspaper* 2 July 1882, *Morning Post* 23 August and 16 December 1882, *Glasgow Herald* 28 and 30 December 1882, 2 January 1883, *Era* 6 January 1883, *Dundee Courier* 7, 9 and 15 February 1883, *Newcastle Courant* 16 February 1883, *Sheffield & Rotherham Independent* 17 and 20 March 1883, *Liverpool Mercury* 12, 15 and 28 May 1883; on the death of Marian, see *Era* 26 January 1884, *Aberdeen Weekly Journal* 29 January 1884 and *Hampshire Telegraph* 9 February 1884.

The Birmingham Midget:
IPN 6 September 1884; *Morning Post* 22 August 1884, *Birmingham Daily Post* 25 August 1884.

The Strange Death of the Earl of Lauderdale:
IPN 23 August 1884; *Caledonian Mercury* 25 August 1860, *Morning Post* 14 August 1884, *Huddersfield Chronicle* 16 August 1884, *Liverpool Mercury* 23 August 1884.

Elizabeth Lyska, the Russian Giantess:
IPN 23 November 1889; *Berrow's Worcester Journal* 21 September 1889, *Era* 9 November 1889, *Pall Mall Gazette* 16 November 1889, *Reynolds's Newspaper* 17 November 1889, *Westminster Budget* 2 February 1893, *Leeds Times* 4 February 1893; *Popular Monthly* 31 [1891], 355–8; www.thetallestman.com and letterology.blogspot.co.uk.

Barnum's Freaks in 1897:
IPN 6 November and 18 December 1897 and 21 January 1899; *Era* 2 October and 27 November 1897, *Daily Mail* 29 November 1897; on these performers, see Drimmer, F., *Very Special People* (London: Brownhills, 1973), Hornberger, F., *Carny Folk* (New York: Citadel, 2005), Bondeson, J., *Freaks* (Stroud: Tempus, 2006) and Hartzmann, M., *American Sideshow* (New York: Penguin, 2006).

Machnow the Giant:
IPN 18 February 1905; *The Times* 10 February 1905, 15 May 1924, 11 March 1936, *Penny Illustrated Paper* 18 February 1905, *Daily Mirror* 28 March 1905 and 19 June 1908, *Daily Express* 27 January and 13 February 1905, *Daily Mail* 4 and 9 February, 7 and 24 March 1905, 5, 18 and 22 June 1906, *Dundee Courier* 10 March 1906, *Burnley Gazette* 1 August 1908, *Manchester Courier* 9 November 1908, *New York Times* 21 February, 17 and 21 June, 16 July 1905, *Otago Witness* 14 June 1905, *Feilding Star* 25 March 1905, *Evening Post* 9 April 1905, *North Otago Times* 11 June 1910; www.thetallestman.com and viola.bz/fyodor-makhnow-the-tallest-person-on-earth.

3 Hermits and Misers

A Welsh Hermit, and His Menagerie:
IPN 22 May 1869.

A Welsh Hermit Defended by Rats:
IPN 11 January 1879; *Baner ac Amserau Cymru* 1 January 1879, *Pall Mall Gazette* 2 January 1879, *Cheshire Observer* 4 January 1879.

The Postman Hermit:
IPN 15 May 1880; *Hull Packet* 10 and 13 May 1880, *Daily Gazette* 11 and 13 May 1880.

The Peckham Miser:
IPN 8 September 1883; *Lancaster Gazette* 1 September 1883, *Graphic* 1 September 1883.

The Bethnal Green Miser:
IPN 2 October 1886; *Berrow's Worcester Journal* 18 and 25 September 1886, *Lloyd's Weekly Newspaper* 26 September 1886, *Reynolds's Newspaper* 26 September 1886, *The Times* 23 September 1886.

Two Norwood Children Shot by a Hermit:
IPN 9 and 23 July 1897, *Daily News* 2 July 1897, *North-Eastern Daily Gazette* 2 July 1897, *Lloyd's Weekly Newspaper* 3 July 1897, *Reynolds's Newspaper* 3 July 1897, *Standard* 15 July 1897.

4 Ghosts

The Manchester Ghost:
IPN 12 June 1869; *Manchester Times* 5 June 1869, *Liverpool Mercury* 5 June 1869, *Dundee Courier* 7 June 1869, *Derby Mercury* 9 June 1869, *York Herald* 12 June 1869.

The Jumping Ghost of Peckham:
IPN 28 December 1872; *Lloyd's Weekly Newspaper* 9 June, 1 and 8 December 1872, *Huddersfield Daily Chronicle* 6 January 1873.

The Ghost of Berkeley Square:
IPN 23 December 1874; Bondeson, J., (*Fortean Times* 335 [2015]. 28–35) and its references.

The Haunted Murder House near Chard:
IPN 22 and 29 March, 31 May and 20 December 1879; *Bristol Mercury* 7 March 1879, *The Times* 7 May 1879, *Trewman's Exeter Flying Post* 7 May 1879, *Reynolds's Newspaper* 1 June 1879; *A History of the County of Somerset*, Vol. 4, article on Knowle St Giles on 'British History Online'.

The Mystery of Sarah Duckett:
IPN 15 October 1881 and 25 November 1882; *Manchester Times* 8 October 1881, *Reynolds's Newspaper* 9 October 1881, *Graphic* 22 October 1881, *Birmingham Daily Post* 31 October 1881.

The Hackney Ghost:
IPN 31 August 1895; *North-Eastern Daily Gazette* 23 August 1895, *Lloyd's Weekly Newspaper* 25 August 1895.

The Fairwater Mystery:
IPN 18 July and 22 August 1896; *Pall Mall Gazette* 11 July 1896, *Lloyd's Weekly Newspaper* 12 July 1896, *Huddersfield Chronicle* 18 July 1896, *Hampshire Telegraph* 15 August 1896.

The Plumstead Ghost:
IPN 6 November 1897; *Daily News* 29 October 1897.

The Fighting Ghost of Tondu:
IPN 17 September 1904; *Daily Mirror* 9 September 1904, *Daily Mail* 9 and 12 September 1904; Ives, G., *Man bites Dog* (London: Jay Landesmann, 1980), 97.

5 Dogs

Newfoundland Dogs to the Rescue:
IPN 4 July 1868, 30 March 1872, 18 November 1876 and 8 September 1883; Bondeson, J. *Amazing Dogs* (Stroud: Amberley, 2011), 162–88 and *Those Amazing Newfoundland Dogs* (Woolfardisworthy: CFZ Press, 2012).

A Famous Detective's Life Saved by a Dog:
IPN 8 May 1897; Dilnot, G. (Ed.), *Trial of the Detectives* (London: Geoffrey Bles, 1928), Bondeson, J., *Murder Houses of South London* (Leicester: Troubador, 2015), 13–8.

A Dog as a Witness:
IPN 27 May 1871, 23 November 1878, 27 September 1879, 30 October 1880 and 19 March 1904.

The Sagacity of the Dog:
IPN 27 December 1884; Bondeson, J. *Amazing Dogs* (Stroud: Amberley, 2011), 16–34.

The Ratting Monkey of Manchester:
IPN 4 September 1880; *Dundee Courier* 19 August 1880; Bondeson, J. *Amazing Dogs* (Stroud: Amberley, 2011), 206–27.

Lady Florence Dixie and Hubert the St Bernard Dog:
IPN 31 March 1883; Bondeson, J. *Amazing Dogs* (Stroud: Amberley, 2011), 200–2 and *Ripperologist* 124 [2012], 99–101.

A Welsh Greyfriars Bobby:

IPN 3 March 1894 and 28 December 1895; Bondeson, J. *Amazing Dogs* (Stroud: Amberley, 2011), 130–48 and *Greyfriars Bobby* (Stroud: Amberley, 2011).

The Dog of Valencia:

IPN 18 August 1906; Bondeson, J., *Greyfriars Bobby* (Stroud: Amberley, 2011), 123–39.

6 Animals

Cats with Nine Lives:

IPN 6 July 1867, 9 May 1868, 12 August 1882; *Era* 5 August 1882, *New Zealand Herald* 30 September 1882, *Le Petit Cettois* 11 August 1882.

The Trouble with Polar Bears:

IPN 12 March 1870, 22 January 1876 and 23 November 1878; *Reynolds's Newspaper* 9 January 1876, *Dundee Courier* 8 November 1878, *STV Dundee Online* 2 January 2014.

Help, My Child was Just Taken by a …:

IPN 17 September 1870, 17 November 1870, 12 June 1880, 2 July 1881.

A Child Carried Off by an Eagle:

IPN 7 August 1869, 1 May 1880, 23 March 1889, 13 August 1898, 14 May 1904, 2 April 1910; *Glasgow Herald* 1 February 1869, *Dundee Courier* 6 July 1888, *Daily Express* 9 May 1904, 22 and 23 March 1921, *The Times* 20 May 1921 and 11 December 1939, *Scotsman* 7 June 1932, *Gloucester Echo* 17 March 1943, *New York Times* 26 August 1881, 22 April 1882, 18 October 1885, 22 December 1889, 13 September 1899, 20 May 1904 and 15 June 1912, *Albuquerque Journal* 18 July 1937, *New York Daily News* 19 December 2012; Maruna, S., 'Avian Abductions' on biofort.blogspot.com, *Foaftale News* 33–4 [1994], 13–15, Mayer, D., (*Film History* 21 [2009], 336–45), Michell, J. and Rickard, R. J. M., *Living Wonders* (London: Thames & Hudson, 1982), 138–43, Tömmeraas, P. J., *Ørnen – en barnerøver* (Trondheim: Strindheim Trykkeri, 1997).

Alas, Poor Jumbo:

IPN 4 March 1882, 26 September 1889, 16 November 1889; Bondeson, J., *Animal Freaks* (Stroud: Tempus, 2008), 93–140.

The White Gorilla:

IPN 6 February 1886; *Birmingham Daily Post* 27 January 1886, *York Herald* 28 January 1886, *Moonshine* 6 February 1886, *Daily News* 8 February 1886, *Berrow's Worcester Journal* 13 February 1886, *Hampshire Telegraph* 13 February 1886, *Standard* 26 January and 20 February 1886, *Fun* 24 February 1886, *Era* 12 December 1885 and 27 March 1886, *Liverpool Mercury* 29 December 1885, 4 and 12 January 1886, *Young Folks* 12 June 1886; Martinez-Arias, R. et al., (*Pigment Cell Research* 16 [2003], 307–11) and *Spotlight* 48, August 2004.

7 Strange Performers

Vincent de Groof, the Flying Man:
IPN 21 June 1873, 18 July 1874, 24 August 1895; *Morning Post* 13, 15, 17 and 24 July 1874, *Pall Mall Gazette* 13, 17 and 24 July 1874, *Penny Illustrated Paper* 7 October 1876 and 4 August 1888; Holme, T., *Chelsea* (London: Hamish Hamilton, 1972), 191–2, Haining, P., *The Compleat Birdman* (London: Robert Hale, 1976), Hart, C., *The Prehistory of Flight* (Los Angeles CA: University of California Press, 1985).

Zazel and Zaeo:
IPN 14 April 1877, 8 November 1879, 14 February 1880; *Morning Post* 26 April 1877, *Era* 29 April 1877, 22 December 1878, 2 February 1879, 18 January and 14 March 1880, 20 August 1881, *Dundee Courier* 26 and 27 May, 9 September 1879, *Daily Mirror* 23 January 1928, *Daily Express* 14 December 1937 and 11 February 1938.

Horsewhipping Salvationists:
IPN 3 September and 22 October 1881, 25 April, 27 June and 17 October 1885; *The Times* 10 December 1880, 8 and 13 March 1881, 12 April and 12 September 1882, 7 and 13 February 1883, 25 August and 23 September 1884, 12 June 1885; Bailey, V. in Donajgrodzki. T. (Ed.), *Social Control in Nineteenth Century Britain* (London: Croom Helm, 1977), 231–53, Walker, P. J., *Pulling the Devil's Kingdom Down* (Berkeley CA: University of California Press, 2001), 223–34.

Leona Dare:
IPN 7 June 1879 and 16 June 1888; *Standard* 1 June 1888, *Era* 15 September and 6 October 1878, 29 September 1888, *Reynolds's Newspaper* 1 June 1879, *North-Eastern Daily Gazette* 7 September 1888, *Leicester Chronicle* 8 September 1888, *New York Times* 9 June 1879, 26 November 1880, 23 November 1884 and 25 May 1922.

Teddy Wick:
IPN 22 October and 12 November 1887; *North-Eastern Daily Gazette* 8 November 1887, *Pall Mall Gazette* 3 August 1889, *The Times* 5 December 1893, *Huddersfield Chronicle* 9 December 1893, *Taranaki Herald* 29 December 1887, *Sydney Morning Herald* 13 January 1894, *Poverty Bay Herald* 10 March 1894, *West Australian Sunday Times* 24 September 1899.

Tragic Death of a Parachutist:
IPN 14 December 1889; *New York Times* 24 November 1889, 14 September and 26 October 1930; Metcalf, B., (*Queensland Review* 13 [2006], 33–49); www.blongerbros.com and the 'Van Tassel Family History Homepage' on freepages.genealogy.rootsweb.ancestry.com.

Succi, the Fasting Man:
IPN 20 November 1888, 26 April 1890, 3 May 1890; *Lancet* i [1888], 434 and 845, *British Medical Journal* i [1890], 1444–6, *New Review* 2 [1890], 409–17,

Sources

Lincolnshire Echo 30 May 1918, *Sunday Post* 3 November 1918; Vandereycken, W. et al, *Hungerkünstler* (Zülpech: DTV, 1990), 92–105, Oettermann, S. & Spiegel, S., *Lexikon der Zauberkünstler* (Offenbach am Main: Edition Volker Huber, 2004), 330–1, Gooldin, S., (*Body & Society* 9(2) [2003], 27–53), Nieto-Galan, A., (*Social History of Medicine* 28 [2014], 64–81).

Lion Wagers:

IPN 8 and 15 June 1895, 21 September 1895, 30 November 1895, 7 January 1899, 3 March 1900, 15 March 1902, 11 May 1907 and 1 February 1908; *Sheffield & Rotherham Independent* 28 January 1890, *Nottinghamshire Guardian* 24 August 1894, *Cheshire Observer* 14 September 1895, *Leicester Chronicle* 8 June 1895, *North-Eastern Daily Gazette* 21 November 1895, *Evening Times* 16 April 1910.

Lively Goings-On at a Trance Show:

IPN 10 October 1895; *Birmingham Daily Post* 8 December 1891, *Jackson's Oxford Journal* 12 December 1891. *Cheshire Observer* 10 October and 14 November 1895, *Dundee Courier* 30 September 1896, *Berrow's Worcester Journal* 3 October 1896, *Reynolds's Newspaper* 4 October 1896, *Era* 27 May 1899 and 3 February 1900.

Tommy Burns, the Champion Diver:

IPN 17 July 1897; *Wrexham Advertiser* 22 February 1890, *Morning Post* 20 June 1890, *North-Eastern Daily Gazette* 8 August 1890 and 21 December 1896, *Era* 6 August 1892, *Blackburn Standard* 12 November and 31 December 1892, 12 August 1893, *Penny Illustrated Paper* 25 March 1893, *Dundee Courier* 8 August 1893, 18 September 1895, 30 January, 13 April and 7 July 1897; www.tommyburns.org.uk and www.rhylhistoryclub.wordpress.com.

Paul Tetzel:

IPN 25 June 1898; *Daily News* 17 June 1898, *Lloyd's Weekly Newspaper* 19 June 1898, *Sheffield & Rotherham Independent* 5 December 1900, *Penny Illustrated Paper* 12 April 1902, *Capricornian* 23 April 1898, *Mataura Ensign* 18 June 1898, *Manawatu Herald* 9 August 1898, *Yea Chronicle* 23 July 1903, *Wanganui Herald* 18 January 1906.

Strange Performers at the Royal Aquarium:

IPN 1 October 1898; *Pall Mall Gazette* 20 June 1890, *Standard* 20 June 1890, *Reynolds's Newspaper* 20 July 1890, *Bristol Mercury* 20 September 1898, *Era* 8 October 1898, *Black and White Budget* 2 November 1901, *West Gippsland Gazette* 10 December 1901 and 21 Jan 1902.

Terrible Parachute Fatality:

IPN 31 May 1902, *The Times* 21 May 1902, *Sheffield Daily Telegraph* 21, 22, 23, 24, 26 and 29 May 1902, *Sheffield Evening Telegraph* 22, 23 and 26 May 1902, *Sheffield Independent* 21 May 1902, *West Gippsland Gazette* 22 July 1902, *New Zealand Herald* 5 July 1902.

8 Strange People

The Cat Woman of Rottingdean:
IPN 1 June 1867, 17 August 1872; about the Cat Woman and her career, see also *Liverpool Mercury* 24 May 1867, *Derby Mercury* 28 April 1875, *Reynolds's Newspaper* 25 October 1874, *Glasgow Herald* 13 and 14 February 1874, and *Birmingham Daily Post* 3 September 1874; on animal hoarding, see the papers by Davis, S. E., (*California Lawyer* September 2002, 26–9), Berry, C. et al., (*Animal Law* 11 [2005], 167–94) and Patronek, G. J. and Nathanson, J. N., (*Clinical Psychology Review* 29 [2009], 274–81).

Suicide from the Clifton Suspension Bridge:
IPN 4 and 11 September 1869, 15 October 1870, 17 August 1872; *Leeds Mercury* 11 May 1866, *Bristol Mercury* 12 May 1866, 30 December 1871, 10 August 1872 and 2 December 1896, *Penny Illustrated Paper* 19 May 1866, *Standard* 30 August 1869, *Reynolds's Newspaper* 5 September 1869; Nowers, M. and Gunnell, D. (*Journal of Epidemiology and Community Health* 50 [1996], 30–2), Bennewith, O. et al., (*British Journal of Psychiatry* 190 [2007], 266–7).

The Strange Case of Boulton and Park:
IPN 7, 14 and 28 May, 2, 16 and 30 July 1870, 13 and 20 May 1871; also Roughead, W., *Bad Companions* (Edinburgh: W. Green & Son, 1930), 149–83, Pearsall, R., *The Worm in the Bud* (London: Weidenfeld & Nicolson, 1969), 461–6, Upchurch, C., (*Gender & History* 12 [2000], 127–57), Senelick, L., *The Changing Room* (New York: Routledge, 2000), 295–325, Diamond, M., *Victorian Sensation* (London: Anthem Press, 2004), 120–3, and McKenna, N., *Fanny & Stella* (London: Faber & Faber, 2013).

Mynheer van Klaes, the King of Smokers:
IPN 18 May 1872; *Pall Mall Gazette* 4 May 1872, *Star* 23 June 1877, *Dominion* 23 July 1919, *Hobart Mercury* 5 April 1923, *New Yorker* 19 September 1931; *Lancet* i [1872], 663, *Notes & Queries* 4s 9 [1872], 466 and 4s 10 [1872], 136.

Tragic Effects of Practical Joking:
IPN 1 January 1876.

Laura Julia Addiscott, the Female Wackford Squeers:
IPN 16 August and 27 September 1879; *Lloyd's Weekly Newspaper* 18 May and 1 June 1879, *Reynolds's Newspaper* 18 May 1879, *Morning Post* 25 September 1879, *New Zealand Herald* 5 July and 30 August 1879; the trial of Laura Julia Addiscott is on www.oldbaileyonline.org.

Daring Robbery at Maria Marten's Cottage:
IPN 25 August 1883, *Bury and Norwich Post* 21 August 1883.

The Lichfield Yeomanry Outrages:
IPN 28 June 1884; *Glasgow Herald* 17 June 1884, *Leeds Mercury* 18 June 1884, *Lancaster Gazette* 21 June 1884, *Era* 21 June 1884, *Bury and Norwich Post* 23 June 1885.

Dick Schick, the Female Errand-Boy:
IPN 30 October and 27 November 1886; *Daily News* 14 October and 13 November 1886, *Morning Post* 14 October 1886, *Observer* 17 October 1886, *Lloyd's Weekly Newspaper* 17 October 1886; Hindmarch-Watson, K., (*GLQ* 14 [2007], 69–98).

Mystery at Mr Cooke's School of Anatomy:
IPN 8 October 1887 and 9 April 1925; *Daily Mail* 2, 3 and 4 April 1925; the article by Bondeson, J., (*Ripperologist* 132 [2013], 37–42) has a full list of references.

The Sleeping Frenchman of Soho:
IPN 9 April 1887; *Morning Post* 30 March and 7 April 1887, *Standard* 31 March, 2, 5 and 8 April 1887, *Lloyd's Weekly Newspaper* 17 April 1887, *New York Times* 1 May 1887, *Te Aroha News* 18 June 1887, *Southland Times* 20 May 1887, *Auckland Star* 25 June 1887; *Lancet* i [1887], 736–7, 740–1, 808, 1004.

Miss Vint and her Reincarnated Cats:
IPN 8 October 1892; *Royal Cornwall Gazette* 6 October 1892.

The Strange Tale of Professor Beaurigard:
IPN 6 October 1894; *Western Mail* 28 September 1894, *Dundee Courier* 29 September 1894, *Marlborough Express* 23 November 1894, *Western Mail* (Perth, WA), 8 December 1894, *New Zealand Herald* 29 September 1900.

9 Misdeeds of the Rich and Famous

A Dismal Tale from the Peerage:
IPN 9 November 1867, *Newcastle Courant* 8 November 1867; Wyndham, H., *The Mayfair Calendar* (London: Hutchinson, 1925), 129–46.

The Strange Story of the Countess of Derwentwater:
IPN 10 October 1868, 27 November 1869, 29 January 1870; *Morning Post* 22 August 1866, 8 and 10 October 1868, 15 and 22 May 1869, 18 January, 17 February and 8 March 1870, 28 February 1880, *Manchester Times* 10 October 1868, *Reynolds's Newspaper* 11 and 18 October 1868, 23 January 1870, *Leeds Mercury* 16 and 21 November 1868, 15 May 1869 and 20 September 1870, *Dundee Courier* 17 March and 19 November 1869, 9 June 1870, *Hexham Courant* 25 May 2002, *Northern Echo* 31 August 2012; Longstaff, W., (*North-Country Lore and Legend* 14 [1888], 165–70, Humphries, A. L., (*Notes &*

Queries 11s. 10 [1914], 311–3; Milne, M., *The Strange Story of the 'Countess of Derwentwater'* (Newcastle-upon-Tyne: Frank Graham, 1970), Dickinson, F., *The Castle on Devil's Water* (Stocksfield: Spredden Press, 1992).

A Bonaparte on Trial for Murder:
IPN 15 and 22 January 1870, *Pall Mall Gazette* 11, 12, 13, 15 and 19 January 1870, *Morning Post* 12 and 13 January 1870, *Lloyd's Weekly Newspaper* 16 and 23 Jauaryn 1870, *Reynolds's Newspaper* 16 January 1870, *Graphic* 22 January 1870.

The Gooch Scandal:
IPN 23 and 30 November 1878, *Ipswich Journal* 4 June 1872, 4 November 1879 and 22 June 1888, *Dundee Courier* 18 March 1879, *Leeds Mercury* 20 March 1879, *Bury and Norwich Post* 4 November 1879, *Birmingham Daily Post* 17 August 1881, *Lloyd's Weekly Newspaper* 20 May 1888, *Aberdeen Weekly Journal* 1 1893, *New Zealand Herald* 18 January 1879 and 11 August 1888, *New York Times* 9 December 1878.

The Fearneaux Frauds:
IPN 25 February, 4 and 11 March, 13 May 1882; *Morning Post* 24 February, 4 March, 9 May 1882, *New York Times* 27 February 1882, *Evening Telegraph* 26 July 1894, *Australian Weekly Chronicle* 8 April 1882, *Guardian* 9 May 2014.

The Garmoyle Breach of Promise Case:
IPN 11 August 1883, 22 March and 22 November 1884; *York Herald* 14 February 1884, *Standard* 2 July and 20 November 1884, *Pall Mall Gazette* 20 November 1884, *Morning Post* 21 November 1884, *New York Times* 21 November 1884 and 20 February 1885; Wyndham, H., *Blotted 'Scutcheons* (London: Hutchinson, 1926), 127–48.

The Dunlo Sensation:
IPN 2 and 9 August 1890; *New Zealand Herald* 28 July and 9 September 1890, *New York Times* 30 May 1891 and 1 Jan 1907; Wyndham, H., *Society Sensations* (London: Robert Hale, 1938), 233–69.

Spiritualism and Animal Hoarding in Thomas Carlyle's House:
IPN 13 August and 17 December 1892; *Pall Mall Gazette* 15 January 1889, *Standard* 5 August 1892 and 17 June 1893, *Morning Post* 11 and 18 August 1892, *Daily News* 17 August 1892, *Daily Chronicle* 5 September 1893, *Woman's Signal* 5 May 1895; Anon., *The Homes and Haunts of Thomas Carlyle* (London: Westminster Gazette, 1895), 108–14; Blunt, R., *The Carlyles' Chelsea Home* (London: George Bell, 1895), 41–8, Lumsden, G., in the *Illustrated Memorial Volume of the Carlyle's House Purchase Fund Committee* (London: Carlyle's House Memorial Trust, 1895), 1–26.

The Strange Case of Lord William Nevill:
IPN 26 February 1898; *New York Times* 5 December 1897, 25 January 1898, 16 February 1898, 14 February 1903 and 14 March 1907, *Auckland Star* 15 January 1898 and 15 March 1907.

The Poulett Claimant:
IPN 4 and 18 February 1899; *Lancaster Gazette* 23 February 1878, *Daily News* 3 February 1886 and 27 January 1899, *Standard* 19 March 1886, *Lloyd's Weekly Newspaper* 21 March 1886 and 29 January 1899, *Hampshire Advertiser* 4 September 1889, *Penny Illustrated Paper* 8 June 1895, *Western Mail* 26 December 1898, *Manchester Times* 27 January 1899, *Graphic* 4 February 1899, *New York Times* 24 February 1886, 24 July 1903 and 10 October 1909, *Daily Express* 26 November 1901 and 25 July 1903.

10 Crime and Mystery

The Great Speke Mystery:
IPN 1, 22 and 29 February 1868, 29 May 1869; *The Times* 3, 6, 7, 10, 13, 14, 24, 25, 26, 27, 28 February, 4 March 1868, 24 April 1869, 25 February 1881, *John Bull* 25 January and 1 February 1868, *Pall Mall Gazette* 5 February 1868, *Observer* 1 March 1868, *New York Times* 12 March 1868; *Lancet* i [1868], 236, 294, 325, 335, Jacob, F., (*Belgravia* 6 [1868], 45–9), *London Society* 36 [1879], 437–48, O'Donnell, E., *Strange Disappearances* (London: Bodley Head 1927), 257–280 and Liddle, D. in Maunder, A. & Moore, G. (Eds.), *Victorian Crime, Madness and Sensation* (Aldershot: Ashgate, 2004), 89–104.

A Thieves' Supper:
IPN 5 February 1870 and 13 December 1884; *John Bull* 29 January 1870, *Punch* 7 January 1871 and 27 January 1872, *Reynolds's Newspaper* 5 February 1871, *Standard* 17 November 1871, *Liverpool Mercury* 3 April 1865 and 6 January 1873, *Hull Packet* 31 July 1874, *Lloyd's Weekly Newspaper* 8 October 1876, *Morning Post* 19 November 1879, *Daily News* 3 December 1886, *Dundee Courier* 9 December 1891, *New Zealand Evening Post* 7 April 1870, *New Zealand Star* 20 April and 9 May 1870, *Sydney Morning Herald* 8 April 1873, *Daily News* 28 July 1908, *Western Gazette* 31 July 1908; Wright, N. *The Story of My Life* (London: Hodder & Stoughton, 1873).

The Great Twiss Mystery:
IPN 23 March 1872; *The Times* 1 March 1872 and 14 March 1872, *Morning Post* 1 March 1872, *Saturday Review* 16 March 1872, *Pall Mall Gazette* 14 and 16 March 1872, *Lloyd's Weekly Newspaper* 17 March 1872; A. Chaffers, *The Twiss Libel Case* (London: Privately published, 1872), Wyndham, H., *Famous Trials Re-Told* (London: Hutchinson, 1924), 215–26 and *Dramas of the Law* (London: Hutchinson, 1936), 47–82, Sparrow, J. et al., (*The Brussels Museum of Musical Instruments Bulletin* 1(1/2) [1971], 41–78), Fitzmaurice, A. in Dorsett, S. and Hunter, I. (Eds.), *Law and Politics in British Colonial Thought* (London: AIAA, 2010), 109–26.

The Harley Street Mystery:
IPN 12 and 26 June 1880; *Times* 7 June 1880, *Morning Post* 8 and 15 June 1880, *Reynolds's Newspaper* 6 and 13 June 1880, *Lloyd's Weekly Newspaper* 6, 13 and 20 June 1880; Spurgin, P. B., (*Transactions of the Medico-Legal Society*

25 [1930–1], 120–37), Oates, J., *Unsolved Murders in Victorian and Edwardian London* (Barnsley: Wharncliffe, 2007), 83–7, Hughes, T., (*Marylebone Journal*, Feb/March 2010, 57–60), Bondeson, J., *Murder Houses of London* (Stroud: Amberley, 2014), 185–8, Kelly, J. and Hoffbrand, J., *The Crime Museum Uncovered* (London: I. B. Tauris, 2015), 31.

The Mystery of Lieutenant Roper:
IPN 19 and 26 February 1881; *The Times* 15 and 22 February 1881, *Essex Standard* 3 December 1881, *Birmingham Daily Post* 14 October 1892, *Nelson Evening Mail* 31 December 1881, *New Zealand Herald* 10 December 1892, *NZ Truth* 8 February 1908. The revelations about Lieutenant Stothert are in *Pall Mall Gazette* 10 January 1885 and *York Herald* 7 February 1885. See also National Archives WO 25/3915/128, Adam, H. L., *Murder by Persons Unknown* (London 1931), 190–6, Bergess, W. (*The Sapper* 20(8) [1982], 312–3) and www.kenthistoryforum.co.uk.

The Mystery of Urban Napoleon Stanger:
IPN 14 and 21 October 1882, 10 March 1883; *The Times* 19 July, 4, 5 and 12 October, 9, 11 and 12 December 1882, *Morning Post* 2 November 1882, 23 and 27 January 1883, *Daily News* 29 September, 9 and 11 Dec 1882, *Penny Illustrated Paper* 7, 14 and 21 October, 11 November 1882, *Lloyd's Weekly Newspaper* 1, 8, 15 and 29 October, 17 December 1882, *Reynolds's Newspaper* 8 October, 19 November 1882, 4 March 1883, *New Zealand Herald* 2 December 1882; the trial of Franz Felix Stumm is on Oldbaileyonline, see also Harrison, M. (*Ellery Queen's Mystery Magazine* 57 (2) [1971], 59–79), O'Donnell, E. *Strange Disappearances* (London: Bodley Head, 1927), 280–92, and Logan, G. B. H., *Guilty or Not Guilty?* (London 1929), 222–39.

The Ardlamont Mystery:
IPN 9 September, 16 and 23 December 1893; *Morning Post* 30 January 1895 and 29 January 1896, *Standard* 8 April 1890, *Pall Mall Gazette* 6–11 April 1894, *Lloyd's Weekly Newspaper* 3 February 1895 and 2 February 1896, *Dundee Courier* 2 and 6 August 1898, *Dundee Evening Telegraph* 14 May 1919, *New Zealand Herald* 14 October 1893 and 9 November 1935, *Scotsman* 10 September 1998 and 12 December 2005, *Daily Record* 9 April 2002, *The Times* 11 September 2005; National Archives J 77/643/19627, University of Nottingham MSS Ga C20/163, Cotterill, J. M., (*Juridical Review* 9 [1894], 43–57), Monson, A. J., *The Ardlamont Mystery Solved* (London: Marlo & Co., 1894), More, J. W. (Ed.), *Trial of A. J. Monson* (Edinburgh: Hodge, 1908), Roughead, W., *Rogues Walk Here* (London: Cassell, 1934), 1–71, House, J., *Murder not Proven* (London: Penguin, 1989), 67–110.

The Greenwich Bomb Outrage:
IPN 24 February 1894; *Pall Mall Gazette* 16 February 1894, *Reynolds's Newspaper* 18 February 1894; Sherry, N., (*Review of English Studies* NS 18 [1967], 412–28), Nash, C., (*Review of English Studies* NS 20 [1969], 322–7), Burgoyne, M., (*Conradian* 32 [2007], 147–61).

The Nicholls-Popejoy Affair:

IPN 14 May 1898; *Dundee Courier* 9 February 1898, *Morning Post* 23 February, 2 and 9 March, 28, 29 and 30 April, 2 and 3 May 1898, *Standard* 2 and 9 March, 28 and 30 April, 3 May 1898, *Reynolds's Newspaper* 8 May 1898, *Sheffield Daily Telegraph* 16 February 1899, *Western Times* 8 October 1901; National Archives HO 144/274/A60198, Jillings, J. H., *Emily Jane Popejoy* (Bagshot: Privately published, 1997), www.bagshotvillage.org.uk, www.surreyheath.gov.uk, 'Policing the Victorian Countryside' from www.open.ac.uk.

The Presumed Murder of a Fortune-Teller:

IPN 18 and 25 March, 1 April 1899; *Standard* 8, 9 and 21 March 1899, *Morning Post* 9 and 23 March 1899, *Daily News* 9 and 27 March 1899, *Lloyd's Weekly Newspaper* 26 November 1899.

The Case of Kitty Byron:

IPN 22 November and 27 December 1902; *Penny Illustrated Paper* 20 and 27 December 1902, *Daily Mirror* 12 June 1905, 12 February 1906, 5 December 1908, *Daily Mail* 11, 12, 15, 18 and 19 November, 18 December 1902, 24 January 1903, 6 April 1907, 5 December 1908; NA CRIM 1/80/3 and HO 44/687/103296, Adam, H. L., *Woman and Crime* (London: Werner Laurie, 1914), 157–9, Frost, G., (*Gender & History* 16 [2004], 538–60).

The Disappearance of a Lady Doctor:

IPN 24 and 31 October 1903; *Daily Mirror* 6 and 13 November 1903, *Daily Express* 20 and 22 August, 20 October, 6 November 1903, *Daily Mail* 19, 20, 21, 24, 26 and 29 August, 20 and 26 October 1903, *Lancashire Daily Post* 21 July 1927; *Saturday Review* 24 October 1903, *Lancet* ii [1903], 624, 849, 964–5, 1177, 1443–4, *British Medical Journal* ii [1903], 868, 1028, 1083–4, 1105–6, 1312, 1356, 1381, McCluer Stevens, C. L., *From Clue to Dock* (London: Stanley Paul, 1927), 78–86, Collinson, S., (*Psychiatric Bulletin* 14 [1990], 83–6), Brock, C., (*History Workshop Journal* 80 [2015], 161–82).

An Exciting Episode from the Life of Mr Kenneth Grahame:

IPN 5 December 1903; *The Times* 25 and 26 November, 3 and 15 December 1903, *Daily Mirror* 25 and 26 November, 3 and 18 December 1903, *Daily Telegraph* 10 February 2008, *Daily Express* 18 February 2008; Green, P., *Beyond the Wild Wood* (Exeter: Magnolia, 1982), 135–6.

11 Victorian Weirdness

Stratmann, L., *Cruel Deeds and Dreadful Calamities* (London: British Library, 2011) traces the history of the *IPN* to the end. See also Bondeson, J., Introduction to Logan, G., *The True History of Jack the Ripper* (Stroud: Amberley, 2013), 12–21 and *Fortean Times* 318 [2014], 40–6 and 319 [2014], 30–8.

Index

Index